In Command of France

In Command of France

*French Foreign Policy
and
Military Planning,
1933-1940*

Robert J. Young

Harvard University Press
Cambridge, Massachusetts
and London, England

1978

Library of Congress Cataloging in Publication Data

Young, Robert J   1942-
    In command of France.

    Bibliography: p.
    Includes index.
    1. France—Foreign relations—1914-1940.
2. France—Defenses.   I.   Title.
DC369.Y68   327.44   78-4875
ISBN 0-674-44536-8

For Kathryn

PREFACE

It may be better to beg a reader's indulgence at the end of a book, but I have listened to contrary advice. Stephen Leacock once recommended that an author begin on a personal note, so that "some of the blame for what he has done is very properly shifted to the extenuating circumstances of his life." There is, however, another reason for mentioning that I was born a Canadian in the course of the Second World War.

It was Croce who likened the writing of history to men traveling on a river of generations, each surveying the same unchanging mountain from a succession of different perspectives. So it is with us now, looking back on the 1930s, a decade that has remained changeless for forty years but that lends itself to new perspectives for every ensuing generation. Thus it is not for entirely trivial reasons that one divulges age or confesses nationality; both are liabilities as much as assets, or they are neither one nor the other.

The events recalled in this book are not of my times, however pervasive and enduring their effects have been on the unfolding of my times. Similarly, for all my affection for the people and countries with which this book primarily is concerned, my perspectives are necessarily different from theirs. I cannot say precisely how either time or place of birth has shaped my response to the history of the European interwar period. But I take it that the two together have done so, that they have left me with a perspective and distance of which any reader has a right to be aware.

So it should also be said how much I have relied upon the assistance of others.

In France, I express my thanks to the following: Monsieur de La Fournière, Ministre Plénipotentiaire, for permission to use the archives of the Ministère des Affaires Etrangères; the Archives Nationales, where the papers of General Victor Schweisguth have been deposited by the Fonda-

Preface

tion Nationale des Sciences Politiques; Mesdemoiselles Bourdin and Chevignard, and Madame Faure, all of whom assisted my work on the Daladier and Blum papers at the Fondation; General Hayez and General Christienne of the Service Historique de l'Armée de l'Air; Colonel Le Goyet and Commandant de Gouberville of the Service Historique de l'Armée; Messieurs Masson and Audouy of the Service Historique de la Marine; General Olivier Poydenot, who allowed me to use his memoirs; the late Guy La Chambre for granting me access to his private archives; the late Georges Bonnet and the late General Jean Petibon for information communicated by correspondence; and Professor Patrick Fridenson of the University of Paris X-Nanterre for his invaluable advice and assistance.

In Britain, where the original idea for this work was first conceived under the direction of Professor Donald C. Watt at the London School of Economics, I was equally fortunate. For their assistance over the years, I express my thanks to the Public Record Office, the British Museum Library, the Institute for Historial Research, the Foreign Office and War Office Libraries, the Air Historical Branch, the Imperial War Museum Library, and the Press Library of the Royal Institute of International Affairs at Chatham House. To Lady Liddell Hart I acknowledge my indebtedness to her late husband, who so kindly granted me access to his private archives, just as I acknowledge my gratitude to Mrs. Bradford of the Archives Center, Churchill College, Cambridge, for permission to consult the papers of Sir Eric Phipps and Sir Maurice Hankey. So too my thanks are extended to Major C. A. De Linde and Air Marshal Douglas Colyer, both of whom allowed me to discuss with them their work as service attachés in Paris, and to Colonel H. F. Heywood for recollections of the attaché career of his brother, Colonel T. G. G. Heywood.

Like many other Canadians, I owe a very special debt of thanks for the extensive financial aid provided by the Canada Council, and I am grateful for the support rendered by the University of Winnipeg.

Finally, I thank Professor Gerald Friesen for his careful and perceptive reading of my manuscript, Professor Hubert Mayes for his advice on translations, and my wife, Kathryn, for everything.

CONTENTS

"So it's us as lost the bloody war? Pore bloody second-line crocks. Is that what you mean?" "What I mean is," said the sergeant, "that you buggered off in face of the enemy and surrendered France.

"Saw it all a-coming a long time ago, I did—only had to look at you, the lads of '40, skulkers, the lot of you, pretty boys without an ounce of discipline . . . Think we had leave in '14?" "Course you did!" "How d'you know that, kid? Didn't happen to be there, did yer?" "I didn't, but me old man did, and he told me!" "Must've fought his war at Marseilles, your old man, 'cos we had to wait two years, and then some, before we got any leave."
. . . "All right, all right," said Lambert, "we don't want to hear the story of yer life." "I'm not telling you the story of m'life. I'm just explaining how it comes we won our war and you lost yours."

Goldilock's eyes were ablaze with anger: "Since you're so clever, maybe you'll explain how you managed to lose the peace?" "The peace?" exclaimed the sergeant in astonishment. There was a babble of voices: "Yes, the peace, the peace, it was you as lost the peace!" "You was the old soldiers, wasn't you?" said Goldilocks: "Well, what did you do for ter see as how your kids should be safe? Did you make Germany pay? Did you see she was disarmed? How 'bout the Rhineland? how 'bout the Ruhr? how 'bout the war in Spain? how 'bout Abyssinia? And how about the Treaty of Versailles?"

—Jean-Paul Sartre

Introduction

Much has been written about the approach of war in the 1930s, but within that body of literature France has won scant recognition. Certainly by comparison with either prewar Germany or Britain, France has generated but modest interest. Small wonder. Its vitality long has been obscured by German diplomatic and military victories; and its weaknesses have been neglected in the unconscious assumption of an English-speaking world that French policy was really made in London. What is more, and bluntly put, the need for a book such as this is evoked as much by what has been written as by what has not. Although fewer studies have been directed to France itself, no one has yet managed to eliminate it from the countless works on international politics in the interwar years; and it is here that one regularly detects the many slips and innuendoes which offer glimpses of a country that has lost its way, that is indefinably but unmistakably degenerate. This is the curse of 1940, that irrepressible need to draw straight lines between the terrible military defeat and everything that had gone before it, to see it, like Sartre's sergeant, "all a-coming a long time ago."

This book is not a study of the 1940 collapse, neither is it a social history of France between the wars. It is a study of foreign policy and military planning, but one based on the premise that the way things ended in 1940 did not carry the cast of necessity. The end of the Third Republic, like its genesis in 1870, may be explained in very large part by

1

military fortunes in the spring of 1940. Of course it is possible to see in the defeat the entrails from which the collapse might have been prophesied but was not. Marc Bloch's at once poignant and burning *Strange Defeat* is not easily countered. Nevertheless, one need not be blind to the shortcomings of the fallen Republic to recognize within it a seriousness of purpose toward the perils at hand, a determination to resist German attempts at hegemony, a willingness to devote enormous care and effort to the cause of national defense. So many of the newly released source materials have suggested to me that France was under control, was under the command of competent if not outstanding civil and military leaders, men who went further than some believed was warranted to avert war, men who did more than was subsequently admitted to prepare for it. These commanders were not great statesmen, not great generals, but they merit more than they thus far have received, more sympathy, more censure, above all more care to outline the problems and alternatives that confronted them in the Nazi years.

To see things in this light does not mean that one must view France in the 1930s as gay, effervescent, content, with all problems in hand. What gaiety there was concealed much unease. Strikes, lockouts, unemployment, inflating prices aggravated by painful deflationary measures and ultimately by successive devaluations of the currency, all testified to anxiety and discomfort throughout French society. To this economic source of tension were added the increasingly acute ideological divisions among Communists, socialists, capitalists, and parafascists; between nationalists and internationalists; between traditional nationalists and the militant, revolutionary nationalists of the extremist *ligues;* between internationalists of uncompromising pacifist persuasion and internationalists of collective security persuasion. And in turn came the menace from abroad: wars in the Far East, Africa, and below the Pyrenees; a revanchist Germany, a resentful, ambitious Italy, a Russian ally still inspired by revolution, vulnerable allies in the east, a Belgium in the west for which France was a symbol of national division, and an England apparently blind or indifferent to all but French hegemony on the continent. Having barely recovered from the colossal costs of the First World War, reckoned either by a million and a half dead soldiers or by a national bill of some five hundred billion dollars,[1] and having just grown accustomed to the proliferation of war memorials and the new allowances for veterans, widows, and orphans, the French thus found themselves on the rim of yet another abyss—that which was opened in the early 1930s by the depression and the dictators.

Precisely how these circumstances shaped the mind and spirit of France in the 1930s is difficult to say—a conclusion based in part on the very ease with which its social psychology has been deduced so often by so many. Surely the popular conception of this France has been rendered indelible: directionless and defeatist, paralyzed by indecision, wedded to Mammon in whose name pleasure seekers were enticed by "salacious cabarets, extravagant restaurants, 'curious' book-shops and well-stocked American bars."[2] Yet one need not debunk this vision in its entirety, possibly by so doing scattering to the winds the makings of a useful social analysis, merely to highlight its unwarranted simplicity. For instance, can this be the France of which William Bullitt wrote in the spring of 1939?

> There is a curious *serenity* from one end of France to the other. There is no vacillation or mourning. The spirit of the people is incomparably better than in 1914 . . . The quiet courage and serenity in France today is the only manifestation in a long time that has made me proud to be a member of the human race.[3]

Similarly, when the British Foreign Office turned to its consulates for a reading of French morale it discovered a France unseen by pessimistic observers in the Paris embassy. As Oliver Harvey recorded in September 1938, "Almost all of these reports are unanimous in saying the French are resolute and resigned to the necessity of making a stand now."[4] Such readings do not dismiss their antitheses. Indeed, they could not, even if one were to cite a hundred such examples. The fact is that different observers took quite different soundings of the national morale, none of which should be reckoned by the measures of right and wrong. What must be granted, therefore, all that need be granted, is that the image of defeatist France, sadly deficient in morale, is by its very precision the product of distortion.

We are entitled to suspect this simple image of malaise-ridden France on other grounds as well, even if the seeds of this suspicion were sown by the same simplicity of judgment. It is one thing to say, as some have, that the history of this period owes much to the fact that so many of the lads of 1914, the best and the brightest among them, were lost to the service of their countries, claimed by death in the millions. It is quite another to regard their comrades who survived as something less than their equals, second-string leftovers into whose clumsy if well-meaning hands the peace was entrusted, a generation that simply had lost the "tough, aggressive spirit so formidable in men like Clemenceau and Poincaré."[5] And yet have we not drifted close to such an awful indictment? How near to calumny are we taken by our imperfect impressions of soldiers and statesmen in the late Third Republic. Laval, Bonnet, Chautemps, were they not all cunning schemers, men who could be counted on to choose the path of least resistance? Weygand and Pétain were commonly regarded in the same almost nefarious light; Gamelin, Flandin, Delbos, Cot, Daladier, all men of the same grey cloth. Of course they were not, but such is as it often appears, however implicitly, in Anglo-Saxon literature. How rich in surly invective is our language when sparked by the Gauls.

> As I waved farewell to the Minister of Public Works [de Monzie] going down in the lift, I seemed to catch a faint final whiff of that sulphureous atmosphere that is commonly supposed to envelop the personage who exercised so unfortunate an influence on the declining days of the worthy Dr. Faust.[6]

How edifying the British Foreign Secretary found this tidbit from His Majesty's embassy in Paris is not recorded.

Although there may be something to it, more than we may care to admit, it would be too shaky a business to suggest that Anglo-Saxon images of prewar France derived mainly from national stereotype assumptions or even from well-tended grievances from the past. Two other considerations merit closer attention. First, it is entirely possible that many of the "defeatist" reports, as Harvey called them, that entered Whitehall through the Paris embassy were in fact responses to English proclivities. In other words, British fears of war may have encouraged them to pooh-pooh the not infrequent rumblings in Paris about the need to resist German terror by force. In any event there is no denying that what was being attributed to the French, the unwillingness to defy the dictators, accorded suspiciously well with the mainstream of official sentiment in England. It is this dimension that must not be missed in Eric Phipps' famous aphorism from 1938, "All that is best in France is against war, almost at any cost." And it is to this phenomenon, what psychologists call projection, that Professor John Cairns speaks when he refers to the "temptation to seek weakness in the French posture, to express mistrust of declarations of determination."[7] The point is more than of mild, passing interest to the historian. Interesting it may well be to speculate on the subconscious responses of men fearful of war and desirous of stability, but at what peril do we now write our histories from such telling but unruly testimony? Are we to see this defeatist France through the lens of Englishmen already impaled on fascist propaganda?

Until very recently it was difficult not to, obliged as we were to rely almost entirely on English archival resources. As a result, historians working in London archives were likely to have had their vision of France shaped inordinately by Anglo-Saxons who were serving a *contemporary* cause. This is our second consideration, the power of Britannia's archives. It may be illustrated with a different theme, for the question of French morale was not the only one that gave rise to inconsistent and competing visions. The same may be said for the state of France's prewar defenses. Throughout the 1930s, and especially following the outbreak of war, English-speaking reading audiences were treated to the most sanguine and comforting assessments of French military preparedness—always to be sure with reference to the famous Maginot Line. In the spring of 1940 France fell, the shock settled in and with it the suspicion, nay the certainty, that those assessments had been lies. Far from being strong, France had been rotten.

Following the publication of the British diplomatic documents, and the subsequent opening of the official archives in 1967, this conclusion drew new vindication. It was found that many professional observers in the 1930s—the diplomats and military intelligence personnel—had tended to be much more reserved, even gloomy, in their private reports on France. Itself exceptional in thrust and tone, one communication from the air ministry outrightly censured the ambassador in Paris for his exaggerated pessimism.[8] However, the point is that the reaction against the bleak science of reporting on France was rare and muted. In general, few official observers took heart from events on the other side of the Channel, although again this tendency may have had its roots in the psychology of the British and not the French. In any event, having been assured by 1940 of all the prewar untruths about French defenses, the historian is all the more susceptible to the carping, *triste*, contemporary assessments which assail him in the British archives, the more so because such appreciations seem so compatible with what came to be the 1940 débâcle. Thus it is, one ventures to suggest, that many of the recent works on British policy tend to reinforce and reproject the image of France as the sick man of Europe, ill at ease and lamentably prepared for war.

I am inclined to doubt much of this testimony, for it consists of sweeping and severe judgments based on too particularistic a documentation. As for French sources and testimony, until recently very restricted, the same may be said to be true. From the Riom trials onward[9] there has been a trend either to damn a group of *responsables* for their defeatism and criminal incompetence or, for those so charged, to retort like General Gamelin that defeat stemmed from a "gradual breakdown of the nation," from the "ineffectiveness of well-intentioned men," from "so many accumulated mistakes" for which "the whole nation" would have to pay.[10] In so many words, all of France, the whole nation, had been sick and ill at heart, leveled by the mediocrity of "a system, a society, a frame of mind, . . . mediocrity of vision . . . mediocrity of leaders."[11] But even if we were to suspend judgment on the validity of such conclusions, it seems clear that the ways in which they were arrived at must be regarded with distrust. Is it not, after all, in the scramble to affix and avoid responsibility that these damning, unforgiving indictments have been recorded?[12] Either there was a necessarily small group of ruling incompetents, poisoned by graft if not by conspiracy, or this unsavory crew was genuinely representative of all that was bad in France. Again, there is an off-putting simplicity in all this. It is dangerous to confuse verdicts with explanations, particularly when the verdicts sweep such a large portion of society and when they are founded on such a body of self-serving evidence.

The preceding reflections have been offered with this in mind.

It is possible, as has been proven repeatedly, to see in French diplomacy of the 1930s all the aimless drifting which the events of 1940 have taught us to look for. More so than in their general direction of foreign policy, successive French governments have been pilloried for their apparently spineless responses to the famous crises of the 1930s. The picture, in other words, is one of the craven, those over-anxious to give Hitler what he wanted so that trouble would be avoided, so that the self-seeking enterprises of business and politics could carry on in abject tranquillity. It is from this same vista that French diplomacy has come close to being identified as not French at all, but British. France, from moral debility, voluntarily surrendered its diplomatic independence to Whitehall, leaving to the British a charge it had not the heart to assume for itself. And if one were to explore this gloomy canvas more closely, one would find in the foreground the hint that the French could have, should have, acted otherwise. This is the crux. Successive French governments bent before Hitler's intimidation when they should have stood resolute. And they should have stood resolute because France throughout the period had a larger and more seasoned army and navy, and for over half the period a much superior air force as well. To bow before Germany, to accept with embarrassed equanimity repeated violations of the Versailles and Locarno accords, constitutes a confession of moral cowardice.

It is here that the concept of appeasement is often introduced, an over-used hat-rack of a word. As a testament to its limitations, one may say that appeasement has never had fewer than two connotations: a peaceful settlement of legitimate grievances through calculated but well-intentioned compromise or a slavish abandonment of principles and interests in the face of terror and threats. To these meanings have been added, in various attempts to explain the operation of British policy: the notion of appeasement as a subterfuge, a deliberate effort to postpone war on the grounds of military unpreparedness; the notion of appeasement based on finance and economics, whereby economic collaboration with Germany seemed sensible and desirable; the notion of appeasement as a capitalist endeavor to freeze out the Soviet Union and impede the course of world communism. Appeasement then can be moral or immoral, realistic or unrealistic, and hence successful or unsuccessful—inspired by the currency of peace or by that of the pound sterling. It is a phantom that we pursue with predictable results.

This conclusion seems all the more valid for the case of France, partly because appeasement has not intruded as much into explanations of French policy, partly because when it has, it has been used in the least sophisticated sense. So it is that one finds very few studies of French diplomacy in the 1930s that have been grounded in the vocabulary of appeasement. Indeed, virtually no Frenchman between the wars came close to emulating the kind of militant pacifism with which we associate Neville Chamberlain—lest it be the much admired Briand or his much reviled protege Pierre Laval. So too, when works of a more general nature do apply the term to France, they tend to do so in a kind of careless, offhand attempt to group the British and French together, in which case the term is usually used as an epithet under which one is expected to read cowardice, drift, and defeatism.

Wary of the morally couched defeatist interpretation of 1940, I am similarly apprehensive about the morally couched interpretation of French diplomacy in the 1930s. At the outset, for instance, the latter is based on a questionable reading of France's physical capacity to resist German demands. If France could have afforded to run the risks of war, confident that Hitler would be defeated, then the charges might be warranted. If such were not the case, if the conviction that France could not defeat Germany grew with the approach of war, then the efforts of French diplomats to avert the military day of judgment might be seen in a more favorable light. It is to this latter possibility that this book turns, and to the relationship between the diplomacy pursued and the national defense resources on hand to complement it.

This relationship provides the book with its central theme. Based on a belief in the genuine command of France, this work uses civil-military planning as a vehicle for explaining France's response to the new German problem. This vehicle, or theme, is a familiar one to students of modern power politics, for it directly addresses the role which force plays in international relations. Indeed, so familiar is it that it has won for itself at least one historical epigram. It was Frederick II who made such short shrift of one disconsolate but uncomprehending ambassador to Paris. The latter had complained that the voice of Prussia was being muffled in France all because the absence of a worthy carriage and pair had reduced him to the indignity of traveling about on foot. The ambassador will remind himself, the monarch retorted, that "whenever he walks through the streets of Paris, behind him march the 30,000 bayonets in the service of His Majesty the King of Prussia."

The reader, however, may find a twentieth-century historical background more useful. With whatever validity, the relationship between the 1930s and the collapse of 1940 has been remarked upon often enough. By this light, the hesitation at Sedan was but the last of a series of fatal inactions, including the failure to protect the Rhineland, Austria, and Czechoslovakia in peace, or Poland, Belgium, and Luxembourg in war. Quite apart from the claims this fabric of events is intended to support, what is immediately clear is the degree of French commitment and involvement across the continent. By the 1930s France had acquired extensive obligations to other European countries—the price of reciprocal assurances to France. Briefly put, moved by the fear of a German resurgence the French had used the 1920s to recruit future wartime allies. What the reader is asked to keep in mind from the outset, therefore, is the

8

sense of peril that had arisen in France from those early moments in 1919 when the Versailles peace revealed the inadequacies of a compromise arrangement. Even with victory in their pocket the French sensed a ruse, sensed that the German problem had been aggravated rather than settled.[13] Second, having been introduced to the principle of France's search for allies, the reader may wish to be acquainted with the general outline of this alliance structure, or what we may term the French security network.

While never quite abandoning its efforts to secure an Anglo-American guarantee of French security, the French Foreign Office, or Quai d'Orsay, looked elsewhere for the requisite assurances of support. The Belgians, Poles, and Czechs proved receptive to the entreaties of a great power committed to the political and territorial status quo established by the various peace settlements. Belgium, with bitter memories of the German invasion six years before, signed a treaty of alliance with France in 1920. A pledge of mutual assistance formed the nucleus of this agreement; and arrangements for the exchange of intelligence information and for regular staff talks gave the accord some practical substance.[14] The alliance underwent slight modifications in 1925, in order to render it compatible with the Locarno accords; but it remained in force until 1936, when Belgium reverted to its traditional policy of neutrality.

Between February 1921 and October 1925 the Quai d'Orsay worked out a political-military accord with Poland. The agreements included a mutual pledge to lend immediate assistance if either became victim of an armed German violation of the Locarno settlement.[15] The "treaty of alliance and friendship" that France and Czechoslovakia signed in January 1924 involved minimal commitments. It merely provided for joint consultation over the defense of their respective territories and future collaboration between the respective general staffs. However, in the following year at Locarno the two nations agreed on mutual assistance in the event that either became victim of an "unprovoked recourse to arms."[16] The letter and spirit of this pact were unequivocal, although its exact relation to the Locarno settlement continued to be ambiguous.

In 1926 and 1927 Roumania and Yugoslavia were drawn more firmly into the French orbit. The Franco-Roumanian treaty, signed in June 1926, allowed for consultation between the two signatories in the event that either became the victim of unprovoked aggression. There was also a provision for joint staff talks, although these were only to be convened when both parties agreed that they were warranted by existing political and military conditions.[17] This treaty, unlike those between France and Poland and France and Czechoslovakia, contained no formal pledge of mutual assistance. The same held true for the treaty of "guarantee and security" that France and Yugoslavia concluded in November 1927. Moreover, this agreement did not include any provision, however ambivalent, for future joint staff talks.[18] Nevertheless, the conclusion of the Franco-Yugoslav accord meant that France had succeeded in drawing to itself a collection of nations whose fears of revisionism corresponded with its own.

It is immensely difficult to define this multifarious assortment of bilateral pacts. It is, however, as convenient as it is simplistic to continue the custom of referring to it as an alliance system, a satellite system, or even more vaguely, a security network. This network's main pretense of unity lay in the fact that each small power shared some common fear with France. Until the mid-1930s the latter had some reason to expect that the policies of these client states would be sympathetically geared to its interests. Until then France might have hoped that an entity like the Little Entente (Czechoslovakia, Roumania, Yugoslavia) would eventually enlarge its framework for cooperation from one of joint opposition to a Hapsburg restoration to one of collective resistance against German, Russian, and Italian influences. But this foreign idea, this French idea, could not be imposed on eastern Europe. The three members of this artificial bloc retained much of their traditional dislike of each other, a dislike fostered by years of cohabitation within the now vanished Hapsburg empire. New grievances based on politics and economics, and exacerbated by the presence of legal territorial boundaries, were added to the old. For these small powers, there was no common enemy, a dilemma which the French never managed to solve.

For their part, the French were never deceived by the facade-like character of the eastern front; however, they did continue to hope that militant German revisionists would think twice before challenging France when it was supported by so many potential allies. And it may even be suggested that this alliance network was a distinct asset to a France that expected to become Germany's initial victim, an expectation the French never wholly discarded at any point in the 1930s. If it would not actually deter Germany from resorting to force, this network did seem to stand as a testament to a continent-wide determination to punish aggression. But if, on the other hand, Germany first turned on the states of central and eastern Europe, the fate of these small allies threatened to become the cause of war between at least two great powers. So was contained the liability of the alliance system. In the event of war the French government would have but two choices. Either it could declare war in the absence of a direct threat to the security of France, or it could renounce its obligations at the eleventh hour, accept the inevitable charges of dishonor, and forfeit much of its claim to great power status. Yet this was only part of the problem. National honor, even national interests, might demand a resort to war, but the subversive voice of reason asked if the allies could be saved. What was to say that these small powers might not be erased from the map of Europe before the white mobilization posters even appeared in France, cruelly if quite inadvertently leaving the French in the lurch? Clearly the honor of France and the fate of her disparate allies depended heavily upon the planning, the capacity, the determination of the French armed forces.

And so one comes full circle, with the mutual needs and objectives of French military and civilian commanders closing around the security of France. Ever convinced of Germany's ill will, and of her potential military superiority, the French had recruited allies to correct the imbalance, thus preserving in the bargain France's dubious pretensions to continued great power status. What this status meant, however, once the German pressure resumed in Eastern Europe was that the demands on French military capacity increased rather than diminished. It was difficult to deter a German drive in the west, but it was that much more difficult to intimidate Germany from moving in the east. Indeed, it could even be said that the more France bolstered its defenses west of the Rhine the more likely it was to encourage Nazi revisionism elsewhere. Once this occurred, the imperfect, but still cherished alliance system threatened to draw France into war rather than ensure against it.

The idea that the conflagration of 1914-18 had been a war to end war did not survive the peace settlement. For the French, what had survived was the German problem and with it the assurance of some future trial of strength. The consequent obsession with *sécurité* in turn inspired constant efforts to alternately prevent and prepare for a new test of arms. Military considerations, whether strategical or tactical, doctrinal or technological, financial or industrial, continually intruded into the realm of foreign policy, raised as they were by professional military commanders

11

or by a disparate civilian command unavoidably attuned to the dictates of modern war. The twenty-year search for peace, conducted with a diligence worthy of no better cause, and the twenty-year quest for military security, thus lent a critical significance to the relationship between diplomacy and military power.

1

Land, Resources, and Strategic Planning

At no time between the wars did official quarters in France discount the possibility of a new German attack. Indeed, it was assumed that Germany would seek to crush the Third Republic as soon as Berlin detected an improvement in the military balance. It is this historically confirmed assumption or, as some would have it, this self-fulfilling prophecy with which this study begins.

Topography dictated the conditions by which any land attack from the east could be undertaken. Broadly speaking, the French had to contend with three extended fronts: their frontiers with Switzerland, Germany, and Belgium-Luxembourg respectively. The French-Swiss frontier, covering a distance of about 255 miles, follows the line of the Jura Mountains between Basle and Geneva. Apart from a soft sector known as the Belfort gap, an area of low ground some 12 miles wide between the southern end of the Vosges and the northern end of the Jura, this front was considered to offer only limited opportunities for a German offensive. Not only would Germany have to assume all the political liabilities attendant on attacking a neutral country, but its communications would be both long and exposed in the mountainous terrain. Moreover, the presence of both French and Swiss forts commanding the Jura passes and the presence of a major fortified area around Belfort—to compensate for the absence of natural obstacles—promised to assure any German invasion a heated reception. Throughout the period in question operational specialists in France and England seem to have regarded this front as potentially the most secure.

The Franco-German frontier comprised two natural sectors, the first running along the Rhine (110 miles) between Basle and Lauterbourg, the second across the Palatinate from Lauterbourg to Longwy on the Belgium-Luxembourg border (115 miles). The Rhine sector, too, was held to be of high defensive potential. On the French side a network of concrete pillboxes arranged in depth from the river bank to the Vosges emplacements afforded an excellent defense against an enemy who first would have to negotiate the Rhine. Equally propitious from the French standpoint, German communications again would be left exposed by the vagaries of nature within a narrow belt of open country between the Rhine and the Black Forest; and the latter, an obvious staging area for troops and supplies, was poorly provided with both roads and railways. Conversely, the Palatinate sector was a natural autobahn, "a great plain, suitable for the passage of all arms and ideal for the movement of mechanized formations."[1] It was here, for historically sterling reasons, that the French were to construct the Maginot Line—along the eastern border not of France but only of Lorraine. What nature had left open the Third Republic would close. By so doing, it was hoped to deny to Germany all but one avenue to Paris, the very one that had taken the miracle of the Marne to seal off in 1914.

This time it was to be different. Balked by Jura, Rhine, and Vosges, by concrete bunkers and Maginot emplacements, Germany virtually would be obliged to retain its 1914 strategy, to try to enter France across the Franco-Belgian frontier.[2] It was this front, over 200 miles in length and roughly two thirds of France's eastern border from Dunquerque to the Rhine, that went largely unfortified until the late 1930s and that belied imaginative press reports about an all-embracing Maginot Line from the North Sea to Switzerland. Why it so remained, apparently vulnerable and inviting, will be touched on subsequently. For the moment it is sufficient to say that the French anticipated that any German attack would come through the Lowlands, either through Holland and Belgium or through Belgium alone. In that contingency, it was reckoned that the boggy, easily flooded land of southern Holland and the wooded Ardennes terrain along the Belgian-German frontier—excepting the Aachen gap (Aachen-Liège), poor in road and rail communications—would so delay an invader as to minimize the possibilities of a surprise

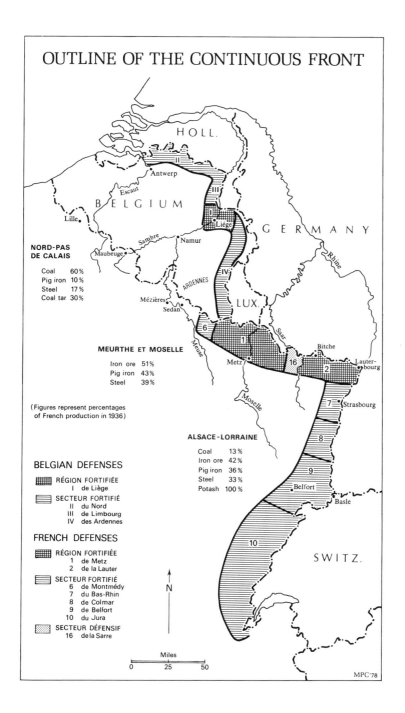

OUTLINE OF THE CONTINUOUS FRONT

HOLL.

Antwerp

Escaut

B E L G I U M

Lille

NORD-PAS
DE CALAIS

Coal   60%
Pig iron 10%
Steel   17%
Coal tar 30%

Maubeuge   Sambre   Namur
Liège

G E R M A N Y

Rhine

ARDENNES

Mézières   LUX.

Sedan

MEURTHE ET MOSELLE

Iron ore 51%
Pig iron 43%
Steel   39%

Meuse

Metz   Saar   Bitche

6   1   16   Lauter-
                bourg

2

Moselle

7   Strasbourg

(Figures represent percentages
of French production in 1936)

ALSACE-LORRAINE

Coal   13%
Iron ore 42%
Pig iron 36%
Steel   33%
Potash   100%

8

BELGIAN DEFENSES

▦ RÉGION FORTIFIÉE
   I   de Liège
▤ SECTEUR FORTIFIÉ
   II   du Nord
   III de Limbourg
   IV   des Ardennes

9

Belfort

Basle

FRENCH DEFENSES

▦ RÉGION FORTIFIÉE
   1   de Metz
   2   de la Lauter
▤ SECTEUR FORTIFIÉ
   6   de Montmédy
   7   du Bas-Rhin
   8   de Colmar
   9   de Belfort
   10 du Jura
▨ SECTEUR DÉFENSIF
   16 de la Sarre

N

10

S W I T Z.

Miles
0   25   50

MPC'78

15

attack. Thus it was that by this scenario the next battle of France would be fought along the Meuse; this time in Belgium.

The alternatives afforded by topographical features, however, are only apparently equitable. What they offer one side may not be identical to what they offer the other. For instance, it is neither by accident nor by partisanship that the potential aggressor and the potential defender have been identified with such single-mindedness. Undeniably, Germany had not been treated lightly by the Versailles architects. Germany was aggrieved and was therefore profoundly and bitterly revisionist in its aims and outlook. Undeniably, France felt equally aggrieved; but it did assume the mantle of a satisfied power in 1919, deeply committed to the preservation of the political and territorial status quo. France was to defend what had been done, Germany to challenge it. This is not to say that such respective roles necessarily dictate the tone of the military strategy each is to adopt, that offensive planning is inconsistent, even incompatible, with objectives that are essentially defensive. Indeed, the Schlieffen Plan, with which Germany launched its assault on Belgium and France in 1914, can be interpreted as the working of a defensive strategy, designed to prevent Germany from being crushed by the Franco-Russian military pincers. However, it is hardly novel to suggest that revisionist powers are more likely to require and thus adopt the instruments of offensive destruction. By this admittedly modest rule of thumb, some correlation may well be seen between France's defensive aspirations in Europe and its de facto renunciation in military terms of the offensive initiative.

In fact, there were far stronger reasons behind France's refusal to court or accept precipitately a new war with Germany. Much of this reticence derived, quite understandably, from the experiences of the First World War. There was a desire, a determination, to avoid a repeat performance of those four years of butchery. But there was, too, a growing awareness that France was imperfectly equipped to continue its martial traditions under the conditions of twentieth-century mass warfare. As topography set certain iron conditions, so also did demography. Germany's population in the 1930s was roughly a third greater than that of France, a serious deficit of some twenty million citizens in a country where birth rates were static at best. By itself this discrepancy was serious enough, particularly in an age that had learned so recently to count army divisions by the hundreds. Was it not obvious that Germany would field a third more divisions and thus make the odds against French survival too poor to be contemplated? But in the temptation to maximize divisional strength there lay yet another and perhaps greater danger. Understandably concerned about comparative field strengths, by the very proximity of this powerful and resentful neighbor, the French still could not afford to forfeit to their armies the critically limited labor resources of their industrial workers. Certainly the British were worried by what they regarded as an unrealistic French goal of seventy-odd divisions in the early weeks of war. Calculations made in London predicted that the curtailment of French industrial production, ensuing from the massive conscription of workers, would mean that close to half of the mobilized divisions could not be supported in the field for more than a month. To strengthen such contentions with true dramatic punch, it was pointed out on more than one occasion that in the last war "the early loss by invasion of the greater proportion of French industry . . . actually helped the French to keep up the man-power of their forces in the field."[3] For the fact is that France was both demographically and industrially disadvantaged. Despite the revamping of much French industry after 1919 and the very substantial economic benefits that came with the return to France of Alsace-Lorraine, German industrial production was reckoned to be at least twice that of the French.[4] Thus, from the point of view of both demography and industry, the French had reason to fear the implications of yet another and more modern war with Germany.

Yet they seemed convinced that it would come, from the day Marshal Foch captioned Versailles a twenty-year truce. How could such a war be fought against an enemy of superior resources? France had to gamble on a quick victory or bow to the necessity of a long war. It chose the latter, retreating before stakes which only those we now call "hawks" would welcome. Everything that had been learned from the last war, for France a successful one, made the conclusion unavoidable: the poorly prepared, punitive, futile offensive stampedes against machine guns; the heroic, victorious defenses on the Marne and at Verdun; the early loss of France's primary industrial region in the north, which in turn dramatically increased its dependence on foreign producers; in all, the successful contest of arms by a resolute defender against an aggressor whose resources had been superior, whose weapons technology initially had been more advanced, and who had capitalized on the factor of surprise. Such were some of the lessons which the French drew from the war. Such were the kinds of considerations which stifled all talk of marching straight for Berlin. By the 1930s and, one suspects, much earlier, reason could not entertain such thoughts.[5] The risks of a German-initiated lightning war were great enough, particularly if French allies were tardy in their response. But for France to undertake such a war, quite possibly prefacing it by some form of preemptive strike, seems to have been regarded as patently foolhardy. In response to their own fears of German reprisals, and in deference to their potential allies—only too easily offended—the French paid no more than lip service to the notion of the knockout blow. A possibility they accorded to their enemy, they nevertheless denied to themselves.

Rather it was the preparation for a long war to which the French turned, just as Germany swung in the opposite direction. For Germany, a central power with a myriad of potentially encircling fronts to consider, the logic of the swift offensive assault still remained valid. On the one hand the assault had come within an ace of stunning victory in 1914; on the other, it seemed to stand confirmed by the way the German war effort had foundered on the allied blockade after 1917. For the French it was precisely the way in which their rival had been vanquished by a prolonged war of attrition waged by an economically superior allied coalition that had so impressed them. Thus it was that their thoughts turned to ways of perfecting, rather than abandoning, the victorious formula that had been devised after 1914.

Just as the French response to the German problem rested on an awareness of topography and an admission of demographic and industrial inferiority, so too their concern derived in large part from certain specific features of their economic potential for modern war. If France recoiled at the idea of a long-shot, knockout blow against the Reich, it could hardly look with equanimity on the prospects of a long, single-handed war against Germany. Excepting the shortage of skilled industrial labor, alluded to earlier, three areas of deficiency were in evidence.

First, the bulk of French heavy industry was concentrated between the Seine and the Belgian and German frontiers. Roughly three quarters of its coal and textile production and nine tenths of its iron ore, pig iron, and steel output were within easy striking distance of the German army and air force. Similarly, 70 percent of the oil-refining capacity, 30 percent of the coal tar, almost 40 percent of the benzol and 70 percent of the sulphate of ammonia originated in the same vulnerable area—an area that included the national capital, the industrially rich nerve center of the country.[6] In the event of another invasion like that of 1914, following which so much of this region had been turned instead to German exploitation, and without the intervention of powerful allies, French prospects in a long war were negligible.

Thus it was that the protection of this area, only partially shielded by the Maginot Line, became the initial and unalterable goal of French strategy. Yet even with this objective secured, France had other perils with which to contend. The second major deficiency lay in the shortages of certain crucial raw materials and in certain limitations of the manufacturing capacity. The following indicate in percentages (applicable for the mid to late 1930s) the proportions of vital war material imports: rubber (100 percent), coal (30-35 percent), crude petroleum (99 percent), manganese (100 percent), copper metal (99 percent), lead metal (87 percent), zinc metal (40 percent), tin metal (95 percent), and nickel metal (30 percent). And whereas it is true that France could produce virtually all its own wheat, fertilizers, iron ore, and aluminum, it was also seriously short of raw wool and cotton and, to the despair of the munitions industry, of sulphur and pyrites.[7] Between such deficiencies and France's productive capacity there was an inviolable connection: steel production, for instance, being dependent on the importation of adequate supplies of manganese; automobile tires on assured supplies from abroad of either natural or synthetic rubber; electrical wares on the availability of copper, and ammunition on that of cotton, nickel, and lead. But even an assured supply of raw materials was not the only answer, was not enough to overcome the frailties which plagued certain branches of French industrial activity. For example, for most of the period in question the desultory production of the French air industry—frames and engines—meant that hardly more than a handful of military aircraft became operational in any given year, most of them already rendered obsolete by an artisanal system that could not compete with serial production methods employed elsewhere. The plight of France's naval and commercial shipyards was no less grave—contributing to an almost constant decline in merchant ship construction between 1921 and 1937 and a resultant fall into seventh place in world merchant fleets, behind the British, Americans, Japanese, Norwegians, Germans, and Italians.[8] And if, in a more promising light, the French armaments industry headed by Schneider of Le Creusot was one of the biggest in the world, it had a herculean task to equip with ever more modern weapons a "unique" European power which required a large army, navy, and air force "at the same time."[9]

Given these raw material deficiencies and these limitations of manufacturing capacity—raised by this cursory survey—it seems clear that many of the older notions about a Franco-German war could be relegated to history. Though still regarded under the weight of tradition as two vying great powers, certainly by the 1930s the contest had become manifestly inequitable. Should northeastern France be lost either to destruction or occupation, the game was over. Should it be held, everything would depend on France's ability to finance and transport the vital raw materials and whatever foreign manufactured goods were necessary to supplement French production. Quite apart from any consideration of finance, it was obvious that metropolitan France could not expect to wage a long war without the resources of its far-flung empire and without the cooperation of at least benevolently neutral foreign powers. Here is raised France's third major liability in modern war. Not only had France to find the requisite materials abroad, but it had to rely heavily on other powers for their safe transit to France. As one very long note on industrial mobilization stressed, a note prepared in 1940 but which spoke to all the key interwar assumptions:

> We are therefore obliged to call, first of all, upon the resources of the Empire—material as well as human—without overlooking the hazards of sea transport during hostilities. We must then call upon the resources of foreign nations, with all the uncertainty this entails with respect to the geographical location of hostile and neutral countries, to import possibilities, to competition in the world markets and to financial and transportation arrangements.[10]

The empire, the principals of which included Algeria, Morocco, Tunisia, Indochina, French West Africa, and Madagascar, could contribute manpower as well as foodstuffs, iron ore, phosphates, nickel, and lead; so too, at least potentially, it could offer a revenue-producing export trade market for France, although in peacetime the trade balance between metropol and colonies tended to be marginally adverse for France.[11] But if the empire were held to be more politically reliable than truly foreign countries, without overstating the imperial attachments expressed within many native communities of these colonies, the logistics problems attendant on its support were very considerable. On the one hand it was unlikely that the French navy alone could adequately protect commercial shipping in both the Mediterranean and the Atlantic. On the other, it was incontestable that the French merchant fleet could not handle unaided the increased tonnage expected in war circumstances. Indeed, no more than a third of France's total requirements and no more than a seventh of its oil supplies were expected to be carried in French ships. The painful truth was that in the late 1930s English ships carried more goods to and from France than did the French merchant navy. Moreover, almost half by weight of seaborne imports to France was handled by ports between the Seine and the Belgian border, a statistic that further underscored the potential role of the Royal Navy in French strategic planning. Thus while France had to face the problem of ensuring continued supplies from abroad, not all of which by any means could be found within its own empire, it also had to rely on foreign ships to carry almost three quarters of its import-export tonnage and on the British navy not to obstruct this critical traffic.[12]

To these preceding remarks, designed to show at one and the same time why the French planned on a long war, how marginal were their resources and how dependent they were on outside assistance, it is important to add two further observations. First, it is quite true that Germany faced similar problems and comparable deficiencies. Indeed, the grand strategy that was worked out by the British and French in 1939 gave particular stress to Germany's vulnerability to prolonged economic pressure.[13] France lacked adequate coal supplies, and Germany suffered from an acute shortage of iron ore. France's industrial capacity was dangerously concentrated in the northern departments, and Germany's were almost comparably centered in the great Ruhr complex. Both had to import petroleum and its derivatives, pyrites, nickel, copper, cotton, and cereals.[14] Moreover, it may well be that considerations of such a coin were as responsible for the shape German strategy assumed under the Nazis as they seem to have been for that of the French, even though the conclusions drawn from them appear to have been widely divergent. Our concern, however, must be focused on France, and it is to this end that the foregoing has been presented—not to mislead by over-bleak assessments, but rather to underline the basic economic problems confronting a country already exceptionally weakened by the enduring ravages of a world depression.

The second observation is of a different order, expressly singled out because of its underlying importance to French diplomacy and strategic planning in the 1930s. Quite apart from the capacity of the Royal Navy either to impede or facilitate French commercial shipping—and under optimum conditions to join in the offensive war against Germany—Britain and its empire occupied a position of pivotal importance to the French economy. By 1937, 45 percent of all foreign tonnage carried in and out of France was transported under the British flag, a figure that dropped to no less than 32 percent of the entire tonnage, French and foreign. Of comparable importance to French industry was the trade with Britain and its empire, a trade that accounted for roughly 35 percent of French trade by value as opposed to about 25 percent with its own imperial domains. For instance, something like a third of French manganese, coal, and coke imports came from British sources, as did 40 to 95 percent of French requirements in jute, rubber, tin, and raw wool.[15] And whereas in the early 1930s over 50 percent of French petroleum supplies were of American origin, toward the end of that decade efforts were being made to increase imports of British-dominated Persian oil and thus to take advantage of Britain's incomparably larger tanker fleet.[16] Such considerations, combined with Britain's edge in aeronautical and naval construction, in the automotive industry, and in the manufacture of machine tools and precision tools, gave further emphasis to the importance of the United Kingdom in the kind of war for which the French felt obliged to prepare. The following sentiments, expressed in a French war ministry document of April 1939, were in fact symptomatic of French thinking between the wars. "Even today we could only defeat Germany in a war if we were assured, in every possible respect, of total British assistance."[17]

It need hardly be stressed that the circumstances in which such preparations were undertaken were far from ideal. Indeed, it is ironic that the French vision of the next war, with its focus on industrial mobilization and economic conditioning, should have struggled to express itself in the troubled years of the world depression. Although France, as an importer of raw materials, took advantage of the decline in primary prices, its revenue as a principal exporter of manufactured goods correspondingly suffered from dwindling markets in primary producing countries. In fact, France's share of the world's export market was virtually halved between 1929 and 1937.[18] Nor was this simply a reflection of contracting foreign markets. By French reckoning, over the same eight-year period their production had declined by 25 percent, while Germany and Britain had enjoyed an increase of 17 and 24 percent respectively. And in certain vital industrial enterprises the record was even more specifically bleak. By 1937 Germany had overtaken France in automotive and aeronautical production and had increased its steel production by a phenomenal 300 percent compared to a modest rise of 30 percent in France.[19] Thus the combined effect of contracted markets abroad and insufficient domestic production spelled major trouble, for this decline in cash revenues had to be taken as especially serious in a country that placed so much emphasis on the accumulation of a massive gold reserve. Without such reserves, it was asked with very good reason how France could finance the vital wartime imports on which her national security rested.[20] Further to this, the declining value of the franc, after which came inflation and the flight of capital from the national economy, further undermined the financial premises upon which French strategy rested. Moreover, the floundering of the French currency in the mid and late thirties not only produced immediate restraints on government expenditure—including to some degree that on behalf of national defense—but it called into question the nation's capacity to fulfill the requisite financial objectives for a successful war effort.

Partly in response to the diverse pressures generated by the depression and partly owing to the storm clouds brewing over international politics, in March 1938 the French government introduced to the legislature a kind of omnibus national defense bill called the *loi sur l'organisation de la nation en temps de guerre*. Within the brief space of four months this comprehensive legislation was to receive statutory recognition by the law of 11 July 1938, a law that won the unanimous support of the members of both houses. As significant as this ambitious measure was, however, it would be more accurate to see it as the culmination rather than the beginning of nation-in-arms planning. It is true that this bill had been delayed by ten years of parliamentary study and investigation, but it is no less clear that many of its provisions had undergone de facto implementation long before 1938. For instance, the state's right of requisition in moments of international crisis had been exercised since 1935, well before this provision had been written into the law of 1938.[21] Indeed, it is just such examples of the state's already sweeping powers that demanded the formalization of a national program. War was, after all, the enterprise of industrial giants, monsters that could consume hundreds and thousands of men in a single day but whose essential food and drink was coal and steel, iron and gasoline. To train such leviathans to their bidding, governments had to control economic as well as military mobilization. This they had learned to do in the course of the First World War, had been obliged to do in the name of *la patrie* and in disregard of cherished capitalist principles of state behavior. But now, as the French had recognized in the early 1920s when the bill first had been proposed, it was necessary to anticipate this involvement, to prepare rationally and meticulously the state intervention which the First World War had solicited in only piecemeal fashion. To this end the 1938 law either created, confirmed, or refined such state powers as those that permitted the integration of military strategy and industrial planning and that gave the state powers to conscript labor, to assume control over all trade, and to appropriate privately owned materials, "including foodstuffs, raw materials, manufacturing processes and patents."[22] After almost two decades of careful planning and measure-by-measure implementation, France now had "a legal basis for what had been a carefully erected structure": a law for the "economic mobilization of the whole country."[23]

If this law articulated the role and objectives of the state in national defense planning, it was the Conseil Supérieur de la Défense Nationale (CSDN) that was left to prepare the plans and methods of operation and to coordinate all ministerial action in matters pertaining to national defense. Composed essentially of cabinet ministers,[24] this committee was an expression in the 1920s and 1930s of the exalted importance the French had come to attach to joint military-civilian planning and to the integration of military and economic mobilization. To these ends the *conseil's* study commission and permanent secretariat worked for twenty years to articulate through their planning the French way in warfare. Although the *conseil* proper had but a checkered career in the 1930s, meeting irregularly if at all from the mid-decade, the permanent secretariat under General Jamet worked to the eve of war on arrangements for the procurement of raw materials and foodstuffs, for the control of wartime labor and manpower allocation, and for the efficient transition to industrial mobilization in wartime.[25]

Yet another service which the CSDN promised to perform, something implicit in its mandate, was the opening of a dialogue between France's military and civilian commanders. While deliberative powers in the *conseil* were all but confined to the ministers, the chiefs of the French armed forces were expected to attend in a consultative capacity.[26] Here, so it was hoped, desiderata of all sorts could be raised by both civilian and military spokesmen, as part of the underlying effort to maximize all resources for the benefit and support of the fighting forces. Regrettably, however, the CSDN did not fare well in this respect. It may have been too large for useful dialogue, a "monster" as one general called it; and certainly its terms of reference were regarded by many officers as evidence of a perverse civilian determination to resist military influence. What is more, whether or not one accepts as completely judicious the complaint that the CSDN was really the cabinet listening to itself, it does seem probable that the interest in holding frequent meetings was minimized by the fact that the key committee members met regularly in cabinet on matters of similar if not identical bearing.[27] In any event one may divine something more fundamental beneath many of these understandable but hardly profound complaints from the French high command. Whereas the interests of soldier and civilian in one sense were entirely compatible, there was no denying the differences between them in the ranking of defense priorities. Certainly many of the criteria deemed essential by long-range civilian planners, with their emphasis on stockpiling, industrial renovation, and the accumulation of extensive capital reserves, were not calculated to appeal to staff officers whose preoccupation was with current divisional strength and equipment.[28] Whatever the cause, however, it does seem clear that the CSDN contributed little that was positive to the dialogue between France's military and civilian commanders.

Although their roles were assuredly less ambitious than that of the CSDN, the Haut Comité Militaire (HCM) and the Comité Permanent de la Défense Nationale (CPDN) may be mentioned here under the same rubric. Both had a narrower mandate than the CSDN, charged initially as they were with the *direction militaire de la guerre,* and both revealed as a result of that mandate a heavier military composition. However, like the CSDN, both attempted to facilitate the military-civilian dialogue, and more significantly, both discovered through experience what in fact had been the wellspring of their prestigious mentor. Military affairs could not be treated in isolation. So it was that if the HCM (1932-1936) were to coordinate the planning, rearmament, and funding of all three service branches, its records also show how frequently, how unavoidably, its members came to dwell on such questions as industrial mobilization and raw material stockpiling.[29] Its successor, the CPDN (1936-1939), followed the same path, abandoning in practice the theoretical distinction between *direction générale* and *direction militaire.* With a membership identical to that of the HCM, although equipped at last with a secretariat and a direct administrative link to the minister of national defense, this committee not only busied itself with matters of colonial defense and military aid to continental allies but also with the mobilization of labor, the supply of oil and petrochemicals, and the licensing, manufacture, and sale of French arms and war materials.[30] Moreover, the CPDN in fact, if not necessarily in mandate, played a more active watchdog role in French international policy than either its predecessor or the CSDN. As for the matter of military-civilian dialogue, the irregularity and relative infrequency of meetings,[31] exacerbated by the only occasional appearances of the foreign minister or his secretary-general—neither of whom was even an *ex officio* member—clearly minimized the formal occasions afforded by the CPDN to discuss diplomacy in the light of the nation's war strategy and capacity. For all its imperfections, however, the CPDN would appear to have been the most effective and ambitious attempt at interministerial coordination between the wars, a judgment beside which one is tempted to add the caveat: necessarily so. By the summer of 1936, when this committee assumed its functions, a new international trial of strength had become less unthinkable and less remote. In France, Germany's universally recognized potential superiority now seemed on the threshold of being made actual. As such the political circumstances confronting the CPDN were a good deal more menacing than those which had faced the Conseil Supérieur de la Défense Nationale or the Haut Comité Militaire.

By this time the die had been cast as far as French strategy was concerned. And not without irony. From the moment the peacemakers had rested in 1919, the only cause for French rejoicing—apart from the return of the lost provinces—was the escape from defeat. Nothing but this could induce them to suffer so again, within one widow's lifetime. In the name of this goal, at once humble and grand, their leaders effectively committed France to just such a war, a repeat war, a long war of attrition. It was not what they wanted, not what they preferred; for they preferred no war at all. Rather it came to them as the best of several unattractive alternatives. For unless there was to be a return to the old smash and grab notion of the *offensive à outrance,* by now largely discredited, there was but one other alternative—a compromise formula based on an elite corps of offensively oriented professional soldiers backed and supported by the mobilized nation-in-arms. Although this is not the moment to explore the fate of this latter proposal, it certainly must be said that the "official" view of war by no means found universal acceptance. As early as 1923 General Serrigny, a member of the CSDN and himself an expert on industrial mobilization, expressed reservations about some of the implications of this modern, mass war syndrome. What would happen to the army, he mused, if all farmers stayed in the fields and all technicians in their plants and factories. Who but the "vagabonds" would be available for active duty? Far from being curtly dismissed as merely a rhetorical barb cast in the name of vested interest, the general's question warrants attention, for in fact it points again to the potential and paradoxical conflict of interest between active and supportive combatants: armies defending unprepared nations, or nations supporting unprepared armies.[32] And a decade later it was the young de Gaulle who asked in feigned amazement how France could possibly have *planned* to wage war like that again. For him, a junior officer, the strategy of 1917-1918 had been essentially a *pis-aller*, a last resort, one which had ended well but not one which warranted emulation.[33] Nonetheless, these as yet were not de Gaulle's innings, and Clemenceau's had barely passed. War was still too serious a business to be left to the discretion of khakied mandarins.

Serrigny's fears had almost come to pass by the early 1930s. The expansive vision of the CSDN, still hard at work on the organization of the nation in time of war, was effectively committing France to a war of long duration. As a result, and in the short run, offensive punch seemed to require little accent. The day would come when the enemy would have to be destroyed; but until resources permitted, the primary and all important objective was to prevent defeat and ward off invasion. To accomplish this the national strategy comprised the following essentials: the assured inviolability of industrially rich northern France; the mobilization of all domestic resources; guaranteed access to the necessary imperial and foreign markets; and the maintenance of secure routes of communication and transportation. Such were the measures held to be vital to the defense of France. These, together with the indispensable contribution from eventual allies, would reverse Germany's advantage in the course of time and thus lead to its collapse. Little wonder, therefore, that France's senior commanding officers expected the war to open with a defensive siege of perhaps as much as two years in duration. It seemed likely that at least that much time would have to elapse before the resources of France and its allies would be great enough to permit the commencement of the strategic offensive.[34]

By 1933, the outset of the Nazi period, France's three armed services had assumed strategic roles that were deemed consistent with the national strategy. To this war plan, for instance, the navy was expected to make a vital contribution. The demographic deficits of metropolitan France were to be combatted by troops raised from the standing colonial army or from native reserves—troops which would be transported to France by the *Marine.* So too the oil tankers, the coal barges, and the ships bearing manganese, copper, and jute to France's war economy, were to rely on the protective escort of the Republic's navy. Thus, if there was little the latter could do for the defense of Lille or Nancy, it did have a critical role in maintaining the uninterrupted flow of seaborne raw materials to those inland centers. Without a doubt this was one of the key reasons behind the CSDN's recommendation in 1932 that France should aim for a two-power standard: naval parity with the combined German and Italian fleets.[35] And, of course, from the outbreak of hostilities the navy was expected to exert its offensive weight by means of attacks on the enemy's merchant marine and navy, coastal installations, and ports. Certainly within the CSDN's conception of economic warfare the navy occupied an absolutely vital position—one that does much to explain the success of its lobby in securing very healthy shares of government funding. It was this belief in "a powerful battle fleet," as Daladier was to put it, "ensuring control of the seas," which made the navy "the major beneficiary of financial allocations."[36]

Perhaps for the converse reason the French air force experienced a less happy fate. The fact is that its strategic role had become a subject for fierce, even acrimonious, debate. For a variety of reasons, most of which were associated with its overlong bondage to the land army, the air force had to struggle for credit support and for a strategically significant mission.[37] Having only become an independent force in 1933, a full decade after the Royal Air Force, the French service suffered from the rigors of partisan debate. Whereas few officers suffered gladly the traditional army view of air power—at best a tactical support weapon for the land forces—no fewer questioned the quite immodest claims of the Douhetistes who saw modern bombers as the only meaningful strategic weapon. Owing to its speed, mobility, and firepower the aircraft seemed to have a multiplicity of functions and roles, the very attributes which encouraged the French to experiment at such length with all-purpose machines. As a result, however, its strategic role and therefore its place in the national strategy was more open to interpretation. Defying precise and accurate definition, because the debate within France continued unabated, it need only be said at this point that the air force had more than its share of strategic bombing enthusiasts. In this sense, certainly, with its emphasis on the destruction of the enemy's economic superstructure, the air force had—or at least claimed to have—the kind of role that was entirely in keeping with the CSDN's vision of modern war. Furthermore, the air force's strategic role in defensive terms was never questioned, if by that one simply means the protection of France's own industrial terminals. Although again there was a debate over the ways in which this defense could be achieved—fighters against enemy bombers or bombers against enemy air bases—the defensive potential of the French air force was well recognized as a key instrument in the implementation of the national war strategy.

Like that of the navy, the army's role in French strategic planning was assured of great distinction. Placed in the front lines by the presence of the German Wehrmacht, figuratively and literally, the French army clearly did stand guard over the destiny of France. Given the industrialization of modern warfare, which none now denied, to lose the battle for northern France was in all likelihood to lose the war. The whims of nature, manifested in topographical features and the geographical location of industries, meant that the enemy would be strongly tempted to tear right through the heart of modern France. For the defender there was no room for error. It was this recognition of the enormity of the stakes at hand that led the interwar army to its sometimes senselessly defamed doctrine of war. In total conformity with the national strategy, one devised by civilian and military experts alike, this army placed an entirely understandable emphasis on the need for a truly inviolable frontier defense. Only if the enemy were stopped short of successful invasion did it seem likely that he could be defeated in the fulness of time. It is to this reasoning—credible enough within the context of nation-in-arms warfare —that one must turn to understand the thinking of the French high command and its civilian overseers in the 1930s. It is in this light, and perhaps this light only, that one discovers the roots of that terrible French nightmare, namely that premature offensive action might rebound into retreat, ignominious rout, and invasion. In this light, too, it may prove possible to explain the French failure to start shooting each time Hitler defied the League of Nations, without having recourse to the terminology of moral stupor and turpitude.

By now the essential outline of the army's military doctrine should be apparent. The army's own blueprint for war was merely a more particular version of that being prepared by and for the nation as a whole. Stopping the enemy was the first step. In army parlance the force designated for this sacred mission was the *couverture* or cover force. Although it was possible to vary the degree of its strength, depending on how many reserve classes were called up to reinforce the regular army, the minimum *couverture* force amounted to one million men: the regular army plus the three most recently released reserve classes, known as the *disponibles*. It was behind this force, quickly entrenched along the frontiers, that full military and industrial mobilization would be effected. For reasons so recently outlined, no offensive action was to be undertaken until this cover force was in place—an operation requiring up to two weeks to complete. The fact is, however, that such action in the early months of war was almost certain to be extremely limited in scope. The strategic offensive, after all, could not be undertaken until French superiority in war materiel was beyond question. In other words, just as the nation had to undergo a vigorous muscle-building exercise in terms of industrial productivity, so too the army expected to have quite dramatic margins of superiority in weapons and munitions before it would send troops against modern defensive weapons. Only then would one expect to enter the second stage of this so evidently two-part war. Far from being exclusively defensive minded, as so often alleged, the French always insisted that wars were won by offensives. This *doctrine de la défensive-offensive*, like the national strategy it served, made it clear that the enemy would have to be defeated, finished off by a series of stunnin irresistible offensives. Thus the theories of cover and materiel belonged to the unfolding of stage one. Only if they found successful expression under the exigencies of modern war could France expect to undertake the defeat of Germany.[38]

In the first instance, however, everything rested on the successful defense of France, a subject that requires further attention in order to complete this initial discussion of the army's strategic function and the doctrine of war that served as its underpinning. Central to this doctrine, and springing again from the land and the industries of northern France, was the theory of defense known as the *front continu*. Faced with the necessity of rendering the country inviolable and troubled by the memories of the bloody stalemate which had been occasioned in 1914 by two opposing armies strung out across the breadth of France, the French government slowly committed itself in the 1920s to the notion of a frontier defense based on a theoretically continuous front of natural obstacles and artificial fortifications. Beyond a doubt the idea had merit, particularly now that the pre-1914 concept of a flexible frontier defense had been replaced by one which forbade even the whisper of withdrawal. Yet it was the disillusionment and bitterness occasioned by the apparent failure of this continuous front theory that did more damage to the reputation of the French high command and of France itself than any other single aspect of army doctrine or the national strategy. Certainly it was this theory, commonly associated with the apocryphal Maginot Line from Dunquerque to Basle, that does much to explain the shock brought down by the German breakthrough of 1940.

Unless one is prepared to insist that a continuous front should be circular rather than linear, one will accept with grace the notion that what is important about such a defense is its extended length—a feature that makes outflanking maneuvers both arduous and perilous.[39] In effect, the enemy can not go around; he must come through, thus exposing himself to the punishing firepower from prepared defensive positions. Ever conscious of the topographical features with which this study began, the French established their defensive front according to the dictates of terrain. First came the Franco-Swiss frontier and the Franco-German Rhine frontier, over 350 miles in length, furnished with natural lines of defense and supplemented according to need by artificially constructed barriers. This was followed by the Franco-German frontier in the Palatinate, another hundred miles, naturally vulnerable but by the 1930s bristling with Maginot Line defenses. Then, instead of following the Franco-Belgian border, costly and technically difficult to fortify as well as being diplomatically complicated, the French envisioned their front running northeastwards along the natural line of defense offered by the Ardennes forest and the river Meuse, a front that could be extended in the mind's eye for another 200 miles into southern Holland. Such was the outline of France's continuous front, some 600 miles in length, in fact a far cry from being as silly and ill-conceived as the Germans made it appear by their famous race to Sedan.

Nonetheless, if the historical record seldom proves inevitability, the same cannot be said for fallibility. Guided in very large part by considerations of terrain, the French clearly and knowingly accepted a substantial risk by obliging themselves to rely on a front one third of which lay beyond their own frontiers. That they recognized this danger well before Hitler took power in Germany is made manifestly clear by the proceedings of the Conseil Supérieur de la Guerre, the army's senior military committee. Similarly, the implications of their decision were immediately clear, as Marshal Pétain repeatedly emphasized. "A priori, then, the defense of the northern frontier consists solely of determining where to establish a defensive line within Belgium."[40] Ideally, with French cooperation, Belgium would prepare defensive positions along the Meuse, positions into which France's northern armies would move in the event of a German attack. The continuous front, theoretically sound, would be transformed into an effective line of fire, conveniently situated well in advance of France's industrial jugular. Of course, as we now know, the plan failed; and with it went the battle for France. Ironically, had the Wehrmacht retained its original plan the attack would have come where it was expected, in the Lowlands. And it would have been there, as expected, that the battle of France would have been fought. Instead, the Germans were obliged to gamble that the Ardennes terrain would not be as difficult as they themselves had hitherto imagined, thus catching the French army on its way to one of history's most famous unfought battles.

2

Disarmament and the Drift toward Arms Equality, 1933

The national grand strategy to which France had committed itself by 1933 was a response to the German problem, a problem which twice had been expressed in warfare in modern times. Certainly the arrival in power of Adolf Hitler at the end of January 1933 was an extraneous reminder to the French of latent Franco-German antagonisms. After all, French strategy and the armed forces which would execute it had been organized since 1919 on the premise of a hostile and revanchist Germany. Though in the early years of power the Nazis were no more capable of waging full-scale war than the last Weimar government which they had succeeded, they nonetheless did bring to the international scene a new tone if not a new vocabulary of rhetorical invective. It was to this that the French were obliged to respond, to a German regime which spat openly on the Versailles peace, which hailed war as a virtue, and yet which knew how to play the right kind of melodies before the international Disarmament Conference now assembled in Geneva.

Before turning to the French response to Nazi Germany, however, it would be good to conduct a brief survey of the French armed forces in 1933. Earlier remarks have concentrated on considerations of broad strategic significance and, in particular, on the strategic assignments assumed by the three armed services. These remarks have been intended to sustain a general validity or applicability through the entire period under discussion. They do not speak, therefore, to the question of actual capac-

33

ity at any given moment; and they have neglected purposefully many practical details which must be considered essential to any understanding of the French armed forces.

Given French assumptions about the nature of any future war with Germany, the navy's role was at once the most fundamental and the least immediate. It could do very little to assist in the initial defense of northern France; it could do much to ensure Germany's ultimate defeat. As suggested, it was owing to this grand strategic function that the navy did so well financially at the hands of the government. In the last analysis it was the ultimate weapon in the kind of war anticipated by the Conseil Supérieur de la Défense Nationale. As a result, the navy must have entered 1933 in fine spirits. At least it had reason to have done so. Despite the trend toward greater economies in government spending, the CSDN had assured the navy of continued financial support by promoting the objective of a two-power standard. Moreover, the modernization of the fleet was nearing completion. Indeed, a grand total of thirty warships had been completed in 1932—including nineteen submarines—and another thirteen had been laid down. With the bulk of its active forces concentrated in the Mediterranean—some sixty men-of-war—France's naval deployment eloquently expressed the country's concern for the safety of its crucial sea lane, a concern incidentally that drew its chief inspiration from Italy rather than Germany.[1] Accordingly, and in some contrast to the other services, the navy in 1933 not only found itself in good health but obliged to find its chief rival in a country which France as a whole regarded as a potential belligerent of only secondary importance.

The air force was in less happy circumstances. When Hitler came to power, this third and still very junior service remained in apprenticeship to the land army. This meant that its strategic role as an independent striking force was most uncertain, which in turn meant that its grounds for financial claims on the government were left ill defined and shaky. Indeed, its progress toward a mature and independent status had been frustratingly slow, particularly in a country which for years had boasted the largest military air force in Europe. Not until the spring of 1933, in fact, did military aviation achieve legal recognition as an autonomous branch of the armed forces—five years after the creation of a ministry for air and two years after the formation of a Conseil Supérieur de l'Air, comparable to the top level control committees of the army and navy. What is more, even this much needed and belated step had to be taken more by cunning than by audacity, relying on such delightfully ambiguous expressions as

opérations aériennes to carve a conceptual niche for independent air action undertaken by an independently organized air force.[2] Nevertheless,
it is important to realize that the air force had been functioning under
these conditions of imposed stealth for more than a decade. By 1933, to
the extent that the army seriously believed in air power at all, it believed
in it as an auxiliary arm: providing artillery spotting, reconnaissance information, and on occasion, active intervention in battlefield operations.
In short, what France was expected to have in 1933, should have had,
was an air force designed for air defense, army cooperation, and tactical
assault bombing.

By such criteria the land army had excellent reason for satisfaction
at the outset of 1933. With approximately three quarters of its forces
equipped and organized for army cooperation, the air staff could do little
more than dream of some truly ambitious strategic function.[3] For the
time being, therefore, it was prepared to concentrate its resources in
favor of the ground war in the Lowlands or northern France. Moreover,
the maintenance in 1933 of France's long-standing margin of air superiority over Germany no doubt gratified land commanders who thought of
air power primarily within the context of their kind of war. Finally, it
would appear that some grounds for optimism still could be found within
the French aircraft industry. Certainly British observers in Paris scarcely
could contain their astonishment at the progress realized by the industry
in 1932—singling out for comment the recent French experiments on
lightweight but powerful air engines, metal propellers, instrumentation
design, and instrument flying, all of which were admitted to be comparable if not superior to British technology. Indeed, the ambassador was
not above warning his peers in London that recent French achievements
"should provide a spur to the British engine and aircraft industry," underscoring his point by observing that however "remarkable" it may
seem, some French aircraft had speeds "comparable to our latest aircraft."[4]

The air force's self-assessment, however, was considerably less
sanguine—a fact which galled army strategists. The army, it could be
said, was prepared to live indefinitely with an aggrieved air force; indeed
the tension which existed between their respective strategic ambitions
seemed virtually to preclude mutual satisfaction. The phraseology of the
1933 legislation which created the independent air force clearly disturbed
the army staff, fearing as they did—and with much justice—that the continued pursuit of an independent strategic strike force on the part of the

air commanders would lead increasingly to an air force that was less and less suited to army cooperation. In fact the advent of Hitler came in a moment of fierce debate within France. The army frankly demanded "the preservation of the status quo" while the air ministry pressed for the development of a strategic bombing arm. As the minister cautioned the Haut Comité Militaire, "Our bombing arm is no longer capable of carrying out the tasks which it would have to face at the very outset of a conflict."[5] To France's misfortune, this debate over what the agenda cryptically called *l'emploi de l'aviation* was never adequately resolved. The army continued to insist on the organization and equipment of the air force for the purposes of the ground war. The air force continued to promote the cause of the bombing arm, insisting all the while on its absolute fidelity to the principle of army cooperation. To accomplish this hardly modest feat, to serve itself, to allay army misgivings, and perhaps to silence those impassioned speakers at the Disarmament Conference who so disliked bombing aircraft, the French air staff turned with renewed interest to the multipurpose aircraft. Here were bombers in disguise, machines theoretically designed for any of the key missions—Bombardement, Combat, Renseignement—but which in practice proved suspiciously best suited for the missions demanded of medium and heavy bombers. It was at this juncture of French air development that the Nazis intruded, just as the ministry in Paris was moving away from specialization in aircraft design and toward "all purpose machines."[6] It was here, as the march toward these machines picked up pace, as it did in 1933 with the adoption of the BCR experiment, that France encountered Hitler's new regime. Would the *avion à tout faire* prove capable of measuring up to its ambitious nomenclature?

The French army in 1933, like its service counterparts, enjoyed a clear margin of superiority over its German rival. Against Germany's legal entitlement of 100,000 regular soldiers, France had as its nucleus twenty infantry divisions and some five light motorized cavalry divisions in metropolitan France, a standing force which comprised some 340,000 men and officers. Over and above this substantial edge, and a de facto part of the standing army, were thirty battalions of special fortress troops, or *frontaliers,* and four to five divisions of special mobile forces normally stationed in France although nominally part of the overseas forces. Thus even without the 40,000 paramilitary effectives afforded by the Garde Républicaine de Paris, the gendarmerie, and the Garde Républicaine Mobile, France's effective peacetime strength in 1933 stood in the region of 450,000 men and officers.[8] As such, the statistics suggested a four to one advantage in favor of France and against a Germany to whom conscription was still legally forbidden. However misleading such calculations were, a notion enthusiastically marketed by the French general staff, there was good reason to conclude that Germany would not be capable of a major war effort for several years.[9]

Yet the French drew slight consolation from this state of affairs. Such an advantage, altogether ephemeral in the long war that was anticipated, was seen as having but limited significance. The fact is that France had no intention of exploiting the current advantage, provoking Germany to arms then launching a preemptive attack. As Ambassador Sir William Tyrrell observed from Paris:

> French opinion, in face of the new menace, instead of advancing specious reasons for active measures against Germany, has confined itself, in fact, to pointing to the necessity of maintaining France's existing superiority in armaments . . . France has, in fact, fallen back on a policy of extreme caution; she is opposed to any forceful measures which would savour of military adventure. [10]

Having effectively renounced the military initiative, the result of a combined civilian and military decision, the French army occupied itself with questions of a defensive nature. It was here that the security of France and the success of the national strategy ultimately rested; and it was in this ultimate, long-range sense that French anxieties were understandable in 1933. In the first place the French knew perfectly well that Germany was in constant violation of the Versailles arms provisions. In fact, Germany had long since acquired a substantial arsenal of modern and, for it, prohibited weapons, including military aviation; and its effective standing army was significantly greater than its legal entitlement allowed, thanks to clandestine training undertaken in various paramilitary formations.[11] Thus, France's actual superiority in land forces was a good deal less pronounced than the formal statistics would countenance, a conclusion which in no way prompted its spurning of the military initiative but which certainly did underline the perils of complacency. Second, this fear of being duped by official statistics, together with the new presence of an aggressive Nazi regime, revived French misgivings about the gamble they had taken in the north. Surely greater attention would have to be paid to the possibility of defensive installations

37

along the frontier with Belgium. As General Maxime Weygand, vice-president of the army's Conseil Supérieur de la Guerre, admonished:

> Our whole plan of action has been prepared with the aim of bolstering the Belgians on the German-Luxembourg frontier. But if circumstances did not allow him (General Weygand) to arrive soon enough, it would be advantageous to have fortified positions ready for use on our frontier. [12]

Finally, underlying these anxieties was the whole question of French military effectives. Here, a series of mutually competitive desiderata clashed and vied for recognition. Ruthlessly simplified, however, the contest pitted financial restraint against army requirements. Prompted in large measure by the contracting economy, the government was inclined to decrease the overall army expenditure and to make cuts in the number of France's regular effectives. Indeed, in the course of 1933 the army was to suffer a budgetary decline of one seventh (slightly over a billion francs) and a reduction of some 500 officers and 28,000 men. [13] Conversely, the army wished to reinstitute a two-year period of military service—in place of the current, less costly, one-year period—and to increase its contingent of professional soldiers. Looking ahead to the "lean years," when the size of the annual class of conscripts would be reduced by half, the army staff now insisted that the country was on the threshold of extreme peril. [14] For all these reasons, therefore, the French found the present troublesome and the future uninviting. General Weygand is said to have been so on edge that he was afraid to leave Paris for even the briefest of visits for fear that further reductions would be ordered in his absence. [15] In short, while the war minister admitted that the army could do nothing more than protect the country from invasion, France's senior commanding officer bitterly refused to assure even this. [16] For Weygand, as for his most decorated colleagues in the army council, the days of peril were fast returning.

There were also other matters that were troubling the French army in 1933. These included the mobilization and the modernization of the land forces. The former of course was an essential prerequisite for the effective defense of France; as such it demanded constant vigilance, and all the more so in the early months of 1933 when almost anything seemed possible under the intemperate hand of the National Socialists. Basically, three steps preceded the order for general mobilization. First came the *alerte* followed by the *alerte renforcée* during which the frontier fortresses would be fully manned and arrangements would be made for the imminent dispatch of the nearest infantry and mobile divisions to the frontier. Should the situation continue to deteriorate, various supplementary measures were to follow immediately—such as the reinforcement of the *frontalier* garrisons by regular army units and a comparable strengthening of the hitherto skeletal forces manning the anti-aircraft batteries. If all went according to plan the French army would be in a state of reinforced alert within the space of sixty hours. Next came the *sûreté*, a series of measures which promised completion within four days and which included the recall of certain categories of *disponibles* and reservists, the placing of the frontier and air defense system on a complete war footing, and the commencement of the first rail transport of regular troops to the frontier. Finally, if the situation so warranted, a state of *couverture* would be proclaimed, a measure which involved the mobilization of the entire active army, the full three classes of *disponibles* and a limited number of especially trained reserve officers. It was upon the shoulders of these one million men, raised and deployed within the space of two weeks, that the security of France would rest while the country entered the final phase—the general mobilization of perhaps as many as ninety divisions.[17]

There is no denying that this was a cumbersome system, particularly given the kinds of restraints upon military action that were associated with it. To begin with, the system underlined France's perilous situation by making it clear that the regular army on its own was incapable of handling a determined invader. Similarly, the prohibition on premature —that is to say early—offensive action meant that nothing of this sort could be undertaken before the completion of the *couverture* operation. Simply expressed, French army units would not move an inch beyond their own frontiers until they could leave in their place something in the order of a million men—a prerequisite which would take up to two weeks to fulfil. It was not the mobilization scheme which could be faulted, however, for as far as one may judge, it corresponded well enough with all the assumptions that had been made about the army's strategic duties. No one had said, after all, that the army could not or should not undertake limited offensive action of a tactical nature. Rather, what was being said was that such action should not be launched precipitately and without having in place the soldiers of the *couverture*, soldiers who first would have to be pulled out of the nation's economy by the well-publicized distribution of mobilization notices. So it was that any kind of police-type action had to be prefaced by a delay of up to two weeks in length, by an expensive mechanism of mobilizing better than a half million reservists, and by a public process which was certain to be construed in Germany as an unfriendly and highly provocative act. In effect the high command, with the active consent and collaboration of successive civilian administrations, had designed an army for total war, one that was entirely consistent with the CSDN's vision of conflict between industrial juggernauts. It was questionable, however, whether any government would be prepared to risk that war by unleashing this great army in the name of limited objectives. Intended as a deterrent, this massive citizen army was so expensive to raise and so politically provocative that it had no place until it encountered an enemy which remained unmoved by the threat of another general European war.

It is much more difficult to assess the degree of modernization in the French army by 1933, partly because the expression itself resists definition. Certainly by the standards set in the late 1930s this army had many deficiencies to remedy. It had no armored divisions, the makings of but one light mechanized division, only a handful of motorized infantry divisions, and merely the uncertain promise of close support tactical aviation. Given the moment, these omissions were neither singular nor surprising. Advocates of such mobile fire power were encountering opposition everywhere, excepting neither Germany nor England. In France the same was true. Partly because of his short-term military training and partly too because of the nature of his initially defensive role, the recruit's instruction focused on the use of light automatics and machine guns. Admittedly, armored cars and tanks had long been the subject of much study and experimentation, but reservations still were being expressed about their limited potential.[18] Moreover, the army still regarded the tank as a defensive vehicle first and foremost, one which would work in direct liaison with the infantry and artillery to plug breaches opened in France's defensive lines.[19] Not surprisingly, therefore, the French army regarded the tank very much within the context of its strategic function. Given the national strategy, from which that function derived, deep penetration, semi-autonomous armored units would be regarded as something between a luxury and an irrelevance.

Yet there is more to the French grasp of modern materiel than this. Doubtless their cautious approach to armor stemmed as well from considerations that were quite distinct from purely mechanical appreciations. For instance, it seemed likely that extensive mechanization would

have to mean either an increase in the number of long-service, professional soldiers or an increase in the length of military service for all conscripts—some way, in other words, of developing the specialized skills
demanded by armored vehicles. Given the widespread unpopularity of
either alternative, at least until 1935 when the latter was implemented,
the army faced a serious dilemma.[20] At the same time, these years of financial belt-tightening did not lend themselves to costly armor programs, particularly when government cutbacks had eliminated many
field maneuvers, during which such vehicles normally were tested, and
had demoralized future crews by reducing military bounties and pension
benefits.[21] Finally, and one suspects with even greater effect, the French
response to modern materiel was in large part governed by the premise of
the two-stage war. It is this, perhaps, which helps explain why only 10
percent of army spending between 1919 and 1934 went to the development of new materiel and why even essentially defensive arms like anti-
tank guns and fixed artillery suffered from similar neglect.[22] Financially
reasonable, certainly cost-conscious, and absolutely central to French
thinking in the mid-1930s was the idea that really serious rearmament
began with the outbreak of war, for it was then that the most modern
materiel could be produced most quickly and in the greatest quantity by
a wholly mobilized and highly disciplined industrial economy. It was
precisely for this reason, for example, that the army staff spoke to the advantage of the lighter D2 tank over the heavier B1—because mass production could be undertaken on the eve of hostilities "more easily and
quickly than that of the B1."[23] This does not mean, let it be said, that the
French were blind to the implications of this stratagem, that they failed to
realize how the retention of outdated weapons might obviate their
chances of negotiating stage one of the war successfully. It does suggest,
however, that the desire to avoid enormous expenditure on the fortune
wheel of technology and the converse desire to have a technological edge
shortly after the war began were in large part responsible for the prototype system of production. What this meant, in effect, for aircraft as well
as tanks, was that a limited number of chosen prototypes could be developed and refined, perfected as it were, right up to the eve of war.
Then, with adequate planning, such machines could be set up for serial
production—furnishing France with a sudden outpouring of the most sophisticated weapons that technology could produce.[24]

   The theory, once again, was not without merit. But whatever
might be said in its favor, there is no doubt that it exacerbated the na-

tion's sense of insecurity. Here, as in the case of the gamble taken on the Franco-Belgian frontier, the national leadership had felt itself obliged to play a dangerous game of roulette—hesitating to rearm for a variety of reasons in the hope that really extensive preparations of this order could be undertaken within closer proximity of the war's outbreak. With whatever compassion or severity one judges contemporary thinking of this stamp, of one thing there is no doubt. Compelled to run such calculated risks, by the force of their own assumptions, the French in effect reinforced rather than exorcized their fear. The whole venture was perilous from beginning to end. It is this fear, rather than Gallic bloody-mindedness, that lies at the root of the French army's disposition in 1933. By its own reckoning short of adequately trained effectives, altogether too conscious of Germany's clandestine rearmament, and fretful about the implications of their own battle plan—from the fortunes of their mobilization scheme, to the vulnerability of the border with Belgium, to the mechanics of prototype production—this army was remarkably on edge. From this stemmed its irritability and apparent intransigence, characteristics which its chieftains exhibited so consistently in the face of the Geneva Disarmament Conference.

For the fact is that throughout 1933 the burning question for the French armed forces was whether they were to be further run down in troop complements and weaponry. Circumstances were not propitious at the beginning of the year. Some worrisome developments for the French services had come about in 1932. In May the election of a new leftist coalition had brought to power a more conciliatory regime under Edouard Herriot, one that promptly reduced the military and naval estimates for 1933 and that, toward the end of 1932, finally subscribed to the principle of arms equality among nations—providing that adequate security arrangements of an international character preceded the implementation of that momentous principle. So it was that France at last bowed to international pressure—despite her caveats, acknowledging Germany's relentless demand for something called equality of armaments.[25] In point of fact the concession proved to be a little less dramatic than it first appeared.

Although some agreement at last had been reached on the principle of arms equality, it had not come under the formal aegis of the Disarmament Conference. Circumvented yet again by the behavior of the great powers, the conference had no recourse but to pursue its own examination of a French disarmament plan dating from November 1932.

By March 1933, however, the clouds of international discord remained as thick as ever. Germany and Italy would not budge in their opposition to the French plan; and there was no sign that any of the powers intended to seek the immediate implementation of the equality principle agreed upon among themselves in December. Neither within nor outside the conference, therefore, did disarmament prospects appear bright. In response to what they saw as German and Italian truculence, the French simply threatened to abandon further thoughts of disarmament. Indeed, their appraisals of the new German regime augured ill for the future of international reconciliation. Although their ambassador in Berlin suspected that Hitler remained uncommitted to any course of action, he dutifully reported the rumors that Germany intended to withdraw unilaterally from the Disarmament Conference.[26] To strengthen the charge that Germany was contemptuous of the very principle of disarmament came the reports of French air intelligence. By the summer of 1933 Germany's legally nonexistent air force would be in excess of a thousand planes, a third of which would be modern bombers.[27] Thus, as the year approached the end of its first quarter the signs were bleak for those who believed in peace by disarmament, not entirely ominous for those who hoped for peace by armed deterrence.

It was at this juncture that a number of events coincided. Edouard Daladier was now premier of France, as of February 1933, a post he would occupy until November. Himself within the moderate leftist tradition, Daladier not only retained the conciliatory Joseph Paul-Boncour as his foreign minister but brought to international politics a personal sense of mission. "To show you how sensible a man he is," Ambassador Tyrrell reported with evident satisfaction, "he told me that . . . he would be quite prepared to go to Rome and Berlin himself and have a heart to heart talk with both Mussolini and Hitler."[28] With what later would prove another inadvertent essay in irony the ambassador also welcomed the principal change of several which took place within the Quai d'Orsay in the month of March. Philippe Berthelot, the veteran secretary-general of the French foreign ministry, was retiring from office, proof, it was said, "that the French Government realize that he has been to a large extent the obstacle to good relations with Italy."[29] In his place entered Alexis Saint-Léger. Léger, the former director of political and commercial affairs, a man whom his British counterpart welcomed with the candid if unkind assessment, "not in the same class as Berthelot, nor indeed the next class either."[30] Finally, it was at this time too that Benito Mussolini invited

France, Britain, and Germany to conclude a special four-power pact in the name of European appeasement.

The Italian project had grown out of the disarmament deadlock. In its original form, however, it extended far beyond the competence of the much ignored conference in Geneva. Simply put, the signatories would be asked to endorse two principles. First, they would recognize Germany s right to arms equality, as they had done the previous December and again outside the reaches of the conference proper. Second, they would approve the principle of treaty revision undertaken by the League of Nations, again as each already had done by subscribing to Article 19 of the League of Nations Covenant. To this extent the Italian proposal for a four-power pact offered nothing new. It was a proverbial motherhood issue with which any responsible government would agree. When the Italians and Germans so consented, the French accordingly sensed a trap. For the next four months they sought to revise the terms of the pact so that neither explicitly nor implicitly would it exceed the limits of France's previous undertakings. Confronted by a worried legislature, the Daladier government made sure that the wording of the pact in no way associated the principle of arms equality with the illicit practice of German rearmament. Pursued and badgered by anxious representatives from allied states in eastern Europe, the government similarly insisted that no possible allowance should be given in the pact for the belief that the great power signatories intended to conspire on behalf of specific treaty revisions. To these ends the government remained faithful. When the pact was finally signed in mid-July 1933, six weeks after it had been initialed, it was bland enough for any palate. For over a month the Germans had argued, correctly enough, that the French version was little more than a hymn to the status quo. But in the end they all joined in, praising peace and equality and responsible change, France and Germany momentarily locked in perfect disharmony.

Several months before this interlude came to its benign end, the discussions in Geneva had taken a new direction. By the spring of 1933 it was clear that the French plan of the preceding November, with its provision for a kind of international police force to combat acts of aggression, had run its own course to oblivion. Indeed, it had been this very failure to agree on the French proposals that had prompted the Italian project. Consequently, while negotiations ensued in connection with the four-power pact, the Disarmament Conference concentrated its attention on the principle of arms supervision. If agreement could not be reached on some system for punishing treaty violators, perhaps it would be possible to devise an international control or supervisory system to head off such violations before they occurred. In the course of several rounds of Anglo-French conversations in June and July 1933, Premier Daladier slowly relented. By the time of their next exchange, on 18 September, the premier was willing to make the following commitment. If, after a trial period of four years a permanent supervisory commission could report no alteration in the current arms balance, France would dispose of its heaviest artillery (above 155 mm) and tanks (above 30 tons) in the ensuing four-year period. Moreover, it would contemplate a 50 percent reduction in its air force and a graduated decrease in its period of military service, the latter to accord with the proposed transition of the German Wehrmacht from a long service professional force to a short service militia army. Four days later the premier repeated this offer to Sir John Simon, the British Foreign Secretary, in fact sweetening the conditions by promising to move toward complete arms equality with Germany in the second four-year period—providing of course that complete satisfaction had been recorded during the initial probationary period.[31]

As the French saw it, they had conceded much in the year and a half of the Disarmament Conference. They had done nothing more than complain about German arms violations, a restraint all the more remarkable in the light of cutbacks in their own armed forces. They had accepted the principle of arms equality and more recently had committed themselves to scrap important components of their firepower on the understanding that Germany would refrain from further rearmament. These were not unimportant gestures of compliance by any means, for not all French politicians shared in the spirit of reconciliation generally articulated by men like Herriot and Daladier; and certainly not all Frenchmen had fathomed the possibilities of Franco-German economic cooperation as carefully as the three great magnates of coal, steel, and chemicals —respectively Messieurs Peyerimhoff, Wendel, and Duchemin.[32] Indeed, by the autumn of 1933 talk of preventive war was again in the wind. Pierre Comert, the recently appointed director of information in the Quai d'Orsay, suggested that if the talks failed to produce agreement, responsible quarters in France certainly would contemplate military action.[33] Whereas it is likely that the menace behind Comert's comments and the promise behind those of Daladier had been crafted for mutual reinforcement, it would be folly to see this threat of war merely as a tactical ploy. However much the civilian and military community balked at the idea of preemptive strikes, there was no discounting the possibility that desperation would act as the instrument of conversion.[34]

As the Germans saw it, of course, the French had conceded nothing of substance. They wanted to retain the exact status quo for several years to come, neither disarming themselves nor allowing German rearmament. Only then, after this uneventful interlude, would France begin to implement the principle of arms equality—an expression that defied precise definition in any event. Indeed, one is tempted to think that Germany may well have been right in her decision to abandon the game. Either France and Germany had to contemplate literal equality of arms, a concept the French rejected because of Germany's greater war potential, or the latter factor would be used to justify a continuation of France's actual superiority of arms, a condition that had drawn German fire since the Versailles peace settlement. Thus it was that the fate of European disarmament rested from the start on the blameless notion of equality, a notion, however, that was defined by the Germans as actuality and by the French as potentiality. The chasm was never bridged. On 14 October 1933, Germany announced her withdrawal from the Disarmament Conference and the League of Nations. To have to wait for four years, with nothing more than the cold principle of arms equality from which to draw comfort, was more than Germany was prepared to accept. It would continue to rearm, ostensibly still in the name of arms parity, more openly than ever before.

With that, French objectives grew more remote than ever. Now, one of the principal arguments of French diplomacy had to be that Germany's departure made a disarmament convention imperative; for failure to devise some agreement was likely to add a note of legitimacy to the German withdrawal and, more disturbing still, to German rearmament. Above all, it was the latter that France wished to avert, a wish rendered less realizable now that Germany had discarded yet another bond to the international community. Consequently, Germany's unilateral action in October was hardly a victory for French diplomacy. France's refusal to make further concessions—repeated again by the new premier, Albert Sarraut, in the middle of November—in effect had provoked the German withdrawal and was expected to encourage even further German rearmament. What was wrong with the French in 1933, according to some observers who would live long enough to find quite different faults in the future, was their stubborn intransigence. Consider the implacable verdict of Robert Vansittart, a man seldom accused of Germanophilia.

The French have filled me with despair for many years, during which they have lived in a totally unreal world of juridical technicality. They have missed every boat that ever wailed its own departure, and are greatly responsible for the advent of Hitlerism and the collapse of democracy in Germany . . . They are persevering in consistency—the hobgoblin of little minds—till the very bitter end.[35]

One is inclined to think that such a view might have been received with some enthusiasm by the French chiefs of staff. For them, Vansittart had reached all the right answers, despite having used all the wrong reasons to get there. In their eyes, 1933 truly had been a year of lost opportunities, impotently recording German troop increases while being powerless to halt the budget cutbacks and general neglect within their own forces. On the basis of Germany's own statistics it was clear that its arms expenditure in 1934 would be up by 40 percent over those of 1933, with the proportion of its general budget allocated for military affairs rising since 1932 from 10.5 percent to 21 percent.[36] France, it seemed, was being duped, its anxieties flagrantly ignored. Reports from all quarters carried the same disconcerting message. French air intelligence could now report that the Reich had constructed at least five hundred modern military aircraft in the course of 1933 and had raised its production rate to the equivalent of that in France: forty frames and sixty engines per month. With this in mind the air chief of staff, General Denain, wrote that the Luftwaffe was an established fact "waiting only to be called what it really is."[37]

The vice-president of the Conseil Supérieur de la Guerre, not one to conceal his feelings, was more than usually incensed. As the country's senior commanding officer, General Weygand emphatically warned the conseil in December 1933 that France had reached a "dangerous crossroads" (un tournant dangereux). While he retained his "great confidence" in the French army, there was no denying that its capacity for war had been "seriously impaired."[38] Recent French intelligence, with which British calculations generally complied,[39] demonstrated that the German army was growing steadily. Indeed, the latter now admitted, with its still accustomed modesty, that it had transgressed its 100,000 man limit by some two thousand.[40] French official statistics, even those marshaled with relative restraint by the delegation in Geneva, told a different story. Germany, it was said, now had a standing army of 200,000 with a trained reserve of better than a million and a half men. This state of affairs, combined with what was termed "the descending curve of French effectives and the rising curve of German effectives," lay at the roots of Weygand's alarm.[41] For him, the disarmament policy of those like Paul-Boncour had been criminally irresponsible, a sentiment which no doubt lends credence to the former foreign minister's admission that his relations with the general staff had been "extremely painful."[42] This was such an integral part of the French tragedy, two men seeking to preserve peace and *sécurité* by two quite different means: the politician by seeking to eliminate the weapons of war, the soldier by keeping them at the ready.

Such acrimony was not rare in France during the highly troubled months of early 1934. This issue, by now only one of several, had come under close public scrutiny. Impassioned debate fueled by sheaves of statistics became commonplace. General Niessel, for example, warned the readers of the influential *Revue des Deux Mondes* that Germany now could rapidly mobilize some 1,200,000 men, a figure privately endorsed before the French cabinet by the venerated Marshal Pétain.[43] What they were saying in effect was that the German army now could raise a force comparable in size to the French *couverture* force. With that, the long-held fears of a sudden German attack, an *attaque brusquée*, at once assumed threatening proportions.

Germany, so some figures suggested, was busily engaged in converting its potential superiority into actual equality followed by actual superiority. Precisely what kind of demands the Nazis would make in the future still seemed uncertain, according to the tentative reports transmitted from Berlin by Ambassador André François-Poncet; but it was already beyond doubt that Hitler "had awakened the German military instinct and appetite for domination."[44] French intelligence circles heartily agreed. In the first half of 1934 their estimates underwent a sharp revision: from ones which predicted a "full-size" German army by 1938 to ones which jumped the date ahead to the end of 1935. By then Germany was expected to be capable of mobilizing a total of one hundred divisions.[45] Expectations or nervous over-statements? Pricked by the tips of their own assumptions about the nature of the next war, the French already were in the process of anticipating an enemy which had yet to materialize. Besides, there was also a natural tendency to exploit the German menace as a tactical device to support the demands of the French forces. But by magnifying the German peril, if only in the interests of proclaiming it, they were in fact distorting it, making it less real, flirting with the paranoid's world of imaginary menace.

Although much has been made of the differences between General

Weygand and General Maurice Gamelin, principally in connection with their meteoric descent in 1940, those differences in temperament and outlook were put to fortuitous use in 1934. Both were men to whom military authority came easily, Weygand the designate generalissimo in time of war, Gamelin then chief of the army staff. Yet they were men whose private interests led them more often than not to history, to philosophy, to art and architecture. Certainly neither would have been mistaken for a General "Blimp" on intellectual or cultural grounds; and their physical statures, too, entirely contravened that famous English epithet. Slight of build and fine featured, these two commanders conveyed the impression of alert, articulate, and remarkably intelligent professional soldiers. But it was easy to overlook their similarities: Weygand, the cavalryman, of dark complexion and mercurial temperament; Gamelin, from the infantry, fair-skinned and glacial; the former renowned as the soldier who talked back; the latter as one who never made waves. That they disliked each other and "quarreled persistently" is true, but for the moment immaterial. What is of interest, however, is the way in which both expressed the concerns of the army in their two distinct but mutually reinforcing ways.

Weygand, fittingly, was direct, agitated, and disinclined to underestimate or understate German arms progress. In the spring of 1934 he launched a new assault on the war ministry. "The imminent, if not immediate, capacities of Germany are in the order of between 28 and 30 active divisions, well led and highly trained, and from 40 to 50 divisions of *Grenzschutz*, all these units capable of being ready within 4 or 5 days." What was needed, the general demanded, was "an immediate rectification."[46] General Gamelin was much more phlegmatic, a man who surely never did anything on the run, and one who in his own time was compared unfavorably to Weygand, as a pillow to a wall.[47] In January 1934 he undertook a calm, dispassionate but still disturbing report on France's strategic situation in Europe.

France, he began, had to be capable of containing both the German and Italian armies, and of doing so without help from allies whose intervention would be neither direct nor effective in the opening days of war. In any event, with the sole exception of Poland, the eastern allies could do nothing more than concentrate on their own defense—an effort the success of which might well be determined by the attitude of the Soviet Union. Similar uncertainties prevailed in the Mediterranean basin. The freedom of passage through the Dardanelles and the preservation of

French interests in the Near East rested heavily upon Turkey. The security of the Mediterranean sea lanes, the stability of North Africa and the continued independence of Austria depended greatly on the behavior of Italy. Having completed this *tour d'horizon* the general itemized the army's missions. France had to be immediately capable of defending itself and of assisting in the defense of Belgium and Switzerland. After a short delay France would have to be able to exercise offensive pressure on Germany in the interests of a beleaguered Poland or Czechoslovakia. Finally, it had to be ready to attack Italy at any time, in the event that Yugoslavia should fall victim to Italian aggression. In all, it was a reasoned survey, clear and concise, followed by an almost clinical outline of the demands which government policy had imposed upon the army.[48]

The problem, as Gamelin saw it, was the large void between French commitments and French capacity. To handle such assignments France had to have more heavy tanks of the 30 ton range and more howitzers of the 155 mm and 220 mm calibre—precisely the weaponry that was under sentence of some future disarmament convention. In other words, without increases in French mobility and firepower, France could not lend adequate aid to even its immediate neighbors, never mind those to whom it had commitments in eastern Europe. In military terms, the much heralded alliance system was now only barely compatible with French military resources. Moreover, by the general's reckoning, this alliance system was no less at odds with the whole of French strategy, for now there was virtually no effective assistance that could be expected from it. Implicit in this note, therefore, is one subtle but obvious recommendation. If France wished to decrease the liabilities currently contained in its obligations of mutual assistance, without renouncing those commitments in their entirety, it would have to contemplate an extension of the alliance system to include Italy and the Soviet Union. Above all, however, France would have to face up to the necessity of its own rearmament.

It was in this very tense atmosphere, made infinitely worse of course by the famous domestic turbulence of February 1934, that seventy-two year old Gaston Doumergue ended the almost two-year reign of assorted left-leaning governments. Touted from the start as a kind of national front government, bristling with the names of Philippe Pétain, Edouard Herriot, André Tardieu, and Louis Barthou—not to mention the new premier, Gaston Doumergue himself, a former president of the Republic—here was a government from which it was hoped decisive leadership could be expected. On its disposition might rest the fate of the disarmament issue—with those like Weygand no doubt hoping for a regime that would have no further truck with disarmers, but with others anticipating a government that would be "strong enough to reach an agreement with Germany over disarmament."[49] In any event, the "gay and gallant old gentleman" with the perpetual grin was back at the helm, Monsieur Doumergue with his crew of equally "old gentlemen," "forced to come together by mobs of exasperated and mostly middle-class Parisians."[50] And from the first, the pressure was on. The army was clearly restless; and Weygand was sometimes given to reckless talk. He had been caught musing about tough action in the past, "spanking" Germany for her arms violations by seizing control of the Rhine bridgeheads;[51] and once more feelings were running high. Hardly had Louis Barthou assumed direction of the Quai d'Orsay than he was paid court by the maverick Belgian senator Dorlodot. More talk of preventive war, but fragmented and seemingly unreal. Dorlodot certainly took it seriously enough, as did the Belgian government, but Barthou in fact did nothing more than express interest—leaving the senator with the patently hopeless task of either toppling the Belgian administration or forcing it to stiffen its attitude toward German rearmament. In the end nothing happened.[52] But the rumors of preemptive strikes continued to circulate, with all their attendant promises and fears; and as usual, Maxime Weygand's name was associated with such bold projects. Provoked by the nervous inquiries of the Belgian ambassador, France's peacetime commander-in-chief reportedly retorted: "Why not a preventive war? Today France still has the military advantage. Soon she will not."[53] Clearly, matters could not be allowed to drift for much longer. The disarmament issue demanded some kind of resolution.

3

Security First, 1934

By April 1934 the temper of the times had hardened perceptibly. Was there a Frenchman who had not come to believe that his government had been hoodwinked and gulled by a German regime whose cunning matched its malevolence? One had only to read the newspapers and the journals of the day to follow the stunning rebirth of the German Reichswehr—a renaissance which was to draw much fire from angry and alarmist feature editorials penned variously by anonymous "friends of the army" and officers like *général trois étoiles*. There was a mood of nervousness across France, accentuated by inflammatory press reports which presented the German peril as imminent rather than as merely potential. Within the corridors of power, where such distinctions could be made, feelings were hardly less intense. The burden of expectation rested on the Doumergue government. It was expected to do something, to regain the nation's confidence, to stop the drift against which the French commander-in-chief had come to speak with such vehemence. The Doumergue cabinet, conscious of domestic political expectations and looking as a result like an abbreviated *Who's Who*, had to reassess its foreign policy with direct reference to the current military situation. The fate of the Disarmament Conference hung in the balance.

At this moment reports from a variety of quarters seemed to suggest that a disarmament convention was a luxury France could ill afford in the face of German rearmament. The Belgians again were proving awkward, balking at the notion of constructing fortifications in locations judged appropriate by the French general staff.[1] The Poles, too, were troublesome; not only because they had concluded a recent nonaggression pact with Germany, but because they seemed to have done so partly out of a declining confidence in the alliance with France.[2] From south-central Europe information arrived of a mixed character. Whereas the Little Entente powers at long last seemed to be working out a plan to contain Hungary, the uncertainty of relations between the French army staff and those of Roumania, Czechoslovakia, and Yugoslavia candidly was acknowledged as was their heavy dependency on French military provisions.[3] In the face of such signs of erosion within the French security bloc came the incessant reports from Berlin and Geneva on the progress being made by Germany in land and air rearmament. Finally, in late March, François-Poncet informed the Quai d'Orsay of the very substantial increase contained in the recently announced German arms budget.

It was on this that Premier Doumergue fastened, the final straw. Yet it would be wrong to suggest that it was grasped with either suddenness or temerity. For almost three weeks the government was to ponder its course of action, evidently preoccupied with the manner in which it could respond to the latest British proposals on disarmament.[4] For in fact, it was the British who by now were really creating France's dilemma. The Germans were neither practicing nor discussing disarmament; their successful defiance already had registered adverse effects within the ranks of France's allies; and Weygand was now simply refusing to countenance further arms reductions without foolproof political guarantees. In short, disarmament was neither logical nor, should the army's case be granted, possible. But would the British accept this reading? Could this country, whose active participation in a long war was so pivotal to French grand strategy, be made to understand?

By 16 April Foreign Minister Barthou was in receipt of several potentially vital communications. First, on his own request a Commission (spéciale) d'études de la Défense Nationale had met to discuss France's proposed reply to Great Britain. Although failing to develop any firm recommendations, the commission's hearings gave General Weygand yet one more opportunity to decry further talk of arms reductions.[5] Further concessions on the disarmament issue were certain to be met by spirited and unflinching resistance from this quarter. Second, Doumergue himself had advanced some very pointed suggestions about the tenor and contents of the forthcoming French reply. Germany's flagrant disregard of the Disarmament Conference, recently underscored by its new arms budget, seemed to have dispelled all doubts from his mind. What France must do, the premier proposed, was to accept the responsibility "of concentrating on her own security. This security has become the first priority."[6] Doumergue had had enough, an attitude Barthou had good reason to believe would be well represented in the cabinet meeting scheduled for the following day. Finally, on the eve of that meeting Barthou also had in hand a curious and perplexing note from the Quai d'Orsay's René Massigli. Following a recent chat with Mr. Eden, the British minister responsible for League affairs, Massigli ventured the view that the British secretly believed that the anticipated French reply would close the file on disarmament, following which "the conclusion of an Anglo-French accord should then be sought."[7] Precisely what Eden had intended by this is not certain, but it would appear that he expected a strong note from the French and perhaps even welcomed the prospect. Certainly a month later he claimed that he had understood the reasoning behind the French reply and that "furthermore he is counting on German rearmament and the anxiety which it creates in England to hasten the rapprochement of the two countries."[8] Whether or not his meaning was accurately gauged by his French interlocutors, there is little doubt that the latter discerned in Eden a sympathetic figure and an attitude in view of which the risk of a forceful note on disarmament might be run. At long last there seemed an outside chance that the British would understand what France had to do.[9]

If such indications relieved some of the pressures on Barthou, they did not make any more palatable for him the kind of dramatic gestures being planned in other official quarters. He did not want France to make any kind of declaration which might burden it with responsibility for the failure of the Disarmament Conference, an attitude which may well have had the reputation of France more at heart than the fate of the disarmament issue. Certainly such a reading would be consistent with Eden's impression of Barthou as the wily and unsentimental practitioner of international politics—a "bristly and foxey . . . old gentleman who has certain affinities with D[avid] L[loyd] G[eorge]; a nasty old man at heart."[10] In any event word reached London from a variety of quarters—including the Quai d'Orsay—that Barthou had opposed the policy statement which came to be approved in the cabinet meeting of 17 April and which was communicated later in the day to the British embassy.[11]

Attributing responsibility to Germany, and in particular to the increase of some 350 million marks in its defense budget for 1934-1935, this famous note insisted that the repeated violations of the Versailles conventions made present negotiations impossible. Now France had no choice.

> Even before seeking to discuss whether an agreement can be reached on a system of guarantees effective enough to enable the signing of a convention which would legalize Germany's substantial rearmament, France must place in the forefront of her preoccupations the conditions of her own security, which she sees as including that of other interested Powers.[12]

France did not intend to leave the Disarmament Conference. Negotiations were still possible, although the preliminary work should be done outside the conference itself.[13] But Germany would have to return to the League of Nations before any convention could be concluded. In the meantime, France would rely exclusively on its own resources and on those of its allies. French *sécurité* was no longer up for sacrifice on the altar of internationalism.

As the British saw it, Doumergue had forced Barthou to fall into line.[14] They certainly did not believe the latter's official assurances that the note was the product of a unanimous cabinet decision.[15] How much credence they placed in Weygand's professed ignorance of the government's decision making is less certain. In fact, it warranted little. France's supreme commander had struck while the iron was hot. Not only had he balked more forcefully than ever before at the prospect of further arms reductions, but he had conspired actively against the more cautious approach preferred by Barthou. Sensing the minister's line of thought, from inquiries received about permissible levels of German rearmament, Weygand had combined with Herriot and Tardieu, the two powerful ministers of state, to produce what eventually became the note of 17 April 1934. In contrast to his denials at the time, the general later made no secret of the fact. He had helped draft the April note, so he later testified, because of his alarm over a "type of sophism which amounted to ignoring the fact that Germany had not fulfilled the conditions of the peace treaty." Given his active role in the formulation of the note, it is not surprising that he was "overjoyed" when Barthou finally agreed to use it as the reply to the British proposals.[16]

The minister's consent appears to have come more as a concession than a conversion. Those who had wanted a strong policy had stolen the march. The premier wished to free France from any further disarmament obligations. So did Tardieu and Herriot, by now both long-time *minis-trables* and the latter leading a nominal bloc of six Radical Socialist cabinet portfolios under Doumergue. Louis Marin, currently in charge of national health, could have been expected to support this line for he, like Tardieu, was widely recognized in press and parliament as an unofficial spokesman for the French armed services. Much the same could be said for Georges Rivollet, currently minister of pensions and secretary-general of the Confédération générale des anciens combattants. Moreover, the sentiments of the high command could have been expected to find wide expression within this cabinet in even more direct ways. Of the three service ministers, two were serving officers and Monsieur Piétri already had distinguished himself as one of the most forceful advocates of closer civil-military planning.[17] General Denain, who as air minister had so recently warned Barthou of German aerial rearmament, continued to hold the appointment of chief of air staff. The war minister was none other than the venerated Marshal Pétain. Credited with the victory of Verdun, the suppression of the 1917 army mutiny, and the creation of the continuous front, the marshal enjoyed a reputation that was unrivaled by any of his highly accomplished cabinet colleagues; and certainly this man had stood in the vanguard of those who had been warning recent French governments of Germany's military revival. These were the principals against whom Barthou spoke in vain and whose collective influence combined to thrash out the policy declaration of 17 April.[18]

Whatever its claims to the contrary, this note did deliver a poorly aimed *coup de grâce* to the Disarmament Conference. Indeed, its demise was almost embarrassingly slow. But consent to German rearmament had remained as delicate and dangerous as it ever had been; and not even the Doumergue government with its galaxy of notables found the strength to associate itself before the French public with such a concession. Moreover, military intelligence warned that such consent would be an unwarranted and quite needless genuflection to German militarism. Hitler would do as he liked, with or without French approval. Of course, this was precisely the argument which Barthou reversed and used against the wording of the April note. Personally opposed to this declaration, more likely because he saw it as a tactical blunder than because he still entertained serious hopes for a disarmament convention, the minister reportedly concentrated on the argument that the note would be irrelevant in any event. It would not deter Hitler from pursuing his publicized goal of a 300,000 man army. Rather, it was diplomatic showmanship, flashy and ostensibly assertive—likely to win some hoped for kudos from the French populace, but likely too to reinforce the view long circulated in international circles that France was seeking to scuttle the Disarmament Conference, and absolutely certain to leave the Germans quite unmoved. Yet the minister did not resign. Mindful of the consequences his resignation could have on a new government in a still volatile domestic situation, Barthou submitted to the views of his cabinet colleagues.[19]

The foreign minister soon was called to account for "his" policy. Léon Blum, the socialist leader, attacked the government for having overturned the conciliatory policy of its predecessors. The charge was untrue. Barthou vehemently denied that there had been any change in policy.[20] That too was untrue. The note of 17 April did not repudiate the idea of a disarmament convention, nor did it discard the larger idea of collective security. It simply stated that in the absence of any viable expression of either principle France would ensure its security by more traditional means. To this point the message was clear; but there was a trace of ambiguity. The note was supposed to be a new statement on the type of guarantee which the French government could find acceptable. It drew its inspiration from Germany's determined rearmament, from the "fear," as Doumergue admitted, which that determination had evoked in France.[21] Yet it did not recommend any method of preventing or retarding that rearmament. Blum was quite right to have asked why this was so; and he was right to have detected a change in policy, although "in" should have been the operative word. The Doumergue administration had not exchanged one policy for another. Disarmament and rapprochement were not ruled out. But the direction and emphasis of French diplomacy had been modified.

It was this that the British discerned immediately. The government, so the embassy believed, was "thinking first and foremost of a general tightening-up of the bonds uniting France and her allies, while other Powers would be left to their own salvation."[22] France had reactivated its policy of alliances. Instead of offering a positive solution to the problem of German rearmament, the April note reemphasized the deterrent value of an anti-German coalition. The government's conclusions were clear, if implicit. The more Germany rearmed, the higher the price France might have to pay for any misguided reliance on the efficacy of international support mobilized under the auspices of the League.

As the military factor conditioned the atmosphere from which the April note emerged, so did it preach the wisdom of maintaining reliable allies. The French economy was slipping into the throes of depression. Increasing unemployment, salary reductions, and a general decline in the index of industrial production put a tight squeeze on government finance. Price decline meant reduced revenues, which in turn necessitated a reduction in expenditures. Moreover, although government salaries were cut, the increases in unemployment benefits forbade significant savings.[23] The financial malaise naturally had an impact on ministerial budgets. A jittery and cost-conscious parliament zealously scrutinized each ministry's expenditure. Consequently, the need for greater financial stringencies to some extent collided with the need to keep abreast of German rearmament. There was also a problem of human resources. The country looked with dread on the approach of those lean years when the annual contingent of conscripts would be reduced by half. The high command would reap the first bleak harvest from the war years in 1935; but already, apparently responsible statesmen now claimed that Germany had an army of 600,000. To whom could France turn in order to relieve the pressures of finance and the predicted scarcity in manpower?

The underlying significance of the April note has been blurred too frequently by a spurious refinement of its central message. The note did announce France's intention to defend its own security but did not include the often attributed passage "by her own means." The Doumergue government certainly did not intend to begin, as this passage could suggest, a policy of political and military retrenchment behind its new frontier fortifications. France's allies were not to be abandoned; perhaps more to the point, these allies were not to be relieved of their obligations to defend France. Quite the reverse. The April note reaffirmed the importance of the alliance system by reasserting the conviction that the defense of France could not be separated from the security of other "interested Powers." In the face of German rearmament, economic depression, and a shortage of military manpower, France increased its dependence on the deterrent effect of alliances.

The April note therefore promised to be of pivotal importance to the future conduct of French diplomacy. Given the note's wording, it seems clear that the Doumergue administration had come down decisively on the need for retaining the alliance system. But what were the military and diplomatic implications of this decision? General Gamelin had said in January that the military capacity of the eastern satellites was inadequate without the support of Russia and Italy and that the military capacity of France was inadequate without further rearmament. If the alliance system was to be retained and even extended, one might expect to see French overtures to Moscow and Rome. However, the diplomatic and military implications of 17 April could not be separated. If France were to secure the cooperation of these two great powers, it in turn would have to increase its own commitments. Yet Gamelin had pointed out the already significant gap between French commitments and French capacity. Moreover, in order to assure itself of Russian and Italian cooperation, France would have to convince Stalin and Mussolini that the guarantee of mutual assistance was a credible one. The more the diplomatic structure was extended, the more dependent it became on the army's capacity to mobilize, transport, and employ its forces.

Bolder in appearance than in substance, the April note nevertheless did signify a policy reorientation. It conveyed under Doumergue's leadership the impression—clear if only arguably well founded—"of an entirely new situation, . . . a kind of resurrection of French virility."[24] As such it quickly invoked some high expectations of subsequent and perhaps equally dramatic adjustments on the part of the Quai d'Orsay and the French war ministry.

By early 1934 the latter was much on edge, its nerves frayed by the alarming appraisals only too readily proffered by General Weygand and the Conseil Supérieur de la Guerre.[25] The progress of German rearmament, the constant whittling of French effective strength, the demoralizing cutbacks in French defense spending—the most recent of which saw Pétain himself bow to a 20 percent reduction in current expenditure—and the inroads made in the French alliance system by the German menace, such were the familiar roots of the army's anxiety. But by now, particularly in the wake of the latest disarmament note, what was rapidly returning to prominence was the old dilemma of fixed fortifications versus battlefield mobility. Without the latter capability France would lack not only the mobile units requisite for modern defensive war but as well the offensive pressures without which its diplomatic assurances of military support meant little. This was, of course, precisely the point both Weygand and Gamelin had stressed prior to April—not only the deficiencies in French military standing, but the growing hollowness of an alliance system for which France was growing ever ill equipped.

But by 1934 the most prominent, most heralded symbol of French military preparation was nearing completion. The Maginot Line, a fixed line of fortifications, stretched out for miles across the Palatinate. While it is important to dispel certain misconceptions about the Line, both contemporary and historical, it certainly is worth repeating that these fortifications were extremely sophisticated, gargantuan, and expensive—characteristics which made them an almost instant legend. By the time in question, the original installations of the Line were in place: the Rhine defenses—a lighter type than those employed elsewhere—running from Mulhouse to Haguenau; the Lauter fortified region, heavy fixed fortifications extending east of the Haguenau forest from the Rhine to Bitche; and the Metz fortified region extending from Têting on the river Nied to the heights immediately west of the Moselle river and subsequently, as the result of a 1930 decision aimed at protecting the Briey mining basin, from the Moselle to Longuyon.

Incorrectly referred to as a "wall," these original sections hardly broke the earth's surface. The underground galleries were so extensive in fact, that linked end to end they would have stretched from Paris to Liège, a distance approaching 150 miles. By 1936 some seven billion francs had gone into this herculean venture, covering the labor and material costs attendant on a project that employed better than 15,000 workers and military engineers and that saw some 12,000,000 cubic meters of earth removed in the interest of nearly 2,000,000 cubic meters of concrete and 50,000 tons of steel plate. Yet volume was matched by technological finesse. Beneath the metal and concrete "crust," carefully engineered to withstand the impact of three 500 mm shells striking simultaneously, lay a nether world of Wellesian proportions. Electrically operated devices ensured against contamination from poison gas attack and similar devices prevented the escape of carbon monoxide from the gun chambers. Reliable communications with the outside world were guaranteed by means of telephone lines buried in five meters of concrete slab. Two alternate lines with different circuits were installed, while the telephone exchanges were located at a depth of 150 feet below ground. Miniature railway lines, independent water supplies, electric generating stations, and air conditioning systems all added to this technological wonder. And for the men who manned these defenses, the *écrivisses de rempart*, every possible measure was employed to ensure their comfort and their fighting efficiency—from modern hospital facilities, to cinematic theaters, to quickly collapsable surface huts in which men could take peacetime refuge from the subterrestrial, depressed state of mind which the French called *bétonite* or "concretitis."

Although this was a static line of defense, it was hardly passive. Attacking infantry would encounter land mines and barbed wire long before they reached the fortifications. Enemy armor would find its own difficulties in the form of the "asparagus beds," networks of steel rails driven into the ground with their points upward. Any tank trying to negotiate such carefully deployed obstacles would quickly expose its vulnerable undercarriage to the fire of the defenders' anti-tank guns. Assuming, however, that some tanks eventually would break through, the French accordingly planted a second bed of defense, the "asparagus farci," the protruding rails of which were armed with an explosive charge. Disregarding the effect that the fortress armaments would have on any attacker seeking to pierce such field defenses, the French defense specialists then went on to provide additional insurance against the arrival of enemy sappers on the fort's superstructure. Light machine guns were positioned to cover the visible portions of every casement. The result of all these elaborately conceived construction efforts and mutually supporting fire zones was a truly formidable line of defense. The price of a frontal assault on such defenses was expected to be extremely high.[26]

Details of this order assuredly have a significance beyond that which would interest engineers and military buffs. For if there was such a thing as Maginot-mindedness, the roots of it are surely to be found as much in the technological triumph as in the original and perfectly understandable desire to block the most direct route of German invasion. Were one to explore the latter first, it may be readily concluded that there was little in this desire which would support the popular definition of Maginot-mindedness. The line was built not out of lethargy or apathy, cowardice or defeatism, but to cope with and at the same time to exploit the topographical features along the Franco-German border. Nor does there seem the slightest reason to believe that the Line engendered a false sense of security in France, at least not in official circles. The fact remained that most of France's eastern border was as yet largely unfortified. Nonetheless, what was true and undeniable was that on its border and that of its principal enemy France clearly had established a defensive position, one that miles of concrete fortifications and billions of francs accurately foretold would not be used for staging an early offensive push. Whereas it is true that the Saar gap, between Téting and Wittring, had been left as a maneuvering area between the Metz and Lauter fortified regions—an area through which an offensive could be directed—there is little evidence to suggest that anything more than the most modest and tentative advances were contemplated in the early stages of hostilities. Certainly the current mobilization Plan D, operative from 1933 to April 1935, gives us no reason to think otherwise.[27] What might be concluded then, with some confidence, is that the Maginot Line unquestionably did symbolize France's defensive posture in the face of the German peril. If this is Maginot-mindedness, so be it. It is also one of the principal keys of French grand strategy, cut in accordance with a whole series of critical assumptions about the nature and dimensions of any future war with Germany.

There is, however, something more to the contemporary references to Maginot-mindedness, something grandly ironic. Simply stated, French land strategy—of which these fortifications were a central part—consisted of forcing the Germans to try their assault through Belgium on whose unhappy soil the next war was to be waged. Such a stratagem placed a high premium on the speed with which French forces could move to occupy the defensive front within Belgium, a stratagem therefore which insisted on mobility: motorized infantry, light mechanized and heavy armored units. In short, the high command had accepted the immobility of the Maginot defenses, deemed truly impenetrable,[28] so that it could use its mobile forces first to plug breaches in the less fortified frontier zones and second to carry the northern armies across the Belgian frontier. Thus the Maginot Line was not intended to deny mobile warfare, but indeed to render it possible. This is why it is not at all surprising to find Weygand and Gamelin recommending the expansion of French mechanized and motorized forces, although to be sure French strategic assumptions placed such forces in an initially defensive context rather than in the offensive context mistakenly perceived by some. The irony was, however, that the almost instantly contrived legend of the Maginot Line served to impede the cause of mobility. So major an undertaking was this Line, so expensive, so well-publicized, and ultimately so exaggerated, that these fixed fortifications seemed to obviate the need for mobility. The general staff had created a beast for its own sustenance, only to discover that the beast had a will and presence of its own. Consequently, what one discovers in the early 1930s is not only the requests for expensive motorized and mechanized units, but the requests—many from frontier communities—for equally expensive extensions of the existing fortified regions.[29] In 1930 it was the decision to cover the distance from Longuyon to Montmédy and to extend the Lauter district from Bitche to Wittring on the River Saar. There was, then, an apparently growing tendency to perfect what already had been developed at such great labor and cost, to protect the investment in fixed and immobile defenses. Thus it may be more accurate to see the French high command as victim rather than as practitioner of Maginot-mindedness, inadvertently thwarted by one miracle of modern technology from developing with requisite speed the possibilities offered by technology in the field of armored mobility.

Accordingly, it was not easy for the high command and the war ministry to adjust either rapidly or profoundly to the demands implicitly contained in the note of 17 April.[30] In a sense what that note called for was increased mobility within an offensive context, so that French international commitments might acquire a new credibility which in turn might elicit new expressions of allied fidelity to France. What the army called for, so the evidence suggests, was increased mobility but within a defensive context. In this respect, it seems, the April note did not prompt the high command to revise its objectives, and this despite the fact that this very note had been partly inspired by the army's pointed observations on the discrepancies between its current capacities and France's diplomatic obligations. In fact, neither the demands implicit in the note nor those made explicit by the general staff were carried to their logical conclusion. Indeed, the key development under Pétain's war ministry came in July with a fixed credit allocation for 1934-1935 on behalf of extensions to the Metz and Lauter fortified regions. No new sums of money were made available for land rearmament in 1934, although the Conseil Supérieur de la Guerre did approve the adoption of the B1 and D2 tanks and the 25 mm Hotchkiss anti-tank gun.[31] Again, one is led to conclude that the army found it tough going to advocate rapid motorization and mechanization—partly for fear that too dramatic a shakeup would weaken the army further in the short run, partly too because Weygand was reluctant to commit the army to "a precise program which might deny us any flexibility in our planning."[32] Finally, however, one must appreciate the difficulties of convincing politicians, even war ministers, that armored fighting vehicles were *de rigueur* when the army's key doctrinal pronouncements concentrated on the supremacy of artillery and infantry and when Weygand himself continued to repeat that the value of fixed fortifications was one of the two principal revelations of the First World War.[33] Tanks, armored cars, troop carriers, and aircraft would still warrant development, but for the time being such vehicles would be in fierce competition for attention and funding with the equally pressing demands for extending and equipping those immobile defenses in the east.

On the diplomatic front the challenge was no less great; and again, as Barthou had feared from the outset, the ambitions of the April note were at once elusive and overlarge. Publicly proclaimed, they put the minister under pressure from the start, pointing as they did to the more traditional diplomacy of alliances but one already fraught with problems, and impeding a policy of rapprochement with Germany by having piled doubts on the sincerity of France's interest in reconciliation. These were disadvantages that Barthou did not need, or invite; but after 17 April they were his to work with.

— Barthou is not an easy man to read, plagued as we still are by remarkably thin archival resources. On the surface this is less apparent. Seventy-two years of age when he entered Doumergue's cabinet, Barthou was instantly regarded as a patriot of proven qualities, experienced and conservative, a leading member of a center-right coalition which intended, as Tardieu expressed it, to rescue the destiny of France from "the hands of weak-kneed Governments which had adopted a policy of internationalism."[34] Physically Barthou bespoke tradition, from the white goatee to the pince-nez of an earlier generation; culturally too he was a man who loved the past, as an academic and historian, as an ardent bibliophile and lover of great music; personally, he had been associated with some key developments of the recent past, from the introduction of three-year military service under his premiership in 1913 to the famous Ruhr occupation a decade later, an act which as president of the reparations commission he had advised and prepared.[35] By the lexicon of our own day he would have been regarded as a hard-liner in so far as Germany was concerned. And it is exactly to this that Geneviève Tabouis has him speak, a reportedly direct quotation on the eve of his appointment to the Quai d'Orsay: "I am an old-fashioned Frenchman. That is, I belong to the generation of good horse-sense. All these League of Nations fancies . . . I'd soon put an end to them if I were in power . . . it's alliances which count."[36]

Certainly this is the Barthou who emerges in one of the clearest contemporary analyses of his diplomatic efforts following the April note. It was Maurice Gamelin, first at Riom and later in his memoirs, who articulated most precisely Barthou's self-confessed goals and objectives. The roots of his entire policy, Gamelin recalled, lay around the fact "that for him it was essentially a matter of returning to the pre-1914 policy." In other words, Barthou was out to contain Germany by isolation and encirclement. To this purpose Barthou reportedly outlined several essentials. He was determined to retain good relations with Britain, hoping to open Whitehall's eyes to the menace of German rearmament and thus to induce effective Anglo-French military cooperation. So too was he determined to revive the spirit of collaboration between France and Belgium, with at least one eye fixed on the goal of convincing Belgium to develop its frontier fortifications. In eastern Europe he wanted to strengthen the ties with the Little Entente and to secure some improvement in Franco-Polish relations. Furthermore, and on lines identical to those contained in Gamelin's own memorandum of January, Russia and Italy would have to be brought into rapprochement with France. Finally, relations with Spain demanded improvement in view of its strategic hold on vital French communications with North Africa. Such, said Gamelin, was the essence of Barthou's diplomacy—a diplomacy which undeniably betrays a different thrust and tone from that which had characterized official French policy toward the Disarmament Conference.[37]

This analysis does accord closely with the diplomatic diary of events between April and October 1934. The minister certainly did launch a major diplomatic offensive, having witnessed within France the withering of any serious belief in disarmament and having detected abroad growing doubts about the efficacy of an alliance with France. Indeed, the pace of German rearmament was having deleterious effects on both fronts. Thus, even before the issue of the April note had been resolved, Barthou had turned to face the at once delicate and thorny question of relations with Belgium. On the one hand, this country had been made critical to the security of France—not by its own choosing but rather by the dictates of French grand strategy. On the other, its own government looked askance at the prospect of inviting German hostility simply by virtue of its ties with France. By the time in question, Belgium was already backtracking from its 1920 military convention with France. Pleading, with much justice, that this convention had become a symbol of the domestic divisions between Walloons and Flemings, the government was now actively engaged in trimming its commitments to France. It would not countenance a French military advance into Belgium without explicit invitation. It virtually repudiated the notion that such an appeal would ever come during a period of diplomatic tension, before hostilities actually occurred. It made it clear that nothing short of the invasion of Belgium by Germany was likely to trigger a request for French help and that no consideration whatever would be given to lending Belgian territory or facilities for the purpose of allowing France to aid its allies in eastern Europe.[38]

Against such pronouncements Barthou could do very little, as is evidenced by the meager returns occasioned by his brief visit to Brussels at the end of March 1934. Contrary to current rumors, so Premier Hýmans assured his guest, Belgium did intend to fulfil its obligations in the event that Germany flagrantly violated the 1925 Locarno agreement—the agreement with which Belgium preferred to replace the military convention as the touchstone of relations between France and Belgium. But beyond that, France could expect little more. Indeed, the premier suggested that not even the appearance of German soldiers in the demilitarized Rhineland would be sufficient cause for war, despite the fact that such an occurrence certainly could be interpreted as a flagrant violation of the 1925 accord.[39] Thus Barthou came away with little to his credit, a plight which the subsequent April note did nothing to assuage. For it was not soft talk of rapprochement and disarmament that Belgium feared, confident as it was of French determination to rally to its defense. Rather it was the tough talk, the whispers of preventive war gratuitously orchestrated by a troublesome Belgian senator, and the defiant thrust of the April note that disturbed the government in Brussels.[40] As a result, and again as Barthou had feared, the Doumergue government's adoption of a more forceful posture had little to contribute to the stability of Franco-Belgian relations.

If the April note had brought any satisfaction to Warsaw, there was little in evidence when Louis Barthou arrived there on 24 April. The Polish foreign minister, Monsieur Jozef Beck, did not bother to receive his prestigious guest until later in the day—leaving the reception at the Warsaw station to the government's official opposition. Marshal Pilsudski, the chief of state, bluntly told Barthou that while he was pleased by the recent French decision he knew that France would continue to yield. Thus, if the Belgians were inclined to take the April note too seriously, the Poles refused to take it seriously enough. Yet the French were no more willing to believe the Poles. Certainly Barthou kept pressing Pilsudski and Beck on the subject of some possible secret convention in the German-Polish accord of January, despite their repeated denials openly wondering what in the published agreement could have induced Germany to sign. And in spite of Pilsudski's warm and friendly welcome there were other signs of tension between the two states. The old question of Polish-Czech relations, though discussed once more, remained unresolved; and thus the dilemma of having two mutually antagonistic allies in the east left Barthou as baffled as it had left his predecessors. Finally, Barthou made little ground on the one issue which may well have been the *raison d'être* of his diplomatic journey.[41]

Barthou it seems was preparing the way for a rapprochement with the Soviet Union, a country for whom Poland retained an unrelenting animosity. By the spring of 1934 certain steps had already been taken in this direction, although largely under the aegis of Barthou's predecessor, Paul-Boncour.[42] Following the initial Soviet offer of a bilateral alliance with France, which came in the summer of 1933, the Quai d'Orsay had sketched the outlines of a larger regional security pact for eastern Europe within which the proposed alliance might be established. It was this project, to which the idea of German membership had been attached, that Barthou floated before the skeptical and unenthusiastic gaze of his Polish hosts. He may even have raised the possibility of a Franco-Russian alliance outside the proposed multilateral pact, although assuredly still under the auspices of the League of Nations.[43] In any event, he clearly did press the case for revising the Franco-Polish military convention—theoretically with a view to bringing it up to date, but practically in order to free France from any commitment to join forces against Russia. Not surprisingly, the Poles greeted this proposition with ill-disguised *froideur*.[44] In fact, Barthou was to get from Warsaw little more than he had received from Brussels—some inspired and misleading publicity about the warmth of Franco-Polish relations, and Poland's assurance that its ties with Germany did not go beyond what met the eye.

Had anyone suspected that the April note or Barthou's visit to Warsaw had restored relations to a sound footing, their illusions were soon shattered. Hardly a month had elapsed since his return from the east when Barthou struck viciously at Polish pretentions. "There are great powers . . . and Poland," he scowled at Beck over a formal Geneva luncheon. "Poland we all know because we have been told is a great power . . . a very, very great power."[45] It was a studied insult, provoked or not, and as such served no purpose but to exacerbate matters. Certainly before another month had passed Barthou admitted, with unconcealed fury, that the recent League session in Geneva had exhibited the most deliberate Polish attempts to disassociate themselves from French diplomatic endeavors.[46]

It was during this same session that Barthou met Litvinov, the Soviet commissar for foreign affairs. With Czech if not Polish approval, the two men met on 18 May to discuss the principle of regional security pacts for eastern Europe, the Pacific, and Mediterranean.[47] Eastern Europe occupied most of their attention. The two ministers soon agreed that the proposed pact would have to include Russia, Germany, Poland, Czechoslovakia, and the Baltic states and possibly Finland and Roumania. This pact in turn would be complemented by a bilateral Franco-Soviet pact of mutual assistance. To make Soviet participation compatible with the wishes of the smaller powers, and indeed, with those of France, Barthou insisted that the USSR should become a League member.[48]

The Franco-Russian negotiations led to a general agreement in early June. All the proposed signatories, excepting Roumania, would be asked to participate in an eastern pact of mutual assistance. France and the Soviet Union would conclude a separate pact by which France would guarantee Soviet security, through the latter's membership in the eastern pact, and Russia would guarantee the Rhenish clauses of the 1925 western Locarno agreement. The French cabinet approved the Barthou-Litvinov plan on 5 June. Significantly, however, the Doumergue government stipulated that the pact with Russia was to be an integral part of the eastern project and was not to be considered an alternative to it. Barthou had no mandate to pursue negotiations solely for an alliance with Russia.[49]

The Barthou-Litvinov proposals encountered a cool reception in some quarters. Czechoslovakia expressed approval but Poland, as was foreshadowed by Barthou's visit to Warsaw, remained suspicious and reserved. Reaction in Germany was typified by ambassador von Hoesch's remarks to Sir John Simon on 12 June. Germany, he suspected, had been invited to join the eastern pact simply to lend credence to the professions that no attempt was being made to encircle it. But the Russians, in particular, expected a German refusal "hoping thereby to throw the blame on Germany."[50] The British government, too, entertained some doubts about the desirability of increased Franco-Soviet contact. There were even reports that Simon was thinking of making some new arrangements with Belgium and Germany in view of French flirtations with Stalin's regime.[51] However, on the day that the plan was submitted to Germany, Simon was moved to suggest British willingness to consider the Franco-Russian proposals.[52]

Barthou was not oblivious to the effect his project might have on Anglo-French relations. In a conversation with the British ambassador to Paris he tried to remove any misunderstanding. The security of Europe, he declared, rested firmly on the principle of Anglo-French solidarity.

British observers should not misconstrue his policy by wondering whether the eastern pact was in any way designed as a possible alternative to the Anglo-French entente. He even hinted that German acceptance of the pact might lead to some sort of French recognition of Germany's right to rearm—a proposition which he admitted carried his personal stamp rather than that of the entire cabinet. Finally, the minister ventured that the Ango-French entente could be strengthened in the form of joint participation in some future Mediterranean Locarno agreement. Whatever his sense of initiative and independence, this seasoned politician was not about to sacrifice the entente with Britain for the sake of new and untried allies.[53]

Barthou was due to put his case before the British foreign secretary in early July. By that time European reaction to the eastern pact had clarified. The German, Polish, and Italian attitudes ranged from unconcealed reluctance to reserved skepticism. Direct opposition involved a responsibility none was eager to assume. On the other hand, the countries of the Little Entente had demonstrated united support for the principle of regional security pacts. In the third week of June Barthou had barnstormed through Roumania and Yugoslavia soliciting support for the plan which he and Litvinov had presented.[54] The trip had been highly successful. Bucharest and Belgrade agreed to back both the eastern pact and the idea of a Mediterranean Locarno. Barthou it seemed had managed to breathe some new life into the alliance system, enough at any rate to mobilize some necessary diplomatic support. Moreover, by repledging France to honor its commitments in eastern Europe, he had received in turn the requisite reciprocal assurances of allied fidelity to France.

Sir George Clerk warned Whitehall of the new spirit which this sprightly French minister had rekindled in various parts of Europe. Barthou, the ambassador observed from Paris, represented an avowedly nationalist administration in which the right-wing traditionalists like Tardieu and Marin were dominant. Security, he reported, "has now taken first place . . . with disarmament a bad second," a trend which in part revealed the greater influence now enjoyed by the general staff. Typical of this change in spirit, Clerk continued, was "the intensive action undertaken to revive the satellite system." As for the French press descriptions of Barthou's policy, "strong and positive": "This may be interpreted as meaning that France is no longer looking for favour or subordinating its policy to pressure from Great Britain, the United States or Italy, but that she is seeking to assume the initiative in Europe."[55]

Clerk's analysis soon received solid confirmation. Barthou had no intention of jeopardizing relations with the United Kingdom; indeed, he was especially anxious to recruit British support for the eastern pact. In particular, he wanted the MacDonald government to recommend the pact to Germany, Poland, and Italy. He therefore was prepared to countenance some of the suggestions advanced by Simon during their London meeting of 9 July. On Simon's lead Barthou accepted the notion that France might guarantee Germany as well as Russia, should a request to that effect come from Berlin. Similarly he could see no reason why the Soviet Union should not extend its guarantee of support to Belgium and Germany, although the fact that Brussels had yet to recognize the Soviet regime was expected to complicate matters. However, on one issue Barthou was prepared to make only the slightest compromise. Berlin could be told that the successful conclusion of the eastern pact *might* lead to a reconsideration of her right to rearm. But the pact was not to be made conditional on the principle of legitimizing German rearmament. On this it was Simon and not Barthou who relented, the foreign secretary finally agreeing to lend Britain's diplomatic support to the pact in exchange for the most modest of gestures from Barthou.[56]

On Simon's instructions the British embassies in Berlin, Warsaw, and Rome set to work on the promotion of the eastern pact. Highly satisfied, Barthou returned to Paris. He had made a good bargain. Germany was unlikely to accept the invitation to join the Franco-Soviet pact. If she refused the eastern pact might well collapse, a regrettable development but one that would place full responsibility on the Wilhelmstrasse; and that would be a turnabout over which the minister who had opposed the April note might have chuckled. Furthermore, the British initiative had served another useful purpose. Barthou had carefully refrained from committing France to recognize Germany's right to rearm. But he had made appropriate if vague noises. Now, if the eastern pact failed France might charge Germany with a breach of faith and thus attribute to it the failure of the last chance to negotiate an arms convention. The liabilities of 17 April might yet be expunged.

It is unnecessary to recount the series of futile negotiations that eventually led to the abandonment of the eastern Locarno project in the summer of 1935, long after Barthou's tragic death. France, Russia, Italy, and Czechoslovakia ultimately supported the plan. The Baltic states also expressed their approval, a politic decision given their proximity to the Russian colossus. Germany and Poland held out, unwilling to subscribe to the proposals but reluctant too to assume responsibility by rejecting them. There matters stood, unresolved; Barthou thwarted once again, suffering from yet another embarrassing diplomatic episode. Or perhaps this is no more than a reading of surface gestures, muting a diplomacy of substance for a diplomacy of appearance.

Barthou could hardly have mistaken Polish intentions. The principle of a Franco-Soviet rapprochement had been received coldly in Warsaw from the beginning. Then in June, when the first draft of the pact appeared, it was clear that Poland would try to stall indefinitely. This draft stipulated that each signatory would assist any member victimized by the aggression of another member.[57] But in view of Poland's blighted relations with such neighbors as Russia, Lithuania, and Czechoslovakia, such a pledge threatened to dissolve in ridicule. Another article of the pact linked the pledge of assistance to articles 10 and 16 of the League Covenant. Consequently, if for example, Czechoslovakia were attacked by Germany, Poland would be obliged to allow the transit of Russian troops bound for the relief of Prague. Barthou was too shrewd not to have appreciated the intensity of Polish feeling against the Red Army. Yet all this notwithstanding, he sought to push the Poles with almost mindless indifference, threatening to go for a direct pact with Russia if Poland rejected the eastern pact. It was curious behavior indeed for a man of Barthou's great subtlety and finesse, acting as if unaware that opposition could be fortified by intimidation. "I can imagine nothing more calculated to exasperate the Marshal," observed the British ambassador in Warsaw, "than putting a pistol to his head in this manner."[58]

Whether this approach was calculated and deliberate depends very much on one's assessment of Barthou's diplomacy toward Germany. Some have argued, along the lines of Gamelin's analysis, that Barthou's policy was that of Delcassé, a policy of alliances and encirclement.[59] Others have maintained that he believed sincerely in the cause of international reconciliation and that the eastern pact really was a device to embrace Germany.[60] The truth may lie somewhere in between. Barthou seems to have been neither so obdurate as to dismiss the possibility of a genuine improvement in Franco-German relations, so bitter as to be unmoved by such a prospect, nor so naive as to idly gamble the fortunes of *sécurité* in the palatial gaming-house in Geneva. He was a veteran politician, coolly pragmatic and unstarry-eyed. As such, Léger may have usurped the thoughts of his minister and close friend when he ventured the view that "if the so-called Eastern Locarno did not materialize France would be more or less compelled to conclude an alliance with Russia."[61] British observers recognized the same possibility. France, Clerk concluded, "has decided to fashion a system of security of her own . . . which, if accepted by Germany, will enable disarmament again to be discussed. If not accepted by Germany, the system becomes automatically the best method of restraining Germany."[62] Such is the pragmatic element, the pursuit of a policy which was likely to end in either one of two satisfactory alternatives. Yet there is no hint of insincerity in George Clerk's assessment of Barthou. In fact, the ambassador was satisfied that the foreign minister preferred to have Germany join the pact.

Barthou may not have been optimistic that Germany would accept the pact; but this is not to say that he dealt with Litvinov on the assumption that Germany would prove intransigent to the end. Certainly until the end of June 1934 he displayed on occasion an earnest, even fervid, desire to see Germany assume a responsible role in the maintenance of European stability. Even the choleric von Ribbentrop, would-be expert on foreign affairs and future minister, conceded that Barthou was "to some extent desirous of reaching an understanding with Germany." Perhaps the Frenchman's words still echoed in his mind: "Please Herr von Ribbentrop, look me straight in the face and believe me when I say that I have a deep understanding for the Chancellor and I believe in his sincerity. I, too, have the most ardent desire to achieve agreement with Germany."[63] Admittedly, however, Barthou's enthusiasm was to wilt in the hot summer of 1934. In another mood, surfacing within days of his chat with von Ribbentrop and as such bringing to mind Eden's impression of the wily fox, the foreign minister publicly despaired over the gulf between Germany's professions of peace and its preparations for war.[64] One can assume, moreover, that the bloody internal purge which was executed in Germany on 30 June did nothing to alleviate the anxieties of a man who personally loathed brutality and violence.[65] In any event, the German ambassador in Paris soon detected that the minister was "much less aggressive and did not show the usual enthusiasm for his own ideas."[66]

What hope Barthou may have retained for a détente with Germany was soon to be dispelled in the month of July. Hitler's alleged involvement in the abortive Austrian putsch and the murder of the Austrian chancellor Dollfuss seemed to have torn open the guise of Nazi duplicity. Even had the minister been personally disposed to persevere with the Nazi enigma, that course of action carried with it mounting liabilities.

Press opinion reflected an incensed electorate. Moreover, in the face of mounting Italian and Soviet resentment toward Germany, the pursuit of a Franco-German détente may have been regarded as potentially too troublesome. Consequently, for a variety of personal, political and diplomatic reasons, Barthou relaxed his efforts to reach some new understanding with Germany. By September he was prepared to condemn Hitler's regime for at last having made it "certain to the world that no one could count on Germany's peaceful intentions or honest purposes."[67] One week later, on 19 September, Germany did all but openly reject the eastern pact proposals. By then the project had ceased to be a major preoccupation of the French foreign minister.

Instead, the rapprochements with Russia and Italy had become uppermost in his mind. With respect to the former, the initial objective was Soviet membership in the League, without which no pact with the Soviet Union could be concluded—multilateral or bilateral. Thus, together with Litvinov, he prepared the ground for Soviet entry into the League. On 18 September 1934, that hurdle was cleared. The Soviet Union at last was a member of the League of Nations. The Geneva forum also enabled Barthou to resume his work on the Italian rapprochement. At least since May he had talked of a Mediterranean Locarno and of his desire to improve relations with Rome.[68] The moment now seemed propitious to accomplish this long-held objective. Italian support for the eastern pact and, more recently, Italian resolution to preserve the independence of Austria, underlined the wisdom of establishing closer ties with Mussolini's regime. Barthou found the Italian delegate to Geneva, Baron Aloisi, to be a genial collaborator. Their discussions about Soviet membership in the League, the approaching Saar plebiscite, and the independence of Austria produced mutual agreement.[69] But the key to a formal détente, as Barthou had insisted, was the state of Italo-Yugoslav relations. Unless the regimes of King Alexander and Mussolini could settle their differences, the durability of a Franco-Italian rapprochement always would remain in doubt. With this in mind, Barthou invited the aging monarch to come to France on a state visit. Beneath the pomp of that occasion the foreign minister hoped to find a basis for an alliance with Italy.

What transpired in Marseilles is well known. On 9 October 1934, King Alexander and Louis Barthou were fatally shot as their motor cavalcade moved away from the harbor. The assassin was a member of a Croatian terrorist society, which, according to reports, was clandestinely financed by the Italian government. Hours after Barthou's death, news leaked of Italian complicity in the plot. Italy's relations with France and Yugoslavia were temporarily shattered. An assassin's gun appeared to have stolen both Barthou's life and one of his greatest aspirations.

Thus ended the first of a series of attempts to revive the French security system in the wake of the disarmament stalemate. The note of 17 April did represent a genuine turning point in French diplomacy, even though it generated more heat than light. Indeed, it was principally a change of spirit. It spoke out more forcefully than ever before against German arms violations, although it offered no equally firm solutions to that problem, certainly none that was novel. Essentially, it pointed to the more traditional form of restraint: coalition politics, which minimally meant diplomacy by crafted voting bloc and maximally meant war by allied armies. But the problems that had bedeviled France's ragged alliance system long before Barthou, refused to simply vanish on his arrival in office—a fact which surely prompted him to resist the April note on the grounds that a heartened public would expect a quick and dramatic revival of an anti-German coalition. In fact Barthou performed creditably and enjoyed as a result some major successes. He had paved much of the way for the two great rapprochements of the following year, those with Moscow and Rome. For the rest, he had preserved the vital ties with England and, with greater difficulty, those with Belgium; he had bolstered the spirits of the Little Entente and he had pursued, albeit with but marginal effect, the dialogue with Warsaw and Berlin. Unlike the case of the war ministry, where the direction indicated by the April note was taken with less vigor and with less immediately obvious results, the foreign ministry had set off with new energy toward the heralded goal of a more independent and decisive foreign policy.

Accordingly, the last quarter of 1934 found the French army in somewhat better spirits than it had been a year earlier. The disarmament issue seemed to have lost its hallucinatory grip on French politicians, certainly those under Doumergue's survey. What is more, the presence of a strong service bloc within the cabinet, combined with Barthou's evident willingness to consult with the high command on matters of foreign policy, had helped ameliorate civil-military relations. Clearly the French commander-in-chief appears to have regarded Barthou with an equanimity that would have astonished Paul-Boncour, the arch disarmer in Weygand's eyes.[70] And although there were contemporaries who saw in Barthou a man truly committed to European appeasement in its most positive sense, it seems no less clear that here was one who would not neglect the more traditional resources from which French security previously had drawn. Certainly his success in maintaining with dignity stable relations with England and Belgium had to be appreciated by the general staff, even if neither the soldiers nor the diplomats could induce the English to accept staff conversations or the Belgians an active application of the 1920 military convention. Similarly, the military also sympathized with the minister's careful efforts to rekindle the loyalty of the Little Entente—without actually extending French commitments—and with his success in retaining the Franco-Polish alliance, without bowing to Polish wishes to tighten up the military convention.[71] Finally, having themselves remarked on the value of Soviet and Italian cooperation, it is clear that the army chiefs supported Barthou in his bid for rapprochement. No one would have said that the German peril had diminished under Doumergue's premiership; indeed, it had continued to mount with Germany's ever more ambitious rearmament. But by November 1934 the French chiefs of staff at last had taken heart; it remained to be seen whether the new Flandin government and Barthou's successor, Pierre Laval, would continue to plot a more independent course for French diplomacy by struggling to keep up with the ringing assurances of April 1934.

4

The Foreign Policy of
Pierre Laval, 1934-1935

The Doumergue government barely survived Barthou's death, although it was the premier's domestic program that really toppled the administration. Before succumbing to the growing unrest in his cabinet, however, Doumergue shifted Pierre Laval from the colonial ministry to the Quai d'Orsay. It proved to be a very important appointment, partly because Laval was to hold this portfolio for the next fourteen months—a long ministry by the standards of the day—and partly because he was destined to arouse such widespread distrust. Before his prewar innings were over, this man had created legions of enemies, French and foreign; even before France could commemorate the first anniversary of his predecessor's death, Laval appeared to have gambled away the modest winnings accumulated by Louis Barthou. When he left office in January 1936, like Doumergue, essentially for reasons of domestic politics, Laval seemed to have forfeited the mantle of Barthou, and with it the dignity, perception, and finesse of his late colleague. So our histories read, with mixed veracity.

In the autumn of 1934 appearances would not have forecast this break in continuity. Admittedly, Laval was a curious man to follow Barthou, reckoned on the basis of past associations. Not of the generation of Barthou and Doumergue, indeed at fifty-one some twenty years their junior, Laval could not have been expected to share their perspectives with perfect fidelity. In fact if Barthou had been received into the cabinet as a traditionalist and hard-liner, Laval long had been associated with the conciliatory policy of Aristide Briand, the man who had engineered the Locarno accords. On the other hand, Laval was no tyro in politics, having held a succession of cabinet posts since 1925 including the premiership in 1931-1932; and he was regarded not as an adventurer but as a man of caution, one who was deemed "unlikely to make the grand gesture" and who, unlike Flandin, could be counted on not to take "too independent a line."[1] As it happens, these expectations were not without foundation. Whatever the elusive inner truth of Pierre Laval, the record that is left to us suggests far more continuity of purpose and approach between Barthou and Laval than is often allowed. It is to this that Sir George Clerk referred when assessing Laval's policy as "different in manner rather than matter from that of Barthou."[2]

There was no denying that the manner had changed, for the personal styles of Barthou and Laval were entirely different. The former was the model of a French gentleman, a man of *haute culture* as well as *bon vivant*. The latter evoked quite another impression. In the minds of so many, Laval was a peasant at heart. Despite the cases he had won as a lawyer, the money he had made as a businessman, and the portfolios he had held as a cabinet minister, Laval never managed to shake—if such were ever his wish—the image and reputation as a simple man of the Auvergne. But of course there was more to it than that. One is reminded of Aneurin Bevan's remark that "we seek to imprison reality in our description of it. Soon, it is we who become the prisoners of the description."[3] One senses that in this lies part of the Laval mystery, for the word peasant has the character of grape-shot. Certainly when the word was applied to Laval, as it was with metronomic consistency, it was intended as a one-word character portrait. Not only did it convey the hint of simplicity and naiveté, but cunning, duplicity, a canny shrewdness—phrases that choked the diplomatic bags in 1935. In particular, Laval came to be regarded by the British with the kind of distant suspicion which the well bred reserve for the well meaning. The squat physique, rather Asian features, and swarthy complexion placed this chainsmoking politician with his famous white ties—reportedly stained—in a world apart from the tailored streets of Whitehall. At the risk of being too severe, one ought to reflect on the at once venomous and patronizing comments which Laval seemed to inspire in London, comments which at least in part were provoked by intelligence gratuitously provided by Pierre Etienne Flandin—a man whose tailor really did reside in London.

Yet it would be foolish to make no allowances for this contemporary and very prevalent description of Laval. Whereas it was too often used as a handy epithet, the word peasant may not be altogether inappropriate if it is used with discretion. What it was frequently used to convey, in a manner that is consistent with the interpretation of Laval's principal English biographer, was a surprisingly simplistic approach to international affairs.[4] By no means an ignorant or shallow man, and already one of no mean political accomplishment, Laval often spoke as if complex matters of diplomacy could be resolved with the direct and matter-of-fact airs assumed by country horse traders. For him, like Barthou, the note of 17 April had been unwise, setting a tone of discord which could serve no useful purpose. Rather, what was needed, was direct and candid talks with the Germans. This is what Laval kept saying until he was forced from office; and it is this sentiment, so genuine and so simple, that encourages one to regard him less as a scheming horse dealer and more as a country man in pursuit of a homespun dream of European peace. Yet to this one should really add two observations. First, if it was his belief in frank dialogue and honest compromise that betrayed his peasant origins, how is it that we do not consider Neville Chamberlain in the same light, a man who is nonetheless remembered for similar ideals, with equal remorse but with less bitterness? Second, in a curious sleight of hand, history seems to have remembered Laval for what he wanted to do rather than for what he did. For all of his musings, all of his simple and benign dreams, this man never did make the much heralded and much feared *voyage à Berlin*.

Restrained by domestic political forces, ones which his sagacity and pragmatism instantly acknowledged, Laval had to confine himself to keeping the idea of a Franco-German rapprochement alive. It was this desire which the British welcomed, at first, and then progressively came to fear as the possibilities for such a reconciliation brightened in the summer of 1935. Having long chided the French for their intemperate opposition to German revisionism, the British government was to grow nervous at the prospect of any new understanding in Europe which might extend their isolation involuntarily. Thus it was the cause of Franco-German friendship, long championed by the British while it was utterly remote and with which Laval was associated, that came to impose a serious strain on Anglo-French relations.

For their part, the Germans also sensed the change of tone which Laval represented, the "manner" as Clerk called it. Amid the political turbulence of November 1934, which saw Flandin's cabinet replace that of Doumergue, Ambassador Roland Köster weighed the new possibilities afforded by the recently appointed Laval and his so newly arrived premier. Having but five weeks earlier warned Berlin that French opinion had hardened on the Saar question, Köster now addressed his superiors with more encouraging news. Laval, he said, seemed anxious to eliminate misunderstanding; "In his opinion, the Saar was one hundred per cent Germany and . . . he personally desired nothing more sincerely than that this territory should return to Germany."[5] Indeed, he hoped to make this question the very key to the establishment of "sincere, honest and good-neighborly relations," a desire endorsed later in the month by Premier Flandin.[6] On the other hand, the ambassador was obliged to report that Laval was pushing for the immediate resumption of negotiations for the eastern pact. While he presented it in a more positive light, as a "unique opportunity for Germany to prove her goodwill," Laval had made it clear that he "fully agreed with Barthou's ideas about the Eastern Pact." However much he emphasized the importance of personal and direct exchanges of ideas, and implicitly played down the utility of diplomatic conventions, he was evidently not about to throw caution to the wind.[7]

This belief in personal diplomacy, in the value of the warm encounter at the summit, was not of course peculiar to Laval. Indeed, the trend had been set irrevocably by the top-floor bargaining engaged in by presidents and first ministers in 1919. But for all that, Laval's diplomacy was far from being as ad hoc in manner and as intuitive in direction as he sometimes led one to believe. As he made clear to Ambassador Clerk, he was not without a diplomatic program, a program incidentally which was as cautious as Clerk's earlier remarks would have caused us to anticipate. First he wanted a multilateral declaration stressing the importance of an independent Austria, followed by a separate Italian pledge of the same order. Then he would go to Rome to negotiate at one and the same time a Franco-Italian accord and an Italo-Yugoslav treaty of friendship and arbitration. Finally, once these issues were resolved, he would aim for the conclusion of the eastern pact, in the wake of which he would be ready to talk to Germany about armaments. Indeed, as if to underline the fact that he foresaw no radical departure from the policy of his predecessors, Laval added that "hitherto the cart had been put before the horse and that it had been useless to talk of disarmament before the several countries were sure of their security."[8] Laval remained attached to the principle of security first.

In a follow-up communication Clerk once more stressed the continuity of French policy under Laval. While it was true that France intended to make no trouble over the Saar issue, "on the question of security, France has not budged. No French Government could at present sign and survive an agreement legalizing German re-armament without first providing for security." Thus, with Laval now well established in the Quai d'Orsay, the ambassador commented:

> I fear that we shall have the greatest difficulty in getting the French to alter either their methods or their tempo. After all, their policy was resolved as a result of the breakdown in April; we blessed that policy in July [Barthou's visit to London]; and in French eyes it has not yet finally broken down and there has not yet been any fundamental change in the situation such as to justify them in discarding it.[9]

The ambassador was quite correct. The Franco-German stalemate seemed certain to continue, with Berlin demanding consideration of the arms issue first and with Paris insisting that the legalization of German armaments should only come after the conclusion of adequate security conventions. Like Barthou before him, Laval had little room to maneuver. Only in late December 1934 did the French government agree to make another slight concession. Barthou had said that the eastern pact might permit negotiation of an arms convention. Now Laval was privately prepared to accept the possibility that the two might be negotiated and signed simultaneously.[10] To go further, as Léger observed, the Flandin government would be torn apart, with ministers like Herriot, Marin, and Maurin leading the revolt.[11]

On this front, therefore, the policy pursued by Doumergue and Barthou remained more or less constant under Flandin and Laval. This the British appreciated, in both senses of the word, for it allowed them to continue their perhaps disingenuous complaints about French intransigence. The moment had not yet come when they feared the possibility of a Franco-German settlement. In Berlin, too, Laval was held in some esteem. He was obviously determined to cooperate on the matter of the Saar plebiscite, and there were some signs, hints, that he might not be averse "to striving for a direct settlement" of an arms limitation agreement.[12] Moscow had less reason for satisfaction. Laval was said to have opposed the rapprochement begun by Barthou;[13] and he now showed very little interest in pursuing these contacts with any dispatch. The most he would do, and that on Litvinov's urging, was to sign the Franco-Soviet Protocol of 5 December 1934, a declaration that merely reaffirmed the intention to retain the original convention for mutual assistance which had been drafted six months earlier. But there Laval called a halt. Nothing more would be done until the fate of the eastern pact had been decided; and by now the minister was determined to leave that issue until after he had negotiated a new declaration with Mussolini on the continued independence of Austria, an undertaking which in turn was to lead in succession to an Italo-Yugoslav treaty and a Franco-Italian political settlement. Thus, in Laval's scheme of things, it was Rome rather than Moscow which commanded priority—an emphasis that may or may not have been different under the guiding hand of Louis Barthou.

What does seem clear is that both Barthou and Laval, assisted by their permanent officials, had devised admirably flexible policies. As contemporaries saw it, Barthou was ostensibly conciliatory but implicitly menacing, characteristics which have earned him praise for his ingenuity and great controversy over which sentiment was foremost in his mind. Laval, it can be said, began his principal diplomatic overture along the same lines, although with Italy instead of Russia. Fundamentally, Laval wanted to reach some *modus vivendi* with Germany, a settlement freely arrived at like his master's Locarno pact. For that purpose Italy had much to contribute, a potential Mussolini had demonstrated in 1933 with his four-power pact. Laval had endorsed that proposal enthusiastically; and now, in charge of French diplomacy, he seemed eager to exploit Italian interest in a rapprochement with France as the first step toward a broader political settlement for western Europe. By working out a common front with Mussolini, the one man in Europe whom Hitler was known to admire, Laval at one and the same time could explain this step as a logical prelude to a Franco-German understanding and yet defend it as an instrument for ensuring Germany's isolation if need be. Simply put, Barthou's approach to Russia suggested the encirclement of Germany, a condition that might either encourage German cooperation or discourage German recklessness. The same sort of motivation could be attributed to Laval; but it rarely is. His unfortunate image as an early and misguided appeaser, unprincipled and devious at that, has denied him the kind of positive interpretation so readily credited to Barthou. Indeed, just as Barthou's image as a traditionalist may have obscured his interest in conciliation, Laval's association with the politics of conciliation may have concealed the traditionalist overtones of French policy in 1935. It is to the latter theme that the subsequent analysis will make special reference, without in any way seeking to deny his very real commitment to the idea of a Franco-German understanding.

Having satisfied himself that the Franco-Italian negotiations had progressed sufficiently, following their resumption some weeks after Barthou's death, Laval undertook his *voyage à Rome*. For four days, between 4 and 8 January 1935, the French and Italian delegations devoted their energies to a series of agreements. In brief, the Rome accords had two aspects, the one colonial and the other continental. The former entailed a renunciation of Italian rights in Tunisia, in return for which France ceded a large portion of desert to round off the southeastern corner of Libya, a strip of coastline for Eritrea, and a block of shares in the Addis Abba-to-Djibouti railroad. On the surface the French had done very well, the settlement on Tunisia being reckoned as more valuable than the undeniably large territorial concessions which they had made in their turn but which Laval privately admitted would not support the growth of "a dozen bananas."[14]

The continental aspect of the Rome agreements also appeared more favorable to French interests. The two signatories promised to sponsor a Danubian pact which would pledge all participants to refrain from interfering in the domestic politics of fellow members. Included in this group were to be Austria, Germany, Czechoslovakia, Hungary, Italy, and Yugoslavia. France, Poland, and Roumania would be eligible for membership on request. Until the pact was implemented, and it never was, France and Italy agreed to collaborate in the defense of Austria—the issue Laval had placed high on his list of diplomatic priorities. Here again, it was Mussolini who appeared to have relented, dropping his support for Hungary's revisionist claims in favor of cooperation with the Little Entente. Given the Duce's antipathy for both Roumania and Yugosalvia, Laval knew that he was asking the Italian leader to swallow a "bitter pill."[15] On the other hand, the pact did offer some hope of stability in southeastern Europe, a consideration of some importance to a fascist regime whose gaze was being drawn toward Africa. Moreover, the pact also promised a measure of consultation between Rome and Paris in the event that Germany violated the letter of the proposed pact by an attempted Anschluss, or its spirit by a program of unrestricted rearmament

As Laval had intended, here was a mutual agreement mutually arrived at, the assurance that even long-standing differences could be rec-

onciled by frank talk and honest bargaining. He returned to Paris well
satisfied, only to discover in the succeeding months that he had been too
clever by half. Just as the French had wondered only a year before what
had induced Germany to sign her accord with Poland, so the diplomatic
community was now buzzing with suspicions about why Mussolini had
proven so pliable. Almost from the start there were rumors of a secret accord between Laval and the Duce. Although it was some time before this
issue would become a *cause célèbre* in Franco-Italian relations, it would
be well to define the debate at the present moment. Did Laval, in his private *tête-à-tête* with Mussolini on the evening of 6 January promise the
Duce a free hand in Ethiopia?

By the autumn of 1935, as Italian operations against Ethiopia began, this question had come to have a critical bearing, not only for the
future of relations between Paris and Rome but between Paris and London as well. In a letter of 5 November 1935, Laval categorically denied
having made such an agreement. To ambassador Chambrun he wrote:
"The Rome accords, far from eliciting French consent for Italian political
designs on Ethiopia, excluded any suggestion of an undertaking against
Ethiopian independence or sovereignty."[16] In his turn Mussolini responded with no less assurance. Having agreed that it was not possible
"to say everything in writing," the Duce reminded Laval, "we admitted
last January the need for a verbal agreement." It was here, the Duce
added, that we mentioned, "on several occasions the 'free hand' which I
was to have in Ethiopia." Lest there be any doubt as to how important he
considered this understanding, Mussolini insisted that it had been "your
consent and your good will" which provided "the point of departure."[17]

On this dispute, one that came to carry with it a grave historical
responsibility, there can be no final verdict, at least not one that is certain. The dispute, after all, focuses on an allegedly verbal agreement between two men whose veracity has never gone unquestioned. The following interpretation is therefore frankly speculative.

The two men discussed the future of Ethiopia and Laval made the
appropriate gestures of compliance. It was to this that Laval referred
when he wrote to Mussolini early in 1936, "The freedom of action which
France thus offered Italy for peaceful purposes, opened to Italy the most
promising possibilities for the future by agreeing to let her realize her legitimate aspirations by means of a civilizing and progressive endeavor."[18]
What he did not do, so he maintains in this spirited defense of his conduct, was give "my assent to the war which you subsequently felt obliged

to undertake." In this Laval was probably quite correct; indeed, Mussolini had never quite said that he had been promised assent for a "war." Very likely, Mussolini's plans for Ethiopia were not discussed in detail in January, an omission which no doubt suited both sides. The Duce had no reason to volunteer such information; and Laval certainly knew how to turn a blind eye, particularly if the fate of a European settlement depended on his doing so. This is not to say, however, that the French minister knew or even assumed that war would be the result of his references to a free hand. He may have taken for granted that Mussolini would be wise enough to accomplish his objectives without war, as his letter to the Duce suggests. Or he may have been prepared to mortgage the future for the sake of an immediate agreement, relying on his talent for sorting out difficulties as they arose. In either event, one is struck more by Laval's naiveté than his treachery. It is safe to assume that he really did not care about the fate of Ethiopia; and he certainly never entertained thoughts of going to war with Italy on Ethiopia's behalf. In this sense, at no time did he think of betraying Italy or the verbal agreement hazily arrived at with Mussolini. But a wink may be as bad as a nod, just as an ill-defined agreement may contain as many hazards as no agreement at all. Almost certainly Laval ended up as the victim of his own cleverness, rather incautiously trusting to Mussolini's sagacity and subscribing to a verbal arrangement which proved harder to repudiate than a written accord.[19]

In January 1935, however, such problems were far from Laval's mind. Indeed, the only embarrassment in Franco-Italian relations was the urgency which Rome seemed to attach to the early commencement of joint staff talks. Laval preferred to stall, fearing to proceed he said before Italo-Yugoslav relations had recorded further improvement, but perhaps more truthfully because he feared that such talks would only exacerbate relations with Germany. For the rest, it was difficult to know where or how to move, Léger freely admitting that for the moment neither Flandin nor Laval had "an idea in their heads."[20] Clearly there was no desire to push the rapprochement with Russia, an attitude which was all too apparent to Moscow.[21] But on the other hand few alternatives were available. While the British still regarded Flandin and Laval as "realists," because they seemed personally inclined to accept the fact of German rearmament and proceed from there, it was true that the prevalent opinion in France, and likely within the cabinet itself, would rebel against the legalization of German rearmament without new safeguards for French security. In the diplomatic vocabulary of the time, that meant the conclusion of the eastern pact—complete with German membership. Yet even those who so insisted seemed to harbor little faith in such a possibility, the obstacles having proven to be so great in Warsaw and Berlin. Thus, as Orme Sargent of the Foreign Office correctly observed, there could be no arms limitation agreement without new guarantees for French security—guarantees that were elusive owing to the British refusal to offer alternate assurances, as well as to the German position on the eastern pact. Hence, by the end of January 1935, a general European settlement seemed as remote as ever, with France being driven "ever nearer and nearer to the fatal solution of a Russian alliance."[22]

This judgment, it should be noted, did not claim ideological inspiration. Rather it was said with reference to that "horrible . . . prospect of a return to the pre-war grouping of Powers." In other words, it spoke to the fear of that old and binding system of alliances which was said to have occasioned such calamitous results in August of 1914. Whether the French were party to this fear remains uncertain, but probable. In any event, at the beginning of 1935 one does find Laval refusing to draw too close to the Italians or the Russians, preferring for the time being to use the prospect of further negotiations with Moscow and Rome as an inducement for Berlin to begin serious bargaining. It was out of this temporary *attentisme* that the English and French rolled a new diplomatic machine, one designed to function in the name of cautious, unspectacular, responsible diplomacy.

On both sides of the Channel the month of January witnessed elaborate preparations for the forthcoming Anglo-French talks in London. For the British this meant warning Paris that the familiar and still inappropriate request for joint staff talks would not be received kindly.[23] For both sides it meant laborious efforts to prepare in advance an acceptable final communiqué which could be released to the public when the conference adjourned. It was in connection with this latter task, a testament in itself to the kind of public pressures that obliged diplomats to prepare agendas and outcomes simultaneously, that a new avenue opened. As matters stood, there was little chance of agreeing on anything that was likely to make the slightest difference to the existing diplomatic stalemate. It was under these circumstances, therefore, that the French appear to have been the first to float the idea of a mutual assistance air pact.[24] The Foreign Office responded with alacrity, no doubt perceiving both the military benefits which might accrue to Britain and the distant possibility of some breakthrough in the current diplomatic deadlock.

Forewarned of the draft plan which Flandin and Laval produced on 1 February, the British were interested in using such a treaty as a new entrée to a more general arms limitation agreement, a use which almost certainly had been intended by the Flandin government. Careful to ensure that the proposed convention would not extend its Locarno obligations, the British government then bargained its support against some new French concession. Like Barthou, Flandin and Laval were to discover that British support for French pacts came with a price tag. France was to declare that the replacement of Part V of Versailles, relating to the military clauses, could be effected as part of—instead of subsequent to—a general European settlement. In fact, the French already had consented privately to such a gesture in December 1934.[25] But what the French public would now see for the first time, as was intended, was not another French concession but the possibility of a new, British-backed guarantee for French security—beside which the acceptance of simultaneous negotiations would pale in significance.[26]

As it happened the proposed air pact was a step sideways rather than forward, certainly as it was first publicly articulated in the joint communiqué of 3 February. Although other versions were to appear for months to come, the original idea was one of a multilateral pact to which Britain, France, Germany, Belgium, and probably Italy would subscribe. Simply put, the signatories were to assist any member who had been attacked from the air by another member. Thus the convention would be useless to French security in the event that Germany chose to attack in the capacity of a nonmember, an indication of the government's willingness to play to public opinion by offering only the semblance of a valuable accord. Furthermore, this attempt to shift the emphasis from the eastern pact to the air pact did not make an arms limitation agreement more likely. The very principle of simultaneity, seized upon as a method of expediting negotiations, in fact threw all pacts and projects into a grand maelstrom, with the most promising left to whirl with the moribund. On the whole it proved to be a weak effort, putting on a public face and saying little in substance that had not been said many times before—with predictable results. It is doubtful, Mr. Wigram minuted, whether these talks

have really facilitated matters with the Germans. The abandonment of Part V is not a concession of great value, so far as Germany is concerned. The hard facts are that we are trying to reconcile positions which—for the

simplest of reasons—are irreconcilable and that we are putting into the negotiations certain concessions and counter-concessions which are unreal,
and are known to be unreal by all parties to the negotiations.[27]

The London conversations therefore had done little to end the current stalemate or dissipate the attendant frustrations. By early March
1935 no breakthrough appeared in the offing. The contemporary view
from Whitehall was openly pessimistic, a perspective which the historian
would do well to keep in mind. It is clear that the decision to try negotiating a number of outstanding issues simultaneously had added greatly to
the complexity of diplomatic affairs. As one Foreign Office minute confessed, the British government really did not know where matters stood
on the eastern pact or the Danubian pact; and it was plain that they had
much thinking to do before "we can be said to know our own minds" on
the specifics of an armaments convention.[28] Within the western and central departments of the Foreign Office there was little doubt that Germany was the principal threat to European stability, an assessment which
brooked little opposition under the steady gaze of the Permanent Under-
Secretary, a man who forever saw natural laws being expressed in German behavior.[29] Russia was regarded as the wolf at the gate, anxious to
sweep France into an overtly anti-German alliance, while Flandin and
Laval still were seen as reasonable men—men who would discuss armaments if they possibly could, men who would negotiate with Germany
but, as yet, men who would continue to reject secret offers from Berlin
for a direct Franco-German agreement.[30] Indeed, for the time being, it
was the unlikelihood of any talks at all that disturbed the British, a mood
that prompted the British government to accept the German invitation
for Sir John Simon to visit Berlin in the spring. There was within the Office a sense of doom, impending or actual, for in fact observers there
were struggling to interpret what was happening around them. Sargent,
for example, was tormented by the prospect of a new Franco-Russian alliance, for him the harbinger of a revived prewar system. A colleague
saw things differently. "For my part, I have long held the opinion that we
are really already back in the days of 'balance of power' and that it is
hopeless to expect anything else in dealing with such protagonists of
'sacro egoismo' as Messrs. Hitler, Mussolini, Pilsudski and Stalin."[31]
As it happened, neither was far from the truth. The pressures
building in favor of more vigorous alliance diplomacy were certainly real
enough. In mid-March Germany publicly proclaimed the existence of its

military air force and, subsequently, its return to compulsory military service in the interest of amassing a total of thirty-six army divisions. Although neither the contents of the two announcements nor their timing came as a surprise to the French government, the German moves did effectively call a halt to the diplomatic marking of time which had governed British and French policy since the Rome accords. In this sense the March announcements clearly marked another milestone in French diplomacy. Laval was compelled to move. The effects of his new initiatives can best be gauged with principal reference to French relations with Italy, Russia, and Great Britain.

To this point Laval's diplomacy had been reckoned almost universally as more moderate in tone and more flexible in substance than that of his predecessor. In fact, appearances had been partly deceptive. Apart from his admittedly frequent expressions of interest in rapprochement with Germany and his low-key handling of the Saar plebiscite in January, Laval actually had done very little that would distinguish his policy from that of his reputedly traditionalist predecessor. Rather it was what he had not done that seemed to mark him as a reasonable man bent on a broad European settlement. He had not bowed to pressure, domestic or external, in favor of an alliance with either Russia or Italy. Nevertheless, he had continued to keep alive the idea of the eastern pact and had declined, along with Flandin, private German offers to negotiate a direct, bilateral agreement. Furthermore, having conceded the principle of simultaneous negotiations, he had refused to do more—never in fact discarding what had been a constant in recent French policy, the refusal to consider an arms convention in the absence of worthwhile political guarantees. While it is possible to view Laval, like countless others, as one who could live with any policy providing it kept him in office, the fact remains that the substance of his diplomacy up to March 1935 suggested a basically conservative attitude which was at odds only with the appearance of a softer, more pliable approach to international relations. From March onward he tried to maintain that appearance—for he surely was committed to the politics of détente—but with increasing difficulty. That conservative substance was demanding more care and attention.

Ever since his return from Rome Laval had stressed the need for caution. He admitted that he had only "a limited confidence in Germany" and therefore urged the chiefs of staff to prepare a new brief for English benefit, "stressing the importance of German armaments and also the necessity for France not to sink below the German level."[32] A month later, in February 1935, the minister was still struggling to slow the pace, this time trying to delay staff talks with the Italians by warning against replying "too quickly to the feelers from Rome."[33] But the general staff had grown impatient, particularly after the latest Italian overture, which suggested discussions relating to French as well as Austrian security.[34] Reluctantly, and with the proviso that such talks should proceed slowly, Laval consented to the recommendations of the Haut Comité Militaire. General Gamelin, the retired Weygand's successor as peacetime commander-in-chief, was to reply to the Italian overtures. He was to mention three contingencies. France might send an army corps to the Italian right flank where it would serve as a liaison unit between Italian and Yugoslav forces—the kind of involvement Laval himself regarded as the "essential condition" for the protection of Austria and the conclusion of a Danubian pact. Italy in her turn might send an army corps to the French right flank, with a view to strengthening the area around Belfort. Finally, the French air staff was to undertake a study regarding the future provision of air bases in the valleys of the Saone and Doubs for the use of the Italian air force. Laval left the committee meeting satisfied, assured that there would be no precipitous rush for agreement that might startle the Germany quarry. Even more telling, when Mussolini temporarily halted these preliminary preparations in early March, Laval seemed far more relieved than anxious.[35]

The next time the Haut Comité convened, following the German announcements of mid-March, there was a perceptible change in atmosphere. Laval and Flandin were there to confront the army. In particular, they wanted to know whether France was capable of undertaking an early offensive on the Rhine should Italy have to rush to the defense of Austria. Preferring the more sanguine response offered by Gamelin to the frankly pessimistic view of Pétain, the ministers promised to convey the general's in fact tentative assurance to Mussolini whom they were scheduled to meet later in the month at the Stresa conference. It was soon after this famous meeting on the shores of Lake Maggiore that the government authorized the opening of formal negotiations with the Italians, although still with the caveat that the venture remain "a strict secret." Clearly, as Italian officials were quite prepared to admit from their side, German rearmament was making staff accords among Germany's potential enemies almost mandatory.[36]

The Franco-Italian air talks, the only ones for which documentation is currently adequate, appear to have been in the vanguard of the accelerating rapprochement. On 9 May General Denain and a five-man delegation from the air ministry left for Rome, with the express purpose of laying the foundations for a commercial air convention and a mutual assistance air pact. For the next four days his two staff officers, Commandant de Dumast and Captain de Vitrolles worked out the basis for an agreement with their Italian counterparts. Briefly put, the officers studied three contingencies: a German air attack on Italy, a similar attack on France, and a simultaneous attack on both France and Italy.

The negotiators discussed the mechanics of the proposed accord on 12-13 May. The normal zones of action in each contingency would place French operations north of the line between Strasbourg and Cheb and those of Italy to the south. Eventually, it was expected that there would be considerable exchangeability, with either force operating on either side of the line. For Case 1, a German attack on Italy, the French air force would commence moving to a wartime footing. Air bases in eastern France, east of the line Lons-le Saulnier-Nancy, would be made available to Italian aircraft, in particular to several squadrons of heavy bombers. In turn, French fighter units would be dispatched to Italy where they would assist in air defense. Case 2, a German attack on France, was to see the early dispatch of some one hundred Italian heavy bombers and a fighter squadron to bases in eastern France. Case 3 was to have both air forces operating from their home bases, athough it was expected that some kind of Italian contingent would operate from eastern France where air bases would allow access to German targets that were ordinarily safe from trans-Alpine bombing runs. With such provisions for future cooperation firmly established, the two air staffs agreed to hold joint conversations at least twice a year and to exchange the requisite technical information in the intervals.[37]

It remains uncertain whether similar accords were reached by the respective army and navy staffs. What is clear is that some six weeks later, on 25 June 1935, the three French chiefs of staff traveled to Italy for several days of discussion with the Italians. The outcome was a rather odd and informal military convention, concluded simply by a series of signatures on the official minutes. By its terms the signatories agreed to a mutual guarantee of their adjacent territories in the Alps and Africa, to an early exchange of small troop detachments at the outset of hostilities, to the dispatch by France of an army corps to the Italo-Yugoslav border and finally to a comparable Italian gesture—one army corps to Belfort and an as yet undetermined number of Italian bombers to bases in eastern France. Seemingly content with such arrangements, by this convention rather imprecisely defined, Gamelin returned to Paris a convinced partisan of Franco-Italian collaboration.[38]

One is hard pressed to explain this rather curious dénouement. There is little doubt that the French dearly wanted a mutual assistance arrangement with Italy. The studies which were made under the auspices of the Haut Comité make this clear. Stung by the sudden interest shown by Flandin and Laval in early April, the military committee had hastened to arrange written responses to the questions posed by the two ministers. All three services appeared to place a high premium on Italian support and cooperation. The army had visions of a gallant Italian defense of Austria, "their left flank on Swiss territory, their right flank linking up with Czechoslovakia." The navy spoke of a future in which Italy would protect French sea routes in the eastern Mediterranean, Red Sea, and Indian Ocean, and perhaps would join with France in the defense of the western Mediterranean and the English Channel. The air force thought fondly of the day when Czech air bases would bring the Italians within striking distance of Berlin, Leipzig, and Hamburg and when French bases would support Italian raids on the Ruhr. But as the air staff observed with characteristic explicitness, "*It is absolutely essential that all these questions be given urgent attention with a view to preparing plans and precise agreements* between the French and Italian General Staffs."[39]

For his part, Pierre Laval shared completely in the belief of Italy's grave strategic importance. In his own words, Italy was:

> the bridge constructed between France and all those countries of central and eastern Europe which were allied with our country . . . It was our chance to benefit, not only from the whole Italian military effort, but to benefit from the military effort of Yugoslavia, Czechoslovakia, Poland and Roumania.[40]

Yet it is doubtlessly true that this same man sent the military delegations to Rome under strict orders of secrecy and presumably countenanced the remarkably informal manner with which the convention was concluded in June 1935. Forced to speculate, one might hazard the guess that this was yet another manifestation of that desire to avoid binding commitments, the kind of commitments with which the outbreak of war had been associated for the past two decades.

Moreover, Laval was still in pursuit of a settlement with Germany, in whose eyes a formal military convention—in this case one explicitly directed at Germany—was sure to be offensive.[41] Nevertheless, it was not a little ironic that Laval should still be insisting on a free hand to deal with Germany when that same and unfortunate phrase was already causing him embarrassment in quite another context. By mid-June 1935, before Gamelin had even gone to Rome, Laval was sure that Mussolini was "aiming for an Italian protectorate over Abyssinia, without fighting if possible, but otherwise using the next incident as a pretext for military operations."[42] If one can accept the accuracy of our earlier analysis of the controversial January accords, it seems the chickens were coming home to roost. France now had the makings of an extremely useful military alliance, the scope of which extended from the Rhine to eastern Europe and across the Mediterranean. Well handled, it could be the shield behind which France could approach Germany; but tossed carelessly on the rocks of some African dispute it was likely to be rendered quite useless.

Just as the German announcements of March 1935 had precipitated the French decision to press on with the Franco-Italian alliance, so too they affected the fortunes of Franco-Soviet relations. For the first two and a half months of 1935 nothing of significance had transpired in those relations. Litvinov had pressed his case for a bilateral accord on every possible occasion, but the French had refused to be drawn—insisting with equal stubbornness that the eastern pact was not yet a dead letter. In fact, Laval, Léger, and to a lesser extent Flandin were loath to end the eastern pact charade, knowing full well that once that game was over the arguments for a Franco-Russian alliance would be insuperable. From mid-March onward, a part of that attitude vanished. The Russians were to be brought from the gate to the foyer, a necessity Laval grasped quickly enough. Several days before the cabinet meeting of 20 March, during which it was decided to resume negotiations with Russia, Laval was talking about the possibility of an early visit to Moscow.[43] At last what had been understood from the beginning, from the days of Barthou, had come to pass. Denied what it really wanted, a European-wide settlement based on German cooperation, the French government was opting for what many regarded as second best. Without question Laval disliked the task before him, remaining personally attached to that policy which, as he saw it, had treated Germany "with every possible consideration in a despairing hope of inducing her to collaborate loyally in the work of appeasement."[44]

However exceptional his attitude, his perseverance, toward Germany, Laval's lukewarm response to the Soviet Union was entirely typical of French official opinion. With the sole exception of Herriot, whose belief in the value of Russia was so strong that it deterred others from sharing it, apparently no cabinet minister was prepared to push for the speedy completion of the mutual assistance pact or an attendant military convention. With rare consensus, "official" Paris indulged in this quite open reticence, the high command proving itself no exception to the rule. Indeed, in the aspirations and anxieties of the professional soldiers one detects most of the elements which constituted the official French appraisal of Soviet Russia and her potential service to French security.

Almost from the beginning, of course, it was the military convention rather than the mutual assistance pact about which feelings were most intense. Indeed, having been prepared in the era of Barthou, the pact proved almost too easy to conclude.[45] For this the general staff was almost certainly grateful, for the principle of the rapprochement had appealed to them since Barthou's day. The motives of the high command no doubt were as diverse as the personalities it comprised; however, with reference to the views of Gamelin, the retired Weygand, and the current war minister, General Maurin, it is possible to offer a synopsis of this motivation.[46]

First, and apparently foremost, the rapprochement with Russia was inspired by a desire to prevent a renaissance of the old Russo-German ties which had obtained for a decade from the early 1920s. Second, it derived from an appreciation of the Soviet Union's war potential, her natural and industrial resources. More than simply denying such resources to Berlin, there was some hope that Stalin might agree to open these resources for French exploitation and to lend or sell requisite materials and goods to French allies in the east. Finally, some thought was also given to the dispatch of French engineers and technicians to Russia for the purpose of developing Soviet military capacity—something the French did not rate very highly. As Clerk quite correctly advised London: "The General Staff . . . hold the view that the Soviet army, though capable of defending Russian soil, will not for many years be in a position to assume the offensive outside its own frontiers."[47] Thus, for these reasons and to this extent, the French high command and by and large the French government were prepared to countenance the long delayed mutual assistance pact with the Soviet Union.

Beyond that, few were prepared to go—yet another trace of that reluctance to accept entangling commitments with which one normally associates the English but seldom the French. Given the contemporary evaluation of Russia's military capacity, there was even less reason to conclude a military convention with her than there might have been with Italy, a country whose value was highly rated but with whom no formal convention would be concluded or ratified. In short, Russia's pledge to assist France was given little immediate import in Paris, a judgment that obviously militated against a convention. Furthermore, although one seldom finds expressions of ideological disgust at these rarefied levels, there is no doubt that anti-communism was an element in the French evaluation of Russia. In particular, what especially offended officers and politicians alike was the activity of Moscow-inspired propagandists in local electoral constituencies and military barracks. Closer contact with Moscow, especially on the part of staff officers, was regarded as something akin to exposing them to a communicable disease, the severity of which could not be predicted with confidence. Finally, it is very likely that many senior officers believed, or at least were influenced by, the kind of warnings regularly issued by Alexis Léger. Mirroring English misgivings with considerable accuracy, the secretary-general kept pleading that closer association with Russia could injure relations with England and thus put paid to the eternal hope of securing closer military cooperation with Great Britain.[48]

Laval returned from Moscow in mid-May 1935, again well satisfied with his efforts. The countries now had a mutual assistance pact but one, on French insistence, that had been placed firmly under the umbrella of the League Covenant, that carried with it no military convention, and that promised to bring into being a sister pact which would entail a Soviet guarantee to Czechoslovakia. Furthermore, Laval also had extricated a statement from Stalin which assured the Communist world of the necessity of French rearmament—an assurance Laval confessed was intended to keep French Communists quiet.[49] With the Soviet deal sewn up on French terms, and with the Italian convention nearing completion, Laval now could concentrate his attention on the problem of deteriorating Anglo-French relations. Indeed, it is clear that the recent decisions to accelerate contact with Rome and Moscow had not derived solely from the German problem—the sole factor hitherto considered to explain the French readjustment toward Italy and Russia. The French, like the Irish, had an English problem as well.

For all that has been written, and believed, about Laval's determination to secure a peace at any price agreement with Germany, if necessary behind the backs of the other European powers, not enough has been said about the role of his English tutors. In early 1935 the foreign policies of both countries were being directed by men who had similar definitions of the current European problem. Both Simon and Laval were reluctant to get the German wind up by raising the bogey of encirclement; and both regarded themselves as men of appeasement, an expression which to be sure was used in the most positive light. In fact Simon prided himself as one who sought "throughout the world . . . peace on a permanent footing by cooperation and improved understanding between nations," a sentiment noble enough to sound like a public pronouncement but which, as it happens, was not.[50] With this goal in mind, and with direct reference to the diplomatic deadlock which had existed since the beginning of the year, the foreign secretary accepted an invitation to visit Germany in early March. In particular, he intended to present his government's recommendations for a positive German response to the Anglo-French communiqué of 3 February.

At this point something akin to a sudden flight of capital occurred in the diplomatic world. On 1 March the British introduced a special White Paper on defense, one which foretold a new rearmament program and which drew as its justification recent arms developments in Germany. Hitler responded by asking Simon to postpone his visit, a request which could be attributed it was said "50% to hoarseness and 50% to choler."[51] Clearly, Hitler was miffed. One week later, on 9 March he announced the existence of the Luftwaffe, an announcement Simon countered by merely repeating his interest in flying to Berlin. Then, on 15 March, the French government introduced a bill providing for the return of two-year military service, a move that was instantly followed by the German return to universal conscription. According to Ambassador Phipps in Berlin, the die was surely cast.

> The fact is that Hitler and Co. now have no intention of binding themselves to any figures, either as regards effectives or aeroplanes . . . ; in fact, their "plafond," if indeed they have one, will be so high as to be indistinguishable from the sky already studded with Goring's latest toys.[52]

Yet it seemed nothing could further impair Anglo-German relations. Not only did the British again reaffirm their interest in the Simon visit, but they quite deliberately failed to consult Paris before sending off a mild protest to Berlin, one which had been drafted with an eye to the "imminence of . . . our Berlin visit."[53] What is more, on the very day of Germany's second announcement talk was already in the wind of an Anglo-German naval agreement, and that at a time when Hitler was complaining that "all his advances [to Laval] fell on deaf ears."[54]

Laval, it should be said, continued to show commendable restraint. That he was angry about British behavior is beyond doubt. It was not that he objected to the principle of the Simon visit or of the guarded British protest to Berlin. Rather, the lack of consultation between Paris and London had implied a break in the Anglo-French front and had given the impression that France again was lagging behind British initiatives. As such he had been placed in an embarrassing position and was now under fire from "Herriot and others for his failure to stop Britain from acting independently." Yet even then, while demanding an immediate tripartite meeting of British, French, and Italian spokesmen, Laval freely admitted having instructed the French press to refrain from criticizing Simon's visit.[55] Hence it was the French who demonstrated enviable restraint in March 1935 and the British who, by the admission of none other than Vansittart himself, had gone "much too fast and too far."[56]

Almost certainly it was this strain in Anglo-French relations that encouraged the French government to increase its diplomatic investment in Italy and Russia, along the lines previously discussed. But the fact remained that no French politician could afford to jeopardize relations with Great Britain, at any rate not to the point of imperiling the basic assumptions of French grand strategy. On the very eve of the tripartite conference in Paris, called on Laval's insistence, the Haut Comité Militaire reviewed a recent brief from the war ministry. This document read in part:

From the practical point of view it is England which could assist us most effectively, not only in the long term, thanks to her great imperial potential and to her control of the seas, but even at the start of hostilities. Therefore, and above all, we must regain and marshal the immediate support of England. [57]

Hence one finds on the eve of the Stresa conference in mid-April the French again pushing for a solid tripartite front; Britain, France, and Italy keeping rank, united against unilateral German revisionism.

In fact, the chances of constructing such a front in April 1935 were very limited. France was already on her way toward the completion of the Russian pact, a liaison which had drawn little sympathy from either London or Rome. Britain was currently laying the foundations for talks with Germany on the subject of a naval convention, long a touchy subject for both France and Italy and particularly at a moment when Britain seemed tempted by secret diplomacy. Italy was sighting her guns on Ethiopia, a metaphorical expression soon to be made literal, while Prime Minister MacDonald as well as Flandin, and Sir John Simon as well as Laval, looked on in professed ignorance of Mussolini's intentions. Indeed, having again condemned German rearmament, again asserted their belief in Austrian independence, and again pledged themselves to Locarno, the Stresa partners also carefully expressed their opposition to unilateral treaty violations of the sort "which may endanger the peace of Europe." For the second time in four months Mussolini had reason to believe that he was being given a green light in Africa.

Inside the space of two months the Stresa front had all but vanished. As yet, Whitehall still saw Laval as a man of peace, a man interested in settling with Germany, not encircling her.[58] But in fact it was not Laval who went to Berlin, it was Simon; and when in early June Hitler opened the first and only series of discussions on an arms convention it was to London and not to Paris that he sent his emissary Ribbentrop. Admittedly, the British had not intended to settle for a bilateral accord. Nonetheless, on Ribbentrop's demand, the two parties agreed on a convention which allowed the German navy to build to a 35 percent ratio of the Royal Navy. The French were understandably upset, and for a variety of reasons. They complained, justly, that Britain had not consulted adequately with Paris and that it had unilaterally discarded the principle of simultaneous negotiations which had been agreed upon but a few months earlier. As matters now stood, it could be inferred that Britain had forsaken its commitment to a broader European settlement; and it most certainly would be inferred in France that *sécurité* again had been "sacrificed on the altar of British egoism," the English having turned their backs on the whole question of a convention for land armaments.[59] For their part, the British responded to these criticisms with little understanding and less sympathy, cryptically dismissing them with phrases like "unduly pessimistic."[60] However seriously one judges the degree of provocation, there is no denying that Laval was profoundly discomfited by this recent British action. "Less buoyant" than ever before, the minister clearly was shaken by the criticism from his own cabinet for the moderation and restraint he had shown toward Britain's diplomatic coup. It was with some bitterness, therefore, that Laval confronted Eden toward the end of June.

> Why should not other Powers now deal separately with Germany? France might have done so. It had not done so and would not do so. France would always inform Great Britain of the course of any negotiations which it undertook and consult with Great Britain before coming to a conclusion. It was the German policy to deal separately with each subject and each party concerned.[61]

As Laval said, the Stresa front was "broken in pieces," a fact made the more clear when Eden returned via Paris from his talks in Rome. Having but a week before upbraided the British minister for the lack of consultation over the naval accord, Laval must have been astonished to discover that in the interval Eden had tried to make a deal with Mussolini over the Ethiopian issue. Little wonder then that "Monsieur Laval was inclined to resent the fact that we had considered offering territory to Abyssinia without previous and detailed consultation with the French government, more particularly since the position of Jibuti would have been affected thereby."[62] By the end of June 1935 the Ethiopian issue was fast becoming the single most threatening storm cloud on the diplomatic horizon. It was not without good reason, therefore, that Laval preferred to be kept *au courant*, particularly as he was having to issue repeated denials "that he had given Italy anything more than a free hand economically." These denials notwithstanding, however, Laval knew that Mussolini was bent on a military conquest. Although in the summer of 1935 it was still too early to foresee all the ramifications of such an action, it is clear that Laval knew the stakes would be very high. He knew that he would have to stay close to Britain, yet he realized too that the loss of Italy would leave France "without allies in Europe"—with the Soviet Union still regarded as too unreliable and with Britain tied to a "traditional policy (which) made it difficult for us to state our position in advance."[63] The last quarter of 1935 thus promised to be a terribly trying one for this man whom George Clerk continued to praise as "by nature a negotiator, a man of compromise" and whom Léger regarded as one "who had no passions save that of a deeply rooted love of peace, . . . a passion in the way that an animal had its instincts."[64]

5

Anglo-French Relations, 1935-1936: Ethiopia and Rhineland

In early June 1935 Pierre Laval succeeded Pierre-Etienne Flandin as premier of France, retaining in the bargain his portfolio for foreign affairs. Indeed, it was said to be an "open secret" that Laval had consented to the premiership only in order to retain his post at the Quai d'Orsay.[1] Almost certainly the new premier believed, quite reasonably, that he was one of few Frenchmen who remained committed to the notion of a Franco-German rapprochement; and it is possible that he hoped for a little more freedom of maneuver once he came to reside in the Hotel Matignon. By the same token, his return to that residence meant that his personal quest for a European settlement would have to warrant greater attention from the chancelleries of Europe. So it was that the British ambassador in Berlin rather nervously reflected on the new appointment and on Laval's "notorious desire to come to some reasonable understanding with Germany."[2] For his own part, Laval never shied away from a reputation which carried with it as many liabilities as assets in French politics. True to form, he prorogued parliament at the end of June with an address that linked the coexisting economic and diplomatic depressions. Recovery, he warned, "is only possible in a pacified Europe. We will pursue a foreign policy of entente and conciliation which, while safeguarding our rights, should strengthen the peace through collective security."[3]

But as always the premier insisted that there would be no back-door diplomacy, no bilateral settlements, no gratuitous abandonment of French demands for adequate security arrangements. While one may argue indefinitely about the genuineness of such affirmations, it is nevertheless clear that he did end up with a cabinet that was even less disposed to a soft approach to Germany than that of Flandin. The increased representation of the Radical Socialists under Herriot suggested a "more definite bias" toward the anti-fascist left, a bias or mood which was expected to restrain the premier, his need for a parliamentary majority rendering him in fact "a prisoner of the Left."[4] Thus, with the likes of power brokers such as Herriot watching his every move, there could be no question of some dramatic, reckless dash for Berlin.

But British suspicions remained impervious to Laval's verbal assurances and to those afforded by his political strait jacket. All too aware of his pique over the recent conduct of British diplomacy, observers in the Foreign Office were becoming jittery, worrying whether Laval truly appreciated "the value of French cooperation with this country."[5] And they had some reason to wonder. By mid-August Laval admitted to being deeply troubled by the prospect of an alienated Italy, precisely the kind of sentiment which accentuated British misgivings about his reliability. At that point it seemed possible that the premier might attempt a direct settlement with Germany in the hopes of heading off an Italo-German rapprochement, the kind of link Italy might seek as a means of breaking its isolation over the Ethiopian issue.[6] The possibility if not the probability of a crisis in Anglo-French relations was now on the horizon. Indeed, for the next ten months relations between the two countries, between the Laval and Baldwin governments, were to fluctuate severely. Through it all, the entente, understood but generally unspoken, rested uneasily—and with it, the whole of French grand strategy.

One suspects that much of the British anxiety over Laval derived from their own failure to escape from the current diplomatic maze. Like the French the British wanted to see Hitler make his peace with the rest of Europe. Yet it is no criticism to say that they wanted such a settlement on their own terms. For instance, and again like the French, they did not wish to throw away what little was left of the Stresa front, lest it be needed as a form of deterrent in the future; and for all their commitment to the appeasement of Europe they were not heartened by the prospect of an Italo-German rapprochement. At a time when Italy and Britain seemed to be on a collision course in the Mediterranean, little could be said in favor of a new diplomatic combination from which Mussolini might draw encouragement. Sir Samuel Hoare, Simon's successor, was in a quandary. When he looked to Paris he found a government under suspicion; when he looked to Rome it was a dictator reckless enough to let legitimate differences over the Ethiopian issue trigger a "mad-dog" bombing attack on British ships and installations in the Mediterranean. When he looked to Downing Street it was to a prime minister who "would think about nothing but his holiday and the necessity of keeping out of the whole business at any cost."[7]

Hoare himself was inclined to back the League of Nations and its already abused Covenant. In particular, he thought it time to determine whether collective security was anything more than a rhetorical catch-phrase; as he put it, "If it were not effective the sooner we know it the better."[8] But the French were hardly enthusiastic about testing such a critical hypothesis on a country which to all intents and purposes was their only ally. The only thing that might have induced them to collaborate wholeheartedly with Britain on the matter of proposed sanctions against Italy was a British assurance that the same determination to punish aggression would be forthcoming in the face of German transgressions. This the British refused to do, preferring they said to take one question at a time. What is more, they would have nothing to do with the view that the League should concern itself with purely European matters —at this juncture a face-saving formula proposed by the French but one that was hardly novel to their view of the Geneva organization. Ignoring arguments from Paris that the Covenant had never been strictly applied to Germany, and conveniently forgetting the care with which the Stresa declaration had been addressed only to the peace of Europe, the British government now denied any distinction "between European and non-European controversies."[9]

By the beginning of September 1935 it was clear in Paris that a major diplomatic crisis was fast approaching. Mussolini seemed bent on conquering Ethiopia by force. On its own, this rather embarrassing enterprise, with which he was associated so closely, was of no great consequence to Pierre Laval. It did not threaten French interests in east Africa and it still could prove to be a useful trade-off to ensure Italian support in Europe. By inclination, therefore, Laval would have preferred to sweep the issue under the carpet: give the Duce a few days of military glory, propose a settlement which at least would transform the African kingdom into an Italian protectorate, then return Europe's attention to the truly pressing problem of the day, that of Nazi Germany. Such would have been Laval's preference, one that would have done little to separate him from the strategy fondly contemplated by many senior officials in Whitehall. For well before the autumn crisis erupted the Maffey committee had advised the Baldwin government that "no vital British interests exist in Ethiopia or adjoining countries to oblige HMG to resist a conquest of Ethiopia by Italy."[10]

It was with this in mind that Eden had been sent to Rome at the end of June to do a deal with Mussolini, to get him to settle for a little less than he intended to take and to induce him to collect his winnings with more restraint than the buildup of his African armies suggested was likely. And throughout the summer and autumn of 1935 talks of a similar nature continued, through the tripartite conference in Paris in the middle of August, to the prolonged negotiations between Peterson and St. Quentin in the autumn, to the famous dénouement that came with the Hoare-Laval proposals in December.[11] The point one wishes to stress in this connection is that the British government, its publicized fealty to the League notwithstanding, shared with Laval the willingness to pacify Mussolini with some form of territorial concession arranged at Ethiopia's expense. The differences between Paris and London on this issue in fact were more those of degree than of substance, a conclusion which makes the more intriguing the undeniable tensions in Anglo-French relations.

This is not the place for a detailed diplomatic narrative of the Ethiopian crisis, a crisis which broke in October 1935 with the military invasion and which dragged on with declining force until the summer of 1936. For fuller information on this crisis the reader would do well to consult some of the excellent studies which are now available.[12] Yet it must be said that most of these studies have focused on the evolution of British policy and perhaps for that very reason have betrayed a greater understanding for the dilemma of the Baldwin government than that of Pierre Laval. The following remarks may help to rectify that imbalance.

French interest in Italy had two derivations. First, Laval long had hoped that the rapprochement with Mussolini somehow would bring him closer to Berlin—either because it testified to a willingness to settle differences or because in the long run it could leave Germany out in the cold. In September 1935 the premier remained faithful to this notion. "His views on reconciliation with Germany had never changed," he told Hoare. ' There would be no peace in Europe until a Franco-German rapprochement was achieved."[13] Historically speaking, Laval's reputation is associated with this notion, one that failed and that therefore caused him much discredit, one that fell entirely into disrepute after 1939 and that therefore sharpened his image as a German lover and quasi-fascist. Yet the fact remains that Laval never perpetrated the act which he was so long suspected of planning. Whether he would have done so under more favorable domestic conditions remains a moot point. What is clear is that he never dealt with Hitler as directly as the English had done, and would continue to do. That he did not inspire English confidence is neither here nor there. Hoare, it is true, found Laval "a queer card . . . with his very cunning peasant mind." But from the Thames all Frenchmen looked alike. Indicative of some unhappy but latent reserve which the English can betray for the French, and seemingly for the Welsh as well, Hoare spotted in Laval precisely what Eden had detected in Barthou. "More than once he reminded me of Lloyd George with his incessant desire to do a deal of some kind behind everyone else's back."[14]

Second, the French placed extraordinary importance on the military value of Italy, an attitude that is often overshadowed by the rather contemptuous remarks which French officers came to make on Italian military competence as relations between the two countries deteriorated in the late 1930s. Indeed, in the judgment of the late Professor Pierre Renouvin, it was this strategic consideration, "the desire to preserve the benefits of the Franco-Italian military accord," which was for the Laval government "the critical motive."[15] As an enemy Italy could employ her air and naval forces to threaten French North Africa, the Mediterranean communications between France and its African and overseas possessions, and the ports, industrial areas, and air bases of southern France. At the same time, as Gamelin and the war minister Fabry stressed repeatedly, the condition of Franco-Italian relations would determine whether or not as many as fifteen French divisions could be liberated for service on the Franco-German front.[16] As an ally, Italy could control the practicability of those long floated notions of an offensive push through the Balkans, just as it could render possible the operations of a French liaison force between Yugoslavia and the countries of the Little Entente. Of even greater importance, its large air force would strengthen considerably French offensive potential against Germany.

Highlighting the tragic dimensions of the Ethiopian issue, as seen from Paris, was the fate of the Franco-Italian air staff talks. Between 9 and 12 September, while Hoare was chiding Laval for his reluctance to choose between Britain and Italy, the second round of air staff talks was taking place in Paris. By then, much progress seems to have been made since the May meetings in Rome. There had been exchanges of information on aircraft fuels, radio equipment, and possible bombing objectives in Germany. French bombs had been sent to Rome for study, with a view to securing interchangeability of French and Italian ordnance. Inspection tours of French air bases already had been conducted by Italian officers in preparation for Italian use; and a small number of their staff officers were expected to arrive later in the month to serve as two month *stagiaires* in the French air force, by which time their French counterparts were already working in Italy.

Now, at this the second round of meetings, further arrangements were made to ensure the cooperation of the two air forces, including the allocation of Italian air bases at Ghedi, Vicenza, and Treviso for French squadrons. Of particular interest was the consideration given to the possibility of securing air bases in other countries. While it was left to the Italians to investigate Austrian air facilities, the French agreed to ask the Czechs for permission to use some of their bases—a proportion of which would be designated for Italian use. Furthermore, while the French regretted the lack of Belgian cooperation in this respect, they entertained wonderful notions of Italian raids on the German Ruhr, "par exemple," conducted from bases in Champagne or the Lille-Douai-Cambrai region. From the French point of view it would be difficult to overestimate the importance they attributed to such remarkably ambitious plans for cooperation.[17]

It is unlikely that the British knew much if anything about these secret conversations. It is equally unlikely that such knowledge would have tempered their attitude in the slightest. As the Mediterranean crisis mounted in the late summer of 1935 there were signs of a growing inclination to put the French in their place. Some in the Foreign Office warned against being "too tender with the French" or "too slow in pushing our views," while others wanted to play "on the French fundamental desire not to alienate us."[18] In fact, so strong was this belief in French dependence that the Sub-Committee on Defence Policy and Requirements predicted on 11 September that, should it come to war with Italy, "France will give whole-hearted cooperation."[19] Prime Minister Baldwin did not believe this, a skepticism which was to his credit. After all, the French had never come close to saying such a thing, and never would. Yet on this day, when Hoare was making a pro-League speech which won acclaim only because it came out more forcefully than he had intended,[20] this same subcommittee was allocating the western Mediterranean to the French navy—in this war with Italy—and with ever growing effrontery was contemplating making France "mainly responsible for conducting offensive air operations against suitable objectives in the north of Italy." Thus at the very moment that the French and Italians were working toward air cooperation against Germany, the British were devising schemes for France to bomb Italy.

But it did not stop at simply taking the French for granted. The fact is that playing diplomacy to a public tune had made the British government surly. It simply was not committed to a vigorous League policy, although vociferous elements in British opinion expected it to be so.[21] Thus it turned to sanctions against Italy as reluctantly as the Laval government, yet justified a cautious application of those sanctions by referring to French reticence, French reservations. Throughout this sorry episode in Anglo-French relations Laval was habitually passed off as the *bête noire*, the foot dragger, the man who unpardonably balked at abandoning the Italian alliance. The version is as sorry as the episode. As the British were never slow to point out, their policy was made in London, not in Paris. If one wishes to understand that policy one would be better advised to look to the British chiefs of staff than to Pierre Laval.

From the beginning of this crisis to the end the chiefs of staff had urged, demanded, pleaded for a cautious and unprovocative policy. In their view, expressed frequently, Britain was not prepared for war in the Mediterranean. By their assessment, the Italians had a powerful air force, a respectable navy and an unpredictable leader. Rubbed the wrong way, that leader might well strike out in some blind "mad-dog" act by ordering the bombing of British ships and installations—most of which were held to be dangerously deficient in anti-aircraft defenses. Moreover, there was no telling what the Japanese and Germans might do in the event of such a contest, conceivably undertaking their own challenges to British interests in Europe and the Far East.[22] Thus, as Captain Roskill quite rightly concludes, the chiefs of staff "had little use for the League and none for the adoption of economic, let alone military sanctions against Italy. To create an enemy unnecessarily on the main line of communications to the Far East, and to encourage Mussolini to turn to Hitler for support appeared to them the height of folly."[23]

Such considerations were paramount, but they had to be met within the existing context of events. Compromise was imperative. Consequently, both Britain and France agreed in November to support the adoption of League sanctions—a decision that pleased the service staffs in neither country and for reasons which were essentially the same. On the other hand, the firm voice of the chiefs of staff meant that the government had to proceed with great care. It was before this dilemma, prodded by public outrage toward sanctions and warned against them by the service advisers, that the British needed French cooperation in a way not experienced since the World War. Should sanctions, or even the decision to reinforce the Mediterranean Fleet, actually lead to war with Italy, there was no doubt whatever what the British expected from the French.[24] Indeed, having already promised themselves such support, all that remained was to wring out French consent. This was to be no mutual compromise. It was to be extracted without any reciprocal British assurances regarding the German menace. Indeed, when Eden met Laval on 3 October he was openly intimidating, reminding the premier repeatedly that his response in this crisis would be the key determinant in the future of Anglo-French relations. Two weeks later it was Ambassador Clerk's turn to tighten the screws. The price of a French refusal of full cooperation in the Mediterranean might well be the end of the Locarno arrangements.[25]

The ambassador must have found this an unsavory task, for he knew Laval's own dilemma. Not only did he appreciate Laval's "passion for compromise" but he understood the political circumstances as well, "the principal features of which all militate against a resolute and decided foreign policy."

> Deputies from country constituencies are returning to Paris with the same story, that the peasants are determined never to fight again unless their country is directly attacked. The difficulties of the foreign situation make no appeal to them; all they ask is a market for their goods. [26]

But orders were orders. Clerk pushed, and Laval relented. In exchange for nothing more than a promise of a reduction of British naval forces in the Mediterranean, and with no reference to British support vis-à-vis Germany, Laval agreed to open French ports to the British fleet. It was the thin edge of the wedge. Within two weeks, by the end of October, the French had agreed to mobilize with Britain in the event of a war with Italy.[27]

Such assurances of cooperation, the fruit of extortion, did little to disguise the poison in Anglo-French relations. As the crisis worsened in November and December 1935, the British clung to their interests with true tenacity, treating their French "ally" with the kind of vigor that ought to be reserved for enemies. French interests and French anxieties seemed to escape notice in Whitehall. Although it moved no one in London, it must be said that George Clerk had provided the information that might have permitted a more sensitive touch. The French general staff, for example, remained as attached as ever to the policy of the Entente Cordiale but were deeply chagrined by recent developments. They perceived, Clerk's dispatch continues:

> the possibility of making a solid barrier to German encroachments through Italy, Yugoslavia and the Balkans stretching right around to Russia. This would ensure that sea communications would be left open to Russia in case of war with Germany . . . They had also come to an agreement by which Italy could through Austria very quickly stretch out a helping hand to poor Czechoslovakia, whose geographical position put her in a position of such strategic inferiority.[28]

For the moment, however, such opportunities would have to be left unfulfilled and untested, early casualties of the Mediterranean crisis.

If French disappointments left the British unmoved, the same could not be said of their reaction to news from Berlin. The ambassador there reported that he was living in an armed camp.

> Except that battles are not being fought, Germany may be said without exaggeration to be living in a state of war . . . That military expansion will be followed by territorial expansion goes without saying . . . It will be seen that the present Ethiopian imbroglio is mere child's play compared to the problem that will, in some not very distant future, confront His Majesty's Government.[29]

This was a sentiment, of course, with which the French long had been in agreement. But so too had the British. For almost two years the British government had accepted the designation of Germany as the ultimate threat to peace, an assessment that does much to explain why there was so much concern about getting involved in a war with Italy.[30] The whims of public opinion to the contrary, official quarters in Britain were determined not to exacerbate the key German problem by provoking a quarrel with Italy.

How Laval could have applauded such determination, had things been but slightly different. But what the French were disposed to call the

"Anglo-Italian" dispute was already a reality; moreover, Britain still refused to strengthen its commitments to French security. It was in the grip of such circumstances that British misgivings about Laval intensified. With the British and Italians now equally inflexible on the subject of increased guarantees for French security, and with the German problem looming larger than ever, it would have been altogether logical for Laval to strike for Berlin. But he did not, although perhaps to his own misfortune he did continue to praise the principle of such a rapprochement. That was still the key issue for him, but as he emphasized to Clerk he intended to search for agreement "only in concert with us . . . There might be, indeed there probably would be, direct contacts of sorts between Paris and Berlin, but he would do nothing behind our backs."[31]

The British did not believe him. Their skepticism arose more from the crisis atmosphere of late 1935 than from anything Laval actually did. One is struck for example by the alacrity with which the Foreign Office pounced on one of Phipps' reports from Berlin in late October. Word had it, in "regular back-stairs intercourse," that the Germans kept in some kind of unofficial touch with Laval through the journalist de Brinon. In London this rumor was received as prophecy come true. It was "only natural that he should be . . . playing with the idea of some agreement." Natural, but ominous too. Instantly, what is envisaged is a "reorientation of French foreign policy" and the abandonment of France's position "as leader and guarantor of the anti-German bloc in Europe." Clearly, Paris would have to be watched closely, to find out what Laval was up to. And since the premier hardly could be expected to answer British questions "truthfully," checks could be made with Herriot, or Flandin, or the journalist Géraud.[32]

As the question of oil sanctions against Italy came to a head in November, and as the Defence Requirements Committee changed its mind about the reliability of France in the event of a Mediterranean war, the tension in Anglo-French relations grew commensurately.[33] As usual, Laval's alleged propensity for doing a secret deal with Germany brought out the finest blend of righteous indignation and condescension. "We cannot of course object to direct contacts between Paris and Berlin . . . but what we do expect is to be kept well-informed" (Wigram). "We must of course accept his assurance that he will do nothing behind our backs, but all the same . . ." (Sargent). "We cannot of course trust any assurance from M. Laval" (Vansittart). That much could be taken for granted, that plus the likelihood that Laval's fall from office "would be an end of all these ideas of a Franco-German rapprochement."[34]

Some Frenchmen were more than a little mystified by British suspicions of Laval. This became evident in the course of a conversation between ambassadors Phipps and François-Poncet, during which the latter took his English colleague to task for Whitehall's insensate attitude. Did they really want to see Laval overthrown, the ambassador wondered? Surely that would mean the advent of Herriot and the very "reversal of that policy of collective security and collaboration which M. Laval and he believed His Majesty's Government desired to pursue." Moreover, could the British not see that: "France had, so to speak, been plunged in an icy pool by Great Britain, who for years had declined even to contemplate sanctions, and was then expected suddenly and without due preparation to express intense pleasure at her rapid transfer into a bath of boiling water."[35]

The simple fact was that the British were too unnerved in November 1935 to trouble themselves with French problems. With an unstable Mussolini overseeing the destiny of the Mediterranean and an avowed appeaser like Laval in Paris, the British were afraid of being left out on a limb. That nervousness provoked the most venomous appraisals of France. Thus the British read into Laval's wish for peace with Germany a willingness to resort to underhanded deals—a conviction that grew stronger rather than weaker with each denial from the premier's office. So too they were to deduce from an address which Flandin made to a party congress in Bordeaux the willingness of France to renounce all its commitments before the threat of war—again a conclusion which simply remained impervious to Laval's own publicly voiced assurances to the contrary.[36] And as yet another measure of the state to which Anglo-French relations had descended, even Flandin's star had fallen. He whose information had been so gratefully received by the Foreign Office over the years was now admitted, "of course" to be "a rogue." It was left to Robert Vansittart to explain with his customary eloquence what was wrong with the French.

> I do not reproach the French government (and nation) for their feebleness and duplicity. What I do reproach them for is not *warning* us in time that they would repudiate all their previous principles, if any risk arose. We should then have been able to look after ourselves, as they intend to do. In other words, the French have not been honest with us or the Italians; . . .

Personally, I would not again put upon them any reliance which might lead us into difficulties—as in this case . . . the French have not had the guts either to repudiate or act up to the League. That is the whole trouble.

Incidentally, . . . the British fleet is in more danger than the French frontier is ever likely to be! And this is largely the result of the French.[37]

It was precisely at this moment, one of division rather than of détente, that the question of staff talks arose. On British insistence the two governments launched a series of joint military conversations, albeit ones the British were prompt to forget when the Italian danger diminished.[38] For the moment, however, the Mediterranean Fleet was in danger; the French were summoned to lend a helping hand.

Appropriately, the first military contacts were made between the two navies. From the end of October into the second week of November representatives of the two naval staffs discussed the Mediterranean situation—the possibility of some wild act by Mussolini and the concomitant plight of the Royal Navy. The French, it seems, managed to keep their distance, wary of the advances of this suddenly insistent suitor for whom war with Italy might be the token of fidelity. Nevertheless, although the *Marine* had warmly recommended such talks to the Laval Government, there was never any question of promising the English too much.[39] Immensely conscious of the dangers of contributing to the outbreak of war, perhaps simply by promising too much in advance, the French naval spokesman, Admiral Decoux, pleaded for time and understanding.[40] France would open its repair and harbor facilities to British ships in such ports as Bizerte and Toulon; it would mobilize with Britain in the event of an Italian act of war; and it would even declare war on Italy in such circumstances if Britain insisted, although from Paris it seemed more judicious to delay such a declaration until French forces were actually ready for action. But beyond that, France virtually could do nothing, nothing that is, for several weeks subsequent to mobilization. Indeed, far from being able to offer immediate assistance, France was more likely to require British naval support for transporting ground troops from North Africa to southern France whence they would be sent to the Alpine frontier. In terms of early assistance, therefore, France presented itself more as a liability than an asset.[41]

For a month there were no further staff conversations. The Royal Navy had got all that it could, and perhaps all that it wanted.[42] The other services were not yet involved. But as November unfolded, and with it the issue of oil sanctions, British agitation increased perceptibly. The Italian menace loomed larger than ever with Mussolini's threat to regard oil sanctions as an act of war; and in its shadow the French seemed too ready to flee. By now, too, the British defense experts had revised their earlier verdict. It was now thought to be doubtful whether the French had any stomach for a war with Italy.

In these anxious circumstances Hoare met Laval in Paris on 7 December 1935, whereupon he urged the immediate commencement of joint air and army talks. Laval agreed, as the British were confident he would. Indeed, earlier in the day the British chief of air staff had completed the instructions for the officer who was to lead the new British delegation, Air Vice Marshal Joubert de la Ferté. He had been chosen less to fathom French capacity as French reliability. The "principal task will be to ascertain French intentions."[43]

Already on record as profoundly skeptical of French reliability, the air staff seemed bent on proving its point. As they had suspected, it was not difficult to find limits to French compliance. Remind the French, the air vice marshal was instructed, that Britain carries the entire burden of air defense over Egypt, Sudan, Kenya, Aden, and Malta. Since the defensive resources in these zones are unlikely to act as a sufficient deterrent, "it is clear that an air offensive against suitable objectives in Italy herself would have the effect of minimizing the attack which the Italians might make against Egypt, Malta, and also against naval ships in the Mediterranean." Putting it bluntly, Air Chief Marshal Sir Edward Ellington proposed, "We expect the French to play the principal part in exerting pressure on the Italian home country." Curiously, Ellington did not know what to expect from the Italians, how they might react to an "air offensive against their home country," although in fairness it should be said that he did not rule out the possibility of retaliation raids against French air bases, the naval establishment at Toulon, or even against cities like Lyons, Marseilles, or Paris itself. No more certain at this moment was the size and composition of the air contingent which the Royal Air Force hoped to send to France. Finally, it was hoped that the British delegation would be able to feel out the French on their reaction to the idea of bombing Sicily and Libya from their bases in Tunis and to bombing central Italy from their Corsican bases. One way or another the French simply had to be made to realize how important such operations might be for the security of the British establishment at Malta.

It is difficult to believe that anyone could have taken such propositions seriously. The British delegation had not the slightest chance of securing any kind of French commitment on this basis. During its three-day stay in Paris, between 9 and 11 December, the French made it clear that such irresponsible notions were not worthy of discussion. As General Denain expressed it, there was a world of difference between the "light risks" which these suggestions entailed for the British Isles, and the "grave and immediate risks" which France was being asked to assume.[44] France would not lend itself to any action that promised to extend hostilities beyond the Mediterranean, the certain consequence of any air raids on Italy. The French would agree to cooperate on an early warning system against Italian air attack; they would explain in detail the key features of their mobilization plan; they would even consider the possibility of bombing Libya and Sardinia, so long as it was understood that British air units would replace those French metropolitan aircraft sent to North Africa for the purpose of conducting such raids. Beyond this, the French would not commit themselves, and rightly so.

For their part, it must be said, the British air staff responded to Joubert de la Ferté's final report—itself free of malice—with perfect *sang froid*.[45] In view of this, it seems likely that his instructions had been phrased with great care. Having criticized the Admiralty for extracting so little from the French, it is possible that the air staff had set insupportable demands in order to squeeze the maximum French concessions. If so, they may well have succeeded on the tactical level, although at what cost it is difficult to say. Whatever the explanation, Britain could not but have revived the ghost of perfidious Albion, and at a time when bitter memories were plentiful enough.

The army conversations that took place in Paris on 9-10 December were much less provocative, although they too betrayed the presence of mutual distrust: the French steeled against becoming executor of Britannia's most aggressive war plans, the British fearful of being left in the lurch by France in the event of a sudden Mediterranean war. Once again the French were perfectly candid, if understandably inclined to underestimate their contribution in a war with Italy. Simply put, the French army was anxious to underline its willingness to cooperate with Britain, but without in any way serving to incite the British to stiffen their attitude against Mussolini. It was an extremely demanding course to follow, as Laval's government well knew. The art, General Gamelin observed, was to avoid giving the British the impression that the French army "can do or wishes to do nothing" while at the same time stressing that "we want to preserve Italian friendship."[46]

Like their air and naval counterparts French army spokesmen promised little and decried all but the most modest forecasts of their future war effort. One by one the British inquiries met with unencouraging replies. There would be no land offensive against Italy, ostensibly because of the winter conditions, in fact because France would not entertain such an action without massive and direct Italian provocation. Equally nonnegotiable was the standing injunction against any kind of offensive operation without extensive mobilization, a position General Denain and Admiral Durand-Viel already had adopted in connection with their respective air and naval forces. In a statement that was soon to acquire greater significance in the light of Hitler's plans for the demilitarized Rhineland, General Gamelin went on record as saying: "The regular army, around which is formed the national Army, can not act on its own; without certain measures of partial mobilization its peacetime strength limits its capacity to simple policing operations in our overseas territories."[47]

In Europe, therefore, the principal area of cooperation for the foreseeable future would be that of air defense. Here, the French army would seek to coordinate its air warning system with that of Britain. But they were chary about talk of operations abroad. They would consider the possibility of an offensive against Tripoli, but not without assurances of an English offensive from Egypt and certainly not with much enthusiasm. They responded similarly to the suggestion of turning their Syrian garrison into a mobile reserve for the Middle East. The principle was fine, but impractical without a major reinforcement of the Syrian detachments. In other words, not possible at present. So too the French agreed on the need to coordinate British and French resources in east Africa, but only under the rubric of a defensive responsibility rather than that of an offensive opportunity. Again and again it was the restraints on French action, and implicitly on Anglo-French action, which the French authorities sought to impress on their British counterparts.[48]

Here the conversations ended abruptly, apart from some final discussions between the respective naval authorities in mid-January 1936.[49] From the outset they had been the product of discord and dissension, instigated on British demand to discuss what the French regarded as an Anglo-Italian dispute, and conducted without reference to France's chief preoccupation, the German problem. Motivated by the absence of mu-tual trust, these talks were then symptomatic of the heavy toll which the Ethiopian crisis had claimed in Anglo-French relations. For the British, they ended with very meager results. They had extracted, it is true, the requisite French assurances of support in a war; but the real question of French reliability remained unanswered. It was precisely to this concern that the December talks had been addressed. Yet when Colonel Hey-wood, the military attaché, submitted his final report, the best he could say was that the French could help "if they wish." In short, the value of those assurances would remain uncertain until the outbreak of war. For the moment, the most promising development was the commitment to coordinate the two air warning systems.

One need not dwell further on France's role in this unhappy episode, so long as it is clear that her conduct really did have something more behind it than a web of lies spun by Laval. The French did not want a war with Italy; indeed, they wished desperately to reconstitute the Stresa front. Hence they were determined to do nothing that might incite a head-on clash in the Mediterranean. Yet the enormous strategic weight which the French had assigned to Britain in the event of a new war with Germany made it incumbent on them to preserve the unwritten entente with the United Kingdom. Thus the French promised the support that was demanded, only to qualify it by the most modest estimates of their own contribution and by the voicing of their misgivings about the entire enterprise. British doubts about French reliability in this sense were seen as desirable in Paris, for they militated against incautious saber rattling. As the French saw it, the great tragedy was the blunt British refusal to ac-knowledge the legitimacy of France's concerns. They appeared indifferent to the fact that France was expected to discard one valuable ally without any sort of compensation for her own fragile security.

By the end of 1935 this question of *sécurité* had acquired an even greater sense of urgency. For months now, steadily throughout the au-tumn and winter of 1935, reports had reached Paris concerning Hitler's intention to remilitarize the Rhineland. Although indisputably German territory, the zone's demilitarized status had been established by the Ver-sailles settlement and confirmed by the 1925 Locarno accord; as such, any attempt to move troops into the area or to fortify it was clearly a breach of international law. Long before the crisis actually broke, in March 1936, it was certain that France would be faced with an awesome responsibility. How was it to act before the open defiance of such treaties?

Thus, as Britain's hour of need came and then slowly passed, that of France rang in its turn. By January 1936 Mussolini's preoccupation with certain military setbacks in Ethiopia seemed to have reduced the likelihood of some reckless attack on the Royal Navy.[50] And since no decision had yet been taken on the imposition of oil sanctions, owing to the Anglo-French agreement to disagree, the African crisis now seemed a little less likely to precipitate a great power blow-up in the Mediterranean. At the same time, Europe was bracing itself for a coup in the Rhineland. Therefore, just as British dependence on France was diminishing with the declining fever in the Mediterranean, French dependence on Britain was mounting with each report coming from east of the Rhine.

But these were not propitious times for French appeals to London. In Whitehall, feelings about Laval had soared to new and bitter heights. As they saw it, he had dragged his heels all the way, conceding no more than was necessary and in the bargain compromising the Baldwin government publicly by leaking word to the press of the latest efforts to find some territorial arrangement that would be acceptable to the Italian aggressor.[51] Moreover, the recent staff talks had dispelled any illusions that France was an unquestioning ally whose obeisance could be controlled like a faucet. In one remark of the day, typically critical albeit untypically and perhaps inadvertently complimentary in its way, Laval was described as "not merely a crook but a clever crook," one who knew how "to look after the interests of France extremely well."[52]

Nevertheless, his days were numbered. His coalition cabinet, grown ever more dependent on the Radical Socialists, was now racked by division. And Laval was at the heart of the troubles, although even the British embassy had to admit that this had little to do with his foreign policy. Rather, there was a growing "personal animosity against M. Laval himself," one that seemed to stem in large part from his rude handling of certain cabinet colleagues.[53] Thus, although George Clerk personally regarded Laval's foreign policy as his most serious failing, he admitted that there was unlikely to be any significant difference in policy between Laval and his eventual successor.

Even from a more distant perspective such as ours it would be difficult, indeed pointless, to deny the failure of Laval's foreign policy. But if such is to be the conclusion, it should be reached for the right and not the wrong reasons. However understandable British resentment of Laval may have been, it would be folly to base a current appraisal on contemporary grumblings from Whitehall. After all, when Léon Blum charged Laval for wanting his cake and eating it too, he could have said precisely the same for the English. They were upset by the ill-founded rumors of a Franco-German deal, yet they ventured nothing to assuage French anxieties about the German menace. They gave not a fig about the collapse of the Franco-Italian alliance, condemning Laval for maintaining his personal contact with Mussolini throughout the Ethiopian imbroglio while at the same time exploiting those very contacts during the months of tiresome Anglo-French efforts to work out a suitable compromise in east Africa.[54] Frankly speaking, when it came to the crunch they expected others to do their bidding—a perfectly natural preference and one the French of course shared in reciprocal fashion.

But in this respect the Laval government was less successful than that of Baldwin. To his profound regret Laval could not get either the Italians or the British to see reason—by which he meant, to patch up their paltry differences abroad with a view to concentrating on European security and the German problem. Here he failed miserably, incurring the wrath of both. But if we should be wary of pinning Laval's failures on what Professor Geoffrey Warner calls "convenient scapegoats"—such as political opponents and foreign governments—so might we refrain from portraying Laval as a free spirit in a free environment, able to choose his directions according to personal dictates. Trapped within a coalition government in which he, as an independent, was vastly outnumbered by ministers from leftist parties and groupings, he was obliged to observe what amounted to alien and often very disparate standards. For most of 1935 the key figure in his cabinet was Edouard Herriot, a man who appears to have lost his earlier faith in a Franco-German rapprochement but who, conversely, applauded Laval's efforts to preserve the Stresa front. Similarly, Herriot backed Laval's attempts to sit out the Ethiopian crisis, in the hope that French ties with both Italy and Britain somehow would survive. But toward the end of that year, the Radical Socialists were themselves in flux, pondering the opportunities and perils of a proposed popular front with the socialists. This leftward orientation in turn meant more vocal support for a steadfast League policy. As a result, Laval's coalition cabinet was further strained by this drift toward the left, while his efforts to prevent an Anglo-Italian confrontation gradually assumed the character of a personal contempt for the League and the principle of collective security. Thus at home as well as abroad Laval's foreign policy had won discredit in certain influential political circles, in this case not because he had abandoned traditional French policy but because he had pursued it.

For the European Left in general the League of Nations was an experiment in the harmonization of international affairs, a goal which was to be reached by both cooperation and collective measures against wrongdoers. With its emphasis on the collectivity of all member states, the League also stood as a negation of the discredited alliance structures of the pre-1914 years. But in 1935 the League in reality was the Anglo-French entente, since neither Germany, Italy, Japan, nor the United States were member nations and since Russia was kept at arm's length for fear of ideological contagion. Thus the League was at once conciliatory and repressive, and a negation and a confirmation of alliance diplomacy. Laval accordingly found himself facing two powerful currents of opposition, one which found his Ethiopian policy to be an affront to collective security, the other which found it inimical to the alliance with Britain. Owing to the latter's unexpected championship of League responsibilities, Laval was vulnerable on both flanks. His attempts to retain some semblance of an independent foreign policy drew fire from all those who knew England was too great a prize to lose. His efforts to impede the course of military and oil sanctions, most assuredly undertaken to prevent a Mediterranean war, earned him the contempt of those who also wanted peace but preferred that it be served on a clean platter from Geneva.

Isolated by the vagaries of domestic politics, and increasingly out of tune with the foreign policy adjustments being made by the Radical Socialists under their new chairman Daladier, Laval was powerless to save his cabinet. The departure of Herriot with four of the six Radical ministers ended speculation about Laval's political chances. In the third week of January 1936 he submitted his government's resignation. His successor was the veteran Radical politician Albert Sarraut, the new head of yet another coalition cabinet, and this time a purely caretaker administration content to keep things in order until the spring elections. Yet to this regime, with the familiar Flandin as foreign minister, would fall the task of handling Germany's coup in the Rhineland. To them would come the responsibility of collecting the fragments from the Ethiopian crisis, the sorry remnants of Laval's earnest if undone efforts in European diplomacy. With Italy and Britain dangerously alienated, both guarantors of the Locarno pact against which Hitler intended to strike, the Sarraut government had every reason to anticipate one of the most serious challenges yet to the authority of France.

It may be useful to record at this point one interpretive issue which is as central to what has gone before as it is to what is to follow. Just as British policy toward the Ethiopian crisis was devised in Britain and according to British interests, French policy during the Rhineland crisis was similarly devised in full sovereignty. The fact that both governments later sought to justify cautious policies by referring to the hesitation of the other ought not to obscure the burden of responsibility. While it is possible that the British in 1935 and the French in 1936 might have acted differently had they been convinced of the other's unqualified backing—a possibility that distinctly troubled both sides at the time—it seems absolutely clear that neither government wished to seize upon the provocative acts of Mussolini or Hitler and so release the dogs of war. In this respect, their willingness to run repeatedly the risk of war gave the dictators a marked psychological edge over the Western powers.

Given the able historical attention which has been paid to the Rhineland crisis over the years, it would seem appropriate to direct this study to some lesser known aspects of the subject.[55] In particular, it may be of interest to concentrate on the French army. This is not to suggest that previous studies have ignored this aspect of the crisis, for it is generally well known that the general staff did nothing to encourage resistance to the German violation. Rather, in the wake of my remarks on the Ethiopian crisis such a focus promises to be especially enlightening.

Looked at from an all too familiar perspective, the crisis of 1935 need not be complicated by matters of a military or strategic bearing. Laval, the double-dealer, gambled away the trust of two cherished allies by trying to be too clever—a diplomatic fling which would hardly have endeared him to the French chiefs of staff. In such a light, from such a perspective, it would be difficult to see anything in common between Laval and his generals. Conversely, if one admits to Laval's acute awareness of the strategic importance of both Italy and Britain, and if one accepts that the French high command wanted to retain both allies, wanted to preserve the Stresa front, and like Laval, wanted to avoid the use of sanctions, the links between officer and civilian are perfectly clear. While it would be an overstatement to see Laval in the pocket of the general staff—since his chief source of inspiration was not of a military character and since his relationship with the generals does not appear to have been especially intimate—his fidelity to the traditional sources of power so cherished by the generals must be acknowledged. From this conclusion, therefore, there emerges more directly than first appearances would allow the question about the high command's role in 1936. Could one expect to see the same consistency between the policy chosen by the new government of the day and the views and advice of the military commanders?

Confronted by so many warnings from across Europe, the army commanders had no reason to doubt the imminence of an attempted coup in the Rhineland. They knew too that it would be justified on the pretext of France's decision to ratify, at long last, the mutual assistance pact with Russia; and they were all too aware of the strategic implications of such a move. Indeed, as a prognosticator General Gamelin knew no equal. Germany will seize the Rhineland, he warned the Haut Comité Militaire in January 1936, in order to "neutralize the French Army by constructing on its western frontiers a fortified barrier comparable to our own . . . Hence, free from any fear of an offensive from us, Germany would be completely at liberty to settle the fate of the Little Entente powers."[56] What was France to do? This clarity of vision, exhibited so often with respect to the enemy's intentions, found a stunning contrast in the dithering and confusion which reigned in army headquarters. Judging from the diaries of General Schweisguth, deputy chief of staff, the months of January and February were given to almost aimless musings— Gamelin wondering whether international contingents could be rushed in to forestall the German coup, or whether the ratification issue could be postponed by sending the pact off to Geneva or The Hague, nominally for consideration of a legalistic order but in fact to deprive Hitler of his chosen pretext.[57]

From the very beginning, therefore, there was good reason to wonder whether this was the man to act in a crisis, his second since succeeding Weygand a year earlier. In certain respects he seemed admirably equipped. At sixty-four years of age, a veteran soldier, highly intelligent, urbane, Gamelin seemed like a man with icewater in his veins. Either that or like a lycée professor, academic, distant, unrattled by the onrushing tide of events. But his command called for more than this, more than the talents of an unflinching seer. Whatever his intellectual gifts, no matter how culturally "plumed" his staff officers, regardless of his former and unquestioned services to the nation under the great Joffre, here now was an elderly general, no longer a decisive man and one who sought to conceal the fact beneath the guise of the laconic and above all obedient soldier. In fact, he had become a bureaucrat, a high functionary, what Harold Laski kindly called a "philosopher general," with a preference for negotiation over resistance, a predilection for compromise, a desire to "bargain, to stall."[58]

All this notwithstanding, the general's feeble efforts to wish the Rhenish problem away did make a genuinely pathetic kind of sense. What he needed to have at the ready was a kind of military flyswatter, supple and relatively unmenacing; instead, military doctrine prescribed a sledge hammer. As Schweisguth was later to remind one cabinet minister, government after government had subscribed to the view that the army need not be equipped or organized for spontaneous offensive action.[59] As matters stood, and as Gamelin barely had finished telling the English in December, there could be no offensive action before the full *couverture* force was in place. More precisely, once the Germans had made their move, no attempt to evict them could be made for something like two weeks. What is more, the final bitter draught, Gamelin was convinced that such action, when finally underway, would only end in a prompt military stalemate, "un équilibre de stabilisation."[60]

What really went on within French official quarters for the first two weeks following the German coup on 7 March is likely to remain a mystery, for while the outcome never seems to have been in doubt, there certainly were some curious and unexpected developments. The Sarraut government was an unlikely one to run the risk of war—a caretaker regime of politicians who were heading into a general election and who knew full well the costly and aggravating implications of even partial mobilization. That they realized any military action required such a measure in advance seems entirely clear, a fact which deflates to more realistic proportions the debate about whether Gamelin or the war minister Maurin or both actually demanded general mobilization.[61] Moreover, it is equally clear that the Sarraut government had made up its mind at the end of February. In the event of a German coup in the Rhineland, France would appeal directly to the League of Nations—a course of action which implicitly meant that France considered the violation to be of a nonflagrant character against which unilateral countermeasures would not be justified.[62] Thus on that famous Saturday when the German troops marched into the Rhineland, the matter should have been settled insofar as French action was concerned. Yet such was not entirely the case. For a fortnight, despite all the earlier signs of the government's intentions and the relative calm reflected in the French press, there were a few indications, ultimately slight and fugitive, that France might yet descend on a tough and uncompromising stand.[63]

The morning cabinet meeting of 7 March revealed that some ministers were leaning toward some form of unilateral military response. At any rate, such was the tenor of remarks made by Sarraut, Flandin, Mandel, and Paul-Boncour—though significantly by none of the service ministers. Gamelin listened with some scorn, and probably with some cynicism. They were talking *généralités* he told them, no doubt noticing in silence that no one had pushed for the immediate adoption of the full *couverture* measures. For his part, the general left the meeting without raising the subject. And so matters stood for the rest of the day. That evening a second cabinet meeting ended inconclusively. There appear to have been more testimonies on behalf of direct action—those which Gamelin dismissed as "theoretical"—but again no decision was made, or request submitted, to throw the cover operation into full gear by calling out the *disponible* reserves.

One day had elapsed. Whatever momentum there might have been for active resistance was fast disappearing. There was another cabinet meeting on 8 March, the mood of truculence still in evidence, with officers commenting on ministers still "very bellicose and full of illusions."[64] Jean Zay, for one, smelled a trap. Flandin, the minister reported, had covered all the options, from a lightning counter-blow in the Rhineland to a simple diplomatic protest. But he had recommended nothing, turning for direction from his cabinet colleagues.[65] General Maurin's moment had come. If it was to be a case of armed force, he said, the army had to go to the brink of general mobilization. In other words, all the premobilization measures up to and including the stage of full *couverture* would have to be invoked.[66] In view of what then happened, it is important to repeat that there was nothing at all new in what Maurin had to say. The active army, and indeed the regular naval and air forces as well, had never entertained the notion of offensive action without very substantial mobilization measures having been taken in advance. Yet Flandin, who moments earlier had been unable to recommend a course of action and who apparently had never pushed for the cover measures during any of the previous meetings, suddenly rounded on Maurin and accused him "of being timorous," a charge he was later to repeat long after the crisis had subsided.[67] Having thus restored his credentials as a resister, the foreign minister then turned in feigned despair to Sarraut. "Monsieur President I see we must not insist."[68] Later that afternoon the Quai d'Orsay dispatched its letter of protest and appeal to the League of Nations. France would act within the conventions of the international community and not as some outraged great power whose security had been placed in direct jeopardy.

From this point on, it is difficult to imagine the government reversing its decision and ordering the army into action, action which to be sure could not have been prompt in any case. Having turned to Geneva, and having thereby interpreted the German move as one of nonflagrant aggression which did not threaten the territorial integrity of France, it would not have been easy to reverse that decision in order to justify a French invasion of the Rhineland. However reasonable this conclusion may be, it does seem to collide with one curious fact. For some reason, the government, or at least the foreign ministry, now asked the army to produce a plan for a Rhenish offensive. Why this had not been done in January or February remains unclear, especially if the talk of resistance was as genuine as we are asked to believe.[69] Be that as it may, the ball was again in the army's court, a condition Gamelin instinctively distrusted.

The general was already fuming over the rumors which credited military advice with responsibility for the government's passive response to the German coup.[70] He knew perfectly well that the government was no stranger to the organizational and doctrinal restraints with which the army had lived for so long. Nonetheless, his indignation was more than a little contrived. Certain entries in the Schweisguth diaries make it clear that Gamelin's own account was not entirely candid. Whereas he tutored his subordinates in the importance of obeying civilian authority, he also ventured the view that such obedience should stop short of action that might lead to "foolhardy decisions"—in which category, incidentally, he placed the notion of sending a French division to Sarrebruck. In short, there were limits to the obeisance which the military technician in all conscience could owe the state. It was in this light that Gamelin freely, if confidentially, admitted to his fellows in the Conseil Supérieur de la Guerre that "the soldiers had been forced to restrain (*freiner*) the politicians."[71] In view of this admission one may wish to judge with greater circumspection his denial of any responsibility for French policy in March 1936. Clearly, he had taken seriously the tough talk which he had heard from cabinet ministers and had determined not to play into their hands. In fact, if our suspicions are credible, he may not have realized until it was too late what sort of hand some of them were playing. They had assumed an air of bravado, almost certainly knowing that the general and his staff would remind them of the military realities—behind which everyone could take cover.[72]

But this still does not explain why the affair was not left at that, why the army was asked on 10 March to produce an offensive plan for some operation in the Rhineland. Here was the French government, three days after the event and two days after its appeal to Geneva, turning to the army for what would have had to be regarded for safety's sake as a preliminary war plan, and knowing that nothing could be done for two weeks—following the as yet unauthorized call-up of the *disponibles*—and that the military experts expected it all to end in an early military stalemate. Nothing seems adequate to explain such behavior, lest it be the Paris meeting of the Locarno powers on that same day, 10 March.[73]

Here, before his Belgian, English, and Italian guests, Monsieur Flandin was to begin the performance of his life. Seldom credited with being either a great statesman or even a man of strong character, Flandin was nonetheless a thespian of no mean stature. Arm still in a sling from a recent automobile accident, the minister slipped into the role of some outraged warrior thirsting for revenge. It was to be expected, and France was lucky to have had someone of his talent, for the government had nothing left with which to negotiate. But for this and subsequent performances the crisis would have been speedily forgotten, and France would have been left with no compensation. It was the latter, one senses, that the foreign minister was after. Thus he began with much surly talk of sanctions—economic, financial, even military—sanctions undertaken jointly by Belgium and the now estranged members of the erstwhile Stresa front. Eden, Hoare's successor as foreign secretary, was surprised. Their appeal to the League notwithstanding, the French seemed bent on tough measures after all. Indeed, when asked specifically whether he was still thinking of military sanctions, Flandin replied in the affirmative, knowing full well that the army was now under orders to produce an offensive plan.[74]

He might also have known that Gamelin would never let such an order get out of hand. The *projet* which the general submitted on the following day, 11 March, was suitably (anodyne,) really a revamped version of two operations which had been on the books since 1932. Immediately ruling out any full-scale plunge into the Rhineland, the general also stressed that even his more modestly conceived operations were sure to be costly, time-consuming, and provocative. Indeed, and as always, nothing could be done without the full *couverture* force.[75] Undeterred, and likely quite untouched by this customary military caution, Flandin repaired to London for further talks with the Locarno partners. Once again he was firm and "very forceful," descriptions which have not often found their way to Monsieur Flandin. For a week he seems to have played his role to perfection, bluffing his way toward some sort of compensation from England, still dropping occasional references to the idea of joint or even unilateral sanctions, and doing so before the astonished gaze of French military observers who could not understand how delegates like Flandin and Paul-Boncour could still believe in France's clear-cut military superiority.[76]

To his credit he pulled it off. On 19 March Britain, for the first time since its fugitive pledge of 1919, formally committed itself to the defense of French security. As part of the bargain, tripartite staff conversations among the British, French, and Belgians were to begin in April. Admittedly, Flandin's victory could be overrated in this version of events, for it might be said that Britain would have defended France in any event, for its own good reasons, and that British capacity for immediate assistance was known to be extremely limited. But for the French minister the appearance was worth almost as much as the reality. Jubilant, he returned to Paris, immodestly forecasting the "consolidation of peace."

Whether or not Flandin deserves quite as much credit as this interpretation would allow, it does seem clear that the French made the most of what was left to them. Having decided for their own reasons not to risk war over the Rhineland, they continued to use the threat of active measures as a means of securing a more formal entente with England. Had those threats not been uttered, it is doubtful whether the British government would have responded as it did.[77] Unlike the British, who had summarily forced them into line in late 1935, the French induced British cooperation by threatening to unleash a war—one into which Britain was likely to tumble willy-nilly and one provoked by a Rhenish issue for which it cared little. One way or another the British got the point. The conduct of Flandin and Paul-Boncour in London, the warnings from Clerk in Paris, leant credence to the barely imaginable—that France might begin marching. At the same time, British intelligence conceded a marked military superiority to the French frontier forces over those of Germany.[78] In other words it was not impossible that the French might be tempted to resort to a trial of strength. Against such a risk the French demands for compensation, for reassurance, seemed quite modest—particularly when to satisfy them would mean the de facto acceptance of German troops and possibly fortifications in the Rhenish zone. It was a good bargain for both sides. In return for France forsaking an offensive, the likelihood of which was far more apparent than real, the British committed themselves to France, an act which presently was also more apparent than real.

That the French knew how to drive a bargain became even clearer as the March crisis subsided. Once the possibility of sanctions finally had been discarded, and in anticipation of the forthcoming staff talks, the French army regained its composure and its spirit of resistance. With almost indecent haste Gamelin determined on a "firm approach." Indeed, given Belgian expectations of French aid, English desires for air defense cooperation and Italian interest in joint planning on the Brenner, Gamelin suddenly seemed to be holding all the cards. It was the friends of France, therefore, on whom this new found firmness was to be employed, in a way reminiscent of British behavior toward France at the height of the Ethiopian crisis.[79] Hardly had Flandin returned from London than Gamelin proceeded to raise the stakes. France, he confided to the British military attaché:

> could fight its own battles and also send some immediate reinforcement to Belgium, but only if it was known for sure that a British Expeditionary Force was on the way. The lack of such a force would mean that France might have to reconsider its commitments in Belgium and leave the latter to fend for itself . . . Such action would mean conceding to Germany potential air bases, and facilities for air raids against England, to which we could scarcely be indifferent.[80]

Clearly, if the French air force could be designated by London as the bombing arm for northern Italy, it seemed appropriate in Paris that the British army should be in the front lines when the Wehrmacht tried to tear through Belgium. Clearly, too, if the British could threaten to scrap commitments to recalcitrant friends, the French were not above playing the same game.

Although there is no evidence of malice on Gamelin's part, it is difficult to believe that he was acting now without some memories of the bitter exchanges that had been occasioned by the Mediterranean crisis. Again on the eve of new staff conversations, the second round in half a year, the two countries remained as bent on mutual manipulation as ever. At the end of 1935 the French had bowed to the demand for conversations, fearful of the commitments which might arise. They thus exasperated the British by minimizing their contribution to a war against Italy and by making everything dependent on the time-consuming mobilization plans of all three services. Four months later, with the focus of attention diverted from the Mediterranean to the Rhine, it was the British who were eyeing their role in some future continental campaign with the same reluctance and with precisely the same references to the time-consuming prerequisites of mobilization.[81]

The parallels between the two sets of conversations are striking, despite British efforts to distinguish between them. Some "staff talks," they said, were held to consider "a perfectly direct issue" for which it was necessary to prepare "details and plans for cooperation." Although it was not said, one was expected to realize that such had been the case in December 1935. Other "staff talks," however, were held to discuss a "hypothetical issue" for which nothing more was needed than a "general interchange of information." Such, it was most assuredly said, was the case of the current talks. Lest the French had missed the point, they were told that the Royal Air Force was not ready for war in western Europe and that the Royal Navy would rely on the *Marine* to assist in the defense of even home waters as long as a clash with Italy remained possible. The British chiefs of staff obviously were determined not to give an ounce of encouragement to French thoughts of direct action—precisely the attitude of their French counterparts in December.[82]

The interesting thing was that the British seemed to have been primed from Paris. Only four days before the staff talks opened in London on 15 April, the British military attaché recorded an extraordinary conversation with Gamelin. The army, the general boasted, was "in excellent shape." Germany was bluffing. If war was to come, better it come now than a year later. All in all, Gamelin "conveyed the impression that should he be called upon to initiate a campaign against Germany at this moment, he would do it with confidence." Flandin himself would have tossed roses. Less than a week before, the same Gamelin had confided to his subordinates that no "clear-cut result" could come from a clash with Germany and that the new Rhenish fortifications would eliminate the possibility of effective French intervention in central Europe.[83]

With the ground so well prepared, the French were able to use the same tactic during the April staff talks, successfully reviving the semblance of confidence and resolution, undaunted by what only appeared to have been a recent humiliation. To this end they worked especially hard to bring out the implications of the German fortification program. While it is true that these defenses were going to compromise French ties with central and eastern Europe, they were also about to provide a strange kind of vindication for the assumptions which underlay French land strategy. Now that the Franco-German frontier was to be fortified from both sides, any attack on France was almost certain to be directed through either Switzerland or Belgium, most probably the latter. It was with this in mind that General Schweisguth suggested the British concentrate on the provision of aid to Belgium rather than to France.[84]

It was a clever ploy and it worked, at least to the extent that Britain would entertain the politically sensitive notion of sending troops back to the continent. As Wigram in the Foreign Office noted, the French had been shrewd to shift attention to Belgium, a country traditionally associated with British interests and one in less disfavor with British opinion.[85] By so doing, the French got closer than ever before to a new British continental commitment. For the next two months contact, *très discrète*, between the two army staffs continued through the offices of the attachés in Paris and London. By the end of June 1936 the British were in possession of detailed information relating to French ports, railways, and roads, telegraphic and telephonic communications, and future barrack facilities on the continent. In turn, "the War Office submitted a detailed order of battle for the British Expeditionary Force."[86] Although formal staff contacts of the sort held in London were not to be resumed until 1939, these exchanges of information at the attaché level appear to have continued sporadically for the next three years. The Anglo-French entente had weathered its most serious storm, not out of natural affection to be sure, but for reasons of overlapping national interests.

The events recalled in this chapter will not appear especially novel to many readers, despite the fact that much important but more familiar material has been excluded in the interests of space. What may appear more innovative is the attempt to explain French policy in its own terms, the policy of a sovereign country and not that of an obtuse and recalcitrant appendage of the British empire. Only those with naiveté intact could fault the British for pursuing their interests with insensitive vigor. But there must be a point beyond which national egoism becomes a liability. The British, it need be said, too frequently trespassed beyond that point, treating the French all to summarily and privately regarding them as wayward delinquents whose fears were puerile and whose integrity was suspect. At no time in the thirties was this more true than during the premiership of Pierre Laval, partly because the British exaggerated his diplomatic independence and underestimated his fidelity to traditional goals, and partly because they were under great nervous strain owing to the explosive potential of the Ethiopian crisis. For their part French officials do not appear to have indulged in the same sort of crass and unedifying characterizations of the English, a judgment based on documentation which is analogous to though certainly not as extensive as that available in British archives. Indeed, one is frequently impressed by the restraint shown by French officials in the face of tactless British behavior. On the other hand, as the record also shows, the French knew that there were times when candor was called for and times when it was not, when threats were more instructive than conciliatory gestures. They were far from artless in matters of diplomacy, a conclusion these two crises should endorse as much as question.[87]

The Ethiopian crisis produced no triumph for French diplomacy, but how it ultimately would affect the now shattered Stresa coalition was not a foregone conclusion. Anglo-French relations were mending by the spring of 1936; and the Italians remained loyal to their military convention with France.[88] Moreover, when all is said and done, the Ethiopian problem was not vulnerable to a simple solution. Laval hung on as best he could, trying to have the best of both worlds; and the Sarraut government continued in the same tradition. As for the Rhenish problem, it too was a grave embarrassment for France but largely because no one wished to admit the truth that it was not worth a war. Consequently, the politicians shirked responsibility by blaming the army for telling them what they knew already. The army did the same, ensuring a safe decision by proffering inflated estimates of German strength and offensive plans designed to end in a stalemate. And from time to time both groups joined together to suggest that France had held its fire only because of the unenthusiastic responses from Rome and London.[89] What happened immediately thereafter, however, was a major diplomatic rally on the part of the Sarraut regime, one that climaxed with a significant détente between Paris and London. After months of mutual distrust, bordering on open animosity, Britain and France appeared to have found new grounds for cooperation and mutual support.

6

The Foreign Policy of
the Popular Front, 1936-1937

By the spring of 1936, as France entered its most famous general election of the interwar period, a full two years had elapsed since the collapse of the disarmament experiment. That interval had produced an uneven record of accomplishment for French diplomacy. Ultimately, in the most fundamental way, it had been successful, for it had managed to preserve and more recently strengthen the entente with England. This had been a veritable feat for contemporary French statesmen. Despite the strains that had been imposed on the entente, successively by the disarmament issue, the French rapprochement with Russia, the Anglo-German naval deal, the Ethiopian débâcle and the Rhineland affair, both countries had managed to set aside their genuine and respective misgivings in the interests of mutual support in Europe, the Mediterranean, and the Far East. In French eyes, in those of Barthou, Laval, and Flandin, this was of paramount importance; and if each of them carried his independence of thought and action to the entente's margin of comfort, not one was prepared to venture beyond. From the French perspective this was healthy and sane diplomacy; and with their assumptions as his touchstone, the historian could not but endorse that view.

What has so confused the issue, what has prompted far less sanguine readings of French diplomacy in this period, is the fact that virtue and vice often defy easy distinction. If the virtue of French diplomacy was its stubborn defense of the vital ties with Britain, its vice was the apparently wilful and even slavish sacrifice of diplomatic independence. For if French sensibilities were offended whenever British diplomats seized the bit and acted without consultation, the same could be said in far bolder script when the roles were reversed. The more independent the French, the more irascible the British. Thus relations between the two countries were most inflamed in the era of Barthou and Laval, as the thrust of their policies spelled out a relative decline in French reliance on Britain—the former by his rapprochement with Russia, the latter by his near alliance with Italy. In the wake of the Rhineland coup, and the contribution made to the entente by the transitional Sarraut government, that inflammation receded. Indeed, under the new Blum government Anglo-French relations continued to improve—a trend that testifies first to the diplomatic continuity which permanent officials in the Quai d'Orsay were able to ensure, and second to the degree of independence which one now could expect from the government of the Popular Front.

Of course, it will be argued that the newly elected Blum and his foreign minister Yvon Delbos, were left with little room for maneuver, that the decision of March 1936 proved to be the crucial diplomatic event of the 1930s and that therefore they inherited a barren diplomatic treasury.[1] But such a view is too understanding, too apologetic. The handling of the Rhineland crisis played almost no role in the conduct or the outcome of the June electoral run-offs, for indeed there really had been no crisis. Or, to be more exact, the Sarraut government had managed to manufacture a crisis as a means of drawing closer to Britain, while internally it did nothing to suggest that it considered war imminent. Despite all the genuine strategic considerations which said that this truly should have been a crisis, it was not; and it is this discrepancy, between what ought to have been and what simply was, that has fueled the historical debate about whether or not the reoccupation of the Rhineland was a critical turning point.

At the risk of appearing too iconoclastic, it may be said that the Rhineland produced no more of a turning point than it did a genuine crisis. The key consideration here is the construction of the German fortifications, that line of defense which, as Gamelin all too quickly conceded, would cut France off from eastern Europe. Yet objectively speaking, it would be at least two years before those defenses had any right to be taken seriously. In short, the events of March 1936 hardly compromised the Blum government in this respect.[2] Where the crisis in a broader sense did occur, and where the turning point, if such there be, was reached, was in the whole series of diplomatic complications which emerged in the course of that year. With respect to these, and to their implications for the future, the Blum government was the incumbent authority to whom all questions of responsibility fairly could be addressed.

In a few words, this government's record in foreign policy was no more distinguished than that of its predecessors—a conclusion which is offered here quite prematurely, and which must be assessed in the light of subsequent remarks in this and the following chapter.

Of the generation of Laval and Flandin, Yvon Delbos went to the Quai d'Orsay in his early fifties, equipped with a respectable if unspectacular reputation as a competent member of the Chamber and as a journalist with a special interest in foreign affairs. A quiet, moderate man of modest political ambitions Delbos was an almost comforting figure, undynamic, untheatrical, uninspiring, yet by the same token, inoffensive to others of greater political appetite, reliable, conscientious, industrious, and loyal. Indeed, in his own way he was rather typical of that political experiment known as the Popular Front—the latter, at once decrying and attesting to traditional policies traditionally conceived; Delbos, a confirmed liberal, "typically middle class," hastening to the call of France's first socialist premier. At a time when wild rhetoric made moderate action imperative, Delbos was an ideal choice. Significantly, in a political world renowned for its gastronomic and alcoholic excesses, here was one, a curiosity, who did not suffer from liver complaints.[3] But he was not the sort of man from whom one could expect either brilliance or novelty in foreign policy. In particular, if he was convinced of France's dependence on Britain, he was slow to appreciate that Britain was similarly dependent on France. Thus if ever he accepted the metaphor of England and France bound like horse and rider, one wonders if he ever saw much point in trying "to avoid being the horse."[4] Without putting too sharp an edge on it, the fact remains that under his surveillance, French diplomacy made no worthwhile advances to either Russia or Italy, at least partially compromised itself over the Spanish Civil War, stood impotent before Belgium's run for the cover of neutrality, and neither advanced nor retreated in an eastern Europe that had been shaken by the restraint shown by France in March 1936. In these respects, if it cannot be accused of failing outrightly, it can be charged with having failed to do much more than it did. Conversely, of course, it was this very restraint, this modesty of action, that so pleased the British and that contributed substantially to the unity of the entente.

But there is no question that this was a high price to pay; for however important British assistance might prove in the long run, in the short haul it was a very expensive commodity. During the April staff talks the extremely limited capacity of the British forces was amply recognized. General Schweisguth's negotiations had turned up very little of substance —an outcome desired and designed by British service advisers but which for all that was not wildly at variance with the actual limitations of the British armed forces. Depending on how the Ethiopian affair ended and how the current program fared for reorganizing and reequipping these services, Britain possibly could send two divisions to the continent— without air support and only after a two-week delay from the actual decision to send them. Following from that, those two divisions, *"if the government in London decided to intervene,"* still could not be operational for another week to two weeks.[5] Within the French psychological environment, where fears of sudden German attack abounded, the qualified possibility of receiving two lightly equipped divisions within a month's time was of limited practical import. Certainly in no way would it rekindle thoughts of an early allied offensive. Indeed, it could only reinforce the standing assumptions of French grand strategy and encourage further preparations for a long war of attrition.

In view of Schweisguth's mission to London, and given the great emphasis which throughout 1935 had been placed on Italian military assistance, it was understandable that the French should have retained their fidelity to the Franco-Italian link. This was especially true in the spring of 1936, first because they already had paid a dangerously high price on its behalf and second because the Rhineland affair had reaffirmed the strategic importance of Italy. While it is perfectly true, as recent events had demonstrated, that France could offer no military guarantee for the safety of her east European associates, it is equally true that French soldiers and diplomats alike continued to believe in the importance of having a second anti-German front in the east. Now, as in the past, Italy was seen as the vital, indispensable link between France and the Little Entente.

This theme of restoring the Italian alliance provided one obvious source of continuity between the Laval and Sarraut governments. Under Flandin's guidance French diplomats worked as hard to lift the sanctions on Italy as Laval had struggled against their imposition. Indeed, if anything, the need to repair relations with Italy was brought home to the Sarraut regime with even greater urgency than before. The Italians now were threatening to scrap the military convention altogether if the League sanctions were not quickly abandoned, and rumors were in the air of a possible Anschluss, the long anticipated act by which Germany would swallow up Austria and against which France and Italy were pledged to resist. Simply put, the French security system was under siege, however much it may have registered a qualified recovery in London. Without the Italians the eastern front would be exposed as chimerical, and without the eastern front the plight of French security could only worsen. As Premier Sarraut admitted, the real meaning of a French divorce from eastern Europe was to be found not in Prague, or Warsaw, or Belgrade, but in Paris. "We would be isolated."[6]

Confronted by this grave situation the French high command hastened to reaffirm the strategic value of Italy and, implicitly, the need to restore relations to a normal footing. The Germans were barely installed in their new Rhenish barracks when the French army staff refloated the notion of some Balkan push, some Salonika-like amphibious operation which, with Italian cooperation, would forcefully reestablish an active French presence in eastern Europe. New studies were under way in this direction by the end of April 1936, for an operation which, however out of touch it may have been with political realities in the Balkans, had the welcome advantages of assuming Italian support and of postponing if not altogether forsaking considerations of a direct offensive against Germany.[7] The simple fact was that France could not lend effective assistance to Poland or the Little Entente without Italian cooperation. Or again, as Sarraut had put it, France was cut adrift.

The new Blum government seems to have been alive to this concern. Certainly it never ceased to proclaim that France intended to remain in eastern Europe with its commitments fully intact. Cognizant of the uncertain authority of France and unavoidably attuned to the strategic importance of an eastern front, this first of the Popular Front governments accepted without question, and perhaps without due reflection, the need for diplomatic continuity in the east. What it did not accept was the role of Italy in this scheme of things, a role which had fascinated every French government since the days of Doumergue and Barthou.[8] In short, while the previous regimes had declined to complement their eastern policies with highly mobile shock forces, they at least had produced an alternative course of action which, however outlandish in some respects, offered Italy as the buttress for France's eastern security bloc. In the case of the Popular Front governments the emphases were reversed. They accepted the eastern strategy, in common with their predecessors; rejected the Italian role; but sponsored a review and reappraisal of France's offensive capacities.[9] Eloquently indicative of this collapse in Franco-Italian relations is the fact that neither country bothered with ambassadorial representation between November 1936 and October 1938. No less so, by February 1937 French defense planners had begun to work on the assumption of a hostile Italy in the event of a new European war.[10]

Why the Blum government, and that of Camille Chautemps which followed it, should have lent itself to such an entirely unproductive policy seems faintly mystifying.[11] Or otherwise expressed, the reasons which have been advanced to explain their attitude seem too trivial to be truly compelling. Delbos, we are told on good authority, declined a series of Italian overtures simply because he "consistently refused to regard the Italian dictator seriously."[12] If correct, this must be regarded as a damning indictment. Mussolini would never have won an award for reliability, but with two thousand modern military aircraft behind him he ought not to have provoked derision or complacency.[13] That he had won the hatred of European socialists is certainly true; and for this reason alone one might have expected to find little genuine affinity between the regimes of Blum and Mussolini. But whether or not ideological fealties properly belong in the conduct of international diplomacy—fealties which all the principal powers eventually would disregard in the face of expediency— Léon Blum ultimately fastened on another reason for having frozen Franco-Italian relations. He had always regarded Hitler and Mussolini as cut from the same cloth, dictators whose alliance was inevitable.[14] When, in the summer of 1936, the two seemed to have resolved their differences over Austria and begun their military intervention in Spain, Blum evidently concluded that his suspicions had been confirmed. With a respect for destiny which some would find disturbing, Blum later testified that he knew Franco-Italian relations were on a collision course. The Duce, he believed, had turned his back on Europe and intended to launch an imperialist drive in the Mediterranean, in which theater he again would encounter the understandable opposition of Britain and France.[15] Having thus assumed a growing antagonism between France and Italy, ostensibly for strategic reasons, Blum thus could continue to denounce fascism wherever he found it and reaffirm French fidelity to the League by refusing to acknowledge Italy's successful conquest of Ethiopia.

It is difficult to be content with such a version, a version by which Blum and Delbos downplay the ideological motive only to offer in its stead one which has the premier taking the Italians too seriously and the foreign minister not taking them seriously enough. What explanations remain? Two that seem remote and one that is prominent. Whereas it is possible that latent anti-Italian feeling on the part of permanent staffers in the Quai d'Orsay, and continued British misgivings about the implications of Franco-Italian ties, may have made themselves felt on the shape of government policy, what appears crucial is the Spanish civil war.

This war, which broke out in July 1936 between forces loyal to the leftist coalition government and the dissident, nationalist forces of General Franco, had two main ramifications for French diplomacy. In the first place, and in the context of the present discussion, it exerted new stresses on Franco-Italian relations. Well before that summer had ended it was clear that Italian policy would be one of direct intervention, fascist denials to the contrary, and that French policy would be one of nonintervention. The latter, predictably, provoked a true *crise de conscience* within the French Left, especially within the ranks of Blum's socialist party but even among the Radical Socialists whose moderate, bourgeois character so belied their name.[16] In plain terms, here was a newly elected government—the product above all else of something loosely called antifascism—hesitantly declining to assist a fellow leftist government against whom allegedly fascist Spaniards were in revolt and against whom openly fascist states like Germany and Italy were prepared to throw men and arms. While defending his decision not to intervene by referring to the need for cautious and responsible diplomacy—the principal object of which was to avoid an extension of armed hostilities beyond the Pyrenees—Blum nonetheless was embarrassed, mortified, by this enforced departure from ideological loyalties. In view of his personal anguish, and given the predicament of his government, now bitterly denounced by all communists and many socialists, it was truly inconceivable for him or Delbos to press on with the fugitive alliance with Italy. What had made sense prior to this war now ceased to obtain, not because the old reasons for courting Italy were invalid but because they had been overpowered by domestic political realities on which the government's very survival depended.

The second ramification of this war, beyond that of its impact on French-Italian relations, was even more directly strategic in nature. By conceding the loss of Italy, France had to revise upwards the strength required of its Alpine armies—a process which in practice meant subtracting a good number of divisions from potential service against Germany.[17] Before the progress of Franco's armies, aided by fascist aircraft, armor, and infantrymen, France had to assess its vulnerability on the southern flank, from Marseilles to Algiers. Here was another potential threat of the first order. If the Italian- and German-backed forces of General Franco overthrew the government of the Spanish Left, the Iberian peninsula could become a third unsympathetic if not overtly hostile front. The Pyrenees in their turn could only be reinforced at the expense of the Rhine and Alpine frontiers. Moreover, a Franco victory could mean a tightening of Spain's strangle hold on the Gibraltar straits by means of German and Italian air and naval bases on the Spanish coast or in the Balearics and Canaries. In that event, the ease with which Britain and France could coordinate the operations of the Mediterranean and Atlantic fleets might be severely impaired. Finally, the exploitation of Spanish bases by pro-rebel forces—nationalist or foreign—could jeopardize troop and munitions transports between France and North Africa. With such a threat to these essential communication routes, there could be no guarantee of being able to ferry North African troops to the metropole; and without those troops the whole of the French mobilization plan would be subject to the most hasty improvisations.[18]

As turned out to be the case in Franco-Italian relations, the Blum government made its decision on Spain in August 1936 and stuck to it. Thus for the remainder of that year and throughout 1937 the Popular Front remained faithful to the freeze on Italy and to its policy of nonintervention in Spain, a constancy which we have suggested derived from mutually reinforcing issues. But it may be taken for granted that the policy toward Italy was much easier to honor than that toward Spain, particularly as Blum's assumptions were further confirmed in the autumn of 1936 by the proclamation of the Rome-Berlin axis. In the eyes of French socialists Mussolini had been a poor risk from the start; that he should betray France now came as no surprise. But nonintervention was a risk of unknown dimension; and from time to time in 1936-1937 it threatened to have been an unwarranted gamble in great power politics. With some 50,000 Italian troops in Spain, their compatriots operating from air and sea bases in the Balearics, and recurrent rumors of a German move into Spanish Morocco, it seemed clear that French fears had ample foundation.[19]

The strategic menace raised by the Spanish war immediately became part of the official French appreciation of that conflict. It could not have been otherwise, for the war introduced several new threats to the security of France. Blum, for instance, was quick to identify the threat to the communication lanes between France and North Africa.[20] And for the remainder of that tragic confrontation, to the spring of 1939, French observers, both uniformed and in mufti, continued to ponder the strategic dangers that were always latent in the Spanish conflict. Indeed, the troubles in Spain were seen as gravely exacerbating the Italian threat to French security and at a time when Italy's naval and air forces were quite menacing enough.[21] Once Mussolini had bases at his disposal on the Spanish mainland or in the Balearics, his grip on the vital French mobilization process would be strengthened immeasurably.

However genuine these concerns, however frequently they were voiced, they were outweighed by other considerations during the heated decision-making process which took place in the last two weeks of July and the first week of August. Significantly, some of these other considerations were also essentially strategic in nature.

The government had to work on the basis of probabilities; and the probable consequences of intervention, versus nonintervention, seemed more dangerous. The official argument unfolded on the following lines. If the Spanish government defeated Franco's rebels, the security situation would remain unaltered. If the rebels won, as expected by the French high command,[22] Franco might then eject all foreign troops from Spanish soil. Not until he proved willing to cooperate with Germany and Italy against French interests in the Mediterranean would the risks of neutrality overshadow the risks of intervention. Conversely, premature intervention would run risks that would be even more certain than the risks attendant on a rebel victory. Above all there was the risk of escalating the war into a major European conflict, which might have one theater on the least fortified of French frontiers.[23] Second, intervention now could force Franco's hand and thus prejudice his resolve to evict his foreign comrades once he had finished with them. Finally, any kind of military operation was sure to be costly in money, materiel, and human energies, diverting French attention from more acute perils on the Rhine and in the Alps.[24]

Thus the military arguments favoring intervention were countered by arguments of no less a military character. And as it turned out, Blum was to use the former to explain his initial decision to intervene, on 22 July, and the latter to justify his decision of 8 August to pursue the line of nonintervention. In point of fact, however, it is doubtful whether his repeated allusions to the strategic menace are enough to explain his conduct toward Spain. While prepared to justify his policy in terms of military exigencies, it seems unlikely that he was so susceptible to their dictates. The stunning fact is that in this crucial three-week period, preceding the nonintervention decision, the government failed to consult the French chiefs of staff on the precise nature of the strategic menace or on the kinds of operations which could be mounted against it.[25]

Having thus outlined the strategic threat from Spain, in keeping with the theme of this chapter, it is proposed not to examine in detail that problem which is known to scholars as the origins of nonintervention. Rather, and again with reference to some of the more recent literature on the subject, there would seem to be an even greater than usual advantage in brevity.

Roughly put, there are two historical schools of thought on this subject. The first tends to emphasize the crowning importance of French domestic politics. Blum and Delbos found themselves with a severely divided cabinet and country. Whereas both men, along with the war minister Daladier and the air minister Cot, were inclined to intervene in Spain by allowing the exportation of French arms and aircraft to the Spanish government, others in the cabinet—like the powerful Chautemps —and the influential presidents of the Chamber and Senate—respectively Herriot and Jeanneney—were inclined to urge nonintervention.[26] Thus, owing to these serious differences of opinion and to the consequent threat to the stability of the government, the viability of the Popular Front's social reform program, and the preservation of civil peace and order, the cabinet at last proposed the idea of an international nonintervention agreement to which all powers would be bound.[27] The second school of thought, led by though not confined to French historians, offers a different emphasis. While acknowledging the impact of these internal divisions, these scholars see another factor as paramount in Blum's deliberations. For them, the French proposal for nonintervention stemmed principally from a deference to Britain's opposition to any form of intervention in Spain. Foreign Secretary Eden and Ambassador Clerk, it is said, had made it clear that Britain wanted no part of intervention and preferred France to follow an equally discreet and cautious course. Thus Professor Renouvin found the British attitude to be the "decisive element" as far as Blum was concerned, just as Professor John Dreifort sees it as "the single most important factor in Delbos' decision."[28]

On balance, looking at the cabinet as a whole, I am inclined to favor the first interpretation. Blum's decision, like the closely related one which his government took with regard to Italy, derived essentially from within France, from within the parliamentary milieu, within the sorely tried coalition cabinet of the Popular Front. To have pressed on with the original decision to aid the beleaguered Spanish government would have meant the strait-jacketing if not the fall of his own administration. The Senate, without doubt, would have mounted a relentless opposition; and the wavering of many deputies, especially within the ranks of the Radical Socialists, would have imperiled the government even inside the newly elected Chamber. As for the British role in this affair, one is inclined to regard it in the same light as the strategic factor. Neither was fictitious nor without consequence, but both appear to have been used to justify a decision that was taken for other reasons. Just as Blum's self-confessed lack of consultation with his military advisers raises doubts about the importance he appeared to attribute to strategic concerns, so too the lack of British pressure in late July-early August simply must weaken the contention that France ultimately bowed to British demands and pressure. There appear to be only two pieces of evidence that speak in any way to the latter. On 24 July the British foreign secretary urged Blum to be "prudent," advice which Mr. Child's extensive research has led him to conclude "was no more than a casual remark."[29] On 7 August, the eve of the French cabinet meeting, Clerk made an unauthorized approach to Delbos during which he expressed the "hope" that France would keep exports to Spain to a minimum, referring then to his "entirely personal" fear that any kind of French involvement might make future Anglo-French cooperation more "difficult."[30] Without seeking to deny what was said to Blum and Delbos, and certainly without suggesting that these remarks were eccentric to the official mood in Britain, it is nonetheless impossible to avoid the impression that the French were decked by a feather. If France chose intervention because of Eden's remark or in deference to the avowedly personal distress of his ambassador in Paris, it was evidently extraordinarily ripe for conversion.[31]

One is tempted to go a step further. Like the Sarraut government which preceded it, that of Blum selected the widely understood and perfectly genuine strategic peril in order to underline the gravity of the situation. Everyone, French and foreign, knew the meaning of the word *sécurité*. It then sought, again like its predecessor, to exploit that peril: first by urging staff talks on Britain; second, given the latter's insistence on caution, by implicating Britain in a decision which was intrinsically French; and third by further attempting to draw closer to a Britain now beholden to a French government which had exhibited such commendable restraint. It is in this light surely that one should view the visit of Admiral François Darlan, the naval chief of staff, to London on 5 August—a mission personally authorized if not actually inspired by Premier Blum and aimed at securing a new round of Anglo-French naval talks. The bait, as it had been in March, was the new strategic menace to Anglo-French interests, a menace which for the moment was entirely theoretical.[32] But this time it did not work, Darlan's opposite number recommending to a receptive government in Whitehall that no such talks be held. Yet by so responding the British government lent all the more credence to the rumors, suggestions, and claims that it had forced the Blum government into line and obliged it to pursue, if not actually propose, the international nonintervention policy. Such an interpretation, to be sure, did nothing to enhance the authority or prestige of the French regime, but it did provide an explanation which most Frenchmen could accept; and it thus distracted attention from the potentially crippling split within the Popular Front cabinet. The British position therefore was a pretext for Blum, superb for its very credibility. The British were not going to intervene themselves; they obviously preferred that France should do the same; and they made that preference clear in Paris. But whether they would have done so or not, under less propitious circumstances, they came nowhere near the kind of arm twisting that had been used on Laval in 1935. Laval had bowed to British pressure, accepting in the end a policy he would not otherwise have pursued. Blum and Delbos used that pressure, as slight and unobtrusive as it was, to explain a policy that had been forced upon them by the overriding needs of the government's survival. France was still sovereign and independent, conducting diplomacy according to its own lights, but doing so in the moderate, unprovocative, cautious manner which seemed most conducive to domestic stability and yet which was so appreciated by His Majesty's Government in London.

Whatever the degree of independence one attributes to Popular Front foreign policy, there was no mistaking the fact that the security situation had deteriorated significantly during Blum's first months in power. For that, one could hardly place the entire burden of responsibility on the government; it had no control over the rebellion in Spain or over the erratic and impulsive behavior of Mussolini. It is evident, nonetheless, that before the summer had ended there were new threats arising in the western Mediterranean, behind the Pyrenees, and along the southern Alps. What is more, if France's eastern policy had been compromised by the Rhineland incident and the decline in French-Italian relations, it certainly found no new inspiration in Delbos. Essentially, his response, and that of the Quai d'Orsay, was to stand pat, reiterating the seriousness of French commitments without revitalizing the eastern bloc either from within or, by turning to Russia, from without.

By the summer of 1936 Franco-Polish relations were suffering from atrophy, a condition which had only been aggravated by the Rhineland affair when Poland appeared to have stood resolutely beside France.[33] But the French had decided not to march, a decision that left their eastern clients with perfectly understandable doubts about the value of their ties with France, and with equally understandable temptations to come to terms with revisionist Germany. As one might expect, the French were no more inclined to tolerate such independent solutions, such everyman-for-himself behavior, than the British had been in the face of those persistent rumors about Laval. So it was that when acknowledging "the misunderstanding which troubles Franco-Polish relations," Delbos did not hesitate to place the blame squarely on Polish shoulders. It was "the result . . . of equivocation in the policy of the Polish government."[34] Moreover, just as it had crossed British minds in late 1935 that Laval's disappearance was likely to solve a lot of problems, so the Quai d'Orsay seriously toyed with the idea of trying to dump Josef Beck from the Polish foreign ministry. But nothing came of it, just as nothing was to come of the French desire to tighten the alliance with Warsaw by whipping the Poles into line.

To this end General Gamelin was sent off to Warsaw in mid-August, on a diplomatic assignment for the Quai d'Orsay. He was to emphasize the value of French support against unprovoked aggression and he was to feel out the Polish government, through the office of the Polish commander-in-chief, General Smigly-Rydz, on its future policy and intentions. With respect to the latter, Delbos hoped that by finding out what military equipment the Poles hoped to purchase from France, what kind of fighting they anticipated and in what sort of terrain, it might be possible to speculate on the future direction of Polish policy.[35] In fact, Gamelin got nothing more than might have been expected. The Polish government was outspokenly opposed to closer ties with Russia, quietly uninterested in improving relations with Czechoslovakia, and tactfully enthusiastic about the alliance with France. The latter position may have been reinforced by the deceptively optimistic strategic appraisal they got from Gamelin, a general who was determined to keep Italy on the right side. "Italian action through Austria would allow us to give a hand to Czechoslovakia: the presence of Italy on our side would permit not only the integration of all the military fronts but the maintenance of links between you and us by land routes and by the Mediterranean."[36]

The Poles required little convincing, intent as they were on arranging a new arms deal with the Third Republic. Two weeks later Smigly-Rydz found himself in Paris, reaffirming, indeed underscoring, the alliance with France by means of the so-called Rambouillet accord: a two billion franc loan in money and materiel in exchange for no Polish commitment to cooperate with the Russians or the Czechs, and no undertaking to either discipline or oust Beck. Indeed, none of the checks which Ambassador Léon Noel had wished to see imposed on Poland, in the interest of the alliance, was attempted by Delbos. The Poles, so to speak, got off scot free.[37]

It may be argued that Delbos' soft and unabrasive approach made at least as much sense as one that tried to intimidate—the more so in connection with a country with whom Nazi Germany had signed one of its earliest accords. And perhaps this is so, perhaps any pressure on Warsaw would have eliminated any possibility of its coming to terms with Prague or Moscow and conversely made more likely a drawing together of Poland and Germany. Such certainly was the French argument right up to the eve of the war; and like any other historical hypothesis it remains impervious to absolute contradiction. To the author, it seems questionable—based on an exaggerated view of how much latitude Poland really had. In general, therefore, the impression we now have of Yvon Delbos' low-key and unassertive demeanor, combined with the published reminiscences of the French ambassador in Warsaw, would lead us to conclude that the foreign minister either missed or rejected an important opportunity to tighten the alliance with Poland in accordance with his repeated verbal pledges to abide by it.

This impression is further strengthened by what seems like yet another instance of his flaccid eastern policy. On two occasions, one in June and one in July 1936, the Roumanian minister Titulescu proposed a new accord with France. Supported by the governments of Yugoslavia and Czechoslovakia, Roumania suggested that France conclude a mutual assistance pact with the Little Entente as one collective entity. In brief, the idea was to extend this entente far beyond its exclusively anti-Hungarian terms of reference; an unprovoked attack on one member from any quarter, including Germany, would call into effect immediate assistance from the other three participating states. It had all the appearances of being the first real opportunity for France to reassert its presence in eastern Europe and at the same time to enlist Roumania and Yugoslavia for the defense of French security. But it could not be done without reciprocal French assurances to Belgrade and Bucharest, in short without an extension of French obligations of assistance. This the Popular Front government declined to do, a decision which to be sure was taken right in the middle of its attempts to introduce and implement an effective non-intervention policy for Spain.

What then happened, however, was a sudden turnabout, or the makings of one. Some two months after the resignation of the sympathetic Titulescu, Delbos decided in October 1936 that such a pact now made sense and should be negotiated quickly, or so he said. In fact, the record of events testifies to lingering French misgivings, just as it suggests that this sudden burst of interest derived more from a desire to stem the rot in the eastern network than from any intent to revitalize or reinforce it.[38] Indeed, it may well be that the real motive behind Delbos' conversion lay in the rumors that Czechoslovakia was putting out feelers to Berlin.[39] In any event, within forty-eight hours of this declaration of interest the Czechs had a draft mutual assistance pact ready for perusal. Two months later the French response was issued, littered with reservations which time alone could satisfy.[40] By then, the spring of 1937 and almost a year after the German coup in the Rhineland, Roumania and Yugoslavia were ill disposed to mortgage their futures further. In March Yugoslavia concluded a nonaggression agreement with Italy. One year earlier such an accord would have been welcomed in Paris as much needed cement for an eastern strategy based on Italy. Now, under the Popular Front and faced with a tense Mediterranean situation, it seemed more like proof of fascist inroads in a French preserve. In any case, this accord is said to have been the *coup de grâce* to the proposed mutual assistance pact between France and the Little Entente, Yugoslavia having come to terms with its own principal adversary.[41]

Pursuing the subject of France's eastern policy a little further, one is struck by what might be termed wilful negligence. It is as difficult to see a French "retreat" from eastern Europe as it is to see any "bold initiative" on Delbos' part.[42] France merely replied to the anxieties of its eastern associates with the customary and now barely comforting assurances of its continuing good faith. Aware of its own inability to lend effective assistance to the east—a condition almost mercifully justified by the German fortifications now under construction in the Rhineland—France would not or could not revitalize the eastern bloc diplomatically, just as it declined to sustain it militarily by exploiting the resources of the Soviet Union.

On this latter issue the views of the army chiefs came to have a special importance, partly because the central question had to do with the value of staff talks and a military convention, and partly because of the enormous significance which politicians and soldiers alike came to attribute to one outspoken military report on the Soviet Union. Indeed, until the outbreak of war this report, prepared by the itinerant General Victor Schweisguth, was held up as the new testament on French policy toward Stalin's Russia. But that report proved to be far more confirmatory than innovative, articulating suspicions which had circulated for years within the war ministry, the Quai d'Orsay, and successive cabinets. In April 1936, long before he made his now famous trip to Russia, Schweisguth had confessed that the Soviet Union had "no military value for France."[43] When he returned to Paris in October of that year he brought intelligence to bear that judgment out, and more besides. He was commended for his perceptiveness, but his prescience really deserved an honorable mention.

145

In the autumn of 1935 General Loizeau had been sent to the annual maneuvers in Russia, an event which he reported on with restrained and certainly well-qualified praise. His superiors in the Rue Saint Dominique were not pleased, an attitude of mind which the newly arrived Schweisguth duly noted. "20 September. General Colson unhappy with Loizeau's interview regarding the Russian maneuvers." The unfortunate Loizeau, it seems, had been carpeted for "eulogizing the Red Army."[44] Whether or not this early experience had any direct effect on him, there is no question that Schweisguth certainly knew the lay of the land long before it was his turn to appraise the Soviet forces. From this point of view, one week in June 1936 had been particularly instructive to him. General Gauché, the head of military intelligence, predicted that staff talks with Russia would only push Poland into Germany's arms and provide Hitler with a new pretext for aggression; Bargeton at the Quai d'Orsay interpreted Russian efforts to buy arms from France as an attempt "to compromise us"; and through the chief of the headquarters staff, General Colson, he learned that their minister Daladier was also opposed to staff talks with Russia.[45] More critical still, of course, were the instructions Schweisguth received from the minister's office in early September, on the eve of his departure for the Russian maneuvers. He was, by his own hand, "to be cautious without being sullen"; and in a telling allusion to the pressures on the Blum government from the Communist party, he was to try to "confirm the accuracy of Loizeau's report which is constantly being cited for political purposes."[46]

The report which Schweisguth tendered on 5 October 1936, following his September visit to the Soviet Union, struck a resoundingly receptive chord in Paris. He devoted relatively little space to the potential of the Red Army. It was, he said, "inadequately prepared for war against any great European power." In any event, the Soviet government did not want to involve itself in military operations, a conclusion which the general substantiated with reference to the fact that the Soviet government "never misses an opportunity to affirm its peaceful intentions." It seemed clear, the report suggested, that the Soviet high command was anxious to secure greater military cooperation with France, even to the point of constructing a true military alliance. However, it was equally apparent that the USSR "naturally would much prefer to have the storm break over France." Indeed, Stalin had a sinister stake in a war between the western powers. "Not only would a war between France and Germany have the advantage of leaving almost all of the Soviet forces outside the conflict, owing to the absence of a Russo-German frontier, but it would leave the U.S.S.R. . . . the arbiter of a drained and exhausted Europe."[47] But the most chilling passage of all was that which contained the prediction that Stalin would seek to promote a war in the west. For example, the Russians might try to convince Germany that France was "an easy prey," or to sell the reverse notion to authorities in Paris. In fact, Schweisguth could see no limits on the possibilities for European Communists to aggravate Franco-German relations—perhaps by inciting France to stiffen its attitude to the Spanish crisis, perhaps by marketing new notions of a preemptive war against an ever strengthening Reich, perhaps merely by persuading Frenchmen of the dangers inherent in a Franco-German rapprochement.

In all, the general's report was received as pleasingly unequivocal by the grand proportion of Paris officialdom. Delbos got a personal copy, as did Albert Lebrun, the president of the Republic. Within the month Schweisguth had learned first-hand from both Léger at the Quai d'Orsay and Daladier at the war ministry that they too shared his appraisal of Soviet military capacity—"a great sham."[48] Such a pleasant consensus, however, was not enough to terminate the stuttering dialogue between France and Russia. This report was to become the official touchstone for French conduct toward Russia, but it could not sweep away the long-standing fears in Paris of some new Russo-German rapprochement, it could not and did not eliminate the potential importance of Soviet war industry,[49] and it certainly could not be used openly to cool Russian ardor for a closer alliance with France. The report thus underscored the importance for France to play a waiting game, an essentially coy game; but it clearly offered no tips on how that game could be played successfully or on where the requisite finesse was to be found.

The Russians, of course, had made their interest in military conversations painfully apparent, most recently by a series of démarches in the early summer of 1936. Shortly after Schweisguth's return to Paris they resumed their pressure. At last, in November, the Blum government bowed to these requests—doing so at a time when Delbos was picking up the notion of a broad mutual assistance pact in eastern Europe, although no evidence has been found to suggest that the two developments were regarded in any way as related. Indeed, the timing of this decision may well have had little to do with either the Russians or the French foreign ministry. As Schweisguth recalled it, the decision to open conversations with the Soviet military attaché in Paris had been inspired by General Gamelin. The latter reportedly had confided within his own headquarters that his suggestion had been designed to outflank Pierre Cot and the air ministry. Cot had wanted to make a personal tour of eastern Europe, principally to sell the theme of a Soviet backed anti-German front; Daladier and Chautemps had balked at the notion; and Gamelin had proposed what appeared to be a compromise but which in fact was made "by General Gamelin so that the War ministry would not lose control of these talks to the Air ministry."[50]

It would have come as no surprise when the army and the war ministry selected for this almost distasteful task their acknowledged Russian watchers, General Victor Schweisguth and Commandant Paul de Villelume, both fresh from the Soviet exercises, both of proven reliability and, incidentally, both keepers of diaries.

Theirs was a sensitive and challenging task, essentially to talk to the Russians without saying anything. They made a good beginning, delaying the opening of these preliminary talks until January 1937, ostensibly so that matters could begin afresh with the new attaché, General Semenov. Then the talks proceeded with flagrant *paresse*, entirely in keeping with the gist of Schweisguth's instructions: "We must drag things out."[51] But Semenov obviously was determined to get to the point. In the course of but a few meetings he laid out his cards. Russia would cooperate with the French air and naval forces; it would send materiel and troops to France and it would give military support to the eastern front if Poland and Roumania were prepared to make this possible. In return, the French spokesmen could only say that when the time came France would act with all its forces—the kind of meaningless counter-offer which compelled the French officers to become more aggressive. They wanted to know exactly what kind of arms purchases the USSR had in mind, why it did not do more to pressure Poland and Roumania into cooperation, and how long it would take the Red army to engage the German troops when and if that cooperation could be arranged. To such inquiries Semenov quite naturally replied with a request for immediate staff talks, so that details of such a nature could be discussed promptly and fully. There matters froze, after a handful of meetings. Semenov was recalled to Moscow around the end of March while his chief, Marshal

Vorochilov, raged against a government which in the words of that popular song, "wouldn't say yes and wouldn't say no."[52]

But if France were biding its time it was not out of complacency. The army, the war ministry, the foreign office, and the government in general simply did not know what to do, caught as always between the fear of Russia and the fear of losing it. For this dilemma, evasion and delay became the chief tactical weapons. Schweisguth himself had difficulty getting to Daladier and Gamelin for the purpose of discussing the stalemate with Semenov; and when he did secure appointments he found, apparently not to his distress, that the main interest was how to stall the Russians, avoid the requested staff talks, and still keep Stalin on the string. To this purpose nothing seemed too trite to consider, including the fact that the Russians had not made their request for staff talks in writing. And in a manner which recalls some of my earlier remarks, the French were not above using English reservations as part of their own internal system of self-justification. Daladier, for instance, returned from London in April 1937 with British views on the subject of Franco-Russian staff talks. In fact, the British had not put their foot down, although they had urged caution. That was quite enough for the war minister, a man who had never been a partisan of closer ties with the Soviet Union. As Schweisguth noted, "In these circumstances he decided to postpone the talks."[53] Again it would seem that British attitudes were being used to justify indigenous French attitudes.[54] Even then, nothing came of this new resolution. One month later, near the end of May 1937, the government decided to free itself without leaving the fence—by holding out the possibility of staff talks in the future while implicitly ruling them out of the present. One month later, near the end of June, Schweisguth learned that the note conveying this decision to the Soviet government had never left the Quai d'Orsay.[55] And so matters stood, changing very little until the spring of 1939.

Although for obvious reasons this embarrassing chapter in Franco-Soviet relations was written principally by the army and war ministry, it is clear for Schweisguth's papers that the Quai d'Orsay was party to this general frame of mind and that Delbos was personally involved in the decision making, such as it was. Furthermore, there is not a shred of evidence to suggest that he deviated from what might be called, without fear of exaggeration, the official French reading of the Soviet

Union.[56] Thus, in a way that was perfectly consistent with his eastern policy as a whole, Delbos did nothing to strengthen France's ties with the Soviet Union and nothing, at least by intent, to weaken them.

It may well be that this view of Popular Front foreign policy is too harsh, too severe in outline. The policy toward Italy made good political sense if little diplomatic sense. Much the same may be said for Spain. French policy did nothing to reassert the authority of France but on balance it may have served French interests more fully than a policy of intervention, judged in the light of domestic stability and the not easily dismissed fear of seeing the conflict escalate to continental proportions. In eastern Europe the Blum government ended up playing an even more cynical game than any of its predecessors, for its continued pledges to honor French commitments in the east were made at a time when France's capacity to so act was known to be increasingly doubtful. But if an obvious alternative now suggests itself, the historian may be sure he has oversimplified. To retreat from eastern Europe, to pull up stakes and renounce past agreements, was really not a solution for a France confident of another German invasion. Such an act would have destroyed at a blow the vestiges of its international authority and made a mockery of its national grand strategy based on an allied coalition. As Delbos confessed to Eden, "We will not abandon Czechoslovakia. We could not do so without disappearing from the European map as a great power."[57] To advance in that theater, however, was an alternative replete with perils. It would have meant increasing commitments in the east, a step toward the gallows if one were to take seriously the Nazi doctrine of *Lebensraum*. It should have meant a military alliance with the Soviet Union, all too obvious a possibility in the light of 1945 but undeniably dangerous given the guiding assumptions and the military intelligence that shaped French attitudes in 1937.[58] To stand pat was also dangerous, but not more dangerous—consistent with France's continued pretensions to great-power status, consistent with its strategic concepts, consistent with the cynical but perfectly understandable hope that one's allies would have a chance to prove themselves assets before they became liabilities. By these lights the policy toward eastern Europe made grim sense, a policy which Delbos again endorsed by his famous tour of reassurance to the eastern capitals, Moscow excepted, in the autumn of 1937. France remained in the east, now involuntarily attached to the lesser of several unattractive alternatives.

Prospects in western Europe were similarly clouded, a condition already attested to by developments in the Mediterranean, along the Pyrenees and Alps, and in the Palatinate. The Blum government also inherited an uncertain legacy as far as Franco-Belgian relations were concerned. Again it was to prove itself competent to steady the boat but incapable of directing it to less troubled waters. By then, by the time it came to office in June 1936, Franco-Belgian relations were in a shambles. On the one hand, Belgium long had occupied the critical strategic role in France's preparations for war in northern Europe. On the other, the alliance of 1920 had served as a constant irritant in Belgian domestic politics, symbolizing as it did the internal split between Flemings and Walloons and of course heightening the chances of Belgium being dragged into a major Franco-German controversy. It was for these reasons, principally, that Belgium at last had pressured France into a diplomatic annullment. On 6 March, only by chance the day before the Rhenish coup, the two countries revoked the alliance of 1920. In the future their relations, including the holding of periodic staff talks, would be determined by the provisions of western Locarno.

That resolution suffered a serious jolt twenty-four hours later. The Germans ripped up Locarno by remilitarizing the Rhineland, the British and French by tacitly consenting to the violation. Now it remained to be seen whether or not Locarno could be revived after having been so badly compromised. On this question, one that plagued European diplomats for months after the German coup, rested the formal definition of Franco-Belgian relations and possibly the future of their joint military planning.

For a time the Franco-Belgian entente limped along on the now uncertain footings of Locarno. It was under the aegis of the latter, for example, that the tripartite military conversations took place in London in April and that the French and Belgian army staffs agreed to further talks in Paris in May 1936. Judging from the latter occasion, the substance of the entente had not been drained by the revocation of the 1920 alliance. Indeed, on the surface, the close meeting of military minds seemed to qualify the seriousness of the more publicized diplomatic differences. The generals, led by Gamelin and the Belgian van den Bergen, discussed some very detailed plans for joint defensive operations against a German invasion—with special attention focused on the three critical sectors, the Albert Canal and the north and south banks of the river

Meuse. However, both sides did seem to appreciate that the glow they were putting on relations between their two countries was at least partly cosmetic. Gamelin, for instance, remained fearful that Belgium would delay an appeal for French aid beyond the point where such assistance could be effective. Van den Bergen, for his part, made an intriguing allusion to the future. For the present, relations between the two countries and the two military staffs would remain unaltered; but in mid-October, he said, the army expected to receive instructions for some as yet unspecified changes.[59]

Although the French were convinced of the Belgian army's sympathy, the summer of 1936 brought little encouragement to the proponents of a firm entente. In Paris it was believed that the real reason for the revocation of the 1920 alliance was the Belgian fear of Germany rather than the fear of domestic upheaval. Consequently, it was believed in turn that Belgium soon would seek to cast Locarno aside as well, and with it the current *raison d'être* for staff conversations. Prodded by these misgivings the French army staff was not above resorting to veiled threats. French aid, they said, was in no sense inevitable and would only be furnished if sufficient lead time were given. For their part, the Belgians remained unmoved, knowing full well that French offers of assistance were at heart "a pretext to stop a German invasion before it reached the French frontier."[60] In fact, France had been snared by its own military strategy. The security of the front between Montmédy and the North Sea, a front still shorn of major fortifications, rested heavily on the orientation of Belgian policy.

By the autumn French anxieties were even more pronounced, aggravated as they had been by Belgium's continued reluctance to rebuild a new Locarno agreement. As usual, the fate of the staff talks lay at the heart of the issue. But the signs were that Belgium was heading for "strict neutrality." In an attempt to head off the Belgian government and its assertive monarch, the French chiefs of staff, seconded by the Quai d'Orsay, circulated a brief to London and Brussels. The thrust of this presentation was to underline the perils of neutrality—for Belgium. In a word, it was a contrivance, referring only on occasion to the plight of France and concentrating with desperate insistence on the certain vulnerability of Belgium. Any relaxation of the bonds with France, the army staff warned, would risk placing Belgium "in a most difficult situation," whereas it would be only "slightly inconvenient" for France.[61] This was whistling in the dark, and the Belgians knew it.

On 14 October King Leopold announced a return to the traditional policy of neutrality. Immediately thereafter, the Van Zeeland administration tried to insist that "independence" was a more appropriate word than neutrality. Belgium was renouncing none of its commitments; and it did not intend to abandon the staff talks with France. Such assurances were of little avail. The Blum government was convinced that the end of Locarno and its provisions for staff talks was imminent, a conviction that was understandably strengthened by Belgian references to the transitional nature of the new policy. Conversely, however, some French authorities were beginning to look upon a new Locarno arrangement with twinges of doubt. There were risks here as well as assets. Such an accord might well ensure the continuation of the Franco-Belgian staff talks, but it was almost certain to prompt German requests for similar talks with the Belgians. In such an event, France might have to tolerate military contacts between its principal adversary and the one power with access to French defense plans in the northeast theater.[62]

It was not until April 1937 that Franco-Belgian relations recovered a measure of stability, as ultimately had to be the case, by partly assuaging their respective anxieties. Briefly put, Belgium was released from its commitment to assist in the defense of France, while new provisions for staff talks were contrived under the aegis of Article 16 of the League Covenant.[63] The Franco-Belgian alliance was dead, and with it Locarno. In their place stood the wizened remains of the League of Nations, now obscenely arranged to provide cover for soldiers' conferences and plans for war. Yet nothing could disguise the truth of what had happened within the space of the year. France and Belgium were no longer allies. The speed with which Belgium might appeal for French aid was more doubtful than ever, as was its willingness to coordinate defense planning with France. Moreover, it was clearer now than ever that Belgium would disassociate itself entirely from any French attempt to intervene militarily on behalf of the eastern allies. Finally, it was now impossible to predict with confidence how Belgium might react to a direct German assault on France.

There is no mistaking the fact that Franco-Belgian relations deteriorated badly in 1936-1937, while the two Popular Front governments under Blum and Chautemps were in office. It is equally clear, however, that this unhappy trend had been gaining momentum for over a decade. That it climaxed when it did says more about the resurgence of German power than it does of the competence of Yvon Delbos. As his own policy toward Russia had amply and now ironically demonstrated, it took two to see eye to eye. Just as the French wished to keep their distance from the Russians, so the Belgians behaved toward the French. And again, Delbos had few alternatives. It was impossible to recommit the so recently freed government in Brussels; but it was impractical for the time being to renounce the whole Belgian strategy before the Franco-Belgian border could be fortified against a German attack from the Lowlands. Thus, once again it was expedient, uncomfortably so, to stand still, to preserve what was left and to hope for the best. In the meantime, the French war ministry issued an appeal for a crash fortification program in the north. The Germans, everyone knew, were not about to stand still.

For the Popular Front governments, like their predecessors and successors, the overriding preoccupation was with the German problem and, as it were, the British solution to it. Otherwise expressed, France's behavior toward other European states in 1936-1937 was predicated on a fear of German power and the consequent resolve not to be cut off from the great wartime potential of the United Kingdom. Daladier certainly was not exaggerating when he told the Comité Permanent de la Défense Nationale that French policy was "presently aimed at complete collaboration with Great Britain."[64] Again, it is this critical feature of French foreign policy that may have prompted and certainly permitted French officials to justify their decisions with reference to the approving gaze of Britain. In the case of Franco-German relations the same syndrome was in operation.

Between the summer of 1936 and the spring of 1937 there were signs that some new French initiative toward Germany might be in the offing. Although the details of this still curious story remain vague, it appears that the opening move came with the visit to Berlin in early August of Monsieur Emile Labeyrie, the governor of the Bank of France. Three weeks later, Dr. Hjalmar Schacht, the president of the German Reichsbank, paid a return visit to Paris, ostensibly for purely business reasons but in truth to promote the "recovery of colonial raw material areas for Germany."[65] To that end he arranged conversations with both

Blum and Vincent Auriol, the finance minister, both of whom were mildly receptive to the idea. On this note the talks ended, with Schacht clearly anxious to avoid fanning French interest before Hitler's approval had been assured, and with Blum equally determined to move only in step with the British.[66] Apart from the September visit to Berlin of the French minister of commerce, Paul Bastid, to negotiate a commercial accord and perhaps to explore German colonial demands, there appear to have been no further conversations directly addressed to this theme of some wide-ranging Franco-German settlement until May 1937. It was at this time that Schacht returned to Paris for the world exhibition of that year and took the opportunity to reopen the colonial question. By then, however, both Blum and Schacht seemed to think that the other's ardor had cooled appreciably.[67] And so it had. Although the idea continued to win some lip service—during the Anglo-French conference of November 1937 and in the course of Delbos' brief meeting with the German foreign minister a few days later—there was never enough momentum generated in any of the three capitals to foster serious negotiations.

Hitler had listened to Schacht's report, applauded his efforts, and promptly forgotten about the idea. For him, it was not a serious proposition. Not only would the British and French end up resisting efforts to separate them from their colonies, but Blum had set some clear preconditions. The premier had insisted to Schacht in August 1936 that there would be no chance of a bilateral deal, and that the broader settlement he envisaged—of which a colonial arrangement would only be part—would have to include an armaments convention. In short, the Blum government had no intention of either breaking rank with Britain or of abandoning the traditional restraints that had characterized earlier French policy. Hitler's reading no doubt was well founded. The bulk of the evidence suggests that the French government was typically if understandably cautious, prepared certainly to entertain new possibilities of productive settlements, but determined to exact conditions that were consistent with Anglo-French interests.

Such a view does not accord well with the impressions left by the American ambassador to France, William Bullitt, without whom this episode would never have attained such proportions. The ambassador, it should be said, was personally committed to the idea of a Franco-German rapprochement, a commitment that fed on his bitterness toward the Soviet Union and his conviction that Stalin would be the only beneficiary of a new European war. He therefore welcomed, and one suspects rather exaggerated, the interest Blum and Delbos manifested toward the idea of a settlement with Germany. One need not look very far to discover, for instance, that most of the details relating to French ideas on an economic settlement based on international business consortiums and a colonial reallocation have come to us from Bullitt.[68] This means neither that the ambassador invented the substance of these reports nor treated the details with great poetic licence. Rather, it is likely that he took more seriously than was intended by his French informants the determination to settle with Germany. If this is correct, it helps explain why this curious chapter in Franco-German relations has achieved as much prominence as it has, and why the emphasis accorded to it by Bullitt seems not to have been matched by other sources.[69]

Central to Bullitt's understanding is the charge that Britain scuttled this promising opportunity for selfish imperialist reasons, a charge to which, as usual, both Blum and Delbos were perfectly prepared to lend credence. But again, as usual, it is the compliance of France rather than the pressure from Britain that is so remarkable. For his part Delbos went out of his way to impress on Phipps that "conversations with Herr Hitler might be all very well, but that they must be joint Anglo-French ones, for any far-reaching tête-à-tête with Berlin would be extremely dangerous and might be fatal."[70] Nor did Eden have to threaten Blum. He merely warned him against the dangers of being caught out by Nazi cunning, against agreeing to anything without reciprocal German assurances, and implicitly, against discussing colonial arrangements without consultation with Britain. To this, what Delbos called "the frown of Britain," Blum "acquiesced good-naturedly, and did not pursue his exchanges with Schacht."[71] Like Flandin in March, Blum did not insist. Having already confronted Schacht with some imposing demands, including those for a general European settlement and for an arms convention, the premier clearly was not of a mind to act recklessly. Eden's remarks merely reinforced this determination, and of course served as a highly convenient excuse for presentation to Berlin. The combined effects of Blum's initial caution, Britain's counsels of restraint and Delbos' personal resentment of German violations of the nonintervention accord for Spain, made it certain that a Franco-German détente was no nearer now than it had been in the recent past. Indeed, judged from a distance, the principal theme of Popular Front foreign policy was containment rather than conciliation, for it was the desire to hold Germany in check that had governed France's relations with Belgium and all the countries of central and eastern Europe.

Having thus examined the general character of French foreign policy across the European continent, it may be appropriate to remind the reader of the assessment with which this chapter opened. The Popular Front governments of Blum and Chautemps, under whom Delbos served continuously, displayed very little diplomatic initiative—except perhaps in connection with their sponsorship of the nonintervention committee for Spain. How critically one should view this depends greatly on how much latitude one believes the French had. I have judged this pedestrian and uninspired diplomacy, the more so for the alacrity with which the French sought to slough responsibility on to Britain. Nevertheless, it was a diplomacy that accorded well with the interests of France, as those interests were perceived at the time by contemporary intelligence of a political, military, diplomatic, and ideological nature.

Where it triumphed, and where Delbos deserves credit, was in its careful cultivation of the Anglo-French entente. On this crucial theme little so far has been said directly, yet much indirectly. The entente had prospered under the Popular Front. "It is pleasant," so the British ambassador remarked from Paris at the end of 1937, to see "the cordiality which marks French relations with Great Britain."[72] The reasons for this cordiality are not difficult to detect, particularly in the light of the preceding survey. There was close agreement on the Spanish issue, with both countries anxious to contain the conflict within the Iberian peninsula. As potentially explosive as the Mediterranean situation remained, the breakdown of Franco-Italian relations and the fascist threat to the Balearics and Canaries meant that both Britain and France were now equally vulnerable to an Italian mad-dog act. Thus, if the Ethiopian crisis had emphasized the differences between them, the Spanish affair served to bring out the similarities.[73] French reticence toward Russia was applauded and encouraged by the Baldwin government and by that of Neville Chamberlain which followed it in May 1937.[74] The same was true of French conduct toward Poland and the Little Entente, with Britain finally reluctant to see a French retreat from eastern Europe—lest it weaken its prospective ally morally and materially—and yet firmly opposed to increased French commitments in that theater.[75] As for the whispers of a Franco-German rapprochement, the British urged caution and left it at that. Nothing more was required, no threats, no intimidation, no pressure. Indeed, there seems to be remarkably little in the British archives on this subject, only the occasional and entirely dispassionate reference to the colonial issue. In view of Laval's experience, it is difficult to believe that such a low key response could have been expected had authorities in London taken such reports very seriously. Again, the ambassador's lengthy report of November 1937 treats the whole colonial project with a total lack of concern. There was no sign whatever that French officials had really believed in such a settlement, partly indeed because "the colonial policy of the Front Populaire government ever since it took office has been aimed at a reorganization and strengthening of the French colonial empire."[76]

In view of the foregoing, little effort is required to see why French policy is often interpreted as a made-in-Britain product. And there is no denying that such an interpretation occupies pride of place because of its very credibility. It is clear that these French governments continued to believe that nothing was worth the price of estrangement from Great Britain, just as it is clear that in each of the cases cited the British government knew its mind and did not shrink from expressing it. Thus when ministers in Paris complained—as they did over Spain, over the eastern mutual assistance pact, over Russia, and over the colonial project—that they had opted for a certain line of policy because they could not afford to lose Britain, the case seemed closed, and on the best of all possible reasons.

By my reading, appearances are deceptive, deceptive when they deprive French policy "of any content and of any purpose: everything being explained by the hand of London."[77] Without denying the importance all French governments attached to the entente with Britain—an attachment this study has underlined repeatedly—I have tried to suggest that there were other reasons for the conduct of French diplomacy, indigenous French reasons, most of which had been marshalled and articulated well in advance of any adjudication from Britain. Insofar as actual decision making was concerned, therefore, perhaps the most that can be said is that the British view may have sometimes swung the balance. If this is what is meant by such expressions as "the decisive element" or "chief factor" then I am inclined to agree.[78] The British often did provide the frosting for the French *gâteau*. Insofar as appearances were concerned, the actual presentation of the decision, there is no doubt at all that the British factor was immensely convenient, however much it may have compromised and indeed degraded the authority and prestige of France. It undermined domestic opposition, partially excused French policy in the eyes of foreign governments, and served as a token of friendship to Britain—under the cover of which new French appeals for joint staff talks normally ensued.[79]

7

National Defense and
the Popular Front, 1936-1937

It was going to take more than diplomatic prudence to win the British prize. In the face of a rearming Germany and a crumbling security bloc, France clung to the hope of Anglo-French staff talks and the kind of joint planning which its entire national strategy made essential. Successive crises brought in their wake some kind of French overture for closer military cooperation. Such was the pattern in March 1936, after the Rhineland coup, in August 1936, after the outbreak of war in Spain, and toward the end of the year, after the Belgian neutrality announcement. Indeed, the latter event inspired hitherto unprecedented pressure, the French Admiralty pushing for closer naval collaboration and the army and air staffs making a series of démarches through the British attachés in favor of air staff conversations. The British, to no one's surprise, declined to take up such suggestions—despite the fact that the French had been careful to avoid any reference to army conversations and the sensitive topic of a British expeditionary force. On the other hand, these overtures were not entirely unproductive. For instance, although actual naval talks remained beyond reach, the two navies did continue to exchange intelligence throughout 1936-1937 on the basis that had been created at the height of the Ethiopian crisis.[1] Moreover, following a series of overtures in January 1937—led principally by General Féquant, the chief of air staff, and Loriot of French air intelligence—the British partly relented. On 12 February 1937, the two governments agreed to the exchange of air intelligence through the intermediary services of the British air attaché in Paris, Douglas Colyer.[2]

Although this British interest in air cooperation was hardly novel —stemming as it did from a desire to exploit the French early warning system—the tone and scope of these new staff contacts were unmistakably different from those of the past. When the first exchanges actually began, in March 1937, attention promptly focused on German industrial complexes and their estimated vulnerability to air bombardment. These contacts through the attaché, therefore, suggested an entirely new offensive character.[3] And the French, with a foot in the door, kept on pushing. By the summer of 1937 they had induced the British to exchange intelligence of a comparable order on Italy. By then, too, they were trying to raise the ante by proposing discussions with Colyer on the deployment of the two air forces in the event of war with Germany. This the British rejected, however much they may have been tempted by the attendant prospect of securing fuller information on the French air force.[4] Nevertheless, while declining offers such as these, it is clear that the British air ministry continued to operate its intelligence exchange program throughout 1937. Indeed, at least one month before the British government finally agreed to actual staff conversations, as it did in April 1938, British and French air intelligence experts already had entered into direct talks on the subject of registering German and Italian industrial targets.[5]

Given Britain's role in French strategic planning, it would be difficult to exaggerate the importance which the French attached to these contacts. But equally clear is the fact that what they had managed to secure after months of badgering remained a far cry from their objective of active joint planning. This they had not obtained, and would not during the reign of the Blum and Chautemps administrations. One was to be grateful for small mercies, but small they were. France and England remained separated by a Channel that was at least as wide figuratively as it was geographically. However much relations were to improve under the guiding, infinitely cautious, hand of Yvon Delbos, this was at best an entente and not an alliance. Until there was a change of heart in Whitehall, France had to face a perilous future alone, a prospect it had pretended to welcome in April 1934 but which now was held in dread.

This peril was of two dimensions. In the first place, there was a kind of strategic *effondrement*. The Rhineland had gone and with it, albeit more gradually, had gone the best avenue for any offensive thrust into Germany. Then it was the war in Spain, throwing up strategic dangers in the south, from the Pyrenees to Algeria, and at the same time confirming the severe rift in Franco-Italian relations. With the latter came the revived threat to the independence of Austria and as well the near bankruptcy of a French sponsored anti-German front in eastern Europe. In return, France could offer nervous allies very little, fearful as it was of losing them yet frightened as it was of being dragged into war because of them. In the face of increasingly aggressive German diplomacy in eastern and southeastern Europe—particularly of a financial-commercial character—France seemed content to stand pat. And again it was this same motif that characterized its behavior toward Russia, behavior prompted by a determination to have Russia as an ally if necessary but not necessarily as an ally. Finally, as the previous chapter has illustrated, the period in question witnessed the loss to France of the Belgian alliance, without any compensating improvement in its relations with Germany. For a country which had clung to alliances with more passion than it had ever embraced the League Covenant, which long ago had ruled out the possibility of a single-handed war with Germany and, conversely, which had predicated its national strategy on a sweeping allied coalition, such a succession of diplomatic body blows registered a stunning impact. Apart from Czechoslovakia, whose loyalty stemmed at least in part from its lack of alternatives, France had no one else in Europe to whom it could look with confidence.

This worsening strategic situation was complemented by a gradual but steady shift in the balance of military superiority. It was this that provided the second dimension to the peril confronting France. Looking at the period 1936-1937 as a whole, there is little doubt that France slowly but irretrievably lost the margin of standing superiority which it had enjoyed hitherto. Or, more succinctly put, both British and French intelligence made it clear that by the end of 1937 Germany was able to boast an actual as well as a potential superiority over the Third Republic.

Since our intention is merely to establish the seriousness of this shift for France, a few examples should suffice. With reference to the land armies, there was no dramatic change in the actual number of regular divisions. In June 1936 the French had some thirty-three divisions in metropolitan France, by their estimate, one division more than the standing strength of the Wehrmacht.[6] By the end of the year this slight lead had all but disappeared. Even by British estimate the Germans were almost up to their target figure of thirty-six infantry divisions, to which they could add their three armored divisions.[7] However, it was in the course of 1937 that the balance shifted markedly, as the Germans began to draw ahead in the number of reserve divisions. Here, British intelligence detected key differences between the two continental armies, both with regard to the speed of mobilization and to the number of divisions which either country could field and, more critically, sustain. On the one hand it was reckoned that France and Germany could mobilize sixteen divisions and thirty divisions respectively within a day of the mobilization order, thirty-three and seventy-eight respectively within a week, and sixty-two compared to eighty-one divisions with the first three months of war. The odds, therefore, purely in terms of numbers, were decisively with the Germans. On the other hand the Germans were held to be doubly fortunate. Not only could they field such a force, but their rearmament progress in 1937 suggested they would be able to sustain such divisions indefinitely. The French were in a different position. Their rate of armaments production was less impressive and their shortage of trained industrial manpower and raw material stocks made it doubtful whether they could sustain sixty divisions in the field for as long as three months. Indeed, British industrial intelligence experts predicted the forced demobilization of some French divisions within a few months of the war's outbreak. Only by some action of this kind, it was believed, could France maintain the majority of its divisions at wartime operational levels.[8]

The same trend applied to the air forces, although the rhythm of its advance is more difficult to estimate. The fact is that the science of counting aircraft is not a science at all but an art, an art that conveys a variety of impressions to serve a variety of ambitions. For instance, in April 1936 the French put their first-line air strength at one thousand planes, a figure the British promptly dropped to six hundred to accord with their definition of modern flying materiel. Then, within the space of two months, the French also were using the figure of six hundred, partly because of a more rigorous definition of modern aircraft and partly because minimizing French air strength in June 1936 gave the Popular Front government a better chance of maximizing their own subsequent contribution.[9] This is but one example among many which illustrate the almost insurmountable problems of assessing the accuracy and reliability of contemporary intelligence. That said, I offer a few tentative remarks based on my reading of those contemporary statistics.

It seems reasonably clear that by the summer of 1936, when the Popular Front came to power, the air balance had shifted in Germany's favor. French estimates put Germany's first-line strength at 1,236 aircraft, compared to their own maximum total of 1,000. British figures, calculated on a different basis, put German strength at 920 and French strength at 600 or less.[10] Similarly, intelligence received in Paris and London emphasized Germany's lead in aeronautical production. By the end of 1936 the indications were that Germany was producing almost 300 planes per month, of which at least 200 were service types. Roughly speaking, such production was better than four times that of France, in service types alone.[11] And the balance of advantage seems to have remained firmly on the German side. By the end of 1937 British estimates awarded Germany 1,737 first-line planes compared to the 1,195 first-line machines in metropolitan France. Pierre Cot's figures are substantially and perhaps understandably higher. But whereas he uses the figures of 1,350 and 2,268 to denote first-line French and German strength in January 1938, his statistics also show that Germany retained roughly a 60 percent margin in first-line planes throughout 1936 and 1937 and in the same period brought its superiority in total numbers to about the same proportion.[12] There was simply no mistaking the fact that Germany had jumped far ahead of France in terms of mass production. As a consideration for international politics, one need only remark that by the end of 1937 Germany's bombing force was at least twice the strength of its French counterpart.[13]

One should not exaggerate the reliability of such computations or confuse them with the "actual" but ever elusive rate of German rearmament. Although postwar findings have tended to lend a rough corroboration to the statistics employed above, there is little doubt that from time to time contemporary intelligence experts were misled and ill informed. More often, one would think, it was a question of basing estimates on quite disparate calculations. Thus in the autumn of 1936 the British believed German first-line strength to be roughly 1,100 aircraft, French air intelligence put it over 1,700 and French army intelligence said it was in the region of 2,200—these striking discrepancies deriving principally from whether all, a portion of, or none of the first-line reserve squadrons were reckoned with.[14] But whatever their limitations the point is that such estimates were the crude stuff with which contemporary strategists and statesmen had to work. Historically speaking, as Sorel long ago observed, what is believed to be true must command the same attention as what we lightly call truth itself. These statistics warrant caution for yet another reason. The intention here has been to establish the presence of a trend and, less surely, the pace of its development, both of which were major preoccupations of intelligence branches in London and Paris. It was clear that Germany had stolen the march; and even if it were not expected to resort to war before 1938, it was conceded that Germany's standing armies now enjoyed a margin of superiority over those of France. But of course this is not to suggest that French foreign policy in 1936 or 1937 should have been conducted with reference to a military imbalance that only fully emerged at the end of this period. The trend which I have identified, in other words, this shift in the power distribution, is far more significant as a condition than a cause. It has been presented here in this sense, as a set of steadily worsening circumstances of which the French were apprised and which heightened and aggravated their sense of peril.

Such was the French predicament. They could not force the pace with their one essential but still only potential ally. They could not put a stop to the rot within their network of allied and associated states, at any rate not without resorting to a cure that promised to be as traumatic as the disease. Finally, they could do little to retard the pace of German rearmament or prevent themselves from being outstripped as the principal land and air power on the continent. The gravity of their plight to be sure was more pronounced by the end of 1937 than it had been in the summer of 1936, but it would be foolish to suggest that the Blum government had taken office under unclouded skies. Such a view not only would clash with all of the preceding remarks, but it would have to either ignore or obfuscate the rearmament program which that government launched soon after its arrival in power. By then the military balance was already in jeopardy and the generally unsatisfactory nature of relations with Germany, Belgium, Poland, Russia, Italy, and even Britain was a cause of worry and complaint. So it was that a government led by Léon Blum, chief spokesman for a party which had prided itself in its social reformism and its anti-militarism, found itself obliged to devote so much of its energies and so much of its sorely taxed capital reserves to the nation's preparations for war.

Before turning to the nature of these preparations, some care should be taken to underline the connection between the diplomatic and the defense efforts of the Popular Front or, as it were, between this and the preceding chapter. As the French realized, much of their difficulty derived from their declining prestige in Europe, a decline that was associated directly with the uncertainties which enveloped their military capacity. Thus, quite apart from the obvious intention to strengthen their own internal defensive resources, there was too a desire to fortify the credibility of the nation's foreign policy by giving new force and direction to its military potential. In turn, by lending renewed authority to the voice of France abroad, it was hoped if not assumed that wavering allies would return to the fold and by so doing would restore to France the possibility of an effective wartime coalition. In short, it was a diplomatic version of that adage about the rich getting richer. The weaker France appeared, and the greater its dependence on allies, the less likely it was to attract and retain them. It was this dilemma that the Popular Front wanted to reverse; and it was by turning with great energy to new national defense programs that the government sought to make sense of a diplomacy which deliberately refrained from major advances or retreats. Subtract the military plight of France and there is lost one important dimension to the conduct of French diplomacy in 1936 and 1937. Subtract France's harried international status, and one loses an essential element of its efforts to accelerate defense programs and to assure the national strategy of the requisite military wherewithal.

The defense efforts of the Popular Front may be grouped into three categories. There was a new frontier defense program, a series of either new or more elaborate preparatory measures for the nation's economic mobilization, and a sharply increased rearmament program. Though clearly related, these categories were sufficiently distinct in nature to warrant separate consideration. Conversely, however, each was wedded to the others by an inspiration and approach which was far more traditional than innovative. Indeed, it would appear that when it came to national defense the Popular Front government was as rooted in long-standing assumptions and as vulnerable to conventional wisdoms as any of its more custom-tested predecessors. As in the case of foreign policy, where an ostensibly radical coalition repeatedly deferred to traditional insights, the Popular Front was to accept with remarkably good grace the guidance and counsels of its professional defense advisers.

The decision to make a new effort in the field of frontier fortifications came as no surprise. Prompted in general by unpromising diplomatic and military circumstances, and in particular by the Belgian drift toward neutrality, the Blum government undertook a new fortification program in late 1936. Although the plunge into Belgium remained the key element in French defensive plans for the northeast theater, it was increasingly clear that the French armies might well require a line of defense to fall back upon if the opportunities for a timely intervention in Belgium did not avail themselves. So it was that for the next three years French military engineers worked to strengthen and extend the fortified zones along the Franco-Belgian frontier. Apart from comparable work on the Rhine defenses between Mulhouse and Pontarlier, the focus of attention was on the northern fortifications between Mézières and Dunquerque. This was not, let it be said, another endeavor of the order of the Maginot defenses in the Palatinate. Basically what Gamelin hoped to establish was a line of defense loosely held together by a series of more heavily defended points of resistance. For this purpose he selected the region centering on Dunquerque, the region comprising the vital industrial complex of Lille-Roubaix-Tourcoing, the region shaped by the forest of Raismes and the region embraced by the Maubeuge fortifications and the forest of Mormal. If the worst came to the worst, the French armies would take cover behind this secondary line of defense—a *pis-aller* to be called upon only if the Belgian operation failed and a German breakthrough was in progress. It was not, therefore, part of the Maginot Line or even an integral part of the continuous front doctrine; and while it may have inspired claims to that effect, it in no sense meant that France was fortified from Switzerland to the North Sea.[15]

In fact, if this new program proved that the French were still capable of adapting to changed circumstances, it also suggested that they would do so in ways that were already familiar. The new defenses were at best an alternative to the Belgian strategy, not a replacement for it. They also seemed to confirm the current belief in the inherent superiority of defensive weapons, tactics, and fixed fortifications—beside which mobile armored units had to labor in an uncertain role. And they were very traditional, too, in the assumptions they reflected about the natural

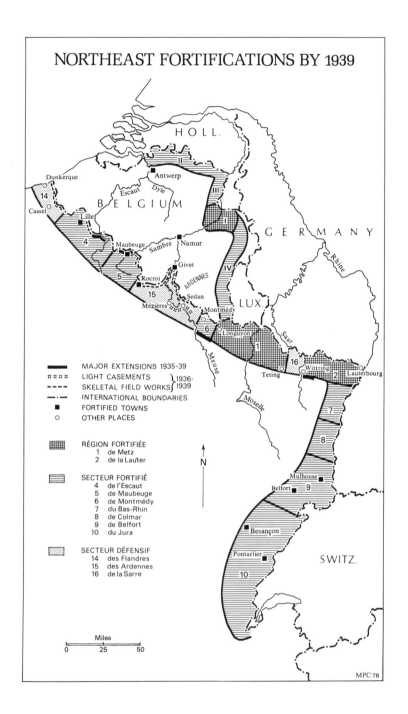

NORTHEAST FORTIFICATIONS BY 1939

MAJOR EXTENSIONS 1935–39
LIGHT CASEMENTS ⎱ 1936–
SKELETAL FIELD WORKS ⎰ 1939
INTERNATIONAL BOUNDARIES
■ FORTIFIED TOWNS
○ OTHER PLACES

RÉGION FORTIFIÉE
  1 de Metz
  2 de la Lauter

SECTEUR FORTIFIÉ
  4 de l'Escaut
  5 de Maubeuge
  6 de Montmédy
  7 du Bas-Rhin
  8 de Colmar
  9 de Belfort
  10 du Jura

SECTEUR DÉFENSIF
  14 des Flandres
  15 des Ardennes
  16 de la Sarre

N

Miles
0   25   50

MPC '78

defensive qualities of the Ardennes. This sector, between Montmédy and Mézières, was never to command the attention which history later proved had been warranted. Although after 1940 few could be found who had believed in Pétain's observations about the impenetrability of the Ardennes, including the marshal himself, the fact remains that no major fortification effort was ever devoted to this region.[16] By the end of 1937 only one third of the gap between Mézières and Montmédy could boast anything like a line of defense, that which ran along the heights between Mézières and Sedan. Apparently confident of the holding powers of the tortuous terrain, forested and threaded with innumerable rivers, the French high command turned its attentions and energies elsewhere. Apart from a string of light casemates which was thrown across its reaches in 1938 and 1939, many of which remained unfinished and unarmed, this remained the Cinderella sector, incapable of competing with the demands emanating from its sister fronts further north or on the Rhine. Though hardly forgotten—it was after all the vital buckle between the Belgian defenses on the Meuse and the French defenses in the Palatinate—the Ardennes sector with Sedan at its center was victimized by its own reputation. It was taken for granted, or hoped, or both, that no sudden attack could come from such a quarter and therefore that skeletal defenses manned by second-class reserves would be adequate for its defense. As General Poydenot recalls, "The impossibility of such an attack was taken as a kind of dogma at General Headquarters."[17] In this respect, what was done under the Popular Front was essentially the same as had been done under its predecessors.

It was with the same fidelity to tradition that the Popular Front pursued plans for economic mobilization. Statistically, the prospects for France were not encouraging. As early as November 1935 Marshal Pétain had warned the Conseil Supérieur de la Défense Nationale that Germany's phenomenal increase in the production of minerals, steel, pig iron, and aluminum was such as to gravely exacerbate the industrial imbalance between France and Germany. The latter, he declared, "in the course of the last two years of accelerated rearmament," had stolen a considerable march (*une avance considérable*) on France's preparations for industrial mobilization.[18] By 1937 the trend was even more marked and alarming. France had fallen behind Britain and Germany in automobile production; it had slumped into fourth place in aircraft manufacturing, from first to fourth in less than a decade; its steel production had increased by a miserly 30 percent between 1932 and 1937, compared to the 300 percent increase enjoyed by German industry; its coal production showed a significant decline over the same five-year period, a development which is largely explained by the return of the Saar coal fields in early 1935 and the consequent increase in German production.[19] Such expansion of Germany's industrial superstructure, combined with the shifting military balance, cast an increasingly dark shadow on France's hopes of resisting a new German bid for continental hegemony.

Yet German production was only one factor in French preparations for economic warfare, albeit one of primary importance. The examples of coal and iron should be sufficiently illustrative. France could produce no more than 60 percent of its wartime coal requirements and no more than 10 percent of the requisite oil tonnage. Even in peacetime these deficiencies had to be made up from importations—in the case of coal, from Germany and Poland, in the case of oil, from the Middle East, particularly from Iran. In the event of war those coal supplies were certain to be eliminated, and the fate of the oil supplies would be determined first by the British government's instructions to the Anglo-Iranian Oil Company and second by the ability of Anglo-French forces in the Mediterranean to hold a belligerent Italy in check. In short, faced with insufficient indigenous resources for supporting France in another modern war, the government had no alternative but to rely on foreign sources over which its control was minimal at best.

But France's predicament did not end here. Not only was it far from being self-sufficient in many fields of production, but so much of this industrial plant lay perilously close to the northern and eastern frontiers. Well within the space of an hour German bombers could be over the lion's share of France's coal, iron, and steel complexes. Minutes later they could be releasing bombs over the Seine basin, the storage region for at least 30 percent of French commercial oil stocks and the nerve center for more than 60 percent of the French aircraft industry.[20] What is more, this question of reserves and stockpiles constituted another dilemma. For example, not only did the new Blum administration have to face the problem of accumulating greater reserves of materials such as aluminum, tin, lead, magnesium, and phosphorous, and not only did it have to weigh the costs of such surplus purchasing against the costs of rearmament, but it also had to balance the arguments in favor of such immediate purchases against those which warned against depleting French gold reserves.[21] Those who adopted the latter position, apparently a majority, argued that France had to minimize its peacetime imports if it were ever to have the financial means to maximize the purchase of crucial wartime imports. Thus it was that the British and French governments actually clashed over the question of French purchases of British coal—with the French anxious to keep their peacetime purchases to a minimum and the British conversely concerned with keeping French buying at a healthy level.[22]

While the preceding remarks do little more than scratch the surface of an immensely complex subject, they should provide evidence enough of France's plight. Not for the first time, the French had been rudely confronted by the dictatorial demands of modern war. The Blum government had not been in office for more than a few weeks before it was presented with two long notes on the subject of industrial mobilization and raw material stockpiling, the first from the army staff's Section de l'Armement et des Études Techniques and the second from the secretariat of the CSDN.[23] Perhaps it was with these reports in mind, both of which stressed the need for greater effort, that war minister Daladier promptly directed the attention of the newly constituted Comité Permanent de la Défense Nationale to the question of industrial mobilization.[24] Indeed, the much broader terms of reference enjoyed by this new committee—compared to those of the now defunct Haut Comité Militaire— were themselves a testament to a growing awareness of the complex demands evoked by modern war.[25]

Although this is not the place for anything more than a few exploratory passes at the subject, it seems clear that the Popular Front governments became deeply immersed in the fine print of national defense. While it is true that they promoted and financed the development of patently military hardware, such as tanks, aircraft, and field howitzers, it is equally true that they initiated or endorsed programs of a less spectacular order. It is under this rough rubric that one might place the policy of stockpiling raw material reserves, of rationalizing, decentralizing, even nationalizing certain key aeronautical and armaments industries, of encouraging the shift of trained workers to more vital branches of industrial production, even of striving for greater financial stability by devaluing an over-inflated franc. Here too one would place a series of efforts and initiatives that were roughly concurrent with those made by the chiefs of staff. Just as the latter pushed for the commencement of joint military planning with Britain, civil ministries and the secretariat of the CSDN made their own démarches to London. While it is true that actual negotiations were not mounted until the spring and early summer of 1938, French initiatives on the subjects of food, oil, and coal supplies were taken throughout the course of 1937. As a result, many of the advance preparations had been completed by the time the British government relented and tentatively accepted the principle of joint planning in April 1938.[26] And again, it is under this same rubric of economic planning that one would place the protracted negotiations of Paul Ramadier with the Anglo-Iranian Oil Company, and with Standard Oil, between July 1936 and the autumn of 1937. Such negotiations, for example, had assured France by the end of 1937 of close to half of its wartime needs in crude oil and had laid the foundations for the Anglo-French oil talks of June 1938.[27]

Although future studies no doubt will have much more to say about this important dimension of French prewar planning, particularly as the papers of the CSDN secretariat become available for research, one modest conclusion now may be offered with some confidence. As in the case of the frontier defense program, the Popular Front governments of Blum and Chautemps continued to uphold the kind of strategic assumptions that greeted them when they took office. There seems not the slightest doubt that they accepted the notion of a long war, waged against Germany by an allied coalition. It was with this in mind, fending off defeat long enough to share in an allied triumph, that the government lent itself to continuing, and in some cases to initiating, preparations of a broad economic and financial character. In this respect at least, it makes no more sense to find in their program some bold and radical departure from past assumptions than it does to accuse them of lethargy and inaction. As in the case of foreign policy, it is the continuity of approach that is most striking.

The third area of Popular Front defense activity, and over which a statistical war has been waged since 1940, is that of rearmament. The volley which follows will not end hostilities, for this is to be a war in perpetuity. For those who saw no French tanks in 1940, there were no such tanks. For those who saw no French aircraft, there were no such aircraft. For the Germans who collected hundreds of them in storage depots, hangars, and vehicle parks there were more than they had imagined. For those who occupied unarmed bunkers in the north, there were no anti-tank guns and few anti-aircraft batteries. For those in Paris who had supervised their production, the numbers were adequate if not impressive. For some, French rearmament between 1936 and 1939 was a failure because it did not match German production and because it was not enough to prevent the fielding of some obsolete tanks and aircraft in 1940. For others, this same output, of an industrially inferior nation, in fact confirmed the success of the French rearmament program, a program which was also responsible for the excellent Morane fighters and the formidable SOMUA tank. Opinions are as legion as memories, and statistics the allies of all.

For my part I am prepared to accept the figures provided by Daladier and Robert Jacomet, the former secretary-general at the war ministry: to accept them, but to use them for no more than what they purport to tell us, namely that a rearmament effort of substantial and certainly respectable proportions was undertaken between 1936 and 1939. By their reckoning French industry produced some 4,500 anti-tank guns—principally of the 25 mm models but including some 500 37 mm and 47 mm models—over 2,000 light and medium tanks, close to 200 heavy assault tanks and about 900 anti-aircraft guns of 75 and 105 mm calibre.[28] Their figures also testify to a comparable growth rate in the French air force. By Jacomet's calculation, different again from that of Cot or of British intelligence, France went from a first line force of 1,200 aircraft in June 1936—of which only 36 percent were regarded as truly modern—to a first line force of better than 1,900 planes in September 1939—of which almost half were reckoned as *avions modernes.*[29] Such statistics, if they may be regarded as accurate in impression even if not in detail, provide ample evidence of the fact of French rearmament as it was initiated to all intents and purposes by the Front Populaire. They say nothing, of course, about whether the rate of rearmament could have been or should have been greater than it was, whether the materiel chosen for special emphasis was technically adequate and competitive with foreign models, or whether such materiel had been designed and ordered with any reference to the kind of mobile armored-air warfare which was winning greater currency in both Germany and Russia.

Having thus affirmed the fact of French rearmament, I would prefer to concentrate on the nature, rather than the numbers, of this rearmament process. Baldly put, did this process reflect the same sort of traditional restraints, assumptions, and loyalties which seem to have characterized the government's effort in frontier defense and economic mobilization? For the purposes of this study special attention will be paid to land and air rearmament, the two service branches that could be expected to exert immediate pressure on a recalcitrant Germany.

The career of military aviation under the ministry of Pierre Cot long has had associated with it a kind of dramatic touch that seems to mark it apart from most of the Popular Front ministries. Though the claims were much exaggerated, Cot's ministry seemed to be a haven for progressives and radicals, men who were attuned to the nation-in-danger notion and who seemed drawn temperamentally to Jacobin solutions. Cot appears to have imposed himself much more forcefully on the air ministry than did Delbos, for example, on the Quai d'Orsay, or Daladier on the war ministry. Certainly he took up his portfolio with considerable panache, making no secret of the fact that the air force was in desperate straits or of his intention to resort to drastic measures. To this end he benefited greatly from an energetic *chef de cabinet*, Colonel Henri Jauneaud, and from the young, recently appointed chief of the air staff, General Philippe Féquant.

Cot, himself only forty-one years of age in 1936, was aggressive and outspoken, a not easily ignored gadfly on the left wing of the Radical Socialist party. While continuing the decentralization and modernization of the French air industry which had begun under his predecessor, General Denain, and while raising Denain's first-line target strength from 1,000 to 1,500 aircraft, Cot was to gain public prominence and no little public odium on other grounds.[30] He was, of course, an outspoken advocate of providing arms to the beleagured Spanish government. He was, too, one of the few non-Communist partisans of a close military alliance with the Soviet Union, an alliance which he hoped to forge through the growth of technical cooperation between the French and Russian armed forces. And he was seen by many as the leading, red-eyed champion of enforced nationalization, a measure by which the state would assert its control over the vital arms and aircraft industries. Finally, it was Cot who at last insisted that the air force should put its cards on the table.

The air force, so he and his entourage proclaimed, was more than an aerial appendage to the land and naval forces. It had to be given an independent role, not for reasons of face but for those of national prestige and security. Without anything like a wholesale commitment to some of the more excessive strategic bombing doctrines which had won currency

174

since the days of Douhet and Trenchard, the French air force simply pointed to the merits of its own case. The land army could not undertake immediate offensive action; bomber squadrons could. The loss of the Italian alliance made the eastern front less credible; bombers could restore French presence in the east by operating from Polish, or Czech, or Roumanian bases, just as they could harass forces on Germany's western front for the benefit of threatened allies in the east. At a time when so much attention was being attracted to the respective industrial resources of France and Germany, the air force again could take direct action—unlike the great naval arm—against Germany's industrial and communication complexes. These were the central issues for which Pierre Cot became famous or, as it were, infamous: an aerial doctrine that was aggressive, ambitious, and insensitive to traditional service roles and authority;[31] a limited experiment in state ownership that was consistent with both socialist ideology and with the patent need to shake up and reorder an air industry fallen on bad days; a foreign political vision that called for the active practice of anti-fascism by resisting fascist incursions wherever they occurred and by sharply strengthening France's ties with the Soviet Union.

In fact, like most reputations that of Cot is overdrawn. Without denying his drive and energy, qualities with which he infected others, his ministry was as traditional as it was innovative, a blend that was partly of his own choosing and partly beyond his power to alter. The strategic bombing doctrine, for example, and the implicit revolt against the army, were new in degree rather than in substance. This storm had been brewing since the end of the First World War and more particularly since 1933 when the air force had achieved a nominally independent status. Once the experiment in multi-purpose aircraft had ended dismally in 1936,[32] it became clear that in the future planes would have to be built that performed, looked like, and were called, bombers. This Cot firmly believed, correctly seeing a modern air force as the closest-to-hand answer to France's worsening international plight. In this sense, therefore, within the ranks of the air force Cot was really a traditionalist, a champion of established truths, however much those on the Rue Saint Dominique and the Rue Royale saw him and his charges as brash arrivistes.

But on this matter, as on so many others, the weight of convention proved too much for Pierre Cot. Ultimately, his efforts to produce a large bombing deterrent foundered on the shoals of interservice discord, desultory production rates, and German aerial supremacy. By the end of 1937, as his ministry came to an end, it seemed clear that France would have to concentrate on the production of fighters, machines that were cheaper and faster to build and which seemed in keeping with France's vulnerability to air attack. What is more, Cot's energies had begun to flag, the result not only of repeatedly bucking the system but of having to bow so often to it. He had to give way on Russia as he had been obliged to give way on Spain. From quarrels with dissident civil servants, many of whom betrayed little sympathy for the Popular Front, he went on to heated meetings with air industrialists who rebelled against state attempts to organize them and yet who balked at the idea of supplementing French production with imports from abroad.[33] To Blum and Daladier he complained bitterly about the absolute shortage of financial credits and about their relative distribution among the three services, a distribution which before 1938 was never to reach a 33 percent share for the air force.[34] He saw himself as an embattled figure, struggling always against the conservative forces within the Chamber, against the encrusted ranks of the Senate's air commission, and against the ubiquitous spokesmen for the private French air industry. To make matters worse, temperamentally he was not inclined to be swayed by special pleading and certainly was illdisposed to lobby support or court favors in the corridors of power. The demands upon him consequently were enormous and, it must be said, they took their toll.[35]

While there is little evidence of this in Cot's own writings, it appears as if his energies were waning even by the end of 1936. Stunned by the malevolent criticisms showered upon him, and tried by uncertain health, the minister succumbed to "a kind of lassitude." In December 1936 "he relented with little resistance" when his request for increased funds was rejected by the Comité Permanent de la Défense Nationale. In February 1937 Schweisguth was assured that even Cot "had resigned himself" to the slow and uneventful sparring with Russia.[36] Later in the month the minister again addressed the CPDN, on this occasion with a project for strengthening French air defenses, the proposed Plan III. Again he was turned down, on the grounds he reports, "I am quoting the exact words of the decision—'that there is no reason at the moment to alter or increase the expansion program of the air force.' "[37] What Cot was never to say, however, was that his own defense of Plan III had been less than spirited. Moments before the decision was taken during this meeting of 15 February Cot is on record as having said that "the realization of Plan III, as proposed by his department, appears impossible to him for reasons of funding, industrial capacity and trained personnel."[38] Strange brief for an appellant, it would seem that Cot had tired of insisting.

Of course it would be inaccurate and unfair to imply that Cot had effectively retired from the fray so many months before he actually left office. On the contrary, it is clear that he continued his efforts to accelerate air production, that he sustained intact his great belief in the deterrent value and military contribution of a revamped air force, and that he complained to the end about the fact that Britain and Germany were spending proportionately more money on their air arms than was France. The thrust of our remarks merely has been directed at the influence which tradition continued to exercise on the French air force—one token of which was the toll it claimed on a young and enthusiastic minister whose commitment to the established order was less profound than that of most of his Radical Socialist colleagues.

In the Rue Saint Dominique the war minister's chair was occupied by Edouard Daladier, veteran minister, former premier, and at the relatively young age of fifty-two an established power within the Radical party. Here was a horse of a different color, or should one say a bull, in customary deference to his stocky, short-necked physique and squarish head. He was known, of course, as the bull of the Vaucluse, partly for reasons of physique, partly owing to Caillaux's terrible jest that this simple, unpretentious, unsophisticated man still smelled of the stable, and partly too for reasons of temperament. The British found him unusually taciturn, for a Frenchman; the French saw him as a blustery figure, rough and menacing on the outside but uncertain of himself within. Cot, for one, regarded him as an obstacle, one who could never hold out to the end against traditionalist quarters in the general staff. "One thought that he was going to say no; in fact, he began gamely by saying no, after which he said perhaps, and then he ended up by compromising if not by giving in."[39] Flandin, for another, saw him as "a weak man," and Tabouis as one who fled from awkward situations "like a schoolboy running away from the classroom."[40] By all appearances, therefore, this was not the man to sweep the cobwebs of tradition from the war ministry, one who would work, certainly, one who in his own way would try as hard as those like Cot, but not one who had the drive, or the confidence, or both, to go against generals who had made war a profession and under whom he himself had served.

Daladier's experience in the war ministry offers certain parallels to that of Cot. Both professed acute alarm at the state of French forces in June 1936. Cot proclaimed the air force a disaster area. Daladier, a trifle more diplomatic, was astonished by the gaps he found in French materiel. While conscious of the thrust of previous budgets—before 1935 "essentially a manpower budget"—Daladier said that he was horrified by the condition of the French army.[41] Despite all the talk of a mobile defense force in the north, to complement the rigid Maginot Line, there were hardly any light tanks or armored cars. Despite the emphasis hitherto placed on anti-tank firepower, the Maginot defenses had no modern guns of the 37 or 47 mm models and no more than a thousand of the older 25 mm models. Despite the proliferation of air scare literature and the concomitant fear of surprise aerial attack, the French army was woefully short of modern anti-aircraft weaponry, possessing no more than some 60 modern guns of the 75 mm model and none of the 105 mm model.[42]

As if such weaknesses were not sufficiently inhibiting of themselves—particularly when they related to weapons which carried the official war doctrine's stamp of approval—Gamelin was quick to stoke the fires of caution. Having been so recently discomfited by cabinet ministers who had pretended to be more ignorant than they were, the general hastened to advise the new minister of two military realities. First, in the words of the army staff: "Even a small-scale operation can not be contemplated with peacetime forces alone. It requires the implementation of the *couverture* measures, followed soon after, if necessary, by general mobilization."[43] Second, the outcome of any clash with Germany would be determined by the extent of allied support—in particular, that of Italy.[44] In other words, France could take no action that might risk war without first having in place the full *couverture* force and without reasonable assurances of allied support. Judging from this, not only had the Rhineland affair failed to prompt a serious rethinking of army planning but it seemed to have taken on the dull glitter of some heroic national event. Far from an embarrassment, it was to be held up as a certificate of good health. As Gamelin assured Daladier, we are now ready to act "just as we were then," both offensively and defensively.[45]

It would be safe to suggest that no one was taken in by such statements, made for the record to exonerate the army from what had happened in March. The fact was that the army was extremely limited in the kind of action it could undertake. Short on speed and mobile fire power, it had to rely on measures of a grander and at the same time more ponderous scale. Thus there was not the slightest doubt about the need for a major rearmament program and for a serious reassessment of the governing, intrusive, war doctrine. The question that directs this investigation, however, is whether either could be conducted with sufficient detachment from past assumptions. Would the weight of tradition again neutralize the sting of a futurist regime led by socialists?

Pressed by the strategic implications of the Rhineland coup, by the pace of German rearmament and by the deteriorating diplomatic situation, the French were impelled to conduct a kind of stock taking in the second half of 1936. From the point of view of army doctrine this meant a review of the arguments in favor of an initially defensive strategy. Here, tradition proved to be insuperable. All the reasons that had been marshaled years before in favor of such a strategy still prevailed: the recognition of Germany's superiority in industry and manpower, the consequent dependence of France on a prolonged allied war effort, the risks of courting an early defeat by gambling on an odds-against quick victory. From this there followed as naturally as it had in the past the reservations about unleashing armored divisions with a mandate for independent offensive action. And from the same wellspring came the army's misgivings about the wisdom of strategic bombing missions which were certain to evoke savage reprisal raids from the Luftwaffe. Conversely, what did seem appropriate and wise was what had been familiar for so long—the need to complement the fixed defenses in Alsace and Lorraine with the mobile defensive power of light mechanized and ultimately heavy armored divisions in the north. And it was these divisions, again in keeping with the old order, that would rush to the defense of Belgium or, in less happy circumstances, would operate defensively from the fixed fortifications now under construction along the Franco-Belgian frontier.[46]

One need not belabor this point for it is assuredly well within the precincts of conventional historical wisdom. It seems as mistaken to view the French army staff as enthusiastic partisans of armored warfare along Panzer lines, as it is to see them as complacently indifferent to the potential of tanks in modern battle. Whether one looks to the opinions of General Bourret, Daladier's military *chef de cabinet*, to the much discussed conclusions of the commission headed by General Alphonse Georges, or to the views communicated to the war ministry by Maurice Gamelin, the same set of assumptions is present. Nothing but hostility was shown toward the notions championed by men like Paul Reynaud and Colonel de Gaulle, notions that involved a more aggressive use of mobile armored forces operating well behind the enemy lines on a bold mission of destruction and disorganization. This the military Brahmins refused to (countenance,) partly because the theory of such a force clashed head on with their own injunctions against dashing but premature light-brigade charges, which if turned could lead the enemy back through the breach, and partly because it implied the division of the army into first and second strings, only the latter of which could be controlled at all times by the supreme general headquarters. Thus, as the army asserted: "In short, the modernization of the French army must not be pursued solely in the *interests of a specialized and autonomous corps* which, though incapable of doing everything itself, nonetheless would threaten to corner all the best units at the expense of the other forces."[47] From this it followed that the land commanders were in no rush to promote the cause of a large and almost certainly more independent armored corps. Rather, or so it was argued, until the number of tanks was large enough to support such an experiment, it seemed preferable to retain them "in a general reserve in order to be able to assign them when needed . . . to the infantry divisions."[48] For the moment, the summer of 1936, it seemed more judicious to continue the theoretical studies of armored divisions, no doubt with reference to their defensive contribution to the cover operations: "ensure the integrity of the defensive line," "counter-attack any enemy unit which might have managed to penetrate between our fortified zones."[49]

Thus the truth of the matter lies somewhere between two extremes, on the spacious plains between two overstatements, the one which has Gamelin as kindred spirit to Guderian and Rommel, the other which has him and his entourage as antediluvian enthusiasts of horse and buggy. The 1936 review commission of General Georges, for example, undeniably paid tribute to the importance of tanks in modern warfare. But it did so within the orthodox context of a tank force that was vulnerable to anti-tank weaponry and limited by considerations of terrain, that was consequently dependent on infantry and artillery support, and that could operate behind the enemy's lines only *after* his defenses had been "sufficiently disrupted."[50] The idea of armored divisions, composed of swift tanks with greatly increased operating ranges, was therefore one that did not generate instant enthusiasm. Gamelin had confessed as much to an appreciative audience of the Conseil Supérieur de la Guerre in April 1936. We have been studying the German experiments with such divisions since 1932, he said, but "the development of the anti-tank weapon has prompted us to reject this notion." "In fact, it seems at the moment that a tank attack can only succeed against a prepared front if it has strong artillery support against the enemy's anti-tank weaponry."[51]

It is true that this attitude was to undergo some change. But at the beginning of 1937 Gamelin was still prepared to predict that a tank force without artillery support would be stopped "by the anti-tank gun, as the infantry had been by the machine gun."[52] And at the end of that year the debate about armored divisions was as unresolved as ever. By then the mood of the CSG was characterized more by an uncomfortable feeling that France should have at least one such division than by a conviction that such a force was indispensable to the French war effort. In short, the land commanders were becoming predisposed to the desirability of such a force rather than intellectually persuaded that it was a necessity. Gamelin presented it as such: "an extremely interesting device," envisaging it as a force "under the control of the Commander in Chief . . . which could make a strong counter-attack." But the inspector-general of tanks, General Duffieux, was not to be swayed. Having already convinced his colleagues that the general tank reserve was essential for military flexibility and therefore should not be depleted for the sake of outfitting a second and third light mechanized division, he now insisted that there were not enough medium tanks in his general reserve, of type B and D models, to support the creation of a heavy armored division. Indeed, he saw little likelihood of having adequate numbers before 1939, an attitude of mind which Gamelin did little to contradict and nothing to shake. As if to narrow the gap which seemed to separate him from his inspector-general, one that was more apparent than real, Gamelin offered this cheery word of compromise. The theoretical studies relating to the formation of such a division should be pursued, he ventured, for it was always possible that this formation would have no effect at all on the Réserve Générale. If such were not the case, he assured Duffieux, "nothing compels us, in every circumstance, to commit the whole Division."[53] The general and his colleagues had not yet abandoned the piecemeal advocacy of armor.

As is attested by the preceding remarks, there is little evidence of any major revision of attitudes or preparations by the army command in 1936 and 1937. This is not to say that no thought was given to the possibility of modifying some of the current assumptions. On the contrary, it is clear that the circumstances of the day made such a reassessment imperative, a review of which the Georges commission is only the most notable example. Nor should one be too quick to assume that the reviews which did take place in 1936 were only window dressing, pro forma inquiries by tribunals which already knew the answers. That it might look this way is understandable, for it is true that the gist of the official findings was broadly self-congratulatory. Certainly the renewed emphasis on infantry and artillery, on anti-tank and anti-aircraft weaponry was altogether obvious, whatever may have been added about the value of tanks and aircraft. With its entire war plan grounded on the need for a successful defense of France, could one have afforded to think otherwise? On the contrary, an unqualified belief in the breakthrough powers of offensive weapons—particularly in the hands of an enemy with superior resources—would have been more than a counsel of despair. It would have constituted a prediction of military disaster. Thus it was that the high command reconsidered, then reaffirmed, its doctrine of war in 1936. So it was too that it drew from the Spanish civil war the lessons which, in a sense, it had to draw. Again and again army and air intelligence explained the victories of offensive weapons in Spain with reference to the inadequate numbers or employment of defensive weapons or to certain peculiarities inherent in this localized war. Conversely, the successes of artillery, anti-tank guns, and anti-aircraft artillery were used to confirm the correctness of French war doctrine.[54]

From this doctrine there emerged a rearmament program in 1936 that was correspondingly orthodox. The original fourteen billion franc program which the war ministry unveiled in September 1936—and which had more than doubled by the outbreak of war three years later—paid homage to traditional interarms priorities. Together, the infantry and artillery branches claimed 40 percent of the war budget, with mechanization and motorization only producing a combined total of 24 percent. And again, Daladier was neither as outdated in his thinking as his critics alleged, nor as visionary and personally assertive as he has led us to believe. By his reckoning at least, the four-year program expressly envisaged the construction of some 3,200 tanks, an extremely ambitious goal by French standards of the day. It is also true that the minister's conception of armored-air cooperation was if anything more developed than that of the senior army commanders.[55] On the other hand, his self-styled image as a maverick, the bull of the Vaucluse, is more than a little contrived. He accepted the established truths about the supremacy of the infantry and artillery arms and shared in the belief that the Spanish experience was confirming the correctness of French tactical procedures.[56] So it was that the minister who presided over the renaissance of French land rearmament was closely attuned to the sentiments and prejudices of his professional advisers. And while it is true that he was expected to receive as authoritative the views of the army staff on war doctrine—as it related to both the choice and employment of military hardware—it would be more accurate to see him as willing collaborator than as hapless victim.

More must be said about the national defense efforts of the Popular Front. But in recapitulating, one would do well to recall several key considerations. First, whereas the foreign policy of the Blum and Chautemps administrations was characterized by a holding action, their defense policy was by design more dynamic. Second, this energy and initiative notwithstanding, their defense policy addressed itself to three traditional sorts of solutions—an extension of frontier fortifications, an acceleration of the nation's economic plans for war, and a refurbishing of the nation's arsenals. Third, with reference to the latter, the fealty to traditional assumptions was equally clear: from the endorsement of the national grand strategy and the army's tactical doctrine to the restraints maintained upon the air force from the point of view of command, employment, and financial backing; from the renewed emphasis on *anti*-tank and *anti*-aircraft weaponry to the lingering commitment to armored units as defensive, *counter*-attacking forces; from the reaffirmed faith in well-armed fortifications with fixed fields of fire to the durable notions about the sovereign pair, infantry and artillery. In view of this, this attitude of mind, it is not surprising that the new armies that were forged in the three years prior to the war were materially but not psychologically better equipped to engage in the kind of war they knew the Germans were planning.

Yet if these conclusions are warranted, they are also derived from a dangerously Hegelian bias. So it is that the nuts and bolts of rearmament spring from a world of the intellect, with attitudes and theories determining which machines will be constructed and how they will be employed. Marx would have seen it another way, and for once at least

183

many French officers might have nodded in assent. For instance, rather than see the French attachment to infantry-armor cooperation as the product of theory, one would do well to remember that the First World War had left the French army with a large number of armored leviathans behind whose slow gait and limited fuel range the infantry could follow with comparative ease. So it was, very likely, that the nature of the machine gave birth to the tactical idea, rather than vice-versa. Similarly, it was this kind of reasoning which General Duffieux used to resist the notion of armored divisions. Flatly unwilling to draw the heavier tanks from his strategic reserve, Duffieux argued that it was foolish to talk about such divisions until the requisite materiel was available in sufficient numbers. It was an idea whose time had not yet come.

Or had it? The problem with this materialistic approach is that it is no more uniformly reliable than its idealistic rival. Our first example may be taken as legitimate, the second much less so. What was critical in Duffieux's case was his refusal to take existing tanks from one force and reallocate them to another. Thus it was not the alleged absence of medium tanks that checked the idea of armored divisions but a belief, the idea of a general reserve which could be thrown into the fray at a crucial moment to choke off a successful enemy penetration. This idea he and his colleagues refused to discard, preferring instead to have both a general reserve *and* an armored division. But, as he said, the latter would have to wait until more tanks were available.

This is but a reminder of the uncertain ground ahead. If it was the belief in the *réserve générale* which long determined the fate of the French armored divisions, and not the number of tanks, was it numbers or attitudes which governed the general pace of French rearmament after 1936? Was the fact that France did not produce more modern materiel more quickly, attributable to the lack of funds, as the generals said, to the slowness of finalizing contracts, as the industrialists said, to the time-consuming antics of civil servants, as labor alleged, or to the inefficient, class-obsessed work practices of French unions, as the bureaucrats complained? In the shadows of this, the Gordian knot would seem simple by comparison. And yet some attempt to unravel this collection of mysteries must be made. Not to do so would mean ignoring one critical dimension of the Popular Front's defense efforts—leaving the story of French rearmament in the hands of those who would tell it solely in terms of intellectual inertia.

First, the question of funds in a depressed economy. Quite clearly, the whole "credit" question was always an abrasive issue between generals and politicians. After 1940, and the allegations of military unpreparedness, the dimensions of this controversy were suddenly magnified. The reputations of individuals and of the institutions they had represented seemed to rest on the ability of one side to discredit the arguments of the other. Gamelin defined the problem. While decrying the lack of adequate funding, he did agree that the military estimates had not been slashed either by parliament or its various service commissions. The government itself, he indicated, had to bear the responsibility for the regular reductions which had been levied on the army's prepared estimates. In his opinion, the war ministers—both before and after 1936—had been too quick to bow to the arguments of their colleagues in the finance ministry. Why else, the general wondered, would they have reduced army requests almost as a matter of course?[57] To this, several ministers responded with conviction. While it was true that the finance ministry could be counted on to exact some cut in the expenditures proposed to it, financial stringencies never became the key to flagging arms production. In fact, Jean Fabry was to admit that there was always more money than could be spent, an assertion verbally endorsed by the Chamber's army commission and, more graphically, by the presence of one unexpended surplus of 60 percent in the 1935 war budget.[58]

For those who remain unconvinced, further confirmation of this reading may be found in Gamelin's own porous postwar testimony. For not only did he admit that administrative and industrial delays had governed the pace of rearmament, but he granted that the army's own rearmament bureau was allocated only enough funds to keep up with current production levels.[59] What is more, the general remained silent before the suggestion, entirely credible as it was, that the high command regularly inflated its initial estimates in anticipation of subsequent reductions. Where the depression of the mid-thirties made itself felt, therefore, was less in the financial domain and more in the general area of national productivity. Depression-sponsored unemployment, strikes, and outmoded industrial plant—now more expensive to replace than ever—helped make limited credits more than adequate. Certainly after the commencement of Daladier's comprehensive program in the autumn of 1936—a program guaranteed by a four-year financial plan—it was the question of productivity which became the operative link between the economic crisis and national rearmament.

The credit question, to be sure, did not disappear entirely from the dialogue between the high command and the ministry for war and national defense. There were further reports of clashes between and among the commander-in-chief, the war minister, and the finance minister in August 1936 and November 1937.[60] However, in view of the fact that thirty-one billion francs were spent on the army's rearmament effort alone between September 1936 and September 1939,[61] it is not surprising that what came to matter was how quickly these francs could be converted into firm orders, and the orders into mass-produced war materiel. The efforts which were made to lubricate the rearmament machine, therefore, should be seen in the light of the Popular Front's quite different approach to the nation's economic plight.

Once in power the Blum administration acted quickly on its pledge to end the policy of retrenchment. Through its Matignon agreement with the employers, the government promised an average rise in workers' salaries of about twelve percent. Subsequent legislation introduced schemes for holidays with pay and a forty-hour working week. Agricultural circles were temporarily pacified by an increase of between 40 and 50 percent on the sale price of their produce. Unemployment was attacked by means of a substantial public works program. However, the increase in government expenditure, combined with the general increase in prices, intensified the administration's need to augment its own revenue yield. But the resulting taxation had to conform, within reason, to industry's capacity to pay, particularly at a time when employers were facing higher salaries and a general shortage of funds for capital investment—a shortage, incidentally, induced in part by their own efforts to spirit capital away to foreign accounts. It became increasingly obvious that some decisive measure was needed to rationalize the whole economic policy. By and large this meant that French prices had to be made competitive with those of the world market. Consequently, in September 1936, the government devalued the franc in an attempt to realign it with the pound sterling and the dollar.[62]

This, and successive devaluations, did stimulate growth in the national rate of industrial production. In fact, by the spring of 1937 France was nearing a state of full employment. However, the stunning fact was that the volume of industrial production was only 82 percent of what it had been in 1929. Owing to a small birth rate, a marked decrease in immigration to France, and a return to the agricultural side of the economy of many disenchanted industrial workers, the labor market could not support the accelerating demands of French industry. The new forty-hour week introduced a further limitation on the productive potential of the available labor force. For a wide variety of reasons, therefore, it seems that France "was less of a manufacturing nation" in 1939 than it had been in the 1920s.[63]

The pressures imposed by rearmament worked in a cyclical fashion on the nation's productive capacity. The rearmament program not only suffered at the hands of a strained economy, but it appealed for measures which in the short run only prolonged the quest for economic stability. For example, the Blum government was obliged to continue the policy of rationalizing and decentralizing the essential war industries, that is to say, streamlining their production and at the same time dispersing their operations away from the vulnerable Paris concentration. New plants had to be installed and workers trained or retrained to keep pace with the most recent technology. Key industries, like those of steel, armaments, and aviation, had to be relocated. Finally, quite apart from the socialist dictates of state ownership, the nationalization of some of these key industries seemed entirely consistent with the accepted need for rationalizing, decentralizing, and regulating their production. But whatever the merits of these ambitious undertakings—and there were many—the magnitude of the changes inevitably produced early delays and disruptions in the rearmament schedules.[64] This does not mean that one must accept the well-rehearsed indictments of Vichy and Riom. That the reorganization of the French war industries produced initial delays is indisputable, but so too is the counter-claim that the framework for modern rearmament, to such a great extent hammered out by the Popular Front regimes, was both sound and ultimately effective. Without the creation of the new coordinating ministry for war *and* national defense, without the fourteen billion franc program, and without a revitalized war industry more actively controlled by the state, it is doubtful whether France could have rearmed as quickly and as well as it did.

Yet if rearmament was more than simply an application of tactical theories, it also entailed considerations beyond the financial and industrial. As might be imagined, the pace of rearmament was also governed by the efficiency of several interrelated but distinct bureaucracies. No new weapon could reach the hands of French troops without having threaded its way through a long, time-consuming, administrative gauntlet. So it was that this, too, along with considerations of an idealistic and materialistic order, became an integral part of the Popular Front's experience in national defense.

The task of determining the basic outline of the army's rearmament program fell to its own Conseil Supérieur de la Guerre. It was here that the tactical doctrine, the idealistic component, could register its greatest impact, for this was the committee that defined the army's general requirements. For example, any question concerning the desired numbers of *divisions légères mécaniques,* or the number and model of tanks which might be allocated to that elusive first armored division, or the exact distribution of anti-tank weapons within an infantry division, came under the aegis of the CSG.[65] In this respect the army commanders had a very free hand, for the war minister seldom bothered to attend its meetings and the CPDN, in which civilians had an edge over officers, rarely turned its attention to details of rearmament. Thus, whereas the cabinet ultimately exercised its judgment on new arms projects, its ministers played a slight role in the early formulation of such proposals. As the soldiers regularly deferred to the politicians as the nation's decision makers, so the politicians appear to have displayed comparable deference to the expertise of their military technicians. Hence the army was comparatively free to set its own rearmament priorities, just as it could partly influence the speed with which its needs were brought to the formal attention of the cabinet.

It was not, however, the sole arbiter of the time factor. Only for a limited period did such control reside within its ranks. On receipt of the CSG's recommendations, army headquarters passed them down to its various technical committees for costing. On completion of that task, General Colson, chief of army headquarters and rearmament executor, forwarded the relevant data to Gamelin, chief of the general staff, then to Jacomet, secretary-general at the war ministry, and finally to the minister himself. Thereafter, responsibility temporarily shifted away from the war ministry. On Jacomet's request the finance ministry then scrutinized the arms program and the costing estimates which accompanied it. Assuming that the financial experts accepted the army's figures—and thus avoided the delays attendant on having to reprocess the estimates—the proposed expenditures would be submitted with the relevant program for cabinet approval, whereupon arrangements would be made to include the new costs in either the ordinary or extraordinary budgets. If the circumstances seemed particularly pressing, as they often did after 1936, more rapid action could be taken by means of the government's power of decree law.

Assured of adequate funding, the army staff reclaimed the initiative. While it is true that Daladier tried to keep his hand in by means of two steering committees, the *comité de surveillance* and the *comité de production*, the onus now rested on the army's own technical bureaucracy. This in itself was no mean affair. Between 1931 and 1933 recommendations on weapon prototypes came from the Conseil Consultatif de l'Armement, a group that included Gamelin, Jacomet, and the inspectors-general of the various army services. The actual experimental work was administered by the *conseil's* own secretariat, an organization called the Cabinet Technique à l'État-Major de l'Armée. In 1933 this system was modified, though hardly streamlined. Stripping the hitherto powerful Direction de l'Artillerie of all functions not expressly related to the artillery arm, the government created the Direction des Fabrications d'Armement (DFA). The latter, while remaining nominally subordinate to the Conseil Consultatif in fact usurped many of its responsibilities—one token of which was the withering away of the Cabinet Technique in favor of the DFA's own Section de l'Armement et des Etudes Techniques. Consequently, after 1933, the administrative procedure which eventually would turn paper estimates to prototypes and prototypes to serially produced materiel operated vertically, up or down, between the DFA's new secretariat and the chief of the general staff. For instance, having been tested by the military engineers, the Corps d'Ingénieurs Militaires des Fabrications, and approved by the secretariat (Section de l'Armement), a prototype tank's performance would be considered and approved by the DFA. The director of this committee would then take the relevant data to the Conseil Consultatif for its recommendation. Following the decision of that body, the matter would be referred to General Colson who, on Gamelin's authorization, would place the initial order with the tank manufacturers.[66]

Bureaucratic inertia was bound to claim its tariff within such a system, not that the French organization was unusually cumbersome by the standards of the day or of the present. Administrative redundancy and competing authorities were certainly part of the problem. The Conseil Consultatif, for example, lost most of its responsibilities in 1933 but very little of its authority. Indeed, it remained next to General Colson on the administrative chain of command. Moreover, Jacomet's presence on this committee seemed to foster army resentment of what they took to be ministerial intervention, and this at a time when Gamelin was finding personally irksome his own lack of control over the increasingly influential DFA.[67] And complaints from further down the chain were even more legion. General Sablet, a former director of the DFA, and General Dassault, once chief of that group's secretariat, were to condemn the time-consuming processes that were demanded in the name of bureaucratic orthodoxy. They attributed these delays, in particular, to the frequent clashes of authority on the part of the kindred agencies to which the DFA was severally responsible. Not only were their programs subject to direction from the Conseil Consultatif, and thus to the delays attendant on its deliberation, but as well from the perfection-conscious inspectorates-general, the secretariat at the war ministry, the minister's own military advisers, and even, on occasion, from the minister himself.[68]

The confusion bred by this plethora of committees and secretariats, by overlapping authorities, and by the quest for technical features capable of satisfying each branch of the service meant that many of the so-called production delays occurred within the war ministry's own internal administration. One example will serve to illustrate this point, for it was by no means unique. In November 1935, on the army staff's request, the French firm SOMUA (a Schneider subsidiary, called the Société d'Outillage Mécanique et d'Usinage d'Artillerie) proposed three types of modifications for its new and impressive twenty-ton S-35 tank. The central idea was to combine the speed of this new vehicle (about 40 kph) with the fire power of the older 75 mm cannon. The army staff approved one of the projects and in December 1936, eleven months later, authorized the construction of several prototypes. However, the actual order for these experimental models was not placed with the factory until June 1937. Even then a continuation of army tests meant that SOMUA did not receive the final details and specifications for the desired optical equipment, radio system, or gun turret until the following November. Fifteen months later the prototypes were ready. These were field tested between February and August 1939 and, at last, thirty-six machines were ordered in November. The entire procedure, from proposal to order, had taken four years of which army administration could account for at least two.[69]

Delays of this sort neither began nor ended with the Popular Front. Indeed, many of the preceding observations are relevant for the

1930s as a whole and not simply for the period 1936-1937 on which our attention presently has been focused. The attitudinal, financial, industrial, and administrative considerations which have been outlined here were as familiar to Blum's predecessors as they were to him—just as one must accept that his own regime proved quite incapable of ridding the system of all the points of resistance. And as emphasized throughout, this continuity of impedimenta of one sort or another—restraining and inhibiting the pace and farsightedness of French rearmament—was complemented by a continuity of approach to the tasks at hand. Thus the French governments in 1936 and 1937 accepted as valid the established vision of the next war with Germany, the strategic precepts which seemed to correspond with that vision, the tactical doctrine which long ago had been developed to support those precepts, and the kinds of military hardware the experts believed to be most consistent with those tactics. In short, the basic assumptions from which permanent French officialdom long had worked, civilian as well as military, stood impervious to surface disturbances such as cabinet reshuffles or even changes in political regimes.

The national defense program of the Popular Front, like that of its diplomatic program, was therefore essentially traditional in character. Belying its radical, innovative, public image, the Popular Front built on what had gone before it as surely as it had fallen heir to the legacy of its predecessors. And what it did in defense matters, on the whole it did well. In terms of the future, its efforts constituted a vital, an essential, reorganization and rebuilding of the nation's industrial resources. This was not, it is quite true, enough to reconcile French military capacity with French diplomatic obligations—not in 1936 or 1937, or even in 1938 or 1939. But it did allow, and one might even say determine, the rapid acceleration of production in 1938, 1939, and 1940 without which the military imbalance between France and Germany would have been as decisively adverse in fact as it has been made out to have been in fiction.

8

Anglo-French Relations, 1938: The Austrian and Czechoslovakian Crises

Despite the lackluster character of French diplomacy, and the frustrations which attended the delays in rearmament, official Paris was mildly optimistic at the beginning of 1938. In the last quarter of 1937 and the first two months of the new year there were signs that Hitler might be obliging enough to challenge France where it would do Germany the least good. Although contemporary German records do not bear this out, while they suggest that Hitler had no wish to precipitate a clash either in the Mediterranean or over French imperial domains, the government in Paris believed otherwise.[1] Temporarily, perhaps even happily, distracted from the problems of eastern Europe, the French fixed their attention on a possible challenge in the southern theater. The continuing reports about German colonial ambitions, and the murderous activity of Italian submarines on behalf of General Franco—to whom Italy and Germany were committing materiel and putative volunteers—suggested to observers in Paris that it was in this theater that Germany, as well as Italy, intended to make its opening bid for supremacy. Moreover, the timing seemed right for such a move. Spurred on by the costs and economic dislocation of their own rearmament effort the Germans and Italians would be tempted to provoke Britain and France before the latter had completed their rearmament. To that end, or so it was anticipated in Paris, the fas-

192

cist powers would go for the imperial jugular—for Britain and France that "source of their hegemony and of so much of their strength." Thus, as Daladier instructed his planners in the CSDN secretariat: "It is by attacking in the Mediterranean region, the seam between the two zones (Atlantic and Far East), that Germany and Italy could secure the most decisive results."[2]

While it may seem unusual for a victim to look upon an anticipated assault with mixed feelings, what must be kept in mind in this case is the promise associated with the threat. For the moment it seemed that Germany might be gracious enough to challenge Britain and France together, the one development that was certain to effect a new Anglo-French alliance. So it was that by the end of 1937 it was hoped in Paris that Germany would give Britain the final shove toward active joint planning with France—the logical culmination as it were of the continuing exchanges of naval intelligence, the joint registering of bombing targets in Germany and Italy, and the tentative initiatives that had been made on the subjects of coal, oil, and food supplies.[3] In short, once Germany challenged British lines of communication with Suez the government in Whitehall was as sure to run to Paris as it had done in Laval's time.

It was from this prospect, a clash in the Mediterranean where British as well as French interests would be imperiled, that the military authorities in Paris drew some heart. Instead of on the Rhine, where the British remained indecisive, or on the Elbe, where they appeared indifferent, the contest seemed likely to come in the Mediterranean. Here, what had held the entente together through the Ethiopian and Spanish crises would endure to forge a true alliance. It was with this in mind that the three service staffs responded with some enthusiasm to government inquiries about their proposed plans of action. Not since the summer of 1935 had there been such talk of offensive strikes, although now against Italy instead of in concert with it. Indeed, the prospect of taking on a lesser opponent, and with British support, struck an all but forgotten military chord. There were only two riders, large enough in fact to qualify substantially what was being said but incapable of dampening the sanguine impressions which would appear to have been the real objective. First, all French plans were predicated on the assumption of direct assistance from the British forces. Second, the naval and air plans in particular seem to have been advanced with a very shrewd eye to increased financial support. In other words, the ambitious undertakings which were about to be outlined were made provisional on the receipt of more money, materiel, and effectives.[4]

But if the substance of what was being said had not altered as much as appearances allowed, there was no mistaking the semblance of a revived audacity. Depending on how events actually unfolded, the air staff had visions of joint operations with the Russians from bases in Czechoslovakia, or of counteroffensive bombing raids against the Ruhr, Bavaria, Milan, and Rome, or of joint air-sea raids to knock Italy out of commission both in the peninsula and in Libya, or even of operations against Spain in the Iberian peninsula, the Balearics, Spanish Morocco, and Rio de Oro. The navy, too, seemed convinced that this was no time to be timid. On the understanding that British support would be assured in advance, and that greater funds would be forthcoming, the naval staff produced equally ambitious proposals. The vital importance of the Mediterranean, it maintained: "calls for . . . the primary objective of knocking out Italy, an enemy of secondary importance, before attempting a decision against the principal foe, Germany."[5] To accomplish this, several kinds of operation were envisaged, from a pincer movement involving land offensives from the Alps eastward and from Yugoslavia westward, to combined service assaults on Libya and Sardinia, and possibly on Spanish Morocco and the Balearics.

Given the thinly veiled pretentiousness of these *projets*, one is inclined to applaud the army staff for having remained resolutely prudent. While postulating land offensives in Africa, either against Tripoli or Ethiopia, the army command made it clear that such operations remained in the "second stage of our planning." In other words, and always, the first task was to look to the French defenses. Thereafter, and expressly with reference to British support from Egypt and Kenya, the French army would play its part in the campaign to eliminate Italy.[6] On the other hand, and again one should say to his credit, General Gamelin took pains to qualify the scope of such a strategy. It made sense, he agreed, so long as the fascist opener really did come in the Mediterranean. But the idea of eliminating Italy first would lose much of its validity if the Germans decided to attack France through Belgium or Switzerland. And one might add that the general was as prescient as he was astute. Not only was he determined to retain some flexibility, but he linked the possibility of a more direct German challenge in the west to the unfolding of events in the east. Germany, he declared, "might be tempted to attack us . . . after having settled the Czech and Austrian questions.'" Nothing, after all, could erase the plight of eastern Europe or the conundrums which France faced there.

To be sure, Austria no longer was much of a problem. Its absorption by Germany had been predicted regularly by French intelligence ever since the Rhineland occupation of March 1936; and certainly since early 1937 French ministers had been willing to concede in private that France would do nothing more than protest against an Anschluss.⁸ Premier Chautemps led their ranks, desperate for cosmetic solutions, for maintaining appearances. When, in February 1938, the government received secret information on the famous meeting between Hitler and Chancellor Schuschnigg of Austria, the premier ordered Delbos to issue an immediate appeal for Britain and France to issue a joint démarche in Berlin against any change in the status of Austria. What was not said with comparable fanfare was that Chautemps' initiative had been prompted by domestic politics—to make it appear that "something" was being done. For his own part, however, the premier subsequently confessed that he "had not been under the illusion that England might join France in such a démarche."⁹ No less indicative of the government's response to the approaching Anschluss was its curt and peremptory treatment of French diplomats in the field. Delbos evidently did not welcome the suggestion which came from Blondel in Rome and Puaux in Vienna to the effect that Italian support still might be enlisted against a German takeover of Austria.¹⁰ Indeed, with untypical choler, the minister branded Puaux's last-minute entreaty as "ill advised" and more or less told him to mind his own business—a puzzling instruction for the French ambassador to Austria.¹¹

The war ministry and the high command displayed an equally stolid demeanor. Now that the tensions between Austria and Germany were reaching a peak, Daladier called upon the counsels of General Gamelin. Judging from the latter's account, it was a true meeting of minds. The general observed that an Anschluss would leave Czechoslovakia vulnerable to invasion from Vienna. The minister observed that since none of the other powers was willing to resist a German move against Austria, the best that France could do would be to look to the defense of its own frontiers. There the discussion ended. Nothing could be done for Austria, despite its critical relationship to the strategic position of Czechoslovakia.[12] Three weeks later, on 7 March 1938, the army staff issued a long directive on the conduct of a future land war, a directive subsequently approved by Gamelin. It read in part: *"An initial French offensive* is only to be contemplated in the event that Germany should first concentrate her efforts in eastern Europe against Czechoslovakia or Poland."[13] In this long document, drafted at a time when an Anschluss seemed imminent, there was not a single mention of Austria or of its threatened independence.

It is unnecessary to dwell on this point, particularly as the reader will find the pattern all too familiar. Like the Rhineland "crisis" of 1936, the Austrian "crisis" of 1938 appeared with the sureness of a Canadian winter and elicited as much surprise. It simply was not an issue over which the French intended to fight, a judgment which is as easy to make now as it was difficult to concede publicly at the time. And so like the Rhineland affair, the takeover of Austria was made out to be a crisis—the cover story for the fact that Austria was not worth the risk of a European war. Domestically, of course, the emergency was well rung. On 10 March, the day before Germany presented its ultimatum to Austria, Premier Chautemps had resigned office owing to mounting political difficulties. Thus, on the eleventh, the cabinet had convened to decide the composition of the succeeding administration. The crisis they had met to discuss, therefore, had to do with the next premier of France and not the next ruler of Austria. To their discomfort, however, the news from Vienna intruded into their deliberations. With what one would guess was some haste the ministers agreed to have Mussolini measured for his reactions—a belated démarche that failed—and to have the defense ministry authorize some entirely unspecified "military measures," which were never taken in any event.[14] There the French response to the Anschluss ended. When Hitler's troops marched into Austria on the following day, 12 March, there was no sign or suggestion of French resistance.

Only then, like the Rhineland affair, could the legend of the crisis emerge. With the event realized and the course decided, the French government turned to disavow all responsibility for what had happened. As usual, it had been the British government which had scotched French hopes of a united front against Hitler. And as usual, this version could carry much weight if it were constructed with an artful blend of what was true and what was merely plausible. Certainly, it was clear enough that the British had no stomach for going beyond purely verbal protests on

Austria's behalf. "What's all this fuss about?" they asked themselves in private.[15] From this came the plausibility of Chautemps' claim that France would have resorted to "military measures" had Britain been disposed to follow—a claim that for all its apparent credibility was certainly fallacious and deceptive. And it is with the same profound suspicion that one must treat Daladier's contention that it had been word of Britain's cheerless advice to Vienna which had caused all notion of resistance to vanish from the French cabinet on 11 March. So far as one may determine, that notion was as diminutive before and during that meeting as it was prominent in the legend which ensued.[16]

Thus the French government, with no express commitment to defend Austria, did not believe that its fate was worth a European war and, in any event, could not decide upon a practical course of military action. Which came first is a matter for historical conjecture, for it is impossible to say whether the French response might have been different under more favorable military circumstances. What is clear is that the French military situation certainly complemented, if it did not actually inspire, the political decision to refrain from overt resistance. In what proved to be an early glimpse of the Czech crisis, itself ushered in with the Anschluss, the service commanders reviewed their options—no longer in the Mediterranean where the picture looked brighter but in central Europe where the same limiting conditions prevailed as before. The navy could do nothing to prevent the Anschluss; it merely could join in the long war such a union might provoke. The army could attack in the west, but for what purpose? All the indications were that Austria would fall long before any decision could be expected in the clash between French and German forces.[17] Like the navy, therefore, the army was really talking about selecting an issue on which the next great war would be fought rather than presenting its services as a deterrent to aggression. As for the air force, that strange mixture of ambition and bravado which had shaped its course under Pierre Cot was swiftly evaporating. With Cot's departure in mid-January 1938 and the conterminous shift in focus from the Mediterranean to central Europe, the mood within the air staff changed perceptibly. From the sanguine appreciations of what the air force would be able to do in the future, emphasis shifted to its present state of incapacitation. It was in this atmosphere, long before the Anschluss and indeed well before he succeeded Féquant as chief of the air staff, that General Vuillemin addressed the first of his chilling forecasts to the new air minister Guy La Chambre. "I am quite convinced," declared this most fêted member of the prestigious Conseil Supérieur de l'Air, "that if a conflict erupts this year, the French air force would be wiped out in a few days."[18] From the moment this officer assumed command of the air force, in February 1938, it was singularly clear that the air staff would do all it could to discourage military adventures abroad. Action against the Anschluss, therefore, either to deter Germany or to exact retribution from it, was not open for serious debate or discussion.

To be sure, the seizure of Austria lacks neither historical interest nor significance. Without doubt it was as illuminating as any of the previous "crises." It underlined the growing impotence of Britain and France in eastern Europe, confirmed the suspicions of a minority that the Nazis were really much better opportunists than conspirators, and suggested that the Wehrmacht still had much to learn about the use and maintenance of its motorized-mechanized vehicles.[19] It was a commentary, too, on the development of the Rome-Berlin axis—as Mussolini grudgingly witnessed the erasure of his interests in Austria—and yet further confirmation of the fact that none of the famous incidents of the 1930s was to catch the French unaware. But its principal historical significance, one would think, lies in the fact that it set the stage for the German seizure of Czechoslovakia, a country with whom France did have a formal alliance and to whom successive French governments had repeated their pledge of assistance.[20] Although in the end the bulk of the German forces did not enter Czechoslovakia from the direction of Vienna, the fall of Austria in March 1938 was seen by all observers as exposing the Czechs to an entirely new strategic menace. It was this that prompted the Chamberlain government in London and the new Blum government in Paris to review their diplomatic and military options in the second half of March 1938.

So far as the British were concerned, the differences between Austria and Czechoslovakia were marginal. Neither enjoyed an alliance with Britain, neither involved British interests on a scale that could justify a new European war, and both undeniably contained large enough German communities to lend some credence to Hitler's irredentist demands. Thus interest and reason together encouraged the British government to see that the approaching Czech crisis did not precipitate a major continental war. Indeed, by Chamberlain's lights a peaceful solution of this problem, including a transference of some Czech lands to German control, promised to serve as a foundation for a new European edifice—one built within an anti-Communist quadrangle linking Berlin, Rome, Paris, and London. The problem of course, as it so often was, was the French.

The French were committed to Czechoslovakia. What is more, they had gone out of their way since the days of the first Blum government to proclaim their fidelity to this alliance. Desirous of maintaining the possibility of a second military front in Europe, of which Czechoslovakia was to be the principal bastion, successive governments in Paris had stayed in the east, neither salvaging nor augmenting their investment; and it was with the same policy that they were caught in the spring of 1938 as the Czech crisis approached. The time for standing pat was almost at an end. It was when France came to face up to its predicament that the British hoped to steer it toward the path of least resistance, the path of compromise, of appeasement at its best or its worst.

It must be said that the British did not underestimate this chosen task. By their reading it was no foregone conclusion that the French would follow like the docile sheep which our histories would later make of them. Certainly not in March 1938 with Léon Blum back in the premier's office and Paul-Boncour returned to the Quai d'Orsay. Indeed, from the Thames it looked very much as if France would honor its obligations should Germany seek to subdue Czechoslovakia by force.[21] No less disturbing was the suspicion that the French were determined to act up to their words partly because they assumed that Britain would have to follow them into war. Delbos had said as much to Ambassador Phipps. France, he had reflected, "will be fighting for her existence, and Great Britain will not be able to stand aside." This state of mind, Phipps judged, was "clearly dangerous," an assessment that may have carried all the more weight among Foreign Office officials who reckoned that the French were probably right.[22] Yet another irritant that had surfaced in Anglo-French relations by the spring of 1938, one which worried the British as much as it annoyed them, was the still skeletal character of French fortifications between Lille and Dunquerque. Unless new construction was undertaken, so the CID advised, the Germans might descend on the Channel ports in some surprise attack. What is more, and this clearly is what angered the British, it seemed probable that such a glaring oversight had been intended by the French as a "deliberate inducement to compel us to intervene on land in order to safeguard an area which we have regarded as vital for centuries."[23] Indeed, with their misgivings fanned by issues such as these, they were in no mood to hear talk of French offensives in North Africa. Already unnerved by these hints of some new vigor in Paris, it would be safe to say that Whitehall found little recompense in Gamelin's hair-raising prediction that "in the future, it may be a question not of bringing divisions to France, but of sending divisions to North Africa."[24] Confronted by such a France, the British again were on edge: a France apparently loyal to Czechoslovakia, a France which assumed a British continental commitment and then too easily talked of peripheral ventures in Africa.

Upset by what they heard from Paris the British did in 1938 what they had done in 1935 and again in 1936. Sensing the tensions in Anglo-French relations, the British suddenly flashed the green light on staff talks. This was becoming a classic response. It was when the French were getting out of line, not the Germans, that the British returned to the notion of joint planning—the bait made irresistible by the dictates of French grand strategy. Thus it was that the stuttering, on-again-off-again decision the British took between 6 and 29 April in favor of staff contacts was not in reaction to Germany's behavior but in anticipation of that of France. The French were to be reined in. This was a decision which was taken against the express advice of the chiefs of staff and which was abjectly defended on the ground that it would be "churlish" to give the French anything less than was contemplated. The talks, after all, would fall under the old March 1936 agreement; they would concentrate on French aid to Britain; they would not be based on the assumption of Italian hostility, and therefore would not involve defense considerations in the Mediterranean or in the Far East. What is more, they would be conducted only at the level of the service attachés and be confined to subject matter that was "purely technical" and "wholly hypothetical." In short, they were to be no more than a modest extension of the periodic intelligence exchanges which had been taking place since 1936. Most assuredly the British were determined to pay as small a fee as possible to ingratiate themselves once again with the French and so to exercise the maximum influence on French decision making.[25]

As it happened, developments in Paris were already lending themselves to such a tactic. While it is true that fidelity to the Czech alliance was *de rigueur*, even within the private precincts of French officialdom, it was equally clear that doubts about the practicality of such a commitment were legion. Having but two days earlier assured the Czech ambassador that France would honor its commitments, Blum went to the

Comité Permanent on 15 March and asked how this was to be done. The response, as he may well have anticipated, was not encouraging.[26] Vuillemin was quick to repeat his prediction that war in 1938 would mean the annihilation of the French air force. In his turn, Gamelin said what he had been saying all along. Any French land offensive would take time to launch and even more time to execute with requisite care and caution; the Russian land army could do little in the east without the full, and most unlikely, cooperation of Poland and Roumania, while operations of the Soviet air force from Czech bases were likely to be thwarted by the early bombing raids of the Luftwaffe.

   The war ministry seconded the observations of its commander-in-chief. Echoing the army's familiar counsels with admirable precision, Daladier's *cabinet* addressed a series of reminders to the premier's office.

> The strength of our *couverture* force limits us to a simple *prise de gages*, one that would be restricted in scope and effect and that would be supported by only limited air action against certain key German centers.
>
> To increase and expand this action will require the participation of *all of our mobilized forces.*
>
> We will then lose the advantage of surprise and, by the time we intervene, if we do, it is likely that the plight of Czechoslovakia will already be very critical. [27]

In other words, there was every chance that Czechoslovakia would fall long before French pressure could be effective and, indeed, before its own forces could be of any value to France. It was this dilemma that so tortured the French, the idea of going to war on behalf of a country whose early destruction seemed likely. And it was precisely this dilemma which Gamelin exploited from March onward, feigning optimism and deceiving no one. It was cold comfort, as he well knew, to raise the possibility of reviving Czechoslovakia at the end of a long European war. It was the peril of the situation, therefore, and not the promise, to which he was really alluding when he addressed Daladier on the day following the CPDN meeting. "In view of this, even if Czechoslovakia should initially find herself in a difficult situation (*en situation difficile*), everything would be settled by the [eventual] peace treaty, as it was in the case of Serbia and Roumania."[28]

   The short-lived Blum government fell in the second week of April 1938, like the premier's first administration and like that of Chautemps, for domestic political reasons rather than for reasons of foreign policy. It was at this juncture that the premiership again fell to Edouard Daladier, a change which the British were to watch with more than passing interest. A change of this order could affect dramatically their chances for insinuating themselves into French policy making. In particular what concerned them was the ministry of foreign affairs. Daladier would do, Eric Phipps adjudged; he was well known and on the whole one who "impresses me favourably" even though those who knew him well jokingly referred to him as *un roseau peint en fer*. What was disturbing, however, was the possibility that Daladier would retain Paul-Boncour at the Quai d'Orsay, "that alarmingly light-weight Paul-Boncour." This unflattering appraisal Phipps did not intend in its obvious sense, for he knew that Paul-Boncour was no pushover. Indeed, that was the problem. The difficulty with the present incumbent, it seems, was his reported advocacy of intervention in Spain, his continued opposition to any rapprochement with Italy, and—one is entitled to guess—his unwavering pledge to Czechoslovakia. None of this pleased the Chamberlain government, an attitude of mind which prompted the ambassador in Paris to make an unauthorized but subsequently commended intervention in French politics. He explained it all in a private letter to Lord Halifax, the man who had succeeded Eden as foreign secretary in February 1938.

> We were nearly cursed by having Paul-Boncour at the Quai d'Orsay . . . I therefore had Daladier and Paul Reynaud informed indirectly that it would be most unfortunate if Paul-Boncour were to remain . . . Paul Reynaud was convinced by my message and used his influence with Daladier in the desired sense. Daladier himself was in full agreement, but hesitated a great deal owing to inevitable considerations of electoral and political expediency. [29]

In the end, however, Daladier was seen to have done the "semi-right thing," which is to say that he had not behaved entirely as Phipps had planned. He had dumped Paul-Boncour, but in his stead he had appointed Georges Bonnet—a man on the right of the Radical Socialist party, an ambitious politician for whom the British had no particular brief but who promised to be safe and solid, "far less dangerous" than Paul-Boncour.[30]

Having settled into office by mid-April 1938 the Daladier administration nervously awaited the Czech crisis. The initiative for the time being lay elsewhere, with the German Sudetenlanders inside Czechoslovakia, with the Benes government in Prague, and with Hitler's regime in Berlin. For its part, the new Daladier government saw no greater room for maneuver than what had been found by previous administrations. Indeed, the circumstances were not at all promising. Much was already clear: that France lacked the military resources either to deter Germany from acts of aggression in the east or to preserve a country like Czechoslovakia from defeat; that other countries in the east lacked either the firepower (Roumania), the political inclination (Poland), or the avenue for intervention (Russia) to support Czechoslovakia in a war against Germany;[31] that the fragile Anglo-French entente would be subjected to intense strain as long as the British feared the French commitment to Prague. These were the factors that obliged the French to listen attentively, receptively, to the compromise proposals that were already being drafted in London.

For the French, however, Czechoslovakia was not and had never been another Austria. The disappearance of the latter had never sparked a crisis in Paris, but the threatened disappearance of Czechoslovakia surely did. A variety of considerations were in play, each of which increased in intensity, rather than diminished, before the mounting German peril. First, the Czechs were allies and for that reason could make a powerful appeal to French *honneur*, an appeal for which Daladier showed great personal sensitivity. As he later candidly admitted in a private letter to Chamberlain: "France is governed by two equally powerful feelings: the strong desire not to have to fulfil its obligations, but also the determination to act honorably if Germany forces its hand."[32] Second, the Czechs had a well-trained army, one which the French had counted on to hold down at least forty German divisions in the east. Indeed, the critical notion of a second military front in Europe rested firmly on the holding power of the Czech garrison. Third, if ever Russia were to be enlisted as a principal component of that second front it would be Czechoslovakia that would seal the bargain—Czechoslovakia being the one country in eastern Europe for whom the Russians were obliged to fight.[33] Fourth, if the Czechs were defeated, Germany would acquire their great industrial resources like the famous armaments works at Skoda; and the oil fields of southeastern Europe would be left exposed to further German expansion.[34] Finally, that which brought the preceding considerations together, the French feared that Germany's drive eastward was primarily a muscle-building exercise to prepare for the final test of strength with the Third Republic. In their eyes Germany still regarded France as enemy number one, the one power against whom Nazi revanchist sentiments consistently had been directed. These were the reasons why France had drawn itself to Czechoslovakia and had persevered in this loyalty, despite all the perils which had surrounded the alliance since France's loss of the Rhineland.

It was the combination of these diverse arguments, those which dictated prudence and those which called for resolution, that shaped the foreign policy of the Daladier government—more or less as it had shaped that of its predecessors. In this case, however, it may be true to say that these two themes came to be identified with two different men, that of resolution with the premier, and that of prudence with the foreign minister.

Georges Bonnet was never regarded as a very attractive figure, the kind of man about whom one almost wishes many things had remained unsaid—and not because they were untrue. What is one to think of a man whose friends would say: "When he walks he does not go straight but moves sideways in such a manner that all one sees of him is a long, powerful nose that seems to scent every danger and every prey."[35] Forty-nine years of age in 1938, Bonnet went to the Quai d'Orsay with an enviable record of career successes. An outstanding student, a veteran decorated with the *croix de guerre*, an accomplished civil servant, a former minister of both commerce and finance, and most recently an ambassador to the United States, here was one whose intellect and industry were beyond doubt. But unlike Yvon Delbos, another Radical Socialist and man of the Dordogne, Bonnet thirsted for power. Indeed, his obituary in *Le Monde* contained the severe judgment that this had been his only goal.[36] It was this too evident quest, in which he is said to have been joined by an ambitious wife wickedly nicknamed "Soutien-Georges," that so offended many of his political colleagues and rankled many others. At any rate, although distantly associated with pro-German circles in Paris, Georges Bonnet seems always to have evoked the image of manipulator and opportunist. By almost all accounts neither a man of principle nor one of great moral character, he seemed at the time to be a far cry from the stern and increasingly intransigent Paul-Boncour. In fact, from the outset he admitted his intention to "undo the work of his predecessor" and distinguished between the public commitment to Czechoslovakia and the "prudent policy" which it would be necessary to conduct behind the scenes.[37] This of course was exactly the line of thought which the British hoped to exploit, a tactic to which Bonnet seemed to fall eager victim.

Daladier, however, must be seen in a different light. In one sense the new premier was much like Maurice Gamelin, reflective and at times agonizingly introspective. "He worried ceaselessly as to what he was going to do, what he was doing and what he had done."[38] In another sense he was like Bonnet, in fact not a man of great internal strength and certainly not the charging bull he let on to be. Indeed, there was something to the joke about this "bull with snail's horns." But if Bonnet's energy and drive were fired principally by personal ambition, Daladier's, ironically, came from self-doubt and a resolution to conquer the hesitation and weakness he sensed within. It was this that André Géraud spied in Daladier's character. "Conscious of his weakness, he feared that all could see it."[39] And to conceal it, he not only blustered in a superficial sense but he also determined to overcome it. In 1938 Daladier was bent on playing the role of the strong and decisive statesman, a role which to his mortification he had abandoned in the heat of February 1934 and which he was now desperate to retake and fulfil.[40] However genuine his strength, therefore, one can see Daladier resolved to honor at least the letter of the Franco-Czech alliance, to prove himself a man of strength, and to expunge the memories and the gibes of past weakness. He had returned to power, he believed, when strength of will was critical to the fortunes of France. Unless stopped in its tracks Germany, he argued, will be able to turn against the western powers if they, through their own weakness, give it the resources to wage the long war for which it is still unprepared."[41]

Yet it was precisely here that the French were vulnerable. For in fact it was not Bonnet and those like him who had dealt Britain the high card, it was Daladier and those of his persuasion. The premier's case rested on the claim that Germany was still incapable of fighting a long war; but the same was true of France, as true in 1938 as it had been in the 1920s when the national strategy had been evolved. Without Britain France could not entertain the idea of such a conflict; without joint staff planning the entente would never mature into an effective military alliance; and without French willingness to consider British formulae for compromise on the Czech issue that planning was likely to be further delayed. This is what was at stake on 28-29 April when the French ministers conferred with Chamberlain and Halifax in London.

At that moment the talks between the Czechs and Sudeten Germans had reached a new impasse; the peace of Europe rested on what they and the great powers might decide to do. Disarmed by a subtly unencouraging brief from Gamelin,[42] Daladier argued with Chamberlain for two days, then finally made his bargain. The British accepted the principle of joint staff talks in all three services—with only the air talks to begin forthwith—and agreed to establish "confidential informal contact" for the sake of discussing the purchase and transport of oil, foodstuffs, coal, nonferrous metals, and textile raw materials.[43] In return, Daladier agreed to back a joint démarche in Prague in favor of additional Czech concessions to the Sudeten Germans. It was an unhappy arrangement for the most part; neither side was pleased about the staff arrangements—the British because they went too far and the French because they did not go far enough—and certainly Daladier resented the notion that it was fine to lean on Prague but not on Berlin.[44] Undeniably, however, the British felt much better with a foot in the door, the entrée to a greater role in defusing the German-Czech dispute; and Bonnet, despite his feigned displeasure over the "murky business" in London, was quick to confide that he had deliberately left "full latitude" to the English—a tactic which the minister was clever enough to have employed in fact or to have invented in fiction. It was, after all, merely a more outrageous version of a tactic that had been practiced by many of his predecessors—concealing a French policy within the folds of an English one.[45]

Furthermore, however, one interprets French motivation, there does appear to have been a shift in responsibility in April 1938. Prior to this conference its commitment to Czechoslovakia automatically made France the arbiter of European peace. The Germans wanted to localize any war that might prove expedient in the pursuit of their aims in the east. Only the French could decide the stakes for which Hitler was to gamble the fortunes of his Reich. Only they could decide whether an attack on Czechoslovakia would be the signal for a war between at least two great powers. But it was now very much open to question whether France had the military means to match this heavy and clearly distasteful responsibility. Confronted by the threat of war, the outcome of which he could not confidently predict, Daladier recoiled before the idea of unilateral resistance; and it would be safe to say that not a shred of military intelligence lay on his desk to contradict him. He turned, as he had to turn, to Great Britain—the natural ally but now an ironical choice. By accepting the bargain of late April, exchanging staff talks for a British mandate in affairs which until now had rarely interested His Majesty's Government, Daladier tied France to a country whose own military advisers were even more adamant than their French counterparts about the need to avoid war. This was the bargain that allowed Britain to be a principal in the Czech drama, one concluded not out of Bonnet's professed desire to use the British but out of Daladier's strategically oriented insistence that war without Britain was unthinkable.[46] Thus it was that the outcome of the two policy themes, that of prudence and that of resolution, was essentially the same—however much the motives behind them may have differed. Whether to shirk its responsibilities, or whether to honor them more effectively, the Daladier government had hitched its wagon to a British star.[47]

Of all the events that are recalled in this book none is more familiar than that of the Munich crisis. Countless articles and books have been addressed to the subject, most of which demand examination in their original form. Chamberlain's famous flights to Germany, the follow-up Anglo-French conferences in London where ministers acted, in Bullitt's words "like little boys doing dirty things behind the barn,"[48] the relentless pressure from both London and Paris to which the Czech government fell victim, the apparently timely intervention of Mussolini to whom credit went for averting war by proposing the four-power meeting in Munich: these are the milestones with which few are strangers today. It is with conscious brevity, therefore, that one offers this summary interpretation of the French role in Munich—that tragic episode in which every care was taken to ensure that the Czechs would surrender, so that Germany would not have to attack, so that France and Britain would be spared from war.

It does bear repeating that this analysis, like the work as a whole, remains focused on the relationship between foreign policy and military capacity. It certainly is not a comprehensive study of France and Munich and, ruefully perhaps, does not satisfy the grand requirements rightly solicited by those like Professor René Girault.[49] Parliament, press, parties, and pressure groups are effectively ignored, set aside, perhaps for some other work at some other time.

Some care has been taken to express the importance which the French government attributed to Czechoslovakia. Were this to be denied, in favor of the view that the Czechs would be abandoned on the slightest pretext, the events preceding the Munich drama would acquire an entirely different cast. Indeed, there would be no drama, no crisis, no debate within France. Munich, like the Rhineland affair or the Anschluss would be no more than a post facto crisis, fabricated for the historical record. But this was not the case. The French had good reasons for being in Czechoslovakia, not even the least of which had much to do with altruism; and certainly one should not exaggerate the facility with which they might have cast off the Czechs as the crisis approached. Even as unsympathetic a group as the British chiefs of staff had concluded that France "having remained inactive in the face of Germany's coup against Austria, will be bound to assist Czechoslovakia against German aggression if it is not to sink to the level of a second-rate Power."[50] And again the reader is reminded that the assumptions which had governed the French decision under Delbos to stand pat in the east, without advance or retreat, still prevailed in the summer and autumn of 1938. The assumptions which had been made about the inevitability of a German attack on France and about the latter's dependence on an allied military coalition—one front of which would be established around the Czech garrison—virtually prohibited any snap judgment from Paris. The peace of Europe and the security of France would depend on it.

It was this, this issue of war or peace, against which the importance of Czechoslovakia had to be assayed. As central as Czechoslovakia was to French strategic planning, could its fate be worth a new European war—particularly when no one seemed sure how long it could resist a combined assault of the Wehrmacht and Luftwaffe? Folklore, of course, barely credits the Daladier government with so much as a momentary pause over this question. Conversely, those who have studied this government's behavior have long been aware of a serious debate within the cabinet—one that was far more pronounced than anything experienced within the Chamberlain cabinet. Although there are differences of detail between the findings of one scholar and those of another, there is a consensus that there was a three-way split. One group, most commonly associated with Reynaud, Mandel, and Champetier de Ribes, consistently denounced the pressure tactics on Prague and vowed to push the cabinet to war in the event of a German attack on Czechoslovakia. For them, all the reasons for which France had committed itself to the Czechs were sufficient to justify a resort to arms. A second group, normally associated with the foreign minister, saw things quite differently. Bonnet and his supporters did not believe that Czechoslovakia was worth a war and for that reason sympathized with and encouraged Chamberlain's efforts to obviate the need for a German assault on Czechoslovakia.[51] A third group, usually associated with Daladier, occupied the middle ground—on the whole disposed to support the Czechs, to go to war should the Germans actually resort to force, but tormented by the *triste* intelligence reports tendered by the military authorities.[52] It was they who wavered in September 1938, who ultimately but grudgingly accepted the need for the distasteful tactics which Chamberlain and Bonnet were determined to use on the Benes regime in Prague, but who may well have rallied to the cause of war had Hitler seen fit to use force. Such, cryptically surveyed, is the kind of division one finds within the Daladier cabinet, a division to which one must refer again momentarily.[53]

Just as one must reject the view that Czechoslovakia had lost its importance for France, that there was no genuine crisis, and that the cabinet had rolled effortlessly into Chamberlain's embrace, so one must rebel against that strangely durable notion that the French high command counseled resistance. To be sure, the longevity of this notion may be explained by the fact that it was eminently logical. Had not this command long defended the principle of a second front, as an integral part of its emphasis on allied coalitions? Who but the strategists had awarded Czechoslovakia such strategic significance, had linked the Czech military potential with the defense of French security? It would have been entirely logical, therefore, for the military authorities to have pressed this strategic factor on the government, to have marshaled the arguments for defending Czechoslovakia, even if it meant doing so from the apparently neutral ground Gamelin, the *technicien*, insisted upon occupying. And just as certainly, it was precisely this approach which the army command subsequently claimed to have pursued throughout the crisis.

Without invoking all the evidence that has been employed elsewhere,[54] it seems clear that this view is mistaken. The army would not abandon its long-standing prohibition against early, ill-prepared offensives and in any event, for that very reason, had not organized its mobile forces for such rapid offensive plunges. Thus it could do no more in 1938 than had been possible in 1936. General Réquin, the officer who would have led the French forces against Germany's western divisions is said to have looked with "absolute horror" on the prospect of such an assignment, predicting that it would mean the "death of a race."[55] Indeed, the kind of advice offered in 1938 was very familiar, exactly the sort of admonitions with which the army had greeted Daladier in June 1936: no offensive move until the *couverture* was in place, and then only operations on a limited scale, what was called a *prise de gages*; nothing more ambitious than this without general mobilization; and no strategic offensive for something approaching two years—by which time Germany was expected to be weakened by the multiple efforts of an allied coalition.[56] Specifically, so far as the Czechs were concerned, the government received no assurance that the Czechs could resist for long, that French action could prevent a quick German victory in the east, or that France could defeat Germany in the ensuing war. Quite the reverse in fact. The principal accounts that have been left to us, those of Daladier, Gamelin, and General Georges, suggest very clearly that no case was made by the military for resisting German demands on Czechoslovakia.[57] Indeed, as I have argued elsewhere, Gamelin's consummately subtle counsels of inaction could not but have strengthened the hands of the Bonnetistes—tacitly endorsing their view that Czechoslovakia was not worth a new European war.[58]

The French air force, of course, had never pretended to be impartial in 1938. General Vuillemin had preached for months against accepting the risk of war; the existence of the air army, he said, was at stake. Germany's superiority was so great that the French air forces would be cleared from the skies within a fortnight, while the cities of France would be left exposed to the caprice of Luftwaffe bombing squadrons.[59] So distraught had this general become that Daladier politely abandoned one interview with him on the eve of the Munich conference. "So upset was he that I decided it was pointless to continue our talk, having thanked him briefly for speaking with such candor and honesty."[60] Clearly, the air staff's reading of the current air imbalance was so bleak and pessimistic that no government could have afforded to dismiss it lightly.

Having outlined the kinds of divisions one finds within the cabinet, and the general disposition of military advice to the government, one has yet to explore the connections between the two. The so-called hardliners, it seems, clung to their position despite the unpromising thrust of the military appreciations. Indeed, whatever may be said of their courage, they really were taking an extremely dangerous gamble: either that Hitler could be outstared or, if he could not, that Britain would follow France into war. Certainly they had no reason to believe from the generals' reports that Czechoslovakia could be saved from defeat or that France could win a single-handed war with Germany. As for the group around the foreign minister, it is doubtful whether they paid any more attention to these daunting military assessments—other than to use them as justification for a policy they preferred to pursue on other grounds. This, one hastens to say, is an essentially intuitive conclusion, for Bonnet was insistent that the military circumstances were prominent in his calculations.[61] But again, without plunging the reader into the details of Bonnet's public and private maneuvering in September 1938, one may simply endorse the general view that the minister was far more preoccupied with how war could be avoided than on what terms and in what conditions it could be fought.[62] Owing to the strength of their respective assumptions, assumptions only marginally based on the military circumstances, neither of these groups appears to have been greatly influenced by professional military appraisals.

It was the third group, ultimately that of the majority, to whom these appreciations came to have genuine significance. These were men who accepted the importance of Czechoslovakia, men who only slowly had drifted away from colleagues like Mandel and Reynaud as a temperamental inclination to resist Germany had been overtaken by a sobering vision of the future. This vision, to be sure, was not inspired by military considerations alone. It is clear, for instance, that one of Daladier's reservations stemmed from a fear that a new war would prepare Europe for a devastating Communist epidemic; and no doubt considerations relating to parties, pressure groups, and personalities played a part in French decision making prior to Munich.[63] But it seems equally certain that this vision of the future did have a military component and that this component did serve as a restraining influence on many cabinet ministers. On the one hand, they knew why the ties with Czechoslovakia had been preserved and were both intellectually and temperamentally disposed to defend them.[64] On the other hand, they could hardly treat with cavalier abandon the grim forecasts offered by the chiefs of staff on both sides of the Channel. Although he refused at the time to use such forecasts as a convenient justification for bowing to British initiative—trying instead to minimize French military deficiencies—Daladier was later to acknowledge the importance of the military situation.[65] His generals, he quite truthfully recalled, had insisted on pegging their confidence to a wartime coalition that did not exist but had declined to say much about the holding power of the Czech fortifications. What is more, he later came to suspect the "flippancy" and the "blindness" of French military intelligence in 1938, complaining that they had exaggerated "the size of the German forces and consistently minimized those of Britain and France."[66] As for the air force, he was to say many times that the air balance "constantly conditioned my thinking . . . we always came back to the same problem," an admission which Gamelin for one took to mean that it had been "the air question which took M. Daladier to Munich."[67]

Yet ultimately what took Daladier to Munich was older than the plight of French aviation, older even than the cautious land strategy which for years had precluded any sudden punch into Germany's industrial midriff. What he was told in 1938, what he had been told since 1936, was that France could not go to war without firm assurances of British support. With this always in mind, and only underscored by the depressing specifics of the situation in 1938, the premier had to turn to London. Having done so in April 1938, it became a race for time with both Hitler and Chamberlain—the prime minister trying to render an alliance unnecessary by getting the Czechs to yield, Daladier trying to induce that alliance by tough talk and the promotion of joint staff conversations. The outcome was never in doubt, for by the arrangement that was made at the end of April 1938 the British were to have a commanding voice in both enterprises—the pace of joint planning, which they preferred to retard, and the degree of pressure applied in Prague, which they were prepared to increase with Hitler's mounting demands.

Doubtless it could be argued that Daladier and the cabinet majority might have regained the initiative simply by calling a halt to their own involvement in the pressuring of the Czechs—even if this had meant the risk of offending Britain and further delaying joint planning. But to what end should this have been done? By ending their pressure on Prague the French would have ensured Czech resistance to the Sudeten demands, an eventuality that would have forced Hitler either to back down or go to war. One may argue forever that the former would have happened, but nothing will dispel the possibility of war instead. And it was on this precise note that Daladier had entered as premier and immediately set out to secure the alliance which all French strategists long had considered indispensable. British policy, therefore, too long exploited as a pretext for French inaction, was fast acquiring the force of a genuine reason—precisely because the threat of war was more real now that it had been for twenty years. At last a French cabinet had within it a majority of ministers who would have defied Hitler had the assurance of British support been readily forthcoming, had that assurance been accompanied by serious staff conversations and, conversely, had it not been scuttled by the entirely pessimistic appraisals of the British chiefs of staff.[68]

The Munich crisis, therefore, did not call up the Anglo-French alliance. Indeed, so far as the British were concerned the strengthening of ties at this moment only would have encouraged the French to be more intransigent. In September 1938 the British government clearly identified its interests with the irresolution and weakness it rightly detected and obviously promoted within diverse French quarters. France had to be guided and manipulated, like some unruly offspring. It was to this tactic that Ronald Campbell of the Paris embassy referred in a "secret and private" note to Orme Sargent in the Foreign Office. Acknowledging how badly the French were being treated by the British government, how badly informed they were kept, Campbell complained that this was no way to keep the French on the "straight path" or to "prevent them taking initiatives on questions which interest us." There is much talk here of how the "initiative in policy" has passed to London. "If we wish to maintain French acquiescence in this state of affairs, we must be careful to *ménager* the French Government."[69] So in fact the French were regarded very much like opponents, the side that could spoil the best laid plans.

Little wonder that joint planning was left to suffer in neglect. Communications between the British and French had been glaringly inadequate. For instance, on the very eve of the Munich meeting, when tensions were highest, an air officer reported on his visit to Paris on 28 September.

> I informed the French that I was not in a position to discuss our various war plans as these depended on so many circumstances which are as yet indeterminate . . . I was informed that owing to various similar indeterminate circumstances . . . they themselves were unable to be precise as to the war plans they would adopt.[70]

The results of such conversations were intended to be minimal. By November 1938 the naval arrangements were being described as adequate for concerted action against Germany, but quite inadequate for operations against Germany and Italy combined. Army conversations had proved even less productive. While logistical work had nearly been completed for getting two British divisions and an Advanced Air Striking Force (AASF) to France, hardly a word had been exchanged on how these forces were to be used and where they were to be concentrated. Arrangements of this kind, it was feared, "would tend to commit us to a part in the French plan." The air talks, it is true, had made substantial progress by the end of 1938, although most of the arrangements had been of a technical nature and although much still had to be done on the subjects of aircraft recognition, the integration of the air raid warning systems, and the assurance of reliable communications between London and its AASF.[71] But the basic problem remained, that of attitude. The British chiefs of staff, the Committee of Imperial Defence and the Chamberlain cabinet simply could not shake the belief that alliance with France was more likely to provoke war than prevent it. Simply put, there is little sign in the last quarter of 1938 that the British had changed their mind on the perils of closer joint planning with France. Munich had not led to a sudden about-face.

Nevertheless, there were some hints that a change was in the making. Some British observers soon began worrying about the implications which Munich might carry for future French policy. In a minute filled with insight and candor, Orme Sargent of the Foreign Office reflected on Munich as a point of departure.

> Til now we have always claimed and indeed exercised the right to intervene actively in the problems of Europe both domestic and international whenever we felt it desirable to do so. For this purpose we have collaborated with the French—or to put it crudely we have used the French army and the French system of alliances as one of the instruments with which to exert our authority on the continent. It is sometimes said that this policy . . . has meant in practice that we have been tied to France's "apron-string." If looked at another way it may with equal truth be said that we have used France as a shield, behind which we have maintained ourselves in Europe since our disarmament.
>
> In any case this state of affairs presupposed an active and positive policy on the part of France and if France now decides, as indeed it must, to abandon this policy we will have to adapt our own accordingly.

Such a change, Sargent went on to say, had many positive features. In particular, the chances of war in Europe were likely to diminish as French policy, became more "passive." In turn, the "need for expeditionary forces ready for service in France will be less apparent and Anglo-French staff conversations will lose a good deal of their *raison d'être*." All this, assuredly, was calculated to warm English hearts. But Sargent had not finished. On a note which the Foreign Office was to sound repeatedly in the ensuing months, this minute ended abruptly with the following:

> On the other hand it must be realised that if, in spite of the change in the balance of power in Europe, we feel bound to answer Germany or Italy next time they challenge us we will do well not to make our calculations on the assumption that we shall be able to count on French support.[72]

There was much bitterness in Paris, as Sargent well understood. Daladier had not smiled at Munich, nor at Le Bourget where to his shame and disbelief cheering crowds had greeted him on his return. He had never shared Chamberlain's notion of appeasement; for him it was an expedient, the wisdom of which he was profoundly doubtful. Furthermore, he believed that he had been taken in by Chamberlain, that "dessicated stick."[73] The staff talks, for which he had paid by supporting British representations in Prague, had remained extremely limited in scope. Now, with Czechoslovakia carved up and its thirty-odd divisions disorganized and scattered, France had lost its most reliable and powerful ally on the continent; and the notion of the eastern front had been all but undermined. As Gamelin put it, there has been "a turnabout in the Central European situation," with Czechoslovakia "virtually incapable of fulfilling her role as a barrier to German expansion in the East."[74] In return France had gained little. There were suggestions that the British were now disturbed by the very weakness which they themselves had helped foment in France;[75] and certainly there was little sign that the recent threat of war had convinced them of the need to accelerate Anglo-French military planning. As Sargent admitted, the French had been used; and they resented it. Now, what was to preoccupy the Foreign Office was not the threat of French resolution, as it had been before Munich, but the threat of French irresolution. Again the fears of a Franco-German deal began to surface, and with them the fears of French passivity in the European Lowlands or toward some future German challenge to the integrity of the British Empire.[76] Thus what one finds in the immediate wake of Munich is the growth of new Anglo-French tensions. It was from these, as had happened so often in the past, that the next step toward a true military alliance would come.

The French clearly were determined to adjust their foreign policy to what Sargent had called the "change in the balance of power." But the exact nature and extent of this adjustment remained uncertain for a time. There were enough signs in the last quarter of 1938 that Bonnet intended to remain on the path of least resistance. Although nothing was to come of the talk about abandoning the Polish alliance, it was evident that Poland and what was left of the Little Entente meant much less to the French now that Czechoslovakia had all but disappeared. Indeed, it was this apparent passivity toward eastern Europe, together with the familiar French distrust of the Soviet Union, that served Bonnet well during his preliminary conversations with Ribbentrop in December on the subject of Franco-German rapprochement.[77] By the same token it was this desire to make Munich a positive point of departure that had moved the minister to sweep his most prominent critics from the Quai d'Orsay and to tangle with Daladier on the subject of an early Franco-Italian rapprochement.[78] Bonnet, in short, had come into the open as an avowed partisan of four-power pact diplomacy and as such stood closer to Chamberlain than to Daladier. The latter, it should be said, had sympathized with Mussolini's proposed pact in 1933 and had even been caught musing about its potential in the immediate aftermath of Munich.[79] However, this man who seemed so conscious and sensitive of his personal dignity and strength of character again had been humiliated by the necessity of Munich and the third-rate role which had been assigned to him there. Partly owing to these bruised sensibilities, one would judge, Daladier simply refused to court Mussolini with the kind of unoffendable eagerness pressed on him by Bonnet and Chamberlain. At the same time, central to his own post-Munich stance was the intention to revive and reaffirm the importance of the French Empire, as a kind of counterbalance to the strategic losses which had been incurred with the sale of Czechoslovakia. This, too, complicated the possibilities of a Franco-Italian rapprochement, for the new imperial emphasis demanded by Daladier did not sit well with the stepped-up colonial claims advanced by Mussolini in November 1938.[80]

Thus there were still two moods in the French government after Munich. The first, that of Bonnet, pressed for conciliation and compromise, working at best from an assumption that the dictators were reasonable men, or at worst from a simple desire to rob them of any pretext for attacking France. The second, that of Daladier, emphasized rearmament, closer military planning with Britain, imperial development, and defiance of Italy.[81] In turn, the confusion over policy that resulted from these disparities in mood was further accentuated by what at first glance seemed to have been muddle-headed military thinking. For senior officers seemed to talk in one breath about rapprochement with Italy and in another about military operations against it. In short, they wanted to enlist Italy in an anti-German front or, if Mussolini opted for the other side, to destroy Italy as quickly as possible.[82] It was perfectly logical in its own terms, but it did contribute to the confusion and uncertainty in French policy. To outside observers, especially to the British, it was unclear whether the greater danger lay in some kind of French action against Italy, or whether the French might settle with Mussolini, slowly retreat into their own splendid isolation, and leave Britain to fend off the imperial pretensions of both fascist dictators.[83] Indeed, the problem seemed all the more complicated to British officials who were gradually moving toward the assumption of Italian hostility while their own prime minister doggedly pursued Mussolini's friendship and cooperation.

Although there is no evidence to suggest that the Daladier government ever entertained the notion of fortress France, the British clearly believed that the risk of such isolationism was there. Something had changed. In the past the Germans had been intent on "trying to separate us from France," but now they seemed more interested in "trying to separate France from us."[84] Ultimately, it was this fear, together with Hitler's mounting effrontery and the acceptance of Italy's probable hostility, that served to forge the Anglo-French alliance in the spring of 1939. For the French it had been a long time coming, for despite the uncertainties that clouded certain aspects of their foreign policy, they had never wavered in their commitment to a strong alliance with Britain.

Just how great this commitment was, how afraid they had been of forfeiting it in September, again was evident in their preparations for the meetings with Chamberlain and Halifax in November. This time the conference was to take place in Paris, as the British saw it—partly to bolster what they feared was a sagging French morale and partly, too, as a more genuine gesture to the importance which France commanded in Britain's global strategy. Nevertheless, if the nature of the relationship appeared to have altered—with Daladier upbraiding Chamberlain for retarding the staff talks and for minimizing Britain's military potential on the continent—it was still clear that the French belief in British support was every bit as pronounced as British belief in the importance of French assistance.[85] Indeed, for the time being it remained more so. The old assumptions were still there and still in the ascendant.

The French, it must be forcefully stated, had never regarded this elusive partnership as anything less than a cooperative venture between two equals. They had not reduced themselves psychologically to the status of a client state, depending on the magnanimity of some powerful guardian. Rather, and in this sense one is inclined to judge them more realistic than the British, they had maintained that the security of Britain, France, and their respective empires was so interdependent that their alliance against the continental or global hegemony of any power was virtually mandatory. The problem as they saw it was that the British perversely refused to admit what was self-evident, thus denying both governments the opportunity to deter the dictators by a united diplomatic front and the facilities with which to manufacture an efficient military coalition. In the circumstances what was especially galling to the French was the recognition that their land armies were regarded as a "cover" force by the British, behind which England hoped to mobilize its economic resources for a *guerre longue*, a "war of attrition" with the dictators.[86] It was the latter concern which had become prominent in Paris by the end of 1938. As the army staff warned their minister and their premier, Edouard Daladier:

> In a word, the only chance the Anglo-French coalition has for victory, and for marshaling its hidden strength in the form of its great war potential, rests on two conditions:
>
> (i) that an early and very serious effort be made to thwart any attempt by a future enemy to end a war quickly by means of a sudden and overwhelming blow.
>
> (ii) that a continual and prolonged collaboration between the two Governments be anticipated and that preparations be made in advance for the sharing of their respective resources.[87]

In the interest of these conditions Daladier was urged to make several recommendations to the British, all of which involved British assistance to France but which also assumed corresponding French support for Britain. For instance, the French wanted enough naval assistance to assure superiority in the Mediterranean, in exchange for which British forces would be given full access to French Mediterranean bases and the prized services of the *Dunquerque* and *Strasbourg*—the only two modern allied battleships in service. By the same token, if France were expected to field a land force approaching one hundred divisions, it seemed appropriate in Paris that the British should accept a serious if not massive military commitment to the continent. To this end the premier was requested to secure this commitment by any means, if necessary by threatening once again to abandon Belgium. Now was the time, so it was argued, for the British to be confronted with some French expectations—"instead of always being interrogated ourselves."[38] As for the air arm, the French command warned the premier against the recent British emphasis on fighter production, a trend which they saw as "inordinately dangerous," and implored him to maximize the number of bombing squadrons which the British intended to operate from French air bases. Indeed, it was in this connection, and with a savage twist on the earlier British proposals of December 1935, that the idea was floated of concentrating the French air force against Italy while leaving the RAF to handle the Luftwaffe.[89] Finally, it was left to the CSDN secretariat to remind Daladier of the imperative need for coordinating Anglo-French economic resources and, ideally, of working toward the creation of a new Commission Interalliée du Ravitaillement.[90]

It was a tall order for Daladier to fill, indeed, an impossible one. Chamberlain had no mandate from his cabinet to draw the strings of alliance any tighter; in fact it had been agreed that French appeals for closer cooperation should be resisted at all costs. Thus the Munich crisis was not to have any immediate effect on the still nascent alliance. Nevertheless, it was responsible for inducing a gradual change in attitude on both sides of the Channel. The close brush with war had reminded the French of the perils of facing it alone, a state of dependency which they had accepted and resented for twenty years. Thus for them Munich reaffirmed rather than questioned the importance of the British alliance;[91] but it also gave expression to bitterness, and it did raise for a time some new possibilities—from a complete pull-out from eastern Europe, to deals with Hitler or Mussolini or both. For their part, the British were alive to these possibilities. In their eyes the Czech situation had been defused and the peace spared only with the grudging support of France. Consequently, they did not underestimate France's loss of thirty Czech divisions just as they did not fail to appreciate the resentment which Chamberlain's proud interventions had let loose within the Daladier cabinet. At the same time they did not expect to capitalize on any gratitude from the Bonnetistes, whose predilection for cooperating with Germany was to become as worrisome to the British after Munich as it had been comforting beforehand. Thus a feeling was gaining expression in British official circles, especially in the Foreign Office, that much greater care would have to be taken with France. It was this resentment and unease, therefore, that Munich had left between Britain and France, that once again would bring them together - as had happened so often in the past.

9

Preparing for War, 1939

January 1939, France was eight months away from a war which now carried the cast of probability. The Anglo-French alliance remained unrealized; the sporadic staff contacts continued under the burden of severe restrictions, little more than technical arrangements designed to confine the Anglo-French dialogue to modest proportions. Even the most explosive of crises, when Europe went to the brink of war in the autumn of 1938, had failed to effect a serious military rapprochement. Indeed, for several months following the prime minister's jubilant return from Munich most of Whitehall remained deeply skeptical of the merits of such an alliance. It was to take time, all that was left of 1938, before its presumed hazards appeared less threatening than its absence. Indeed, as irony would have it, the British were to confess to the dangers of forfeiting that alliance only when they admitted to the vulnerability of France, to the weakness of their continental ally. When they did, at the end of January 1939, the results were dramatic. Within the space of two weeks the British government was to assure the French that it would go to war on behalf of both Holland and Switzerland, and propose an "entirely new and frank phase" of joint conversations and planning. In British eyes, certainly, there was no mistaking the onset of a genuine diplomatic revolution. At no time, so the Committee of Imperial Defence pronounced solemnly, not even prior to 1914, had conversations reached:

the stage of joint Service discussions involving an exchange of views as to the broad strategic problems of a major war, and of joint plans to meet the varying situations which may arise . . . We are indeed assuming a mutual commitment which is even more clear and binding than those existing with some of our Dominions.[1]

Any extensive analysis of this turnabout must be left to studies of a more thoroughly British character. Conversely, it will be appreciated that particular attention is paid here to the role France was to play in British stock-taking. Of premier importance, it may be granted, was the uncomfortable fact that the exercise of appeasement at Munich appeared to have left the dictators unmoved. The recent Anglo-Italian agreement notwithstanding,[2] there was a growing feeling in official London that Chamberlain would never manage to pull off the recruitment of Italy. Instead, a move was afoot in both London and Paris to plan for Mussolini's hostility while doing whatever was possible to ensure his neutrality. As for Germany, even fewer doubts remained of its good intentions. Although only a few openly forecast the final dissolution of the Czech state—what had been left to Prague after the Munich conventions— many others freely predicted future German moves against other European states, both in the west and in the east.[3] Indeed, the burst of everant though exaggerated naiveté which Chamberlain displayed at Heston airport on his return from Munich, when "peace in our time" was offered up to newsreel microphones, concealed a much less sanguine disposition in official Whitehall.

It was this skeptical, pessimistic view that grew in authority during the winter of 1938-1939. In particular, it derived special force from the persistent rumors of an approaching German attack in the west, aimed either at the continental Channel ports or at Britain itself. These rumors, it should be said, had a curious association with French military intelligence—the bulk of them originating within the army's *deuxième bureau*.[4] Prompted by such reports, the British turned with greater interest to the possibility of French support. It is in this light that one may view Chamberlain's suggestion in late November that subsequent staff talks might give even greater attention to the subject of French aid in the event of a German attack on Britain; and one senses, too, a connection between Halifax's admission that such an attack was a real possibility and the ensuing British request for assurance that French air bases would be made available to the RAF in such an eventuality.[5] The new year began on the same jarring note, with French spokesmen making none too subtle reference to the future installation of German air and submarine bases in an occupied Holland, or to Italy's capacity "to bomb our fleet out of effective existence at Alexandria."[6] How much of this belonged to a carefully orchestrated scare tactic may never be known. What is clear is that such rumors, apparently quite ill founded in fact, played havoc with British composure. By the end of January 1939 the government had become unnerved, enough to propose a major and unprecedented step toward the formation of a military alliance. But it had done so not merely in response to a possible German challenge in the west. As usual, much of its motivation stemmed from misgivings about future French action.

The fear that France might foresake the defense of the European Lowlands was hardly new to Whitehall. After all, the French had brandished that threat for years. Unable to see why they should bear the entire brunt of defending the North Sea ports—from which some invasion of England could be marshaled—the French liked to play upon these doubts of their reliability. This was especially true after Munich when Britain's inability to compensate for the loss of the Czech divisions rendered especially offensive any notion that France should do all the fighting in the Lowlands. It was in recognition of this, belated as it may have been, that the British chiefs of staff came to admit in late January 1939 that French support for Belgium was "unlikely . . . unless more substantial support were forthcoming from us."[7] Instead, it seemed possible that the French would not venture from their fortified positions, leaving Belgium and Holland to the mercy of the Third Reich. As no less a person than Alexis Léger shrewdly confided, French foreign policy would be governed in large part by the nature and extent of Britain's military contribution. Unless the Chamberlain government got down to business, Holland might be forgotten by France, and Britain left to recover its own chestnuts from the Lowlands.[8]

To be sure, the British divined what the French were up to. Alexander Cadogan, Vansittart's successor in the Foreign Office, knew perfectly well that Léger was "indulging in propaganda." Nevertheless, he observed, "the facts of the present situation must convince us that there is *something* in it," a judgment rendered the more compelling by a complementary suspicion that France hoped to use British military weakness as "an excuse in preparation for a general policy of retreat."[9] This suggestion that the French were groping for an excuse may have had unusual force in January 1939. Not only had they been hinting of dropping the defense of the Lowlands into Britain's lap, but their own military situation did not appear bright. Indeed, recent reports from Paris indicated that the French military authorities "do not consider that France is now in a position to defend herself against Germany without military assistance from the United Kingdom."[10] In London the Chiefs of Staff Sub-Committee was moving toward a similar conclusion. While it seemed unlikely that a frontal attack could bring Germany an early victory against France, other factors had to be considered. The German air force, for instance, enjoyed such a superiority that French cities would be left to ransom, more vulnerable even than French reserve divisions struggling to move up to threatened sectors on the frontiers. More serious still, a flanking attack by the Wehrmacht, through Belgium and Holland, would bring the Germans against the "weakest part" of the French fortifications—an eventuality in which "France would be less likely to withstand a German attack."[11] So it was that by very early 1939 the British had come to accept the possibility of a German attack in the west, of a French refusal to go beyond the call of self-defense, and even of a successful German invasion of France.

Underlying these anxieties was the presence of an undeniable malaise in Anglo-French relations. Word from Paris was equivocal—repeated assurances of French support for Britain, qualified by the veiled insinuations that barring a greater military contribution on its part Britain could be "more of a liability than an asset to France."[12] Lurking in the background, therefore, was the uncertainty of how France might react, of exactly what it might do in the event of a German attack on the United Kingdom. The fact is that the course of French policy since Munich had suggested a passivity of response which no longer was seen to be in Britain's best interests. As the belief in appeasement waned, and as the assumption of fascist hostility strengthened, the more important it became to have as an ally a France which was determined to resist in western Europe, in the Mediterranean, and in the colonial domain.

But this was not the France that commanded attention at the end of 1938. Equivocation seemed to have reached new heights in Paris. For the French, eastern Europe was more than ever a kind of no man's land where one moved in neither direction. Franco-Czech relations appeared to have "loosened overnight," leaving "little to record" in the diplomatic register for the last quarter of the year. The same was true of Franco-Polish relations. Although the alliance had not been renounced, and although Bonnet sometimes insisted that it would be respected, there was reason to believe that the French had severed psychologically their ties with the east. As Phipps remarked, "There will not be any alacrity here . . . to help Stalin or Beck against Hitler."[13] In western Europe similar uncertainties prevailed, at least in British minds if not actually in French policy. While some reports predicted a continuing French fidelity to traditional obligations, others wondered whether such ties were strong enough to carry France into war, whether French "isolationism" or French "defeatism" were not in the ascendant since the Munich humiliation. As for the southern theater, the big question mark was Italy. Here the French posed two difficulties. First, it remained unclear for a time—at least until April 1939—whether the apparently tough line preferred by Léger and Daladier would hold its own against the more pliant, compromising line favored by Bonnet and the French ambassador in Rome.[14] Second, it was equally unclear as to which of these approaches presented the greatest threat to British interests—that which might lead to a confrontation with Mussolini or that which might produce a Franco-Italian deal to drive a wedge between Britain and France. In general, therefore, the British detected too many uncertainties in French policy to be able to rest easy at the end of January 1939. Placed within this context of general unease, the specific fear that France might abandon the Lowlands or might prove incapable of adequate self-defense gave a special immediacy to British concerns about the future of the Anglo-French alliance. It was against this background of anxiety and, indeed, of distrust that one may view the startling British initiative of 4 February 1939—that which said it was time to strike the alliance.

Even then, one hastens to add, this alliance was not assured of safe or speedy passage. It was to take the better part of two months before actual staff conversations could begin on the basis of a presumed war against Germany and Italy. Roughly speaking, both sides shared equally in the delay. For its part the Quai d'Orday sat on the British invitation for three weeks, a response that surprised and puzzled the British. Several inquiries merely evoked the reply that the delay was being caused by the elaborate security precautions which had been effected to ensure the secrecy of the British *aide-mémoire* and the proposed French reply.[15] While this story may have been substantially true, it seems

225

equally likely that the French were determined to see that this long pursued trophy was now well hooked. Certainly there was no sudden abatement of the reports from Paris stressing the crucial importance of a British continental commitment or of Germany's efforts to back an Italian challenge in the Mediterranean.[16] What is more, a week before the official French reply was issued, papers in both countries were carrying remarkably detailed reports of the forthcoming staff conversations. Word in Whitehall had it that the French, far from being so exceptionally tight-lipped, in fact had leaked the news to the press in an attempt to keep the Chamberlain government honest. As Lord Halifax finally had come to understand, the French really were disturbed by the prospect of British duplicity, by some ruse to get them to fight a war for the British Empire. This time they were unlikely to rush into closer ties unless and until they were convinced that such joint planning was intended to be for the mutual benefit of England and France.[17]

Phipps received the French reply on 24 February. The Daladier government agreed to send the appropriate delegations as soon as a date could be arranged. The initiative again rested with London. This time it was picked up in more desultory fashion, in the old style, with regained composure. In fact, for the time being no precise date was suggested. An extensive strategic memorandum was in the process of being prepared, so the French were informed. Once this document had been completed, it would be sent to Paris for formal written appraisals. Not until British authorities had had the time to reflect on these French responses would actual conversations be initiated. The French, it appeared, had reaffirmed their intent to stand with Britain. For the moment that was all that mattered. Besides, second thoughts seem to have been in vogue in Whitehall during the first two weeks of March. What with the emphasis on the precedent setting nature of the proposed talks, the sudden flurry of reports disclaiming any German threat in the west, and the alleged recklessness of French policy toward Italy, there may well have been a renewed inclination to delay that still feared commitment to France.[18] Indeed, French troop reinforcements to Tunisia had stirred another small tempest in Anglo-French relations, with English appeals for restraint drawing an official French *aide-mémoire* which proved to be much "stiffer" in tone than anything anticipated by the Foreign Office.[19] As matters stood, it was no foregone conclusion that the final step toward that still elusive joint planning would ever be taken. Indicative of the strain between these two almost allies was Phipps' growing distaste for meetings of any kind with the French minister for foreign affairs. "I have had a most persistent bout of influenza which returns with renewed vigour each time I go to see Bonnet!"[20]

As the French had long expected, it would take Hitler to activate the Anglo-French alliance. The old incentive for tentative and fleeting attempts at cooperation, mutual distrust, had to be replaced by a more positive motive. It was no longer enough to recognize the community of mutually supporting interests that linked Britain and France. What had to come was a new incentive, a new purpose, the recognition that the survival of Britain and France might depend on the early commencement of joint military planning. This, the British did not feel deeply enough until the middle of March 1939. The devouring of what had been left of Czechoslovakia on 15 March, the ensuing reports of Roumania's peril, the new rumors of a sudden German assault in the west, the German seizure of Memel, and the almost simultaneous breakdown in German-Polish negotiations over Danzig changed all that. Although hopes for an appeased Germany would still linger in some quarters, to the very eve of war, it was this quite tumultuous two-week period in the second half of March that altered the tone of European diplomacy and that finally issued in Stage I of the Anglo-French staff conversations.[21] On 29 March, two days before Britain and France issued their guarantee to Poland, the Anglo-French delegations met in London to begin planning for war in earnest.

In France there was no parallel to Britain's sudden conversion. While it may not have been true before the autumn of 1938, then and thereafter the French government seems to have concluded that Hitler would have to be stopped before his piecemeal expansion left him invincible. So it was that a kind of siege mentality, preparing for the worst, had been developing since Munich, a mentality which the British sometimes took to mean defeatism and isolationism. It was in this mood that Gamelin assured Vuillemin that air warfare would be accorded "a preponderent position" in subsequent French planning, especially with respect to fighter aircraft and anti-aircraft weapons.[22] So too the general talked about conducting the war from behind the frontier defenses and, in December 1938, of hastening plans for the creation of the first heavy armored division, but a division which he regarded as a kind of anti-siege weapon: a counterattacking force "in the initial period of operations" and thereafter as a reserve striking force, held back for use at a "decisive moment in the battle."[23] Also indicative of this same climate of opinion, in which a clash with Germany seemed likely and greater defensive mobility indispensable, was Gamelin's disturbing admission of the dangers posed by a German *attaque brusquée*. "Until now I was skeptical, now I believe that it could become dangerous."[24] Unless France were to remain constantly alert, the general was saying, its security could be endangered by one surprise assault for which the German high command had assembled a massive local superiority by means of ultra-rapid mobilization and concentration measures.

Thus the French government had no reason to believe that Munich had changed a thing so far as Germany was concerned. Hitler would keep on taking as long as the military imbalance seemed to be in his favor. Certainly the seizure of Prague in mid-March came as no surprise. In fact the Conseil Supérieur de la Guerre had been told in advance that the fifteenth would be the "fateful date" for the Czechs. Eastern Europe, so Gamelin said, would be left to Germany's mercy—Russia considered "incapable of effective intervention in Europe," very much like "the little countries . . . who no longer have much military value."[25] A few days later, with the seizure of Prague an established fact—as real as the six hundred modern tanks which the Germans picked up in booty[26]—the French *état-major* turned to more pressing matters. As Gamelin had warned so recently, the days of the *attaque brusquée* had come. French army intelligence was deeply impressed by the "lightning speed" of Germany's military machine, a capacity which was said to allow for the concentration of thirty divisions within three to four days. "Once this operation is underway, Holland and Belgium could be overrun within one or two days—before their defensive measures had any effect—and our northern defenses engaged."[27] Under these circumstances the British pledge to defend Holland meant next to nothing. What was needed, and needed quickly, was the immediate commencement of Anglo-French military planning. As suggested, the events of the last two weeks of March 1939 enabled the French to get their wish. In their eyes, as Ambassador Corbin put it, the British at last had seen the light and by so doing finally had paid "belated homage to the wisdom of our own diplomacy."[28]

The growth of the Anglo-French alliance, as it was recorded by the various joint planning mechanisms that developed after March 1939, must be surveyed with some care at a later moment. For the time being, the reader's attention is still called to the subject of foreign policy and more specifically to the diplomacy of alliances, which now seemed to be enjoying such a recovery.

Having for so long balked at the idea of getting too close to France and to what had been seen as "French" interests on the continent, the British finally relented at the end of March 1939. The fear of making France too aggressive and independent at last had been overshadowed by the fear of finding it neither aggressive nor independent enough. Although the French would have been mystified by either side of this British *crise de conscience*, it is clear that they welcomed the British invitation to open the first stage of the staff conversations on 29 March. At long last they seemed assured of the one indispensable item in their strategic calculations—British support and involvement in the next war with Germany. What is more, once they had this, theoretically they had much else besides—the opportunity to conduct their foreign policy with fewer genuflections toward the Thames. Although much care has been taken in earlier chapters to qualify the extent of this generalization, enough also has been said throughout this work to support the notion that French diplomatic independence had to be subordinated to the imperious demand of working for alliance with Britain. Once this was assured, however, the scope for greater initiative increased. Again, it was precisely this possibility that had so worried the British Foreign Office in the past, as its operators had sought to keep the French in hand and at arm's length at one and the same time. Once that concern had to surrender priority to the fear of German hegemony, the French could expect satisfaction; and just as surely, once the French were more confident, new initiatives could be expected from them.

In fact, the Quai d'Orsay was not transformed from lamb to lion. But it did demonstrate, it is true, more independence of thought and action than had been apparent in the recent past. Whether this would have occurred simply because of the burgeoning alliance with Britain is not clear. What expedited matters at any rate, if it did not serve as a principal cause, was the bilateral guarantee which Chamberlain extended to Poland on 31 March, in the name not merely of Britain but of France as well. Although it now appears that the French in fact were forewarned of the proposed joint guarantee,[29] they clearly were left with little choice but to go along with this new British initiative. Any failure on their part to have issued immediate and formal approval would have mocked the unity of the new Anglo-French alliance and destroyed the credibility of the old Franco-Polish alliance. Nevertheless, the French had demonstrated little desire to increase their commitments to Poland; and in effect this is exactly what Chamberlain's guarantee had done. Britain really had promised the Poles that France would not abandon them. Hence the French were stuck willy-nilly to an ally whom they had come to distrust profoundly. They detected other problems as well. Both the Quai d'Orsay and the general staff believed that Roumania was in as much danger as Poland,[30] yet the British guarantee had been given without so much as a suggestion that Poland should pledge itself in turn to the defense of Roumania. Moreover, the guarantee did not even ask Poland for an assurance that it would be prepared to cooperate with the Soviet Union. In keeping with the Munich tradition, the one power in Europe that might have lent some practical import to this commitment to Poland had been totally ignored. The French were rightly critical of this oversight. To be sure, they themselves had long dawdled over the idea of closer ties with Russia;[31] but a new guarantee to Poland, this underscoring of old obligations, suddenly and dramatically returned France to the east, highlighted the importance of the Soviet alliance, and in so doing afforded an alternative to paying what would have amounted to protection money to Italy.

One cannot say with assurance that Daladier's hard-line attitude toward Italy stemmed from the recent progress which had been recorded within the Anglo-French alliance. It may have been prompted by the Italian invasion of Albania in the second week of April; and in any event, despite a certain willingness to permit secret though unofficial talks with the Italians, the premier's position even before the consolidation of the English alliance had never satisfied Italophile quarters in France.[32] What can be said with some certainty is that whatever its source, the premier's resolution clearly found expression over the Italian question in the spring of 1939. This time, indeed repeatedly, he refused to give in. While disclaiming any wish to snub Mussolini, Daladier resisted a prolonged campaign that was designed diversely to convince him that the Duce could be won away from Hitler or, at the very least, that he could be used as a counsel of moderation in Berlin. The interesting thing was that those Frenchmen who regarded themselves as his antagonists on this issue took special care to enlist the services—rather indecently available—of sympathetic British diplomats. The often lonely voice of Pierre Laval was added to those of Bonnet and François-Poncet in appealing to the Foreign Office, the foreign secretary, and to Ambassador Phipps to bring the premier into line.[33] The ambassador, in particular, proved a willing convert. On the bidding of Monsieur Bonnet, a man who had turned his stomach only a month before, Phipps welcomed the idea of trying to beard Daladier—"attacking" him as he preferred to put it.[34] But it was to no avail. Fortified by the knowledge of the new staff talks in London, or merely determined to assert his independence in defiance of his past surrenders, Daladier was in no mood to listen. Indeed, the Italian attack on Albania provoked his immediate order that the armed forces be prepared to descend "vigorously" on Italy should it come to open hostilities— "with air as well as with naval forces." To that end he simply informed the English that French aerial concentration would be directed to the southeast and that they in turn should accept "the necessity . . . of protecting themselves more effectively from our territory."[35] He had given the British occasion to wonder, with considerable concern, whether they were witnessing the emergence of "another Poincaré."[36]

For Daladier, the notion of enlisting Italy's support or soliciting its neutrality made little sense. Italy, he insisted to Halifax, was "firmly placed" in the "opposite camp," a status which did seem confirmed by the announcement of the Pact of Steel in May 1939.[37] In any event, with the winding down of the Spanish war, the subsequent evacuation of Italian troops, and the conclusion of the Bérard-Jordana protocol between France and Franco's Spain, the strategic situation in the southern theater had improved enough to remove some of the sting from the demands for a Franco-Italian rapprochement.[38] So it was that Daladier turned instead to the idea of revitalizing a second front in eastern Europe. Indeed, even before France had been flung back to the east by the guarantee to Poland, the premier had tried to nudge the Poles with his prediction that the seizure of Prague would be the prelude to an attempted German seizure of Warsaw; and with equal alacrity Georges Bonnet greeted the March takeover of Prague with a reaffirmation of France's eastern ties and the necessity of closer cooperation among France, Poland, and the Soviet Union.[39] Once the joint guarantee to Poland had been announced, there was nothing in it but to press ahead, working with little conviction and much doubt toward a more visible anti-German coalition. Thus it was that while recovering some of their diplomatic self-assurance elsewhere, the French now were confronting allies to the east who were less receptive than ever to entreaties from Paris and frankly much less impressed by the possibilities of independent French action.

The Franco-Polish conversations of May 1939 attest to the degree of latitude which the French government presumed itself to have. Albeit on Polish initiative, the French did agree to revise the alliance with Poland in accordance with the more recent Anglo-French guarantee of 31 March. To that end, military as well as diplomatic discussions took place in Paris during the first two weeks of May. On the surface, therefore, it appeared as if the French government was prepared to make something serious of the Polish alliance. And if one were to look a little more deeply, that impression would be reinforced by the fact of staff conversations—for the first time in years—and by the Quai's willingness to broaden the existing convention by agreeing to the defense of Poland's "vital interests." In these respects, and to this extent, the appearance of a revived French assertiveness was undeniable. Yet it would be mistaken to make too much of this new energy, for the fact is that whatever else French diplomats and soldiers displayed in May 1939 it was not audacity. Bonnet hedged from start to finish, first by refusing to acknowledge Danzig as a vital Polish interest, second—and absurdly—by then refusing to sign the defused protocol on the grounds that the British had latched upon an even more anodyne formula.[40] For their part, the soldiers qualified their recognition of Danzig as a vital Polish interest simply by making their military convention dependent on the terms and, of course, on the ratification of the political accord. Thus beneath the semblance of a new vigor, French equivocation still had its place and its uses. Despite the enduring commitment to Poland, the Anglo-French guarantee, and more recently still the appearance of this new political protocol and military convention, there was clearly little desire in French official circles to be locked into some irrevocable commitment to Poland. Just as the British had avoided too firm a commitment to France, so the French were afraid that Poland would abuse such assurances of support by becoming even more truculent.

This continued reticence toward Poland had very little to do with British policy. As Bonnet later made quite clear, he had refused to recognize Danzig as a vital Polish interest *before* he had been informed that the subject had yet to be raised in the Anglo-Polish discussions. Rather, it was simply very clear that Chamberlain's sudden reversal at the end of March had not triggered an equally abrupt change in French feelings toward Poland or toward the perils of being diplomatically over-extended in the east. As Bonnet's behavior illustrated, there was no wish to tie the strings of alliance too tightly. As the soldiers' behavior suggested, there was no intention of contradicting either the nation's war doctrine or the key principles of the national strategy simply for the sake of providing temporary and likely ineffective relief to a besieged Poland.

This impression of French military conduct will not surprise the reader for it is consistent with previous remarks on their attitude before and immediately after the Munich episode. The generals supported the idea of securing assistance from the eastern allies but made little effort to alter French war plans in the interest of increasing the speed and effectiveness of their aid to the east. They had not done so in the interval between 1936 and 1938, and they were not to do so in 1939. Only days before the Franco-Polish talks opened in Paris, General Lelong of the French army delegation in London had conceded that providing aid to Poland was a "very thorny problem." "The Maginot Line and Siegfried Line faced each other," he noted, "and France could not seriously attack Germany on land without long preparation. There seemed to be no solution for action . . . other than an advance into Germany through Belgium and Holland"—the latter being a throwaway line utterly removed from political realities in May 1939.[41] To the Poles, in Paris, army spokesmen tried to present a more positive attitude. In fact they promised to undertake an offensive against Germany's western defenses within three weeks of a declaration of war.[42] Yet there is little evidence that the French consciously sought to deceive the Polish military delegation, assuring them of action which they had no intention of attempting. In brief, they were talking about a tentative offensive, undertaken by a force of some thirty divisions, after several weeks of preparation, against a well-prepared defensive line, and from which little more was to be expected than some modest relief for the beleaguered Polish forces. This is what the French were saying in May 1939, despite their self-confessed efforts to put the best construction on what obviously was a forbidding situation.[43] After all, it was hardly in France's interest to discourage Poland into Hitler's embrace. For their part, and this too seems worthy of notice, the Poles could only have been misled with their own assent and compliance. They were not strangers to France's grand strategy; and they would have had to be unimaginably naive or forgetful to think that the French, having suffered a string of reverses in the east, now were determined to launch their own blitzkrieg on Berlin.[44] Nothing so far had made the French depart from the injunction against early, premature offensives; nothing had moved Gamelin to anticipate a major strategic offensive before the expiry of a two-year defensive interval; and nothing the Poles were told in May 1939 would have justified them in thinking differently.

The Franco-Polish negotiations uncovered yet another facet of French policy toward eastern Europe. Although this was to undergo some change in the ensuing months, particularly on the diplomatic level, so far there had been no major attitudinal adjustment toward the Soviet Union. Indeed, the old Schweisguth assessment of Russian policy remained as intrusive as ever.[45] The high command continued to sponsor the view that Stalin hoped to have Germany and the Western powers "cut one anothers' throats" in order to "pave the way for bolshevism in Europe." And there was still plenty of skepticism about Soviet military capacity, especially in the bloody wake of Stalin's purges. The general staff reportedly harbored the notion that Russia's contribution outside its own frontiers "would be virtually worthless"; and the air staff, while not subscribing completely to this evaluation, continued to dwell on the limitations of the Red air force.[46] Owing to perceptions such as these, and fully cognizant of the latent enmity between Russians and Poles, the French government did not try to use the May conversations in Paris as an entrée to some kind of tripartite cooperation among Paris, Warsaw, and Moscow. Certainly from this point of view, the Franco-Polish talks would have to be regarded as another lost opportunity.[47] In a way reminiscent of the Rambouillet discussions in the autumn of 1936, these talks also failed to produce the kind of authority which France doubtless required to bring the Poles into line. Although the Poles again were in Paris as suppliants, after money as well as a guarantee for Danzig, and this time shorn of their nonaggression pact with Germany,[48] neither France's diplomats nor its soldiers showed themselves willing to risk rupturing the alliance by insisting that it be strengthened through the recruitment of Russia. Here again, therefore, while the very fact of these conversations may attest to some revival of French diplomatic confidence and independence, as yet there was little sign of a commanding French presence with respect to eastern Europe.

The same may be said for southeastern Europe where French interest in a Balkan front was as evident as the unwillingness to pay for it. While the Poles were being entertained in Paris, General Weygand was pulled from retirement to head an important mission to Ankara, expressly with a view to preparing the way for a Franco-Turkish alliance. Although the Turks long had occupied a key role in French strategic appreciations in the Mediterranean, they nonetheless had remained outside the French alliance network. In the spring of 1939 there seemed some promise of a change. German economic penetration of the Balkans, and the Italian action against Albania, seemed to have brought home the perils of the Rome-Berlin axis to the government of President Inonu and consequently induced a growing Turkish sympathy for Britain and France.[49] However, the old Franco-Turkish dispute over the Sanjak of Alexandretta and Ankara's doubts about French willingness to make an effective contribution to a Turkish war effort, had left the two countries at a sympathetic but very clear impasse. The first issue the French were now prepared to settle as quickly as possible, but the second was not as easily resolved, despite the recommendations of those like Weygand and Ambassador René Massigli.[50]

From Paris the problem looked only too familiar. Few had any doubts about Turkey's great strategic value for the Western powers, the "key" as Charles Corbin called it, to the Black Sea, the Levant, and the eastern Mediterranean.[51] Turkey's threat to the Italian Dodecanese, its control of the sea gate to Russia, its potential to distract if not defeat Bulgaria, and its ability to expedite troop transports from the Near East to that much thought-about bridgehead at Salonika were all acknowledged and prized. Indeed, these were the reasons why the French were prepared to give way on the Sanjak issue and why they worked patiently toward the completion of the tripartite alliance with London and Ankara in October 1939. But in the early summer General Gamelin was still insisting that Poland and Roumania be given a higher priority in the distribution of what little material aid there was available.[52] Indeed, France's own military plight forbade significant assistance in war materiel to any power, just as the familiar determination to husband the nation's precious capital reserves forbade much in the way of financial subsidies— even to states France was committed to defend. Thus the Turkish alliance, desirable as it was, had to remain unrealized for the time being— despite Turkey's apparent interest in joining an Anglo-French front against the dictators and despite French recognition of Turkey's potential for buttressing the defenses of the Balkan states and for drawing upon the assistance of the Soviet Union.[53]

The latter was already beginning to command French attention in a more direct way. Though it is true that the same negative attitudes continued to prevail within French officialdom, civil and military, the force of expediency, of anxiety, was gaining momentum. Bonnet, we have reported, had been quick to reintroduce the Soviet Union into the rhetoric of alliance diplomacy almost from the moment Prague fell to its new German masters; and it seems clear that through his offices it was the French who took the lead in reestablishing contact with the Russians within a few days of Chamberlain's guarantee to Poland.[54] From the start, therefore, from the spring of 1939, it was the French who tended to press the cause of a tripartite Anglo-French-Soviet combination. With increasing urgency and frequency it would be the Daladier government that encouraged the British toward the very alliance so long spurned by the premier himself. Again, one must say that the French attitude toward Stalin had not changed appreciably; what was different were the circumstances, different enough to warrant gambling on the reliability of a Communist regime. Whereas in the past the suspicion that Stalin intended to "stay out of any conflict" had been used as an argument against a military alliance, now the importance of trying to change his attitude and secure his cooperation had become uppermost in French minds. Besides, disconcerting rumors were already arriving in Paris, rumors of some new Russo-German rapprochement.[55] By the end of May, therefore, the French government had become aware of the peril of losing Russia for good.

It is unnecessary for the purposes of this discussion to relate in detail the tortuous course of the tripartite negotiations for a political accord. Begun in May, these halting, frequently bitter exchanges, unfailingly characterized by mutual suspicion, carried on into the second half of July. Then they were abandoned, not quite finalized, in favor of tripartite military conversations.[56] Over that period, it may be said that it was the French who took the lead for the Western powers, proving themselves more willing than the British to concede points to the Russian negotiators, more willing to search for compromises, above all, more intent on the need for speed. So it was that Georges Bonnet, less than a year from the Munich crisis during which he had regarded Russia through the lens of Schweisguth,[57] could press the utmost dispatch on his diplomatic officers. His instructions to ambassadors Naggiar in Moscow and Corbin in London are full of these appeals for speed, appeals that finally climaxed with his suggestion to the British that their respective ambassadors in Moscow be given the greatest possible latitude "so as not to have to be constantly telegraphing us for new instructions."[58] By then, however, it was too late. In mid-July 1939 the Russians asked that the prospective political accord be shelved until after a military convention had been concluded.

This Soviet decision automatically transferred responsibility from diplomats to soldiers. In the case of France, the task assumed by General Doumenc and his small delegation was not an enviable one. Enjoined by Daladier to bring back an accord at all costs, this hapless contingent departed for Russia as the emissary of a general staff that had never been more than lukewarm about the Soviet alliance, and in the company of a British mission whose instructions were to proceed slowly and prudently.[59] Indeed, if proof were needed that old ideas die hard, it can be found in plenty within the precincts of the French high command. Despite the fact that they could now foresee a war in which the circumstances facing France had never been worse,[60] not even desperation was enough to soften their skepticism about Soviet military capacity or diminish their fear of winning Russia at the cost of losing Poland and Roumania. Nor was it enough to settle their ideological nervousness. Charged with the task of national defense, they found it impossible to sympathize with a Communist movement which condemned militarism on principle, which reportedly sought to foment revolution in the barracks, which openly proclaimed loyalty to a foreign power, and which by its inspired strikes jeopardized the pace of the French rearmament program. Finally, and with a gentle reminder against treating such misgivings with excessive levity, the French chiefs of staff found it very difficult to imagine detailed discussions of French war plans with a nation that was known by August 1939 to be in close touch with Nazi Germany.[61]

For these reasons the ambivalence toward the Soviet Union remained unabated within Gamelin's headquarters; and so the soldiers displayed neither enthusiasm nor remorse over the government's decision to conclude a military convention with Russia. More obvious, however, was the determination to see that the military authorities were not left holding the bag should the Moscow negotiations fail to produce agreement. This long had been one of Gamelin's central preoccupations as commander-in-chief; and he now sought to obfuscate army responsibility with the same sort of care he had demonstrated during the Polish negotiations. In May 1939 he had leaned the military package against the political accord. In August 1939 the task was more difficult, for the Russians had insisted that a military convention precede a political one. All that Gamelin could do was keep his own role to a minimum, an impression which his memoirs have skillfully conveyed by their curt and laconic treatment of the Russian negotiations. Having selected the mission members and given them a short catalogue of instructions—ones which all but ignored the ticklish question of securing Soviet transit rights across Poland and Roumania—Gamelin tried to wash his hands of the matter. From the time of their departure in early August to their return home some two weeks later, the French mission appears to have had little communication with the high command in Paris.[62]

The talks began in Moscow on 12 August. The Soviet negotiator, Marshal Vorochilov, quickly came to the point. Had his interlocutors been empowered to negotiate and sign the proposed convention? It was a bad beginning. General Doumenc replied that he could *traiter* all questions of a military character, an expression which was stretched to include authority to sign. The British Admiral Drax, on the other hand, had to admit that he enjoyed no such powers. No convention could be concluded, therefore, without prior reference to the government in London. Visibly annoyed, Vorochilov reluctantly agreed to proceed with the negotiations. What sort of military operations did Britain and France propose for the relief of eastern Europe? In response, Doumenc quickly sketched French operational plans for the Western theater. Slightly inflated estimates of the French forces helped satisfy the marshal who nevertheless expressed surprise that only forty German divisions were expected to be left in the west. As for the estimates of the British strength and contribution, Vorochilov dismissed them as too derisory to be true.[63] On the following day he presented Doumenc and Drax with the "cardinal question." Would Poland and Roumania allow Soviet troops to cross their territory for the purpose of waging war on the Germans? With his "formidable logic" he warned that further negotiations would be "useless" until this question had been resolved—the very question Gamelin had glossed over in his instructions to the French delegation.[64]

Time, for everyone, was at a premium in mid August 1939. The Russians were afraid of being left alone at the mercy of Hitler's relentless drive for conquest in the east. The Western powers were concerned lest the eastern front fade entirely from the realm of possibility, leaving them to face the full brunt of the German armies. The Germans, in their turn, were disturbed by the possibility of fighting a two-front war—disturbed enough to be in active pursuit of some *modus vivendi* with Moscow. So it was that in reply to a Soviet démarche of 13 August, the Germans proposed the immediate opening of negotiations for a formal Russo-German rapprochement. General Doumenc also recognized the need for prompt action. On 14 August he wired Paris requesting authorization to send one of the mission members to Warsaw, a request firmly seconded by Ambassador Naggiar who stressed "the necessity" of Poland taking "a less negative attitude."[65] If the Polish general staff could be persuaded to give even its tacit approval to the principle of Soviet transit rights, the talks in Moscow still had a chance to succeed. The reply from Paris did not come that day, or the next. Only on 16 August did Doumenc receive the government's negative reply. That day, the Russians advised Berlin that they would accept the principle of rapprochement. The day following, Naggiar again warned the Quai d'Orsay that the military talks were finished unless the Poles came up with a suitable reply, "officially, unofficially, or even tacitly."[66]

In Moscow the French embassy had picked up too many rumors of the surfacing Russo-German entente to be under any illusion that time was on the side of the West. As a result, on 17 August, General Doumenc simply notified Paris that he was sending Captain Beaufre to Warsaw on his own initiative, the object being to press on the Polish high command the absolute need for greater flexibility.[67] Unless the Poles relented, Doumenc warned, the tripartite meeting scheduled for 21 August would only record the failure of the negotiations.

Beaufre's mission demanded the impossible. The young captain found himself in trying circumstances, an only partially authorized representative of France in a capital impervious to the urgency which had taken him there. What is more, his relations with the French embassy in Warsaw were somewhat uncertain. For its part, the embassy was supposed to cooperate. Georges Bonnet had sent up a barrage of instructions, pleading with his ambassador to make the Poles see reason, to make them realize that "the Russian problem" was "a critical part of the more general problem of organizing a defensive front in Eastern Europe."[68] But neither Ambassador Noel nor his military attaché, General Musse, could relinquish the old misgivings. Noel could foresee his long service in Warsaw being nullified by attempts to push the Poles too hard.

Even a new Polish-German agreement seemed a possibility to him. Musse was even less receptive to the appeals from Beaufre and the Quai d'Orsay. He would carry Beaufre's entreaties to the Polish general staff, but he did not expect them to have any effect. Very much indicative of his own reservations, Musse reminded the war ministry in Paris that the Poles resented Soviet blackmail and remained unmoved by Soviet claims of military efficiency.[69] It was not surprising, therefore, that the efforts of these two men on 19 and 20 August failed to elicit the kind of unequivocal response which Vorochilov had set as a condition for proceeding with the tripartite talks in Moscow. In any event, Stalin was growing less and less disposed to wait for the Western powers. By 19 August he had agreed to receive the German foreign minister in Moscow, for the purpose of discussing a Russo-German nonaggression treaty. With this in the wind, and with the Poles as recalcitrant as ever, the tripartite meeting that Vorochilov had set for 21 August was assured of failure.

Although some last minute acts of desperation were still to come, the matter was effectively settled. The attempts, first by Daladier and then by Bonnet, to promise full Polish support—in the absence of such a pledge from Warsaw—left the Russians unmoved and rightly unconvinced.[70] Panicked at last by the prospect of losing Russia, in stunning contrast to the casual indifference so long shown toward Moscow, the French were bounding ahead of the British in a bid to prevent a Russo-German deal. But it was too late. On the evening of 23 August foreign ministers Ribbentrop and Molotov signed the Nazi-Soviet pact of nonaggression. Of special importance to the Western powers, whose delegations were still in Moscow, was the undertaking that neither signatory would participate in coalitions which were directly or indirectly aimed at the other. As Ambassador Naggiar had warned Bonnet several days earlier, the stage was being set for a Russo-German partition of Poland.[71]

Throughout the entire courtship of Russia it was the French who had taken the lead for the Western powers. This should not suggest a major attitudinal difference between Britain and France on the subject of the Soviet Union, for the fact is that their misgivings—political, ideological, and military—were essentially the same. Rather, the more pronounced sense of urgency which one detects on the French side was a direct reflection of France's interests as a continental power in supplementing Britain's air and naval support with the services of a major continental ally.[72] With this in mind, the French were prepared to force the pace, pressing the British and Poles in directions they were not keen to go. Once the Russian episode was over, however, it remained to be seen how and whether this recent assertiveness would continue to be expressed.

Georges Bonnet had been a central figure in this resurgence of French initiative. He, in particular, had led the campaign to bring Britain and Poland into some kind of compromise with the Soviet Union—in the name of which he gradually abandoned his fear of upsetting the Poles or of jeopardizing their interests. By 23 August he had even appropriated the right to speak in the name of the Polish government, falsely claiming that Poland at last had given "full authority" to the Doumenc delegation.[73] When that failed to wash, the minister became vindictive. Enraged by Beck's "incomprehensible, arrogant and treacherous" attitude, he fled to the illogical but comforting conclusion that "any attempt to save Poland would only lead to that country's complete destruction."[74] Without the blink of an eye the minister now contemplated taking independence to even greater lengths. Even before official word of the Nazi-Soviet pact had arrived in Paris, Bonnet had urged Daladier to convene an early meeting of the Comité Permanent de la Défense Nationale. Was it not time, he wondered, to weigh and reconsider the implications of French commitments to Poland? Had he been successful in marketing such doubts to other committee members, Georges Bonnet might have taken France well beyond the threshold of independence—this time, leaving not only the Poles but the British in the lurch.

While never overtly recommending the scrapping of the Polish alliance, Bonnet did open the door for such a retreat on 23 August.[75] But France had not come this far simply to forfeit the alliance with Britain within a few months of its inception. Indeed, it was clear from the early moments of this strange and controversial meeting that the premier and his fellow members of the CPDN had no intention of wriggling out of the commitment to Poland.[76] In fact they quickly agreed that a German attack on Poland would take France into a war, a decision endorsed by the cabinet on the following day. Bonnet's rather clumsy efforts to discredit the Polish alliance, it seems, had been badly timed—for two reasons. First, the military factor had again impressed itself on the Daladier government, possibly even more forcefully than it had at the time of Munich but in a very different fashion. In 1938 French military deficiencies had provided counsel against fighting for the Czechs. In 1939 it was precisely this awareness of France's deteriorating military position on the continent that encouraged, if not actually induced, the government to fight for the Poles. So spoke Daladier, candidly admitting that it now was a question of resisting Hitler or of witnessing "the creation of a more than Napoleonic Empire under Hitler which could attack [the Western powers] at will."[77] So too insisted Gamelin. This, he said, was "the essential point": "Either war now, with Germany first attacking Poland, or the risk of soon being attacked in our turn, with Poland eliminated . . . Now, in the latter instance, given the state of our air power and the extent of German mobilization, we could not accept the risk."[78]

Second, it is clear that this French decision of 23-24 August—apparently taken without direct reference to Whitehall—was predicated on the belief that Britain could not and would not abandon the Poles. Just as the British had believed in 1938 that a German attack on the Czechs would have taken France to war, so the French now were convinced that an attack on Poland would see a British declaration of war. The question for the Daladier government, therefore, was whether it was more perilous to stand with Britain in war or to negotiate an independent peace with Germany. In fact, this was a purely rhetorical question, for there is no evidence that the government ever wavered in its resolution to follow Britain into war—however much it worked to forestall a German attack before the first of September 1939 and despite Bonnet's feverish last-minute attempts to avert war even as bombs were raining down on Warsaw.[79]

In point of fact, by the third week of August 1939 the Anglo-French alliance had acquired an extensive form. Within the space of five months, roughly speaking since the end of March, the Chamberlain and Daladier governments had agreed upon a marked acceleration of their hitherto modest attempts at joint planning. While one should not exaggerate the speed with which long-standing mutual suspicions gave way to confidence, it was increasingly apparent that an awareness of mutual need and dependence had reached unprecedented proportions.[80] From a wide range of ministries and departments, delegates and spokesmen regularly were being sent on trans-Channel missions to solicit allied expertise, intelligence, and material assistance. Although information of great detail is not required here, and although care must be taken not to imply that such planning preempted either government's right of decision, some attention should be paid to the dimensions of this fast maturing alliance.

The joint staff conversations offered only one facet of this alliance. Conducted in three successive stages, principally in the month of April and during the last few days of August, these exchanges ultimately led to the preparation of a common strategy in the event of war in Europe, in the Mediterranean, and in the Far East. Complemented by similar if more specific exchanges between the respective regional commanders around the globe, from Singapore to Aden and Bizerte to Djibouti, these conversations in London slowly clarified allied intent and enunciated their strategic priorities. Simply put, the allies agreed on the need for an initially defensive strategy: holding Germany and Japan at bay as best they could, angling for the neutrality of Spain and Italy, and planning for their hostility merely by directing allied action in the first instance to ensuring mastery of the Mediterranean sea lanes. The principal offensive arm in this opening stage of hostilities was to be that of the navy, the one branch of service where allied superiority promised to terrorize enemy merchantmen and neutralize hostile navies in European waters. Thereafter, if Mussolini did not abandon Hitler, and once their own defensive dispositions across North Africa were fully assured, the allies were likely to descend on Libya as the first step to knocking Italy out of the war.

To this primary objective of averting early defeats, the allied military delegations addressed a wide range of detailed planning arrangements: from those which defined respective operational jurisdictions in the Mediterranean, the Channel, and the Atlantic to those which concerned the embarkation, transport, and accommodation of the six-division British Expeditionary Force now slated for the continent, and from those which spelled out the details of common aircraft recognition and signals communication to those which provided for the caching of British bombs on French soil in anticipation of the arrival of the RAF's Advanced Air Striking Force.[81] And it was arrangements such as these which in turn gave rise to an inter-allied command structure which left supreme control to a Conseil Supérieur, operational control to a jointly staffed Haut Comité Militaire, and the virtually limitless logistical and planning responsibilities to a Comité d'Etudes Militaires Interalliées, which in practice operated as a secretariat for the Supreme Council.[82]

The military circumstances that confronted the allies in the spring and summer of 1939, and the consequent decision to aim first at containing rather than conquering their enemies, guaranteed that the conventional military planning of past campaigns would be insufficient for the task at hand. As they had learned in the four long years up to 1918, raw materials could outrank army corps, just as boffins and bureaucrats could determine the fate of a battle as surely as the fighting forces. Accordingly, and at long last implementing assumptions which had been held in common for almost two decades, the less overtly military aspects of joint planning acquired a renewed prominence in the spring of 1939. Of these, only a few need be singled out for the purpose of illustrating the range and degree of precision to which Anglo-French planning had risen by late August 1939.

There were of course many instances of technological collaboration, the most notable examples being in the field of air engines and of aircraft and submarine detection. In these instances, while chary of simply handing over the manufacturing rights and details to the French, the British did agree to deliver a limited number of fully operational Rolls Royce Merlin III and Merlin X engines as well as working models of the radar and asdic detection systems. Given the conditions of secrecy in which the latter had been developed, it was indeed a testament to the growing force of alliance that equipment of such a nature should have been placed in foreign hands, even on a limited basis. Yet another dimension of joint planning was that which may be designated as "economic pressure." Again, given the kinds of strategic assumptions shared by Britain and France, central to which was the belief that any war with Germany would only be won after a long campaign of economic as well as military attrition, it was natural that discussions relating to economic pressure on Germany would follow quickly from the decision to tighten the bonds of alliance. To this end, men like J. W. Nicholls of the economic section in the Foreign Office conveyed voluminous quantities of economic intelligence to Paris from April onward and successfully induced the Quai d'Orsay to strike a new Comité d'Action Economique à l'Etranger in the month of June. So it was that in the course of an ongoing series of conferences, alternatively in London and Paris, the allies worked out detailed plans for an extensive economic blockade of Germany. On these plans and arrangements would fall the burden of allied offensive action during what, for them, would be the predominantly defensive stage of the war.[83] Finally, there was the even broader dimension of "economic warfare," a term which may be used to embrace offensive economic pressure but which is used here within the context of self-defense and survival. Arising from the modest and tentative exchanges of 1938— relating to food, oil, and coal supplies—a series of stepped-up contacts emerged in the spring of 1939, some of which touched upon relatively new areas like those of shipping, finance, munitions production, and raw materials. While it would be wrong to exaggerate the progress which had been made in many of these areas—for example that of finance, where joint discussions did not begin until the very eve of war—once again the scale of joint action that was envisaged and the confidences that had to be exchanged on the subject of their respective planning, resources, and requirements suggest the emergence of an allied sentiment as well as a mere joint planning mechanism.[84]

By the summer of 1939, therefore, the French did have some reason for satisfaction and some grounds for a renewed self-confidence. Certainly Daladier seemed to believe that at last he was in a position to tell Chamberlain to forget about a Franco-Italian rapprochement,[85] to force the pace of allied overtures to Russia, and to reaffirm France's commitment to Poland without double-checking first with London. What is more, not only did it appear certain that the long-sought alliance with Britain had been achieved, but there was very good reason to conclude that it had been founded on French strategic assumptions. Indeed, for those who still harbor the image of an inept and somnolent France draped on the arm of an alert and attentive Britain, it might be recalled that the strategy with which they entered the Second World War had been fashioned in common—fashioned at the twelfth hour after almost twenty years of independent but remarkably similar planning. The enormous emphasis placed on a long war of attrition had been absolutely central to French grand strategy, war waged by allies whose joint economic resources would permit them to prevail over enemies less richly endowed. The same may be said for the French, and later allied, emphasis on securing the vital Mediterranean sea lanes, the injunction against premature land and air offensives, the notion of opening the allied offensive stage by carrying the war to Italian possessions in North Africa, and the lingering idea of setting up a second continental front in the Balkans.[86] It is worth bearing in mind, therefore, that the French not only succeeded in winning their one indispensable ally but did so on the very terms which their vision of the next war proclaimed to be inevitable.

10

Dénouement, 1940

The general mobilization of the French land, sea and air Armies was decreed on September 1st and a state of siege throughout France and Algeria was established . . . Parliament met on September 2nd and at 5 p.m. on September 3rd France was at war with Germany . . . On September 10th the Minister of Finance said that France and England would win the war because their Empires were the two most powerful in the world.[1]

Like many forecasts, this one left much to be desired. As it happened, France collapsed in 1940, after a generally undistinguished campaign of six weeks duration. It was sudden and dramatic fall for which the reader—like the protagonists of 1940—has been incompletely prepared to fathom. This is as it should be for this collapse was unexpected by all, including the Germans. Without forsaking the historian's well counseled search for continuity in history, one need be wary about writing the 1930s for the sake of 1940. Edifices collapse for reasons other than rotten foundations just as death by violence or misadventure befalls more than the already infirm. Still, autopsies are deemed necessary; and that too is as it should be, for man must draw his inspiration as well as his torment from the question "why?" The following remarks may help explain the nature of this sudden defeat and some of the controversy surrounding it, to make some sense of an occurrence that seemed wholly improbable at the time war was declared.

In the ultimate sense French diplomacy failed in 1939, for it did not prevent the war which had been feared for twenty years. It had succeeded, however, perhaps by subservience, perhaps by guile, certainly by persistence, in securing for France the one essential prerequisite for war: alliance with the United Kingdom. In September 1939 French military policy as yet had not been put to any operational test. How it should be evaluated, therefore, remained uncertain for the time being. However, in 1939, before the 1940 débâcle seemed to erase all traces of sensible pre-war planning, the indications were promising enough. An allied grand strategy had been developed in concert with the British, though only very imperfectly with the Belgians and Dutch, a strategy appropriately founded on the superior economic and naval resources of the chief partners and their respective dominions overseas. Germany was to be blockaded, cut off from its vital seaborne imports, rendered anemic by such deprivation, and then crushed by an all-out allied offensive. Until then, on land and in the air, the allied armies were to hold on the Western front, concentrating on one objective—denying Germany the kind of successful penetration which had nearly ensured its victory in 1914. It is in this light that one must view the so-called Phoney War period, from the autumn of 1939 to the spring of 1940, a period which began with a British request for assurance that there would be no early French offensive in the west.[2] Thus are explained the strategic reasons for the failure to launch a really serious offensive on behalf of Poland, a country whose only hope, Gamelin believed, was "to be resurrected after our final victory."

> I said in the meeting of 23 August that with British aid and American materiel I hoped that by the spring of 1940 we would be able to wage a strong defensive battle. But I did not conceal the fact that we could only win against Germany at the price of a long war and that it was only in 1941 or 1942 that we could take the offensive.[3]

In point of fact this was a sensible grand strategic plan, for which the French armies were generally well equipped by May 1940. Indeed, if German economic inferiority legitimized the concept of blitzkrieg warfare, the canon may be reversed to explain the connection between allied economic superiority and the grand strategic design of a long war. Moreover, the specific strategic plan for the Western theater was at least theoretically sound. Until February 1940 even the German high command had expected to attack where the Belgian Ardennes and the French fortifications in the Palatinate and along the Rhine said they must—through the Low Countries, on a plan of attack resembling the sweeping movement of the old Schlieffen plan. So the notion emerged, long harbored in Paris, of meeting the German invaders along the Belgian Meuse with three allied armies in fixed defensive positions and supported by the bulk of the allies' armored forces. It was not a brilliant strategy, for something so obvious, so consistent with virtually all current military assumptions —French and foreign—and so long contemplated as a result, could hardly merit such extravagant description.

The so-called von Manstein plan, which was to win Hitler's approval in February 1940, was quite another matter. Departing from conventional military wisdom—German as well as foreign—this plan envisaged a violent knockout blow delivered principally not through the Low Countries but through the Ardennes forest via Luxembourg and southern Belgium. The German high command did not like it, convinced as they were that the Ardennes would not permit the speedy transit of thousands upon thousands of armored and motorized vehicles. Even with their original plan of assault fallen into Belgian hands by a freak accident in January 1940, von Manstein's superiors had to be overruled by Hitler whose own intuitive sense again stood him in good stead.[4] After numerous delays, occasioned in part by the successful German assaults on Denmark and Norway, the Ardennes plan was initiated on 10 May 1940.

The results are well known and need hardly be chronicled here. The German feint in the north worked to perfection. Belgium and Holland fell victim to a sudden air and land assault, the signal for the mobile Anglo-French forces in the north to tear across the Belgian border and set up their defensive concentrations just north of the Belgian Meuse. Further south, however, von Rundstedt's Army Group A was already unleashing the major blow between Namur and Sedan, a sector defended by two poorly prepared French armies whose commanders had shared in the knowledge of the "impenetrable" Ardennes. Deprived accordingly of armored units, very short on anti-tank guns and mines, and desperate for the air support which was still concentrating its attacks further north, these armies were stunned by the paralyzing fire power of seven panzer divisions and the terrifying Stukas. The Meuse was conquered in three days, to the astonishment of Berlin, as well as Paris, London, and Brussels. From the Meuse the battle quickened, or rather did the pace of the panzer divisions, now on open ground and heading for the Channel ports with a recklessness that alternately frightened, irritated, and delighted their incredulous warlords in Berlin. Within the space of the ensuing three weeks the Dutch and Belgians were forced to capitulate, and the major part of the British Expeditionary Force was to return from the continent through the fiery gates of Dunquerque. Thus the French were left, strung out along the Somme, faced with a now vastly superior enemy whose mobility enabled him to dash south to envelop the armies still isolated behind the Maginot defenses and at the same time to deliver the final blow on Paris. On 25 June France concluded an armistice.

There are few instances of inevitability in history, and this was not one of them. What was unavoidable, and as certain as things can be, is that French war planning would be discredited by the German victory, discredited sweepingly and indiscriminately. That this planning lay somewhere in the roots of the French defeat may not be doubted, but how this was so, and where, needs to be examined with much care. For instance, so much has been said in this work to explain the *raison d'être* of French grand strategy, with its vision of a long war, that the reader may be properly skeptical of the argument that France should have adopted a short-war concept or that it should have opted for the same formula (not just a formula) for armored-air warfare that had finally broken through the resistance of military conservatives in Germany. Of similar coin is the sermon that France should have paid more attention to the Ardennes, in the 1930s as a whole but at least in March-April 1940 when the Germans were reported to be shifting divisions from north to south. Undoubtedly these were errors of judgment, ultimately lethal, but when one knows that the Germans had changed their plans partly by force of accident and Hitler's intuition, and then only with lingering reservations, the French failure seems something less than extraordinary. As for Gamelin's failure to read his 1940 intelligence reports correctly, one ought to recall that it was never a question of the Germans being either in the north, or in the south, but both at the same time—with Bock's Army Group B furnished with enough fire power and assault force to keep confirmed the allied expectation of attack from the north.

It was this expectation, in fact partly fulfilled, that led the French high command, with British blessing, to commit another error of judgment—again a critical one, although again one that was neither silly nor without reason. Henri Michel speaks of the "insoluble problem of Belgium," and so it was.[5] For good political and strategic reasons the French had to, wanted to, assist in the defense of Belgium. The latter, however, for solid domestic reasons if questionable international ones, refused to engage in active defense planning with the British or French, or to allow the latter to take up defensive positions within Belgium until a German attack was actually underway. Thus, without adequate information about proposed Belgian military operations, or about the defensive works into which their own forces were intended to move, the French were facing the risk of an encounter battle with the Germans, the sort of enterprise that French military conservatism had long warned against. Indeed, was it not this very argument that had stifled earlier talk of offensive projects—for fear that badly prepared offensives might lead to totally unprepared routs?[6] Yet in November 1939 General Gamelin, the allies' supreme commander on the continent, recommended advancing the proposed front in Belgium from the Scheldt-Escaut to the river Dyle.[7] Though this meant protecting a larger area of Belgium than what had been contemplated under Plan E(scaut), and though it promised to shorten the allied front significantly, it also meant a much longer march for both the BEF and General Giraud's Seventh Army in the north—thus delaying the British installation on the northern Dyle and driving the Seventh Army as far north as Holland. So it was that Maurice Gamelin, that cautious commander who had looked so askance at offensive daring, was prepared—against bitter opposition from many of his field commanders—to insist on an act of defensive daring, one that ultimately sent his best forces into improvised and unfamiliar defensive positions or banished them, in the case of Giraud's powerful forces, to northern Flanders, far away from the Dyle, the Meuse, Sedan.

Yet to their lingering discomfort most of the French armies remained "far away" from their attackers—held at bay by their commanders' outdated temporal and spatial conception of modern war, or at least the way the panzer corps and Luftwaffe practiced it. In this, again, the French were not alone. Both they and the German OKW (Oberkommando der Wehrmacht) anticipated that no crossing of the Meuse could be negotiated in less than nine days, three times more than what Guderian and Reinhardt proved was necessary.[8] But the French simply never adjusted thereafter, never managed to anticipate the speed of the next panzer advance and thus never succeeded in marshaling a sufficiently large armored corps of light mechanized and heavy armored divisions to break the back of a reckless adversary who had surrounded himself voluntarily. That the French commanders had not accustomed themselves to think of massed armor is in large part true, and so is raised the matter of military doctrine as well. But even on those occasions when French and German tanks did meet in significant numbers it seemed apparent that the French units had been hastily thrown together and were lacking the complex logistical support—for instance fuel services—which time alone could make provision for. And it was this that the French lacked, lacked it because they sorely underestimated how quickly they had to strike or, conversely, how far back they had to withdraw, in order to defend against this lightning warfare. This conceptual failure, bitterly compounded by an extremely awkward allied command structure and by the chronic failures of an overstrained communications network, meant that the allies were being continually caught off balance by an adversary that had mastered the science of movement.[9]

Thus, as I see it, one has the military collapse of France; a critical error of judgment regarding the Ardennes, to which only a very few did not succumb; a critical error of judgment regarding the risks that were immediately implicit in the Dyle plan; and a critical failure to adjust to the tempo of armored-air warfare—here, one suspects, partly owing to the far grander temporal provisions of allied grand strategy and partly to associated doctrinal caveats of the sort which insisted on opening offensives with artillery barrages and closing them with time-consuming regrouping maneuvers. Certainly without the third failure, what others have less kindly called "sclerosis," the first two may well not have proven fatal. Had the German juggernaut been halted before the end of May, either on orders from a supreme headquarters unnerved by the sight of its conquering forces surrounded by allied armies, or as the result of timely counterattacks from concentrations of allied armor,[10] the war might have developed into the kind of extended struggle which the allied powers had anticipated and for which they had prepared. But it did not. So France fell, and in its wake, the Third Republic.[11]

Then ensued the autopsies, by the thousands, some less honest than others, some to indict, some to vindicate, a few merely to explain. Put together, these inquiries, some official and some private, from the great and the humble, exposed a grand universe of causes and responsibilities for the defeat. Fault finding became a national pastime under the sullen and vituperative Vichy regime,[12] an activity which of course stirred up as much controversy as it settled. And we have not yet reached that point, historically, where passion and partisanship have entirely abandoned the field to more reflective inquiry.

What happened after the battle of France went something like this. Whereas the political elite may have been content to explain the defeat in terms of military operations—covering the gamut from misadventure to incompetence to treason—the officer corps saw matters quite differently.

Though it was now undeniable that mistakes of grand proportion had been committed on the field of battle, the now discredited commanders protested that they had been left in the lurch by the civilian authority. In the face of a rearming Germany they had been expected, so it was said, to guard France and assemble a modern war machine on behalf of a society that had condemned militarism and its attendant expenses and had been misled into associating many of the most modern offensive weapons with military adventurism. The entire nation, Gamelin preferred to think, was at fault—a verdict which many reluctantly accepted as they would a stiff purgative. Sartre has his priest assure those taken prisoner in 1940, "When a man believes that he is the innocent victim of a catastrophe, and sits wringing his hands, unable to understand what has happened to him, is it not good for him to be told that he is expiating his own faults?"[13] So it was that Gamelin came to present the defeat, not, like the priest, something to rejoice in, but something nevertheless deserving, expiating his faults and his regrets in those of others. The defeat, he said, was the final issue

> of all French policy, domestic and foreign, since 1919, the consequences of which unfolded inexorably . . . I am personally convinced that our defeat is not a simple military one . . . but rather the result of many causes. The whole nation has paid for so many accumulated mistakes.

Thus the attribution of guilt was rapidly being broadened from the military and civilian commanders to the people as a whole, the people who as citizen soldiers had been demoralized and in some cases panicked by the unchecked visitations of the enemy.

Complementing these incessant, unedifying but entirely understandable exchanges in mutual recrimination—from which few in French society emerged unscathed—came one of the most extraordinary, most moving, and most influential works in modern French history. So different in character and motive from the more self-seeking inquests being conducted around it, Marc Bloch's *Strange Defeat* (1940) nonetheless did contribute to the growing conviction that such a great defeat required a truly great cause.[15] Whereas Bloch, this immensely gifted professional historian, in fact did devote the bulk of his attention to the performance of the army—ranging from intellectual to bureaucratic to operational considerations—he also issued a carefully worded indictment of the society to which that army had belonged. Thus, together with those partisan

accounts which in the pursuit of guilt sought to purge the country of anything remotely attributable to the defeat—from alcoholism to the Republic itself—Bloch's analysis also embraced *la nation toute entière*. So it
was, particularly within academic circles left grateful for Bloch's scholar-
ship and aggrieved by his martyrdom in the name of France and the Resistance, that the historical tradition of explaining the fall of France
"macrocosmically" was born.

There is not a single reason to disparage such an approach. By intent, surely, it is admirable, particularly under the gaze of a historical
profession which instinctively distrusts anything but multicausal explanations. But there is good reason for such an approach to exact great
caution on the part of its practitioners. It would be well to remember, for
instance, that this seminal work, though written by such an accomplished scholar, was also written in a self-confessed state of anger and
humiliation. A veteran of the proud 1918 campaign, Bloch, like so many
others, was enraged, mystified, and embarrassed by the inglorious campaign of 1940. Though more judicious and temperate, Bloch has a certain
kinship with Sartre's self-styled "biffed, buggered and bewildered" soldiers of 1940, those self-seen "Champs of the running-track, giants of the
open road, speed kings of the Olympic Games."[16] Behind *Strange Defeat*
there is an incensed soldier and an indignant patriot—a scholar who in
calmer days might well have protested against this so personal testimony
being used as clumsily yet so purposefully against the fallen Third Republic.

We have then to be careful about the role of motive in this broadening inquest into the fall of France: witnesses being used and using in
their turn a wide assortment of reasons for ever extending the search for
les responsables. This certainly must not undermine the validity of the
general endeavor, but it does counsel great caution.

So too is caution urged for other reasons. For instance, as was evidenced by Gamelin's testimony, the earliest impetus for macrocosmic
definition came in part from men for whom "destiny" or "inevitability"
were to serve as defense advocates. By their lights, a historical ground-
swell, far more grandiose than a six weeks battle, had swept the whole of
French society against the rocks of misfortune. Thus, together with inquiries inspired by partisanship and by a national pride insufferably
abused came those initiated by the need for some form of psychological
compensation. It is in this context that one may view the extraordinary
rereading of French mobilization in 1939. Then, as war was being de-

clared, public and private reports dwelt on the calm serenity in France and on the unprotesting, responsible manner in which soldiers were answering the call to mobilize. So Ambassador Bullitt assured Roosevelt of the "self-control and quiet courage . . . far beyond the usual standard of the human race." So the Paris correspondent of the *Sunday Times* told of a country standing "the test magnificently," with "nation-wide but individual restraint and self-control." So Genêt wrote of the same national composure.

> There are no flags, flowers, or shrill shouts of "Vive la patrie!" as there were in 1914. Among the men departing now for the possible front, the morale is excellent but curiously mental. What the men say is intelligent, not emotional. Yet all the French seem united in understanding that this war, if it comes, is about the theory of living and its eventual practice.[17]

Indeed, all this was in marked contrast to the euphoric atmosphere which had prevailed in 1914; but in August-September 1939 that difference was regarded as healthy. Was it not understandable that with those four years of butchery so easily within living memory men should have misgivings, and few illusions, about what lay ahead? But they went, with resignation—in Germany as well as in France[18]—to do their duty. Within a year, however, with France defeated, how legion were the seers who looked back to the days of the mobilization only to find more signs of the impending defeat. What had been regarded months before as reasonable, even praiseworthy, now was held up as the first raised head of defeatism. And so more "evidence" that the collapse had been foreordained.

There is too within this effort at a broad inquiry a peculiar and dangerous tendency to focus too particularly on France itself. If it may be said that a microcosmic interpretation based, say, on the military operations, is too narrow, indeed too simplistic, it may also be argued that many "macro" approaches do not go far enough. The failure to plan adequately for the lightning war practiced by Germany, after all was not peculiar to France, however much its collapse overshadowed that of Poland, Denmark, Norway, Holland, and Belgium and the subsequent near escapes of Britain and Russia. The failures (relative and not absolute) of conception, intelligence, and doctrine were of European-wide dimension —failures only belatedly, narrowly, and sometimes only partially averted by Germany's own military chiefs. Furthermore, whereas for a time it appeared that the equipment of the French army had been sadly, disastrously, deficient—an area of preparation which embraced generals and politicians, bureaucrats and technicians, workers and industrialists— it now is clear that only in the air were the allied forces decisively inferior, and there more numerically than qualitatively.[19] Moreover, it would appear that French industry was already on the verge of making up for most of the French air losses by the time the armistice was concluded toward the end of June.[20] Thus even when "macro" history is confined to France itself, it needs to be tailored to the new evidence instead of stubbornly persisting in the old legends.

And this raises one final reservation, again not against the principle of broadening our vision but against the force of assumptions to which much of this kind of work has deferred. It is good to be rigorously inquisitive about historical causation, and it is good to undertake the formidable tasks of broad social analysis; but these must be undertaken without allegiance to cause or commitment. A rigid, inflexible insistence on historical continuity, whereby events unfold in smooth and logical sequence, may carry one into the smothering embrace of determinism. And if one goes that far one is likely to overstate and oversimplify the causal relationship between, in this case, the defeat and the society which suffered it, finding not merely the explanation but the assurance of defeat. From this flows in turn the bitter, incriminating historical analyses which are tailor made to fit the form of defeat. This we must regret and resist for it is an obstacle to more productive and rewarding analyses of which the Third Republic is still in need.

This study, of course, has not been directed at the fall of France, nor is it a social history of the Republic. Rather it is a survey of French diplomatic and military attempts to at once avert and prepare for war. It has not been cut to accord with what happened in 1940; and therein is explained the uneven transition between this chapter and its nine predecessors, between the prewar years and the first year of war, between peace and the unexpected, unforeseen defeat. It may be granted that this need not have been the case, for others have demonstrated the possibility of tying the 1930s to 1940. With whatever justice, this account did not produce such a clear association, although there is no denying that problems which it discovered to be current in the 1930s had grown to tragic proportions by 1940. For instance, French strategic assumptions about Belgium in general and the Ardennes in particular were well rooted in the 1930s and, for that matter, in the 1920s. Similarly, one can hardly hope to grasp either the purpose or the impact of the Maginot Line simply by a hurried look at 1940, although it was ironic that what played so well into German hands in 1940 was not so much the immobility of the southern armies as it was the carefully contrived mobility of the French armies in the north. So too it is in the 1930s that one discovers the progressive canonization of the army's doctrinal pronouncements on the conduct of land and air warfare, pronouncements which eschewed all but the most methodically prepared offensives on the grounds that time—again the critical factor in 1940—could be cheaply bought by defensive firepower deployed on a fixed and elongated front. There is a good deal here, therefore, which throws as much light as shadow on the subsequent tragedy of 1940, however much that defeat extends beyond the focus of this work. Within that focus, up to September 1939 when war had never been more than probable, there seems to be little legitimate call for a severe indictment of French policy, foreign or military. Considered on balance, neither could be reckoned as provocative or incompetent, illogical or baseless, or even manifestly unsuccessful.

We may now hope that this policy, this French policy, has acquired, or rather reacquired, a form and substance of its own. Though it operated within a diplomatic solar system which had Britain at its center, this policy drew its inspiration from many quarters of the universe. Hence one may speak of French policy without intending it as a rather clumsy cover-up for something that in fact was British. The crises of the 1930s do more to confirm than contradict this judgment. To see them as one piece, threaded on one continuum, proof of an unenviable but perfect record of British-invoked paralysis, is to be taken in. The Rhineland (1936) and Austrian (1938) "crises" were not genuine crises at all, at least not to French governments determined to avoid war. The problem here was how to conceal that determination. The Spanish "crisis" (1936-1939) too, reflects a point of view and a pattern of behavior which were easily as much French as British in origin. Not so the Ethiopian (1935-1936) and Czech (1938) crises, when Anglo-French relations suffered from the pressures exerted by the threat of war and by the significant differences of outlook that characterized their respective policies. Thus, in the case of the former, what unnerved the Laval government was the fear that Britain might go to war with Italy; in the latter case, what Daladier found disconcerting was the chance that Britain would refrain from war with Germany. Again, to see these famous crises as a succession of repeat performances is to try to package history in neatly tied bundles—only to discover on inquiry that the string is too fine and the contents too unwieldy. Under these circumstances, therefore, it does not seem too audacious to insist on the intrinsic importance of French policy.

The diplomatic side of this policy reveals a mixed record of accomplishment and failure. Without holding them alone responsible for what did not happen, and without characterizing their behavior simply as motive-free drift, the French clearly did fail to enlist the allied services of Italy and Russia—services that had been demanded by Gamelin as early as 1934. Similarly, the Czech and Polish cases do not reflect well on French diplomacy. The upshot was that the French sold out the powerful Czech garrison—morally as well as militarily discrediting—only to ride out reluctantly the long unpopular alliance with Poland, the alliance which had kept France pinned in the east but which also impeded French chances of enlisting the great power services of the Soviet Union. On the other side of the ledger, and now without holding them fully responsible for what did happen, the French did manage to avoid pushing General Franco into the arms of the Axis—at considerable cost it is true; did manage to retain the sympathies of President Roosevelt, out of which came some much needed technical assistance in the form of military aviation;[21] and did manage to preserve at least satisfactory relations with Belgium and Turkey, both of which occupied vital strategic positions in French grand strategy. Finally, with much perseverance they managed to capture the indispensable British prize. Perseverance matched by good fortune, for what really tied the British to the continent was Chamberlain's determination to remain uncommitted, to remain isolationist: a determination to resolve continental problems before they involved Britain, before they demanded an alliance with France. This sort of intervention the French did not want, or need, but were powerless to prevent. Unable to stop it, they were obliged to wait, to wait until isolationism had imposed too heavy a responsibility on the British government and thus had paved the way for a real alliance. This waiting game the French played successfully, although how cleverly it is frankly difficult to judge.

The military side of this policy offers an equally uneven record. At the levels of tactical theory and operational conduct it appears as if the French underestimated, rather than ignored, the potential speed and firepower of armored-air units working in close cooperation. Ultimately it was this which hindered their attempts to bring the Wehrmacht to a halt after the Meuse crossings in May 1940. On the strategic and grand strategic levels we have found a conceptualization and a planning—appropriately economic as well as purely military—which accorded extremely well with the key military assumptions then current across Europe. If we are to learn anything from Marc Bloch and the respected *Annales* it must be the injunction against anachronistic value judgments —of the sort which tiresomely repeat how the French failed to go beyond the lessons of the First World War. First it is untrue, and second it suggests a signal failure to accept, without the protestations afforded by hindsight, a view of the world which all the events of the Second World War have prompted us to forget.

All in all the military and diplomatic efforts of prewar France, of the fallen and discredited Third Republic, did not constitute a sparkling or brilliant national policy. Deprived for good or ill of the charismatic leadership that seemed to surface in the totalitarian states, lacking the dynamic and aggressive diplomatic thrust of countries hungry and acquisitive, and not obliged by the same force of economic and strategic pressures to develop with commensurate speed and intensity the weapons of blitzkrieg, France of the 1930s has acquired in contrast a pale and pedestrian image. One may never succeed in discarding that impression; and perhaps one never should, for the strengths of this France derived more from the competence than from the charisma of its military and civilian commanders. But it may be hoped that this volume will restore to France a greater measure of independence, of rational and coherent motivation, of sensible planning, of dignity, than hitherto has been the case.

Abbreviations, Notes,
Bibliography, Index

Abbreviations

Private papers cited simply as:
Blum, Daladier, Schweisguth, La Chambre, Poydenot, Liddell Hart, Phipps, Hankey

Anglo-French Colloquium, for the four Colloquia on Relations between France and Great Britain between 1935 and 1939 (1971-1975)
Colloque Daladier, for the Colloquium on *La France sous le gouvernement Daladier* (1975)

ADM	Admiralty
CAB	Cabinet
CID	Committee of Imperial Defense
CPDN	Comité Permanent de la Défense Nationale
CSDN	Conseil Supérieur de la Défense Nationale
CSG	Conseil Supérieur de la Guerre
DDB	*Documents Diplomatiques Belges*
DDF	*Documents Diplomatiques Français*
DBFP	*Documents on British Foreign Policy*
DGFP	*Documents on German Foreign Policy*
EMA	Etat-Major de l'Armée
EMAA	Etat-Major de l'Armée de l'Air
Evénements	*Rapport fait au nom de la commission chargée d'enquêter sur les événements survenus en France de 1933 à 1945*
FO	Foreign Office
FRUS	*Foreign Relations of the United States*
GFM	German Foreign Ministry

Abbreviations

HCM	Haut Comité Militaire
JO	*Journal Officiel de la République Française*
MAE	Ministère des Affaires Etrangères
PRO	Public Record Office
SHA	Service Historique de l'Armée
SHAA	Service Historique de l'Armée de l'Air
SHM	Service Historique de la Marine
WO	War Office

AHR	*American Historical Review*
FA	*Foreign Affairs*
FHS	*French Historical Studies*
IA	*International Affairs*
IR	*International Relations*
JCEA	*Journal of Central European Affairs*
JCH	*Journal of Contemporary History*
JHM	*Journal of Modern History*
RDDM	*Revue des Deux Mondes*
RHDGM	*Revue d'Histoire de la Deuxième Guerre Mondiale*
RIIA	*Royal Institute of International Affairs*
RMG	*Revue Militaire Générale*
RUSI	*Royal United Services Institute Journal*

Notes

Introduction

1. C. Schoenbrun, *As France Goes* (New York: Harper Brothers, 1957), 44.

2. H. Butler, *The Lost Peace* (London: Faber and Faber, 1941), 70. In my view, Shirer's best-selling work, *The Collapse of the Third Republic* (London: Heinemann/Secker and Warburg, 1970), is an excellent example of this conception, an example singled out only because readers will be more familiar with this recent study than with many others.

3. Bullitt to Roosevelt, 23 March 1939, in *For the President: Personal and Secret*, ed. Orville Bullitt (London: Deutsch, 1973), 332-334.

4. Entry of 27 September 1938, *The Diplomatic Diaries of Oliver Harvey, 1937-40*, ed. John Harvey (London: Collins, 1970), 200.

5. Butler, *Lost Peace*, 81.

6. Phipps to Halifax, 12 October 1938, Public Record Office, Foreign Office 371, 22910, C16506/25/17 (hereafter cited as PRO, FO 371 . . .). Transcripts of Crown-copyright records in the Public Record Office appear by permission of the Controller of H.M. Stationery Office.

7. J. C. Cairns, "A Nation of Shopkeepers in Search of a Suitable France: 1919-1940," *AHR*, 79.3 (June 1974), 714. In this connection, Harvey suspected that Ambassador Phipps was "taking no trouble to find out opinions which may be unpalatable to H.M.G.," Harvey, *Diplomatic Diaries*, 195.

8. "You should ensure that your Ambassador is made aware that the view held by the Air Staff . . . is by no means as pessimistic as that which His Excellency appears to have held." Air Ministry to attaché (Paris) 27 September 1938, PRO, FO 371, 21596, C12038/36/17.

9. The short-lived trial of 1942 and the pre-trial investigations which were

initiated by Pétain's Vichy regime to establish the connection between the fall of France and the prewar Popular Front governments.

10. General Gamelin's Mémoire #10, December 1940, Blum, 3BL/Dr12; and Mémoire #2, August-September 1940, Daladier, 4DA24/Dr6/sdr b.

11. Preface by René Rémond to Paul de Villelume's *Journal d'une défaite, août 1939-juin 1940* (Paris: Fayard, 1976) xii-xiv.

12. The case of de Villelume's diary is admittedly different. Its contemporary authenticity is beyond doubt, but so too is its *parti pris* nature. For de Villelume to have seen military incompetence in a war he regarded as utter folly, for him to have seen the defeatism which under another name he himself championed, should not be regarded as remarkable.

13. Only a minority of Frenchmen may have opposed the Versailles settlement in 1919, as Pierre Miquel contends, but their ranks clearly grew steadily thereafter. Cf. P. Miquel, *La paix de Versailles et l'opinion publique française* (Paris: Flammarion, 1972).

14. *League of Nations, Treaty Series*, II, 1920, 127-130 (hereafter cited as *LNTS*).

15. *LNTS*, XVIII, 1923, 12-13; LIV, 1926-27, 354-356.

16. *LNTS*, XXIII, 1924, 165-169; LIV, 1926-27, 360-362.

17. *LNTS*, LVIII, 1926-27, 225-231, 233-243.

18. *LNTS*, LXVIII, 1927, 375-379.

1. Land, Resources, and Strategic Planning

1. "Topographical Factors Affecting Land Operations," 1939, PRO, 9086, CAB 53/45.

2. The French staff officer, General Schweisguth, made precisely this point to General Dill in April 1936. The location of the French defenses, he said, would "direct (*rejeter*) future operations . . . toward Belgium and Holland," Schweisguth, 351 AP6, Dr12.

3. "Topographical Factors," August 1935, PRO, CAB 54/25, 8988.

4. British estimates gave Germany a two-to-one edge. Cf. "Notes on the principal industrial . . . factors," August 1935, PRO, CAB 55/7. Marshal Pétain gave Germany a three-to-one margin. Meeting of 22 November 1935, CSDN, Service Historique de l'Armée (SHA).

5. Even in 1920-21, the offensively oriented Plan P was very modest in its goals, "designed merely to hinder German mobilization and strengthen [France's] diplomatic stance." Cf. J. Hughes, *To the Maginot Line* (Cambridge, Mass.: Harvard University Press, 1971) 86.

6. Cf. "General Survey of National Resources of France," 6 March 1939, PRO, FO 371, 22916, C2737/130/17; Economic Warfare Synopsis (France), July 1939, PRO, FO 837/1B.

7. See "General Survey" in note 6 above; CSDN note entitled "Le potentiel économique de guerre de la France," Daladier, 2DA4/Dr3/sdr a and Dr4. For information relating specifically to French coal requirements, see M. Gowing,

"Anglo-French Economic Collaboration before the Second World War," Anglo-French Colloquium, 1972. (See note under Colloquia Papers in the Bibliography).

8. "General Survey," March 1939, PRO, FO 371, 22916, C2737/130/17.

9. Ibid.

10. "Note sur la mobilisation industrielle," 17 January 1940, Daladier, 4DA4/Dr1. Cf. also J. Regnault, "L'évolution du rôle militaire et maritime de l'empire colonial français," RMG (February 1938) 191-219.

11. See "General Survey" in note 6 above; see also note entitled "Possibilities of the Exercise of Maritime Economic Pressure on France," August 1930, PRO, CAB 47/4; C. J. Gignoux, L'économie française entre les deux guerres, 1919-1939 (Paris: Société d'Editions Economiques et Sociales, n.d.) 187-208.

12. Information on the French carrying trade is contained in a note prepared by Daladier's secretariat on 22 November 1938, Daladier, 2DA4/Dr3/sdr a and from the "General Survey" of March 1939, PRO, FO 371, 22916, C2737/130/17.

13. French awareness of this vulnerability is reflected in a note by air intelligence, "La situation économique de l'Allemagne," 28 September 1938, Service Historique de l'Armée de l'Air (SHAA) Carton B 73; see also Le Goyet, "Les relations économiques franco-britanniques à la veille de la 2e guerre mondiale," Anglo-French Colloquium, 1972.

14. Cf. note on "Economic Situation in Germany, Italy and Japan," April 1939, PRO, CAB 53/45; A. S. Milward, The New Order and the French Economy (Oxford: Clarendon Press, 1970) 28-29, 34-35.

15. Cf. notes referred to in notes 4 and 12 above, August 1935 and March 1939, PRO, CAB 55/7 and FO 371, 22916, C2737/130/17.

16. Cf. notes referred to in notes 11 and 12 above, August 1930 and March 1939, PRO, CAB 47/4 and FO 371, 22916, C2737/130/17. See also minutes of CPDN meetings of 5 December 1936 and 3 November 1937 for information on the work of Paul Ramadier, under-secretary of state for mines, electricity, and liquid fuel, SHA; M. Gowing, "Anglo-French Economic Collaboration," Anglo-French Colloquium, 1972; R. Grandclément, "La politique mondiale du pétrole," RMG (May 1938) 591-623.

17. "Note sur la mobilisation industrielle," 5 April 1939, Daladier, 4DA4/Dr1.

18. W. A. Lewis, Economic Survey, 1919-1939 (London: Unwin University Books, 1966) 100. For French benefits from reduced primary prices, see T. A. Schweitzer, "The French Colonialist Lobby in the 1930s" (Ph.D. dissertation, University of Wisconsin, 1971) 226-229.

19. Undated 101-page report, likely by Robert Jacomet, entitled "Du rôle du secrétariat-général du ministère de la défense nationale et de la guerre," Daladier, 4DA2/Dr2; and "Note sur la mobilisation industrielle," 5 April 1939, ibid., 4DA4/Dr1.

20. For signs of this anxiety consult J. Néré's account of a series of lectures presented to the Collège des Hautes-Etudes de Défense Nationale in 1936-37, in "La France devant la guerre économique," Anglo-French Colloquium, 1972.

21. R. D. Challener, The French Theory of the Nation in Arms, 1866-1939 (New York: Columbia University Press, 1955) 233-235.

22. Cf. "General Survey," March 1939, PRO, FO 371, 22916, C2737/130/17;

Challener, *Nation in Arms*, 233-236; J. Paul-Boncour, *Entre deux guerres* (Paris: Plon, 1945) II, 250-257.

23. "Note sur la mobilisation industrielle," 17 January 1940, Daladier, 4DA4/Dr1. The importance attached to economic warfare after 1919 was complemented by the proliferation of new economic-oriented dailies and weeklies. Cf. R. Manévy, *La presse de la IIIe république* (Paris: Foret, 1955) 160-161.

24. Voting members included the premier or the president of the Republic as chairman, the ministers of foreign affairs, interior, public works, finance, war, navy, and colonies, and one marshal of France. See *League of Nations: Armaments Year-Book, 1934*, 214-215; J. Vial, "La défense nationale: Son organisation entre les deux guerres," *RHDGM*, 5.18 (April 1955) 12-14.

25. Challener, *Nation in Arms*, 192; F. Greene, "French Military Leadership and Security against Germany" (Ph.D. dissertation, Yale University, 1950) 97. The CSDN appears not to have met between October 1932 and March 1935. Its last formal session took place on 22 November 1935. See the CSDN minutes, SHA.

26. Consultants included the under-secretary of state in the premier's secretariat, the inspector-general of air defense, the vice-presidents of the army, navy, and air councils, and the vice-chairman of the CSDN's *commission d'études*. Cf. A. Martel, "Le poids de la stratégie controverses et données contestées," Colloque Daladier, 1975. (See note under Colloquia Papers in the Bibliography.)

27. For examples of these military complaints see M. G. Gamelin, *Servir* (Paris: Plon, 1946) II, 133; M. Weygand, *Mémoires* (Paris: Flammarion, 1957) II, 392.

28. For the misgivings expressed in army headquarters staff see Daladier's testimony, 3 March 1940, Blum, 3BL/Dr15/sdr b.

29. Its usual membership included the premier, the three service ministers, the vice-presidents of the army, navy, and air councils, the inspector-general of territorial air defense, and a marshal of France. In addition to Greene and Vial and *Armaments Year-Book*, see Mordacq's *La défense nationale en danger* (Paris: Editions de France, 1938) 26; and General Albord's article in *La défense nationale* (Paris: P.U.F., 1958) 294-305.

30. Cf. Vial, "La défense nationale," *RHDGM* (April 1955) 17-18; Gamelin, *Servir*, II, 251-252; General Azan, "L'organisation de la défense nationale," *RMG*, 4 (1938) 254; France, *Journal Officiel de la République Française* (*JO*) Chambre des Députés, Documents (January-December 1937) annex no. 90, 4 March 1937, 60-61.

31. Judging from the official minutes for 1936-37, currently the most complete, the CPDN met at irregular intervals but roughly on an average of every two months. Occasionally there were other meetings held under the aegis of the CPDN, designated as *Réunions des Chefs d'Etat-Major Généraux*. Membership comprised the four chiefs of staff (including the colonial arm) and a handful of their most senior staff officers.

32. General Bernard Serrigny, "L'organisation de la nation pour le temps de guerre," *RDDM*, 18 (December 1923) 593.

33. For example, see his chapter on policy in the *Army of the Future* (London:

Hutchinson, n.d.) 61-84.

34. Gamelin, *Servir*, I, 33, and his note 1. See also his replies to the Riom court, 28 September 1940, Daladier, 4DA24/Dr5/sdr a.

35. Naval ministry to Daladier, 27 April 1937, Daladier, 4DA7/Dr5.

36. Daladier's figures suggest a budget distribution for the period 1920-34 as follows: navy (42%), army (31%), air (27%). See his note on "L'armement de la France," Daladier, 4DA1/Dr1. Cf. also Admiral Castex, "L'Afrique et la stratégie française," *Revue de Défense Nationale*, 14 (May 1952) 523-534; Admiral Darlan, "Composition et puissance de la flotte," *RMG* (January 1938) 31-42.

37. See my "The Strategic Dream: French Air Doctrine in the Inter-War Period, 1919-1939," *JCH*, 9.4 (October 1974) 57-76. The debate within the Haut Comité Militaire in March 1933 is particularly illustrative of the tension between the land and air armies.

38. Cf. A. Krebs, "Considérations sur l'offensive," *RMG* (September 1937) 324-365; R. Young, "Preparations for Defeat: French War Doctrine in the Inter-War Period," *Journal of European Studies*, 2.2 (June 1972) 155-172.

39. It seems the French themselves were unhappy with the expression "continuous front," fearing that it falsely implied a linear defense without fortifications arranged in depth. See the meeting of 15 May 1933, *Conseil Supérieur de la Guerre*, XVI, SHA.

40. For expressions of concern about the vulnerability of an unfortified frontier with Belgium, see the meetings of the CSG, 28 May 1932 and 15 May 1933, SHA. Pétain's warning, one of many, came during the meeting of 17 December 1926, Daladier, 4DA1/Dr2.

2. 1933: Disarmament and the Drift toward Arms Equality

1. Tyrrell to Simon, 16 January 1933, "France. Annual Report," PRO, FO 371, 17299, W540/540/17. The Mediterranean ports, principally Marseilles but including Cette and St. Louis du Rhône, accounted for 22 percent of French import trade (nearly 100 percent of imports from North and East Africa, Levant, India, and the Far East) and about 25 percent of French export trade. See Advisory Committee on Trade and Blockade report of August 1930, PRO, CAB 47/4, ATB 91.

2. For evidence of the suspicions aroused by such expressions as "opérations aériennes" and "bataille aérienne" see the minutes of the study sessions by the military members of the Haut Comité Militaire, 20, 21, 25 October 1933, SHA, CPDN "Archives du Général Gamelin."

3. "Note concernant les possibilités actuelles de l'aviation française," March 1934, SHAA, B21. See also General Jauneaud's deposition at Riom, 21 March 1941, Daladier, 4DA15/Dr3. Unlike France, where bombers comprised a third of the air strength, Germany was reported as having two thirds of its total air strength in bombing units. Cf. "Note au sujet des armements aériens allemands," 8 March 1933, SHAA, B21.

4. Tyrrell to Simon, 16 January 1933, PRO, FO 371, 17299, W540/540/17.

5. HCM meetings of 20, 27 March 1933, SHA. General Denain, the chief of air staff, later described French air power in 1933 as "mediocre as far as the technical quality of its equipment was concerned . . . , totally incapable of measuring up to a modern air force," Riom deposition of 21 April 1941, Daladier, 4DA14/Dr1.

6. HCM meeting, 20 March 1933, SHA. See also my "Strategic Dream," *JCH* (October 1974) 57-76.

7. Peacetime strength of one infantry division stood around 15,000 men of all ranks. War footing brought the figure to 18,000, organized into three infantry regiments, two artillery regiments, and assorted companies of engineers, signals, reconnaissance, wireless, and meteorological services. Each division (1933-37) was to have 36 field guns (75 mm), 24 howitzers (155 mm), 350 light automatics, 185 machine guns, 9 close support guns (37 mm), 27 mortars, and some 30 anti-tank guns (25 mm). See *Notes on the French Army*, pp. 50-51, prepared by the British War Office in 1936, with amendments for 1937, WO Library.

8. Tyrrell to Simon, 16 January 1933, PRO, FO 371, 17299, W540/540/17; *League of Nations, Armaments Year-Book*, 1935, 32-37; *JO Sénat*, Debates, CXXIII, 28 December 1935, 1022.

9. A view expressed by Daladier, then premier and war minister, to the CSG, 15 May 1933, SHA.

10. Tyrrell to FO, 19 May 1933, PRO, FO 371, 16729, W4650/320/18.

11. Cf. French note "Infractions de l'Allemagne," 22 March 1933, PRO, FO 371, 16706, C2641/245/18; and "Principaux manquements allemands," 4 August 1933, ibid., 16708, C6942/245/18.

12. CSG, 15 May 1933, SHA.

13. Cf. Annual reports on France for 1932 and 1933, PRO, FO 371, 17299, W540/540/17, and 17660, C317/317/17.

14. *Les années creuses*, or the "lean" years, referred to the period 1935-40 when the annual contingent of French conscripts would be halved from 240,000 to 120,000. This phenomenon, so dreaded by the high command, stemmed from the slaughter of 1914-18 during which well over a million young soldiers lost their lives. The lean years is thus a haunting reminder of the sons these men were never to have, of an unborn generation of *poilus*.

15. Enclosure from Colonel Heywood, Tyrrell to Simon, 18 March 1933, PRO, FO 371, 16706, C2626/245/18.

16. The minister (Daladier) "thinks . . . that our current resources will allow us to defend the country, but that initially it will not be possible to do anything more than ensure our territorial integrity." CSG, 15 May 1933, SHA.

17. Cf. note under cover Gamelin to Daladier, 10 July 1936, Daladier, 4DA1/Dr4/ sdr b; Gamelin, *Servir*, II, 199; General Maurin's testimony in *Rapport fait au nom de la commission chargée d'enquêter sur les événements survenus en France de 1933 à 1945*, V, 1265 (hereafter cited as *Evénements*, Testimony or Report). The figure of 90 divisions was used by Weygand, ibid., VI, 1637.

18. Meeting of CSG, 4 June 1932, Daladier, 4DA1/Dr2.

19. Cf. discussion on mobile forces, agenda item 2, CSG meeting of 13 May 1933, SHA. "Tanks are restricted to a short attack on a narrow front and no independent role is ever assigned to them." *Handbook of the French Army*, 1932, WO Library, 169.

20. For instance, the French Left and Center Left disliked on ideological grounds the idea of a professional, mercenary army which they feared would be unresponsive to the nation's democratic will. They also disliked, however, extending the period of military service for fear that the conscript would become too militarized—a sentiment warmly endorsed by many future conscripts although not necessarily for the same reasons. Finally, either measure would be expensive, difficult then to justify when money was tight and when the foreign danger was still more potential than immediate.

21. Tyrrell's annual reports for 1932 and 1933 indicate that financial pressures had led to a cancellation of the army's regular autumn maneuvers in 1932 and the elimination of all "large-scale maneuvers" in 1933 (i.e., above divisional level). Cf. note 13 above.

22. Cf. Daladier's undated note on rearmament, Daladier, 4DA1/Dr1. For the shortage of anti-tank weapons in 1936, see his testimony of 27 February 1942, Blum, 3BL/Dr14/sdr d. As for the artillery, "We did very little to modernize our artillery service," deposition of General Georges, 21 August 1940, Daladier, 4DA14/Dr5.

23. CSG meeting, 24 March 1934, SHA.

24. French technicians estimated that even an anti-tank gun would require an average of 55 months to go from the initial studies to serial production, including 18 months from prototype to series. Hence the temptation to delay serial production, partly to limit financial outlay and partly to limit obsolescence of weapons produced too far in advance of war. Cf. Daladier's testimony, 27 February 1942, Blum, 3BL/Dr14/sdr d. For one critical view of this "fruitless cult of perfectionism," see J. Weygand, *Weygand, mon père* (Paris: Flammarion, 1970) 237.

25. French acceptance of this principle came in a five-power agreement of 11 December 1932, signed at Geneva but outside the formal authority of the Disaramament Conference. The powers included Britain, France, Germany, Italy, and the United States.

26. François-Poncet to Paul-Boncour, 15 and 30 March 1933, *Documents Diplomatiques Français*, ser. 1, vol. II, no. 413, pp. 809-822, and vol. III, no. 70, pp. 118-124 (hereafter cited as *DDF*).

27. "Note au sujet des armements aériens allemands," 8 March 1933, SHAA, B21.

28. Tyrrell to Simon, 30 March 1933, PRO, FO 800 (Simon) 251-253. One may note that Daladier later referred to "my work" in connection with disarmament, "nullified, frittered away, overturned" by the subsequent Doumergue government. See his testimony, 27 February 1942, Blum, 3BL/Dr14/sdr a.

29. Tyrrell to Simon, 16 March 1933, PRO, FO 800 (Simon) 288. It was ironic

that these two men should have been so described in 1933, Daladier, who would be forced to go to Munich, Léger, who was to acquire the reputation of a bitter Italophobe.

The other changes included Bargeton's replacement of Léger as director of political and commercial affairs; the creation of two assistant posts in this directorate, filled by Robert Coulondre and René Massigli; Charvériat's replacement of Bargeton as director of the European department; Renom de la Baume's replacement of Coulondre as subdirector of the commercial relations department; and the appointment of Pierre Comert as head of the Information and Press department. The ambassadorial changes saw Claudel move from Washington to Brussels, Corbin from Brussels to London, Clauzel from Vienna to Berne, and Alphand from Dublin to Moscow.

30. Minute by Vansittart, Tyrrell to Simon, 28 February 1933, *PRO*, FO 371, 17301, W2301/2301/17.

31. Cf. memo 18 September 1933, *Documents on British Foreign Policy*, ser. 2, vol. V, no. 399, pp. 600-606, and record of conversation, 22 September 1933, ibid., no. 406, pp. 612-621 (hereafter cited as *DBFP*).

32. These proponents of Franco-German cooperation were identified for Wigram by Pierre Etienne Flandin who "has informed me regularly for the last five years . . . These men believed in a Franco-German commercial and industrial combine (and) were quite indifferent to German rearmament, provided it was effected in agreement with France." Memo (Wigram), 21 November 1933, PRO, FO 371, 16710, C10307/245/18.

33. Memo (Charles Peake), under cover, Harvey (Paris) to Vansittart, 19 September 1933, PRO, FO 371, 16709, C8343/245/18.

34. One may note in this connection that in 1933 Daladier ordered the commander of the sixth army corps at Nancy to prepare plans for a limited offensive in the Rhineland. Cf. "Notes manuscrites," Daladier, 1DA6/Dr6/sdr b.

35. Minute by Vansittart, permanent under-secretary at the Foreign Office, 8 December 1933, PRO, FO 371, 16712, C10759/285/18.

36. Cf. note on "L'armement de la France," Daladier, 4DA1/Dr1.

37. Denain to Barthou, 23 February 1934, *DDF*, ser. 1, vol. V, no. 427, pp. 804-806; "Note sur les possibilités comparé des aviations lourdes françaises et allemandes," 8 March 1934, SHAA, B21.

38. CSG meeting, 18 December 1933, SHA.

39. Colonel Bond (WO) to Wigram, 15 November 1933, PRO, FO 371, 16710, C9893/245/18. British figures "compare very closely with the conclusions reached by the French General Staff."

40. Cf. *Armaments Year-Book*, 1935, 401.

41. Note of 6 January 1934, *DDF*, ser. 1, vol. V, no. 201, pp. 417-419.

42. Cf. Weygand, *Mémoires*, II, 383-393; *Evénements*, Testimony, Weygand, I, 232-240, 243-246; Paul-Boncour, *Entre deux guerres*, II, 182-325; *Evénements*, Testimony, Paul-Boncour, III, 785-790.

43. Niessel, "Les effectifs de l'armée allemande," *RDDM*, 19 (January 1934) 35-50; E. Herriot, *Jadis*, II, *D'une guerre à l'autre* (Paris: Flammarion, 1952) 399-400.

44. François-Poncet to Paul-Boncour, 27 December 1933, *DDF*, ser. 1, vol. V, no. 172, pp. 354-365.

45. Clerk (Paris) to Simon, 14 June 1934, *DBFP*, ser. 2, vol. VI, no. 456, pp. 757-758. The British did not accept this conclusion, believing instead that Germany was unlikely to pose an offensive threat before 1938. Director of Military Intelligence to FO, 5 July 1934, PRO, WO 190/262.

46. Note of 11 May 1934, under cover Weygand to Pétain, 17 May 1934, Daladier, 4DA1/Dr2/sdr a.

47. Daladier, it was said, had once remarked, "Weygand, c'était un mur. Gamelin, c'est un édredon." General O. Poydenot, "Mémoires" (unpublished) pt. 2, p. 5.

48. A transcript of this survey may be found in J. Minart, *Le drame du désarmement français* (Paris: Nef de Paris, 1960) 69-71.

49. Phipps (British ambassador, Berlin) to Simon, 14 February 1934, PRO, FO 800 (Simon) 289.

50. Eden to Simon, 18 February 1933, ibid.

51. Tyrrell to Simon, 30 October 1933, *DBFP*, ser. 2, vol. V, no. 508, pp. 732-737.

52. R. de Dorlodot, *Souvenirs* (Bruxelles: Ad. Goemaere, 1964) II, 27-39, 134-148, 170-171, 192; *Evénements*, Testimony, Dorlodot, III, 829-832; Cabinet meeting, 24 April 1934, *Documents Diplomatiques Belges*, vol. III, no. 127, pp. 359-361 (hereafter cited as *DDB*).

53. The remark was reported by Ambassador de Gaiffier and was aired during the cabinet meeting of 24 April, *DDB*, vol. III, no. 127, pp. 359-361.

3. 1934: Security First

1. Cf. General van Overstraeten, *Albert I-Léopold III: Vingt ans de politique militaire belge, 1920-1940* (Bruges: Desclée de Brower, n.d.) 90-115.

2. Note from the EMA, 17 February 1934, *DDF*, ser. 1, vol. VI, no. 401, pp. 737-740.

3. General Pétin (Bucharest) to Pétain, 8 April 1934, ibid., no. 70, pp. 176-181; General Lepetit (Belgrade) to Pétain, 12 April, ibid., no. 85, pp. 210-211.

4. See French request for time to reflect on German budgetary increases, Barthou to ambassadors, 6 April, ibid., no. 64, pp. 160-162.

5. Compte Rendu (Commission spéciale) 14 April, ibid., no. 93, pp. 220-237.

6. Doumergue to Barthou, 16 April, ibid., no. 97, pp. 246-247. For the premier's consultations with Tardieu, Pétain, Herriot, and Marin, see J. Minart, *Le drame*, 72; J. Chastenet, *Histoire de la troisième république* (Paris: Hachette, 1962) VI, 96.

7. Note (Massigli) 13 April 1934, *DDF*, ser. 1, vol. VI, no. 87, pp. 212-213.

8. Cf. Massigli's two notes of 15 May 1934, ibid., no. 208, p. 477, and no. 211, pp. 479-480.

9. For other signs that the French believed British opinion was ripe, see Weygand's *Mémoires*, II, 419, 421. For evidence of British embassy sympathy see

Campbell to Simon, 30 April, *DBFP*, ser. 2, vol. VI, no. 415, pp. 681-682. And although there may have been "a painful disappointment," Simon too treated the matter very calmly. Corbin to Barthou, 26 April 1934, *DDF*, ser. 1, vol. VI, no. 145, pp. 361-364.

10. Eden to Simon, 18 February 1934 and 17 May 1934, PRO, FO 800 (Simon) 289.

11. Eden's note, 12 May 1934, PRO, FO 371, 18525, W4691/1/98; his report on talk with Massigli, 15 May, ibid., W4714/1/98; Lord Avon, *The Eden Memoirs: Facing the Dictators* (London: Cassell, 1962) 89.

12. Barthou to Campbell, 17 April 1934, *Négociations relatives à la réduction et à la limitation des armements* (Paris: Imprimerie Nationale, 1934).

13. While one may be skeptical of such assurances, the scheduled second meeting of the special commission did take place on 17 April in order to discuss the topic of disarmament. The meeting convened after the cabinet's decision on the note, with neither Herriot nor Tardieu saying anything to the commission about that decision. Compte Rendu, 17 April, *DDF*, ser. 1, vol. VI, no. 197, pp. 275-283.

14. FO minute (Leeper) 1 May 1934, PRO, FO 371, 18524, W4152/1/98. François-Poncet's account is more graphic. Doumergue, it is said, prevented Barthou from reading his proposed reply. "No, my friend. Keep your plan and take this one; it's better. It was jointly prepared by me and the two Ministers of State. This is the text that we will propose to the cabinet." *Souvenirs d'une ambassade à Berlin* (Paris: Flammarion, 1946) 178.

15. Barthou to Ambassadors, 8 May 1934, *DDF*, vol. VI, no. 183, p. 433. Barthou was more candid with the Chamber, claiming that he and Doumergue had been agreed but adding: "if there had been differences of opinion, it perhaps would be awkward for me to say so." *JO Députés*, 25 May 1934, II, 1261.

16. For Weygand's denial of involvement see Campbell to Simon, 2 May 1934, *PRO*, FO 371, 18524, W4154/1/98. For his admission see *Evénements*, Testimony, Weygand, VI, 1595. Cf. also Herriot, *Jadis*, II, 410-411; O. Abetz, *Das offene Problem* (Cologne: Greven, 1951) 56. Interestingly, Weygand's *Mémoires* do not mention this role.

17. The records of the Haut Comite Militaire make this very clear. However, it may be noted that Chastenet singles out Flandin, Laval, and Piétri as opponents of the note. Cf. Chastenet, *Histoire de la troisième république*, VI, 96.

18. No cabinet records were taken in this period. Consequently, one is dependent on contemporary utterances, private and public, and subsequently on postwar testimonies and published memoirs. The result, often, is a series of accounts which differ wholly or in part. Herriot, for instance, never conceded Barthou's opposition to the note, a recollection that is at odds with most others.

19. Campbell to Simon, 17 and 30 April, *DBFP*, ser. 2, vol. VI, nos. 394 and 415, pp. 630-631, 675. Cabinet minutes, 24 April, *DDB*, vol. III, no. 127, p. 358; Gaiffier to Jaspar, 13 June, ibid., no. 133, p. 386; Flandin, *Politique française, 1919-1940* (Paris: Les Editions Nouvelles, 1947) 72; *Evénements*, Testimony, Lebrun, IV, 958.

20. *JO Députés*, Debates, 25 May 1934, II, 1260-1261.

21. Campbell to Simon, 30 April, *DBFP*, ser. 2, vol. VI, no. 415, p. 678.

22. Ibid., 679.

23. Cf. W. A. Lewis, *Economic Survey*, 99; M. Wolfe, *The French Franc between the Wars, 1919-1939* (New York: Columbia University Press, 1951) 73-137; *Evénements*, Testimony, Lebrun, IV, 954-956; ibid., Reynaud, I, 83-88.

24. Campbell to Simon, 30 April, *DBFP*, ser. 2, vol. VI, no. 415, p. 682.

25. One suspects that such warnings were being used to ensure against further defense cuts. One knows that Gamelin was less exercised than Weygand. "We will see," he confided to François-Poncet, "how long it takes the Germans to catch up to the 20 billion francs which we have spent on our armaments," to which Poncet adds, "In this period our military chiefs believed sincerely that we had a considerable advantage in materiel over the Germans and that Germany would never have the means to finance a large rearmament program." *Evénements*, Testimony, François-Poncet, III, 762. This has been supported by General Tournoux, *Haut commandement: Gouvernement et défense des frontières du nord et de l'est, 1919-1939* (Paris: Nouvelles Editions Latines, 1960) 199, but denied by Castellan, *Le réarmement clandestin du Reich, 1930-1935* (Paris: Plon, 1954) 517, n.4.

26. R. Leurquin's article in *The Times*, 17-18 August 1938; article by Poulaine in *Le Temps*, 1 August 1935; V. Rowe, *The Great Wall of France* (London: Putnam, 1960) 60-79; P. Bénazet's report of 28 June 1934, *JO Sénat*, Debates, CXX, 848-850.

27. Cf. Tournoux, *Haut commandement*, 336-337. He alludes to "a relief operation in the Rhineland" but only after "a certain delay," like Plan C only after having assured the defense of "our land frontiers," and finally only as a counter-offensive move to release some of the German pressure on eastern Europe.

28. Although it was not yet so judged in June 1934. Indeed, the French were said to fear a German seizure of the newly completed fortresses, which, although replete with arms and ammunition, were unmanned and only lightly guarded. Military attaché (Heywood) to WO, 18 June 1934, *PRO*, WO 32/3594.

29. Also in evidence was the tendency to assign more and more recruits to the fortified regions, even though the special *frontalier* units had been created in 1931 to free recruits for service in the regular divisions. Weygand, *Mémoires*, II, 416.

30. A fact confirmed by both Weygand and Gamelin, ibid., 426, and Gamelin, *Servir*, II, 133.

31. Cf. Daladier's note "L'armement de la France," Daladier, 4DA1/Dr1 and the CSG meetings of 24 March and 3 September 1934, XVII, *SHA*.

32. CSG meeting, 24 March 1934, SHA; Tournoux, *Haut commandement*, 205, 208.

33. The other being the superiority of defense over attack. Campbell to Simon, 2 May 1934, PRO, FO 371, 18524, W4154/1/98.

34. Campbell to Simon, 30 April 1934, *DBFP*, ser. 2, vol. VI, no. 415, p. 677.

35. Cf. E. Bonnefous, *Histoire politique de la troisième république* (Paris: P.U.F., 1962) V, 285; F. Goguel-Nyégaard, *La politique des partis de la troisième république* (Paris: Editions du Seuil, 1946) 136.

36. G. Tabouis, *They Called Me Cassandra* (New York: Scribner's Sons, 1942) 197.

37. Gamelin, *Servir*, II, 126, 131-133.

38. P. van Zuylen, *Les mains libres: Politique extérieure de la Belgique, 1914-1940* (Bruxelles: L'Edition Universelle, 1950) 274-284; P. Hymans, *Mémoires* (Bruxelles: Institut Solvay, 1958) II, 602-636.

39. Compte rendu, 27 March 1934, *DDF*, ser. 1, vol. VI, no. 141, pp. 105-111; *DDB*, vol. III, no. 121, pp. 335-338.

40. As ambassador Gaiffier observed, "The logical outcome of the April 17 note ought to be war," *DDB*, III, no. 135, p. 394. For reference to Senator Dorlodot, see my chapter 2.

41. Laroche to Quai, 24 April, *DDF*, VI, no. 133, pp. 333-336; Barthou to Corbin, 7 June, ibid., no. 299, pp. 637-640; Clerk to Simon, 5 May 1934, *DBFP*, ser. 2, vol. VI, no. 418, pp. 688-689; Herriot, *Jadis*, II, 442-424; J. Laroche, *La Pologne de Pilsudski* (Paris: Flammarion, 1953) 154-155; J. Beck, *Final Report* (New York: Speller and Sons, 1957) 54-56.

42. Cf. note of 16 April, *DDF*, vol. VI, no. 100, pp. 258-262; W. E. Scott, *Alliance against Hitler* (Durham, N.C.: Duke University Press, 1962) 134-152; Clerk to Simon, 14 June 1934, *DBFP*, ser. 2, vol. VI, no. 455, pp. 753-756.

43. Tabouis, *Cassandra*, 207. Tabouis was one of the journalists who accompanied Barthou to Poland.

44. See note of 24 March 1934, *DDF*, vol. VI, no. 37, pp. 97-98. For General Debeney's unsuccessful trip to Warsaw see his report, 25 June 1934, ibid., no. 385, pp. 782-784; Laroche, *La Pologne de Pilsudski*, 166-167, and "La collaboration franco-polanaise, 1933-1939," an unpublished, undated study by the SHAA, Cote C/2.

45. Avon, *Facing the Dictators*, 94-95.

46. Barthou to Laroche, 22 June 1934, *DDF*, vol. VI, no. 373, pp. 764-765.

47. Unlike the differences encountered in Warsaw, Barthou's visit to Prague in April was said to have been "unclouded by any shadow." Clerk to Simon, 5 May 1934, *DBFP*, ser. 2, vol. VI, no. 418, p. 689; Barthou to Corbin, 7 June, *DDF*, vol. VI, no. 299, pp. 637-640.

48. Compte Rendu, 18 May 1934, *DDF*, vol. VI, no. 221, pp. 496-502.

49. Herriot, *Jadis*, V, 437-438; report by M. Torres, *JO Députés*, Documents, 10 December 1935, 161-169.

50. Simon to Phipps, 12 June 1934, *DBFP*, ser. 2, vol. VI, no. 450, pp. 746-747.

51. Davis to Secretary of State, 2 June 1934, *Foreign Relations of the United States*, 1934, I, 95 (hereafter cited as *FRUS*).

52. Simon to Phipps, 12 June 1934, *DBFP*, ser. 2, vol. VI, no. 450, p. 747.

53. Clerk to Simon, 14 June 1934, ibid., no. 454, pp. 752-753. For British interest in France's value as an ally, see the note on the German air menace by air chief of staff Ellington, 11 July 1934, PRO, CAB 53/24, COS 344.

54. For information on this visit, see *DDF*, vol. VI, no. 366, pp. 752-753, and no. 432, pp. 878-879.

55. Clerk to Simon, 20 June 1934, *DBFP*, ser. 1, vol. VI, no. 463, pp. 764-768.

56. See French note, 11 July 1934, *DDF*, vol. VI, no. 457, pp. 940-944; and British record, 9-10 July, *DBFP*, ser. 2, vol. VI, nos. 487-489, pp. 803-822.

57. "Eastern Pact," Cmd. 5143, Miscellaneous no. 3 (1936) *Correspondence Showing the Course of Certain Diplomatic Discussions Directed towards Securing a European Settlement, June 1934 to March 1936*, 7-8.

58. Erskine to Simon, 3 July 1934, *DBFP*, ser. 2, vol. VI, no. 479, p. 783.

59. Avon, *Facing the Dictators*, 98; Flandin, *Politique française*, 71; Scott, *Alliance against Hitler*, pp. viii, 257; C. A. Micaud, *The French Right and Nazi Germany* (Durham, N.C.: Duke University Press, 1943) 33-34; F. L. Schuman, *Europe on the Eve* (New York: Knopf, 1939) 95-100; P. Renouvin, *Les crises du xxe siècle*, II, *De 1929 à 1935*, Histoire des relations internationales, (Paris: Hachette, 1958) 77.

60. Although once having described the logical consequence of 17 April as war, Ambassador Gaiffier later concluded that "Barthou does not want, as we first believed, the death of the (Disarmament) Conference," *DDB*, vol. III, no. 133, p. 386. Cf. also W. d'Ormesson, *France* (London: Longmans, 1939) 120-128; O. Aubert, *Louis Barthou* (Paris: Librairie Quillet, 1935) 196-197; Herriot, *Jadis*, II, 444; Brinon's testimony in *Les procès de collaboration* (Paris: Editions Michel, 1948) 55.

61. Köster to Berlin, 4 July, *DGFP*, ser. C, vol. III, no. 57, p. 124. It is Tabouis who recalls the Barthou-Léger friendship, in *Cassandra*, 199.

62. Clerk to Simon, 20 June 1934, *DBFP*, ser. 2, vol. VI, no. 463, p. 765.

63. Fröhwein to Schonheiz, 23 June 1934, *DGFP*, ser. C, vol. III, no. 31, p. 81.

64. *Le Temps*, 26 June 1934.

65. W. Herzog, *Barthou* (Zurich: Verlag die Liga, 1938) 94-95.

66. Köster to Berlin, 20 July 1934, *DGFP*, ser. C, vol. III, no. 101, p. 199.

67. Straus to Secretary of State, 4 September 1934, *FRUS*, 1934, vol. I, no. 1183, pp. 572-573.

68. For his earlier interest in rapprochement, particularly with reference to his insistence that it be induced slowly and in consultation with Yugoslavia, see *DDF*, ser. 1, vol. VI, nos. 116, 209, and 478.

69. H. Lagardelle, *Mission à Rome: Mussolini* (Paris: Plon, 1955) 93.

70. Weygand, *Mémoires*, II, 410-420. It must be said, however, that the committee structure for civil-military consultation was poorly utilized under Doumergue's regime. The CSDN proper did not meet that year, nor did the CSG—although a number of military study meetings were called by Weygand. The HCM seems to have met only once, in March 1934.

71. Cf. Laroche, *La Pologne de Pilsudski*, 166-167; Léon Noel, *L'agression allemande contre la Pologne* (Paris: Flammarion, 1946) 256.

4. The Foreign Policy of Pierre Laval

1. Campbell to Simon, 30 October 1934, *DBFP*, ser. 2, vol. XII, no. 156, pp. 182-183.

2. Clerk to Sargent, 17 December 1934, ibid., no. 299, pp. 333-335.

3. Aneurin Bevan, *In Place of Fear* (London: Macgibbon and Kee, 1961) 34.

4. G. Warner, "The Decline and Fall of Pierre Laval," *History Today*, 11.12 (December 1961) 817-827. Warner later concluded his major study of Laval with the remark: "The greatest flaw in his character was not deviousness, but a frightening tendency towards over-simplification." Cf. *Pierre Laval and the Eclipse of France* (London: Eyre and Spottiswoode, 1968) 422.

5. Köster to Berlin, 30 September 1934, *DGFP*, ser. C, vol. III, no. 228, pp. 552-554. Versailles had compelled Germany to surrender the valuable coal region of the Saar for 15 years, leaving it in the interval under the direct authority of the League of Nations. At the end of this period a plebiscite was to be held in the Saar Territory, enabling its citizens to vote either for a continuation of League government, annexation to France, or a return to Germany.

6. Köster to Berlin, ibid., no. 307, pp. 587-591. For Flandin's views see memorandum, 22 November, ibid., no. 344, pp. 656-658.

7. Köster to Berlin, 5 December 1934, ibid., no. 374, pp. 707-709.

8. Clerk to Simon, 13 December 1934, *DBFP*, ser. 2, vol. XII, no. 288, pp. 322-323. Significantly, Laval did not mention the USSR or suggest that he would push rapprochement as a priority issue.

9. Clerk to Sargent, 17 December 1934, ibid., no. 299, pp. 333-335.

10. Anglo-French talks, 22 December 1934, ibid., no. 311, pp. 352-356.

11. Herriot and Marin were Ministers of State. Maurin was then serving as war minister. Clerk to Simon, 18 January 1935, PRO, FO 371, 18823, C593/55/18.

12. Memorandum (Neurath) 16 November 1934, *DGFP*, ser. C, vol. III, no. 330, pp. 633-634.

13. Herriot, *Jadis*, II, 437.

14. Straus to Secretary of State, 16 January 1935, *FRUS*, 1935, I, 175. Also, G. Warner, *Pierre Laval*, 66-71; D. C. Watt, "The Secret Laval-Mussolini Agreement of 1935 on Ethiopia," *Middle East Journal*, 15 (Winter 1961) 69-78; W. C. Askew, "Secret Agreement between France and Italy on Ethiopia, January 1935," *JMH*, 25 (March 1953) 48-49.

15. Straus to Secretary of State, 16 January 1935, *FRUS*, 1935, I, 175.

16. Laval to Chambrun (Rome) 9 November 1935, *Daladier*, 1DA6/Dr4/sdr a.

17. Mussolini to Laval, 25 December 1935, ibid.

18. Laval to Mussolini, 23 January 1936, ibid. This document is reproduced in *DDF*, ser. 2, I, no. 99, pp. 145-147.

19. The Quai d'Orsay later put most of the blame on Laval. One report of January 1939, prepared on Georges Bonnet's instructions, reads in part: "There is no doubt that in the course of the talks the French premier [sic] also agreed to give Italy a free hand for the conquest of Ethiopia." Daladier, 2DA5/Dr2/sdr a.

20. Clerk to Simon, 18 January 1935, PRO, FO 371, 18823, C593/55/18.

21. Cf. report by Wiley to Secretary of State, 16 January 1935, *FRUS*, 1935, vol. I, no. 354, pp. 176-177.

22. Note (Sargent) 28 January 1935, PRO, FO 371, 18825, C962/55/18.

23. Harvey (Paris) to Simon, 25 January 1935, ibid., 18823, C655/55/18.

24. Ibid. The idea appears to have arisen first in a conversation between Campbell of the British embassy and René Massigli around 23 January.

25. Cf. my note 10 above.

26. For the British record of these meetings, 1-3 February 1935, see PRO, FO 371, 18824, C893/55/18.

27. Minute on Phipps to Simon, 8 February 1935, ibid., 18825, C1076/55/18.

28. Minute (Peterson) 25 February 1935, ibid., 18827, C1463/55/18.

29. "The true German," Vansittart observed, "and the true Germany, has always become arrogant and impossible with success." 17 January 1935, ibid., 18823, C435/55/18.

30. For a British reading of the USSR see Sargent's comments, 8 March 1935, ibid., 18828, C1720/55/18. For references to German feelers to Paris and London, see minutes by Eden and Simon, 28 February 1935, ibid., C1724/55/18. For French domestic restraints on Laval and Flandin, see Herriot, *Jadis*, II, 498-499.

31. For minutes of Sargent and Collier, 26 February 1935, see PRO, FO 371, 18827, C1558/55/18.

32. HCM meeting, 23 January 1935, SHA.

33. HCM meeting, 20 February 1935, SHA.

34. Gamelin mentions Italian proposals of 25 January and 4 February in *Servir*, II, 163-164.

35. HCM meeting, 20 February 1935, SHA; Gamelin, *Servir*, II, 165.

36. Quai d'Orsay to Denain, 2 May 1935, SHAA, B80; air attaché (Rome) to Denain, 18 April 1935, ibid.

37. This material is drawn generally from SHAA, B80. In particular, see "note pour le ministre" 20 or 21 July 1936. Also see Kuhlenthal (attaché) to Berlin, 14 May 1935, German Foreign Ministry Archives, 5606H/E401746 (hereafter cited as GFM).

38. Cf. Gamelin to Fabry, 29 June 1935, Ministère des Affaires Etrangères (hereafter cited as MAE). Two notes, undated, one a p-v of a Badoglio-Gamelin conversation, the other for Denain entitled "Exposé du Général Gamelin," SHAA, B80. Also see Gamelin, *Servir*, II, 167-169; note from army staff, 9 July 1936, *DDF*, ser. 2, vol. II, no. 419, pp. 643-644; Kuhlenthal to Berlin, 3 July and 16 August 1935, GFM, 5606H/E401763 and 5606H/E401772-74; *The Times*, 6 July and 5 and 7 September 1935.

39. The responses of the three staffs, dated 8 or 9 April, can be found in the CPDN records, "Archives du Général Gamelin," SHA.

40. P. Laval, *Laval parle* (Paris: Librairie Béranger, 1948) 245.

41. It also appears to have suited Italy's purposes to be able to deny a formal alliance, particularly as the appeal of an Italo-German rapprochement increased. Cf. note, 22 October 1935, *DGFP*, ser. C, vol. IV, no. 373, pp. 765-767.

42. Clerk to FO, 17 June 1935, PRO, FO 371, 18846, C4768/55/18.

43. Although he assured Campbell that "any agreement which France might make with Russia would remain open to Germany's accession." Campbell to FO, 17 March 1935, ibid., 18830, C2146/55/18.

44. Ibid. Consistent with his attitude was his attempt to present the Russian pact to Germany as part of an effort to "induce Russia to abandon the idea of bolshevizing Europe." Köster to Berlin, 27 July 1935, *DGFP*, ser. C, vol. IV, no. 231, pp. 493-494.

45. The actual time taken for the discussions could not have exceeded two weeks, although technically they were in progress from the end of March to the end of April. Cf. Scott, *Alliance against Hitler* and Clerk to Simon, 30 April 1935, PRO, FO 371, 18837, C3527/55/18.

46. For Maurin, see Köster to Bülow, 30 November 1934, *DGFP*, ser. C, vol. III, no. 365, pp. 692-694. For Weygand, see Bankwitz, *Maxime Weygand and Civil-Military Relations in Modern France* (Cambridge, Mass.: Harvard University Press, 1967) 249-252, 260-261. For Gamelin, see *Servir*, II, 132-133, 166, and his Mémoire #10, December 1940, Blum, 3BL/Dr12.

47. Clerk to Simon, 28 March 1935, PRO, FO 371, 18833, C2656/55/18.

48. For Léger's view, see Clerk to Simon, 28 February and 4 March 1935, ibid., 18827, C1558/55/18 and 18828, C1734/55/18.

49. Charles (Moscow) to Simon, 15 May 1935, ibid., 18840, C3922/55/18. For reports of Laval's personal problems with Communists in the Seine department, see Köster to Berlin, 12 February 1935, *DGFP*, ser. C, vol. II, no. 489, pp. 924-926.

50. Simon to Phipps, 12 March 1935, PRO, FO 371, 18829, C1995/55/18.

51. Phipps to Sargent, 9 March, ibid., C2013/55/18.

52. Phipps to Simon, 14 March, ibid., C2071/55/18.

53. Simon's record of talk with Ambassador Corbin, 18 March 1935, ibid., 18831, C2309-10/55/18. For French resentment, see Campbell to Simon, 19 March, ibid., 18830, C2212/55/18.

54. Phipps to Simon, 16 March 1935, ibid., 18829, C2122/55/18.

55. Cf. three dispatches from Campbell, 19 March 1935, ibid., 18830, C2261-62/55/18, C2212/55/18.

56. Vansittart's minute, 19 March, ibid., C2071/55/18.

57. "Note sur la situation relative des forces allemandes et françaises," HCM meeting, 22 March 1935, SHA.

58. Cf. three dispatches from Phipps plus attached minutes, 10 and 28 May and 12 June 1934, PRO, FO 371, C3834/55/18; 18834, C4302/55/18; 18846, C4684/55/18.

59. Léger was particularly outspoken in his talk with Clerk, unburdening "his heart with great frankness." Laval was said to be "much discouraged." Clerk to FO, 15 and 17 June, ibid., 18846, C4725 and C4768/55/18. Jean Fabry saw this as "further proof of the off-handedness with which England treated us." *De la Place Concorde au cours de l'intendance* (Paris: Editions de France, 1942) 67. Cf. also A. Géraud, "France and the Anglo-German Naval Treaty," *FA*, 14 (1935-36) 51-61.

60. This attitude, unbending to the point of perversity, is reflected in a series of documents from June 1935. In addition to the minutes on Clerk's dispatch of 15 June, one should note the patronizing and self-righteous minutes on the dis-

patch from Strang, 21 June, 18846, C4904/55/18 and the War Office memorandum on French complaints, 25 June, PRO, WO 190/337.

61. For the first Eden-Laval talk, see Eden's dispatch, 21 June and that of Clerk of the same date, FO 371, 18846, C4901/4902/55/18 and C4904/55/18.

62. For the second talk, following Eden's visit to Rome, see Clerk to FO, 27 June, ibid., 18847, C5031/55/18.

63. Eden to FO, 19 August 1935, ibid., 18850, C6077/55/18.

64. Clerk to FO, 14 June and 29 July, ibid., 18793, C4714/33/17, and 18849, C5700/55/18.

5. Anglo-French Relations, 1935-1936

1. Clerk to FO, 14 June 1935, PRO, FO 371, 18793, C4714/33/17.

2. Phipps to FO, 12 June 1935, ibid., 18846, C4684/55/18.

3. *Le Temps*, 30 June 1935.

4. Clerk to FO, 7 June and 24 October, PRO, FO 371, 18793, C4626/33/17, C7226/33/17.

5. FO minutes, 29 July 1935, ibid., 18849, C5700/55/18.

6. Cf. Eden's dispatch and FO minutes, 19 August, ibid., 18850, C6077/55/18.

7. Hoare to Chamberlain, 18 August, PRO, FO 800 (Hoare) 295.

8. F. W. Deakin, "Anglo-French Relations and the Italo-Ethiopian Crisis, December 1934-December 1935," Anglo-French Colloquium, 1972, 24.

9. Ibid., 16.

10. Ibid., 8, 13. Under the chairmanship of Sir John Maffey, this interdepartmental committee reported in June 1935 after a four-month investigation.

11. For the negotiations between Maurice Peterson of the Foreign Office and René St. Quentin of the Quai d'Orsay, and for the Hoare-Laval project, see ibid., 27-36; Peterson's *Both Sides of the Curtain* (London: Constable, 1950) 113-124; G. Warner, *Pierre Laval*, 115-126; H. B. Braddick, "The Hoare-Laval Plan," in Gatzke's *European Diplomacy between Two Wars, 1919-1939* (Chicago: Quadrangle Books, 1972) 152-171.

12. Some of the more recent of which are R. Parker, "Great Britain, France and the Ethiopian Crisis, 1935-36," *English Historical Review* (April 1974) 293-332; A. Marder, "The Royal Navy and the Ethiopian Crisis of 1935-36," *AHR* (June 1970) 1327-1356; A. Goldman, "Sir Robert Vansittart's Search for Italian Cooperation against Hitler," *JCH* (July 1974) 93-130. For a study more directly focused on France, see F. D. Laurens, *France and the Italo-Ethiopian Crisis, 1935-36* (The Hague: Mouton, 1967).

13. Hoare to FO, 16 September 1935, PRO, FO 371, 18850, C6516/55/18. Yet it was clear to the Germans that Laval intended to refuse bilateral agreements, to work through normal diplomatic channels and to keep in tandem with Britain. Memorandum by Bulow, 5 September and dispatch by Köster, 18 November 1935, *DGFP*, ser. C, vol. IV, no. 287 and no. 415.

14. Hoare to Lord Wigram, 14 September 1935, PRO, FO 800 (Hoare) 295.

15. P. Renouvin, "Les relations franco-anglaises, 1935-1939," Anglo-French Colloquium, 1971, 7-8; "Note envisageant les répercussions possibles du conflit," EMA (2e Bureau) 9 September 1935, MAE.

16. Including 10 infantry divisions and 2 cavalry brigades normally assigned to Alpine service, and 4 North African divisions. Cf. Fabry's testimony, 2 July 1941, Daladier, 4DA14/Dr3; and note of 18 January 1936, DDF, ser. 2, vol. I, no. 82, pp. 116-117.

17. Cf. Chapter 4, n37. In particular see the note "1ère réunion des représentants des états-majors de l'air français et italiens," 9-12 September 1935, SHAA, B80.

18. FO minutes on Clerk's dispatches of 8 and 29 July, PRO, FO 371, 18793, C5313/33/17; 18849, C5700/55/18.

19. Report of 11 September 1935, ibid., 19198, J4971/3681/1.

20. Deakin, "Anglo-French Relations," Anglo-French Colloquium, 1972, 23; Templewood, Nine Troubled Years (London: Collins, 1954) 169-171. Two weeks had barely passed when Hoare was instructing Eden not to hasten the discussions of sanctions in Geneva. Avon, Facing the Dictators, 293.

21. "Even though the Minister for League Affairs was not taking the lead at Geneva, all the world thought that he was." Cabinet meeting, 16 October 1935, PRO, AIR 8/190. Eden later admitted that his own "tentative methods" had been bested by Laval's natural "ingenuity." Eden, Facing the Dictators, 293.

22. Memo by chief of the naval staff, 3 September 1935, PRO, Air 8/188/8647; joint memo by Admiralty and Board of Trade, 10 September, PRO, FO 371, 19198, C9071; memo by Chiefs of Staff Sub-Committee, 16 September, PRO, Air 8/188/8647.

23. S. Roskill, Hankey: Man of Secrets (London: Collins, 1974) III, 183; Hankey to Phipps, 2 January 1936, Phipps, I, 3/3.

24. The principle of sanctions was accepted implicitly on 7 October when the League Council declared Italy in violation of the Covenant. The arms embargo was effected immediately. A selective embargo on exports to Italy, excluding iron, steel, coal, and oil, came into effect on 18 November. The reinforcement of the British Mediterranean Fleet began in late August.

25. For the Eden-Laval talks of 3 October see PRO, Air 8/189/8647. Cf. also Parker's account of the Clerk-Laval conversation of 16 October, "Great Britain, France and the Ethiopian Crisis," English Historical Review (April 1974) 309; French naval attaché (London) to Admiral Decoux, 17 October 1935, MAE.

26. Clerk to Hoare, 24 October 1934, PRO, FO 371, 18793, C7226/33/17.

27. See Marder, "The Royal Navy and the Ethiopian Crisis" AHR (June 1970) 1347.

28. Clerk to Hoare, 26 October 1935, PRO, FO 371, 18807, C7245/5527/17.

29. Phipps to Hoare, 13 November, ibid., 18851, C7647/55/18.

30. For the key conclusion of the new Defence Requirements Committee in February 1934, see K. Middlemas, Diplomacy of Illusion (London: Weidenfeld

and Nicolson, 1972) 33.

31. Clerk to FO, 7 November, PRO, FO 371, 18816, C7465/7/18. This assurance Laval repeated to the Paris correspondent of *Frankfurter Zeitung.* "Laval declared that he neither could nor would do anything without the British." Köster to Berlin, 27 November, *DGFP*, ser. C, vol. IV, no. 430, p. 859.

32. Phipps to FO, and accompanying minutes, 25 October PRO, FO 371, 18816, C7266/7/18.

33. Marder, "The Royal Navy and the Ethiopian Crisis," *AHR* (June 1970) 1348-1349.

34. Clerk to FO, and accompanying minutes, 7 November, PRO, FO 371, 18816, C7465/7/18.

35. Phipps to Hoare, 19 November 1935, ibid., 18851, C7762/55/18.

36. Clerk to Hoare, 19 November 1935, ibid., 18794, C7717/33/17. The report of Flandin's speech drew a barrage of minutes, of the sort indicated in the text. Laval's radio speech of 26 November, however, went virtually unnoticed by the Foreign Office. See Clerk to Hoare, 27 November 1935, ibid., C7907/33/17.

37. Vansittart's minute on Clerk to FO, 19 November 1935, ibid., 18794, C7717/33/17.

38. These conversations evidently were not considered to have been significant in the gradual progression toward extensive staff talks in 1939. See "Summarised History of Staff Conversations," March 1939, PRO, CAB 29/159.

39. Durand-Viel recommended the talks in a letter to Léger of 22 October 1935, IBB 8/602, Service Historique de la Marine (SHM). Part of the reasoning seems to have come from a desire to offset France's dependence on Italy. Cf. P. Masson, "Les conversations militaires franco-britanniques, 1935-1939," Anglo-French Colloquium, 1971.

40. For French concern about fanning British belligerence, see naval attaché (Rome) to Piétri, 20 October 1935, 1 BB 8/602, SHM and the HCM meeting of 31 October 1935, ibid.

41. For the Chatfield-Decoux talks see Masson, "Les conversations," Anglo-French Colloquium, 1971; Marder, "The Royal Navy," *AHR* (June 1970) 1347; Roskill, *Hankey*, III, 182-185. Cf. also Defence Policy Requirements paper #45, "Franco-British Naval Cooperation in the Mediterranean," November 1935, PRO, Air 8/190/8647.

42. The air staff obviously felt that the Admiralty had been too soft with the French. See their note, 5 November 1935, PRO, AIR 8/190/8647.

43. The text of these instructions of 7 December 1935 can be found in PRO, CAB 21, FA/6/13, 420.

44. Note by Denain's military cabinet, 9 December 1935, MAE.

45. See the précis of this report, 10 January 1936 in PRO, Air 8/199. The naval attaché's draft report is in PRO, ADM 116/3398. Cf. also J. Lecuir and P. Fridenson, "L'organisation de la coopération aérienne franco-britannique, 1935-mai 1940," *RHDGM* (January 1969) 43-71.

46. As recorded by the deputy chief of staff, General Schweisguth, in a diary

entry of 12 December 1935, Schweisguth, 351/AP2/Dr6.

47. The French records of these meetings may be found in PRO, FO 371, 20159.

48. See Colonel Heywood's report, 18 December 1935, PRO, Air 8/199.

49. See admiralty circular, 25 January 1936, PRO, ADM 116/3398; and Peake to FO, 30 May 1936, PRO, FO 371, 20161, J5071/15/1.

50. Parker, "Great Britain, France and the Ethiopian Crisis," *English Historical Review* (April 1974) 326.

51. This was in reference to the famous Hoare-Laval plan of December 1935, following which Hoare was obliged to resign in favor of Eden. Again one refers to the excellent account of this issue, particularly from the French side, in G. Warner, *Pierre Laval*, 115-126.

52. Wigram minute on Clerk to FO, 10 December 1935, PRO, FO 371, 19168, J1945/1/1.

53. Clerk to Eden, 31 January 1936, ibid., 19855, C656/1/17.

54. The British disliked these contacts because they underlined the split in French loyalties. But Laval used them to avoid wasting time on proposals Mussolini would not even consider. This sort of tactic the British found offensive, certainly, but expedient as well. In this connection, the British asked that the French use these contacts to present the Anglo-French staff talks to Italy in the least provocative light. See source in note 48 above.

55. Some of the more recent of which are, M. Baumont, "The Rhineland Crisis," in N. Waites, ed., *Troubled Neighbours* (London: Weidenfeld and Nicolson, 1971) 158-169; G. Sakwa, "The Franco-Polish Alliance and the Remilitarization of the Rhineland," *Historical Journal*, 16.1 (1973) 125-146; T. Emmerson, *The Rhineland Crisis, 7 March 1936* (London: Temple Smith, 1977).

56. HCM meeting, 18 January 1936, 1 BB8/602/Dr9, SHM.

57. Entries of 18 and 24 February, Schweisguth, 351/AP3/Dr7. Further confirmation of this dithering within Gamelin's bureau is found in Poydenot, pt. 1, 45-46.

58. Without citing all the sources which have contributed to this impression, I would pay special thanks to General Poydenot for his charming recollections of Gamelin and for permission to use the Poydenot memoirs. In addition to Minart, Ray, and Géraud (see the Bibliography), Le Goyet's recent biography of Gamelin must be mentioned here—*Le mystère Gamelin* (Paris: Presses de la Cité, 1975). Laski's article is from the *Daily Mail*, 27 September 1938.

59. Entry of 17 March 1936, Schweisguth, 351/AP3/Dr8.

60. Entry of 19 March (Rapports), ibid.

61. *Evénements*, Report, I, 30, and Testimony, IV, Maurin, 908. Since there could be no action without partial mobilization, including the *couverture* stage, and since thereafter there was nothing left but general mobilization, it is the question of timing that is at issue. Did the generals demand immediate general mobilization—possibly but unlikely—or did they simply say that it was necessary to prepare for it, i.e., by invoking full *couverture?* Almost certainly it was the latter case.

62. Cf. note from Flandin, 27 February 1936, *DDF*, ser. 2, vol. I, no. 241, p.

339. Unlike Versailles, which simply used the expression "hostile act," Locarno distinguished between flagrant and nonflagrant violations—the latter meaning that there was no intent to use the violation as a prelude to a major act of aggression. Should the victim interpret the violation as nonflagrant, it was obliged to inform the League, then await a League decision on whether there had been a violation and what kind of punitive action was called for.

63. For the French press, see *Le Temps*, 9-10 March (which include reviews of leading French newspapers); *Manchester Guardian*, 10 March; *The Observer*, 22 March; *New York Times*, 19 April; *News Chronicle*, 21 April. Cf. also A. Fabre-Luce, *Vingt-quatre années de liberté* (Paris: Juilliard, 1962) 160; Micaud, *The French Right*, 86-97; Forster to Berlin, 13 March 1936, *DGFP*, ser. C, vol. V, no. 96, p. 132.

64. Entry 10 March (Mémentos) Schweisguth, 351/AP3/Dr8.

65. Zay was under-secretary to Premier Sarraut. Cf. his *Souvenirs et solitude* (Paris: Juilliard, 1945) 66.

66. This is an interpretive version of Maurin's remarks, based on considerations discussed in note 61 above.

67. Entries of 10 March and 21 April, Schweisguth, 351/AP3/Dr8.

68. Paul-Boncour, *Entre deux guerres*, III, 35.

69. On balance, this does not seem to have been done. Flandin suggests that he badgered the military about preparing a plan in February (*Politique française*, 195-196) but his account is vague and imprecise and not entirely consistent with what is left of the HCM archives. The HCM meetings of 7-8 February indicate that he did refer to the need for determining French counter-measures, but there does not appear to have been a formal request to prepare an offensive plan. Gamelin's version has the minister wanting to know under what conditions France could *accept* the German occupation of the left bank (*Servir*, II, 197-98). The relevant volume of *DDF* also seems to indicate that little pressure was put on the armed forces to have an offensive plan at the ready.

70. "He considers it intolerable that they should say that the soldiers would not march on 7 March." Entry of 22 April, Schweisguth, 351/AP3/Dr8.

71. Entries of 9-10 March (Rapports), ibid.

72. A month later Sarraut gave Gamelin a true Judas kiss. Referring to a recent press report that had attributed French passivity to military advice, the premier condemned whoever had been responsible for, in effect, leaking the truth. Cf. meeting of 5 April 1936, *DDF*, ser. 2, vol. II, no. 23, p. 46.

73. Flandin's formal request is dated 11 March (*DDF*, no. 390, pp. 501-502) but his verbal request to Gamelin, through Maurin, came on the tenth. Gamelin, *Servir*, II, 204.

74. See Flandin's communiqué, 11 March, *DDF*, no. 380, pp. 493-494 and Avon, *Facing the Dictators*, 348-350.

75. Army staff note, 11 March, *DDF*, no. 392, pp. 504-506. For French concern about providing adequate air cover for the mobilization and adequate protection for cities such as Paris, see *Evénements*, Testimony, IV, Maurin, 908-909, and *DDF*, ser. 2, vol. I, nos. 392 and 525 and vol. II, nos. 23 and 138.

76. Entry of 17 March (Mission à Londres) Schweisguth, 351/AP3/Dr8. From

Paris Clerk was reporting that economic and military sanctions were still possible and that Gamelin's aide, Petibon, had assured him that Hitler would not "get away with it." Clerk to Eden, 12-13 March, PRO, FO 371, 19855, C1743/1/17, 19891, C1838/4/18.

77. While Eden had pledged Britain on 9 March to defend France and Belgium during the course of the forthcoming negotiations with Germany, the declaration of 19 March—including a reciprocal French and Belgian guarantee to England—was to be in effect indefinitely. See Eden's note, 30 March 1936, PRO, FO 371, 19899, C2528.

78. French intelligence had 300,000 German troops in the zone, including 90,000 regulars. British intelligence could find less than 100,000, including 45,000 regulars. With French frontier forces reckoned at 145,000, the British detected a French superiority of roughly two to one, while the French believed in a German superiority of the same margin. See Clerk to Eden, 13 March, PRO, FO 371, 19891, C1838/4/18; DDF, ser. 2, vol. I, no. 392, p. 505; WO to FO, 13 March, PRO, FO 371, 19891, C1848/4/18, C1850/4/18.

79. Entry of 24 March (Mission à Londres) Schweisguth, 351/AP3/Dr8.

80. Enclosure from Lieutenant Colonel Beaumont-Nesbitt, in Clerk to Eden, 21 March 1936, PRO, FO 371, 19896, C2203/4/18.

81. Minutes of the COS Sub-Committee, 13 March, PRO, Air 9/73 and the memo from the committee, 1 April, PRO, FO 371, 19899, C2608/4/18, and CAB 53/27.

82. For the British record of these staff talks, 15-16 April 1936, see PRO, Air 2/1758. Schweisguth's recollections are in his papers, 351/AP3/Dr12/Dr13. His final report to Maurin, 20 April, is in DDF, ser. 2, vol. II, no. 97, p. 164.

83. For the attaché's report, see Clerk to Eden, 11 April 1936, PRO, FO 371, 19902, C2864/4/18. For Gamelin's remarks to his staff, see entries 4 and 7 April, Schweisguth, 351/AP3/Dr8.

84. As Schweisguth told Dill, recorded in annex 4 of his final report (not reproduced in DDF), these fortifications would "direct future operations toward . . . Belgium and Holland." Schweisguth, 351/AP3/Dr12.

85. Wigram minute on Cabinet Conclusions, 22 April, PRO, FO 371, 19903, C3103/4/18.

86. Schweisguth, 351/AP3/Dr12/sdr a; and EMA, 4e Bureau, "Note sur les ports," 4 May 1936, SHA, 0179, 2.

87. That anglophobism could be found in France is amply documented by S. H. Osgood, although in general his conclusions about French and British officialdom respectively seem to endorse my findings. See "Le mythe de 'la perfide Albion' en France, 1919-1940," Cahiers d'Histoire, 1 (1975) 5-20.

88. Note for the minister, 18 July 1936, SHAA, B 80.

89. For example, "England had refused to let us take military action in the Rhineland in 1936." Flandin, Politique française, 245.

6. The Foreign Policy of the Popular Front, 1936-1937

1. Cf. J. E. Dreifort, Yvon Delbos at the Quai d'Orsay (Lawrence: University

Press of Kansas, 1973) 198; J. Colton, *Léon Blum: Humanist in Politics* (New York: Knopf, 1966) 200.

2. Although there was clearly something to be said for Blum's contention that the coup of 7 March "already had constructed, in our minds, an early Siegfried line which separated us from the rest of Europe." *Evénements*, Testimony, I, Blum, 127.

3. Cf. Dreifort, *Yvon Delbos*, chap. 1, 1-20.

4. The metaphor is Paul-Boncour's, *Entre deux guerres*, III, 84.

5. See Schweisguth's report of 20 April 1936 in *DDF*, ser. 2, vol. II, no. 97, p. 159, or in the Schweisguth papers, 351/AP3/Dr12. The phrase is underlined in the original.

6. Record of a meeting, 5 April 1936, *DDF*, ser. 2, vol. II, no. 23, p. 46.

7. Ibid., nos. 23 and 138. The idea of a Balkan offensive through Salonika and in support of the Little Entente countries derived of course from the military campaign between 1915 and 1918. Schweisguth several times refers to the workings of the Salonika study group. See entries of 20/10/36 and 22/2/37 in Schweisguth, 351/AP3/Dr10 and Dr11. For subsequent French planning in 1939 see Poydenot, pt. 2, pp. 12, 33-39.

8. Although it is true that Delbos initially expressed interest in restoring the Italian link. Eden to FO, 26 June 1936, PRO, FO 371, 19877, C4645.

9. See Chapter 7.

10. CPDN meeting, 15 February 1937, SHA. Even so, as late as December 1936 Gamelin was arguing that the tie with Italy remained "the key to the preservation of peace," and the Salonika study group continued to meet. Entries of 22 December 1936 and 22 February 1937, Schweisguth, 351/AP3/Dr10 and Dr11.

11. Blum's first government fell at the end of June 1937. Chautemps, a Radical Socialist, became premier while Blum remained as vice-premier and Delbos as foreign minister.

12. Dreifort, *Yvon Delbos*, 180.

13. Cf. General Féquant's "Note pour le ministre," 3 August 1936, SHAA, B 81.

14. Cf. record of Eden-Blum talk, 15 May 1936, PRO, FO 371, 19880, C3693/92/62, and Blum's *L'histoire jugera* (Montreal: Editions de l'Arbre, 1945) 100-102.

15. *Evénements*, Testimony, I, Blum, 220.

16. See Dreifort's useful breakdown of the cabinet, *Yvon Delbos*, 49.

17. Cf. Chapter 5, n16.

18. For a detailed analysis of the technical problems facing France, see report by attaché Kuhlenthal on his visit to Morocco in October 1935, GFM, 5606H/E401841-90, also the Joint Planning Committee memo of 20 August 1936, PRO, CAB 55/10.

19. For evidence of plans for counter-strikes against Italian attempts to seize those bases on a permanent basis, see entry of 7 November 1936 (Mémentos) Schweisguth, 351/AP3/Dr10.

20. Straus to secretary of state, 31 July 1936, *FRUS*, vol. II, no. 696, p. 450; Welczeck to Berlin, 6 August 1936, *DGFP*, ser. D, vol. V, no. 499, p. 880.

21. Monsieur Masson refers to a naval document of 6 July 1936, in "La marine

française et la guerre d'Espagne," Anglo-French Colloquium, 1973. See also Admiral Darlan's note, dated both 17 October and 15 November 1938, MAE.

22. Phipps to Eden, 5 July 1937, PRO, FO 371, 20696, C4888/82/17. Gamelin later admitted, "Need I add that for reasons of sentiment and conviction, the sympathies of the soldiers were always with Franco." Mémoire #10, December 1940, Blum, 3BL/Dr12.

23. *JO Députés*, Debates, 4 December 1936, 3327-3330; *JO Sénat*, Debates 23 February 1937, 189; Delbos' article in *Sunday Times*, 12 June 1938. For an estimate of French weaknesses on the Pyrenees, see Heberlein (Spain) to Berlin, 13 November 1937, GFM, 1568H/383223-237.

24. For British views on this French concern, see Phipps to Eden, 26 October 1937, PRO, FO 371, 20712, C7386/3/18; Phipps to Eden, 3 November 1937, ibid., C7576/3/18.

25. Blum later referred to some consultation with Admiral Darlan (*Evénements*, Testimony, 218) but he claimed not to have known the views of the other services—a condition borne out by Gamelin's memoirs, Schweisguth's diary, and the minutes of such bodies as the CSG and CPDN. Blum's *chef de cabinet*, Monsieur Blumel, was to admit that the government knew that the generals were "instinctively unsympathetic to the aims of the Blum government" and by direct inference, to the Spanish republicans. See Wilson to secretary of state, 30 August 1936, *FRUS*, vol. II, no. 776, p. 503.

26. Again see Dreifort's remarks on the cabinet divisions, divisions which finally hardened on 8 August with Blum, Delbos, and Daladier all drifting to the side of the noninterventionists, *Yvon Delbos*, 48-49.

27. For example, see C. J. Child, "Great Britain, France and Non-Intervention in Spain, July-August 1936," Anglo-French Colloquium, 1973; D. Carlton, "Eden, Blum and the Origins of Non-Intervention," *JCH*, 6.3 (1971) 40-55; and G. Warner's often neglected study, "France and Non-Intervention in Spain, July-August 1936," *International Affairs*, 2 (April 1962) 203-220.

28. P. Renouvin, "La genèse de l'accord de non-intervention dans la guerre civile espagnole, août 1936," Anglo-French Colloquium, 1973; Dreifort, *Yvon Delbos*, 50-51.

29. *Evénements*, Testimony, I, Blum, 216. Child assures us that there is no record in the British archives of any offical talks on the subject of Spain during Blum's July visit to London, and nothing in the Baldwin papers at Cambridge to suggest that the matter was discussed by the two prime ministers. Child, "Great Britain, France and Non-Intervention," Anglo-French Colloquium, 1973.

30. Clerk to Eden, 7 August 1936, PRO, FO 371, 20528, W7964/62/41. It is difficult to see this intervention as a "grave warning" (Dreifort, *Yvon Delbos*, 47), just as it is difficult to ignore the impression that Delbos, in Child's words, "was manifestly pleased with this remarkable intervention."

31. There appears to be no record of this remark in the British archives, and Eden himself neglected to mention this allegedly pivotal meeting in his memoirs. He does say, however, that Blum "and Delbos knew only too well that any other course of action would sharply divide France, while open intervention by the

great powers could lead to a European war. We agreed with this French decision of policy." Avon, *Facing the Dictators*, 401.

32. For this meeting see *DDF*, ser. 2, vol. III, no. 87, pp. 130-133 and PRO, FO 371, 20527, W7781/62/41. It is amusing that Darlan had no specific intelligence on this threat to the Balearics, despite his claims, and that Lord Chatfield had, despite his denials. Cf. W7781 above and Masson, "La marine française et la guerre d'Espagne," Anglo-French Colloquium, 1973.

33. Cf. G. Sakwa, "The Franco-Polish Alliance," *Historical Journal* (1973), and R. Debicki, "The Remilitarization of the Rhineland and Its Impact on the Franco-Polish Alliance," *Polish Review*, 14.4 (Autumn 1969) 51.

34. Delbos to Noel, 30 July 1936, Daladier, 1DA7/Dr2/sdr e.

35. Ibid. Daladier had scribbled the word *naif* beside this passage of Delbos' communication. Blum later admitted that Gamelin had been chosen because he could "short-circuit" Beck by dealing directly with Smigly-Rydz. Lloyd Thomas to Strang, 20 August 1937, PRO, FO 371, 20764, C6041/981/55.

36. Gamelin to Daladier, 14 August 1936, Daladier, 1DA7/Dr2/sdr e. Included here is his statement to Smigly-Rydz of 13 August from which the quotation is taken.

37. Cf. *DDF*, ser. 2, vol. III, no. 259, pp. 377-378. Although Léon Noel was not invited to these meetings, his own full account is found in *L'agression contre la Pologne* (Paris: Flammarion, 1946) 139-145.

38. Ambassador Corbin had brought this stabilizing goal to Eden's attention. See Eden's memo of 5 February 1937, PRO, FO 371, 21136, R838/26/67.

39. Mr. Hadow (Prague) reported on 10 February 1937 that France was "being held up to a mild form of blackmail by M. Benes' threat of negotiations with Germany," PRO, FO 371, 21136, R968/26/67. For Lacroix's misgivings, see his note to Delbos, 27 January 1937, *DDF*, ser. 2, vol. IV, no. 359, pp. 620-622. Cf. also G. Weinberg, "Secret Hitler-Benes Negotiations in 1936-1937," *JCEA*, 19 (January 1960) 366-374.

40. Delbos to Lacroix, 11 January 1937, *DDF*, ser. 2, vol. IV, no. 281, pp. 465-468; Dreifort, *Yvon Delbos*, 134-135; Paul-Boncour, *Entre deux guerres*, III, 58-69.

41. This accord may have been a response to the proposed mutual assistance pact, Italy regarding it as "an anti-Italian quite as much as an anti-German move." Drummond (Rome) to FO, 12 February, PRO, FO 371, 21136, R1014/26/67. If such were the case it illustrates effectively not only the diversity of interest within the Little Entente but how immensely difficult it was for France to hold such a collection of states together.

42. Cf. respectively, A. P. Adamthwaite, "French Foreign Policy, April 1938-September 1939" (Ph.D. dissertation, Leeds University, 1966) 61, and Dreifort, *Yvon Delbos*, 139.

43. Clerk to Eden, 6 April 1936, PRO, FO 371, 19901, C2737/4/18.

44. Cf. General L. Loizeau, "Une mission militaire en U.R.S.S.," *RDDM* (15 September 1955) 252-276. Entry 20 September 1935 (Mémentos) Schweisguth, 351/AP2/Dr5.

45. Schweisguth entries, 24, 25, 27 June 1936, ibid., 351/AP3/Dr9. See Colonel Beaumont-Nesbitt's excellent report on the attitude of the French high command toward Russia, 14 October 1936, PRO, FO 371, 19880, C7262/92/62.

46. Entry, 4 September 1936, Schweisguth, 351/AP3/Dr10.

47. This report is in *DDF*, ser. 2, vol. III, no. 343, pp. 510-514 and in Schweisguth, 351/AP5/Dr7. Cf. also P. W. Blackstock, *The Soviet Road to World War Two: Soviet versus Western Intelligence, 1921-1939* (Chicago: Quadrangle Books, 1969) 269-270.

48. Entries, 8 and 31 October 1936, Schweisguth, 351/AP3/Dr10.

49. For instance, French air intelligence estimated that Russia's maximum peacetime production with current plant could reach 8,000 military aircraft per year. See report on Soviet air production, EMAA (2e Bureau) April 1939, SHAA, B 89.

50. Entry 7 November 1936 (Mémentos) Schweisguth, 351/AP3/Dr10. Some three weeks earlier Gamelin had said that he would resist staff talks with Russia as long as he was chief of staff. Lloyd Thomas (Paris) to FO, 16 October 1936, PRO, FO 371, 19880, C7389/92/62. Cf. also Le Goyet, *Le mystère Gamelin*, 196-212.

51. Entry 8 January 1937 (Mémentos) Schweisguth, 351/AP3/Dr11. This word came directly from Gamelin who was about to crack down on Communist propaganda in the army. He was soon to forbid in the barracks any publication that attacked the country, the regime, the army, or the officer corps.

52. The fullest account of these highly secret talks is still that of Commandant de Villelume, the military adviser to the Quai and liaison officer between it and the war ministry. Cf. his testimony in *Evénements*, IX, 2742-2744. His diary has recently come to light, a portion of which has been published as *Journal d'une défaite* (1976).

53. Entry 25 April 1937, Schweisguth, 351/AP3/Dr12. While in London, Daladier had boasted to a German informant that he had been largely responsible for preventing Franco-Russian staff talks. See Woermann to Berlin, 5 May 1937, GFM, 621/250420-25. Daladier's own dossier on Franco-Russian contacts is very fragmentary and filled with unsigned, undated, unaddressed documents, few of which reveal much of his own attitude. See Daladier, 1DA7/Dr5/sdr c-d.

54. Although the distinguished French scholar, Henri Michel, has concluded otherwise, seeing the British attitude as "the principal reason for French behavior." See "Le Front Populaire et l'U.R.S.S.," Anglo-French Colloquium, 1971.

55. Entries of 26 May and 23 June 1937, Schweisguth, 351/AP3/Dr12 and Dr13.

56. For two reports on Delbos, see Chilston to Eden, 11 May 1937, PRO, FO 371, 21095, N2712/45/38, and the FO note, 15 May 1937, ibid., 20702, C3685/532/62; also see Dreifort, "The French Popular Front and the Franco-Soviet Pact, 1936-37," *JCH*, 11 (1976) 217-236. For Léger and the Quai, see the remarks of his secretary, de Croy, Wright (Paris) to FO, 28 December 1937, PRO, FO 371, C8880/532/62/. *DDF*, IV, V, VI (November 1936-September 1937), throws little light on this subject. There is little on Russia, and what there is originates in Mos-

cow rather than Paris.

57. FO memo, 15 May 1937, PRO, FO 371, 20702, C3685/532/62.

58. Central to this intelligence in 1937 was the belief that Stalin's purges of the armed forces in general and of the officer corps in particular had effectively eliminated any possibility of serious operations for many years to come.

59. Cf. *DDF*, ser. 2, vol. II, no. 217, pp. 322-329. See also the excellent study by D. Kieft, *Belgium's Return to Neutrality* (Oxford: Clarendon Press, 1972), and *Les relations militaires franco-belges, 1936-40* (Paris: CNRS, 1968).

60. Kerchove to Van Zeeland, 23 April 1936, *DDB*, vol. IV, no. 76, pp. 208-213; and to Spaak, 25 August 1936, ibid., no. 104, p. 258.

61. Cf. note of 30 September 1936, *DDF*, ser. 2, vol. III, no. 300, pp. 437-444. Gamelin told the British, however, that a change in Belgian policy could necessitate a major revision of his plan of campaign in the north. Lloyd Thomas to Eden, 19 October 1936, PRO, FO 371, 19853, C7382/7284/4.

62. Delbos to Corbin, 21 October 1936, *DDF*, ser. 2, vol. III, no. 388; Laroche to Delbos, 26 October 1936, ibid., no. 411, p. 628; Delbos to Corbin, 4 November 1936, ibid., no. 440; Laroche to Delbos, 7 November 1936, ibid., no. 454, p. 711.

63. "Franco-British Declaration of April 24th 1937," in *The Official Account of What Happened* (London: Evans Bros., n.d.) 56-57; Van Overstraeten, *Albert I-Léopold III*, 258.

64. CPDN meeting, 15 February 1937, SHA.

65. Foreign ministry circular, 4 December 1937, *DGFP*, ser. D, vol. I, no. 56, pp. 95-96; H. Schacht, *My First Seventy-Six Years* (London: Wingate, 1955) 379-380.

66. Blum-Schacht interview, 28 August 1936, *DDF*, ser. 2, vol. III, no. 213, pp. 307-311.

67. Interview of 28 May 1937, ibid., vol. V, no. 470, pp. 806-811. By this time Poncet already had recognized the "impasse" while Schacht himself admitted "nothing more could be done." See Poncet to Delbos, 21 May 1937, ibid., no. 442, p. 754, and Schacht's interview with Auriol, 27 May 1937, ibid., no. 462, p. 793.

68. Cf. Bullitt to secretary of state, 20 February and 27 May 1937, *FRUS*, 1937, vol. I, nos. 250-254, and nos. 689-690, pp. 106-107. See also the key letters to the president of 24 October and 7 and 20 December 1936 and 10 January 1937, in O. Bullitt, *For the President*, 173-176, 194-196, 200-202, 203-207. One may also note the claim that Bullitt had "brought" Schacht to Paris. B. Farnsworth, *William C. Bullitt and the Soviet Union* (Bloomington: Indiana University Press, 1967) 159.

69. For a detailed summary of the colonial question and its role within a broader European settlement, and for evidence of one French view that was less intransigent than the English, see the Quai d'Orsay note, 27 August 1937, *DDF*, ser. 2, vol. VI, no. 362, pp. 640-645.

70. Phipps to Eden, 2 May 1937, Phipps Papers, I, 1/19.

71. Cf. O. Bullitt, *For the President*, 201; Avon, *Facing the Dictators*, 502;

Eden to FO, 20 September 1936, PRO, FO 371, 19859, C7626/5740/18.

72. Phipps to Eden, 26 November 1937, PRO, FO 371, 20684, C8134/18/17.

73. This was generally if not strictly true. From the spring of 1937 on the British, led by Chamberlain and encouraged by the COS, were moving toward some kind of rapprochement with Italy—principally as a means of reducing the possibilities of a simultaneous conflict with Germany, Italy, and Japan. The French, however, were assuming Italian hostility and planning accordingly. On the latter point see my "Le haut commandement français au moment de Munich," *Revue d'Histoire Moderne et Contemporaine*, 24 (January-March 1977) 110-129.

74. The British chiefs of staff had themselves concluded that: "The policy of the Soviet remains fundamentally opposed to everything for which the British Empire stands," Joint Planning review, 21 July 1936, PRO, FO 371, 19910, C5356/4/18.

75. The British certainly did not care for the mutual assistance pact proposal; and some in the Office believed that Britain should "exercise a definite control over her [France's] policy in the east of Europe"—in this case by disapproving of any new French commitments. See memos by Sargent and Eden, 29 January and 5 February 1937, PRO, FO 371, 21136, R501/26/67, and R838/26/67.

76. Phipps to Eden, 26 November 1937, ibid., 20684, C8134/18/17. Even less notice was paid to this subject by the naval attaché in his long report on France, 26 October 1937, ibid., 20687, C7348/18/17. For the empire's crucial role in French strategic planning see the long note of 19 June 1937, from the colonial ministry to national defense ministry, SHAA, B1; and W. B. Cohen, "The Colonial Policy of the Popular Front," *FHS*, 7.3 (Spring 1972) 368-393.

77. Cf. F. Bédarida's excellent study, "La 'gouvernante anglaise,' " Colloque Daladier, 1975, 3.

78. Expressions employed by Renouvin and Michel respectively. See this chapter, n28 and n54.

79. For information on Anglo-French staff contacts and the attempts to secure actual conversations, see Chapter 7.

7. National Defense and the Popular Front, 1936-1937

1. Entry 21 December 1936, Schweisguth, 351/AP3/Dr10. See British resumé of these contacts, June-July 1938, PRO, ADM 1/8583.

2. Clerk to Eden, 7 December 1936, PRO, FO 371, 20738, C1141/271/18, Clerk to Eden, 2 March 1937, ibid., C1759/271/18; Perowne (Paris) to Strang, 26 March 1937, ibid., C2471/271/18.

3. Perowne to Strang, 26 April 1937, ibid., C3172/271/18. See French note, apparently of June 1937, PRO, Air 9/20. Air ministry to Strang, 21 September 1937, PRO, FO 371, 20734, C6609/185/18. This interest in compiling bombing targets corresponds well with the newly established (1936) British Air Targets Intelligence Sub-Committee.

4. For one of many complaints about the difficulties of securing information

on the French air force, see FO memo, 6 October 1937, PRO, FO 371, 20738, C6941/271/18.

5. See meeting, 3-4 March 1938, between 2e Bureau representatives and Squadron Leader C. G. Burge, secretary of the Air Targets Sub-Committee, SHAA, B 71. Minutes are now reproduced in *DDF*, ser. 2, vol. VIII, no. 316, pp. 611-615.

6. The French total of 33 is calculated on: 20 infantry divisions, 3 cavalry, 1 light mechanized, 4 North African, 1 White Colonial, 3 Senegalese Colonial, 2 Spahis brigades, and the 16 infantry and 9 cavalry regiments of the fortified sectors. To which one could add the Réserve Générale (11 tank regiments, 9 cavalry regiments, 25 artillery, and 12 engineer regiments). The German total is based on 29 infantry and 3 armored divisions. Cf. "Situation de l'armée française," Daladier, 4 DA1/Dr3, and "Le problème militaire français," 1 June 1936, ibid., 4DA1/Dr4/sdr a.

7. WO to FO, 2 October 1936, PRO, FO 371, 19946, C7007/3790/18; CID report on German army, 13 January 1937, ibid., 20731, C1134/136/18.

8. COS report, 12 November 1937, PRO CAB 24, CP 296 (37); WO note, 3 March 1937, PRO, WO 190/520; Deputy Chiefs of Staff, "French Armament Factories," 14 December 1936, PRO, CAB 54/3.

9. CID memo, 15 July 1936, PRO, FO 371, 19871, C5391/172/17; COS, Joint Planning note "Man Power in Certain Foreign Countries," 11 February 1937, PRO, CAB 55/9; Pierre Cot, *L'armée de l'air* (Paris: Grasset, 1939) 113-114.

10. French estimates are found in CID memo, 9 June 1936, PRO, FO 371, 19946, C4274/3928/18, and British air ministry figures in note of 12 June, ibid., C4317/3928/18. French estimates are based on the figure of 12 aircraft in a German squadron, the British on the figure of 9, the remaining 3 regarded as first line reserve.

11. French estimates are reported in air ministry note to FO, 2 December 1936, PRO, FO 371, 19870, C8598/140/17. As for French production, Denain claimed 50 planes a month by the end of 1935, while Cot gives an average between 1934 and 1936 of about half that figure. Cf. Denain's deposition, 21 April 1941, Daladier, 4DA14/Dr1, and Cot's *Triumph of Treason* (New York: Ziff-Davis, 1944) 321-322.

12. COS report, 12 November 1937, PRO, CAB 24, CP 296 (37); FO memo, 27 November 1937, PRO, FO 371, 20694, C8434/122/17; Cot, *L'armée de l'air*, 111-114. Cot gives France 607 first line planes in July 1936 and 1,000 to Germany; in January 1938, 1,350 to France and 2,268 to Germany. His aircraft totals show France with 1,500 and Germany with 1,630 in July 1936, and France with 3,157 and Germany with 4,800 in January 1938.

13. Germany's long- and short-range bomber force (above or below an operational radius of 350 miles) was reckoned at 1,000 aircraft, that of France at 456. Cf. COS report, app. 3, 12 November 1937, PRO, CAB 24 CP 296 (37).

14. Cf. note 10 above, also FO memo, 18 November 1936, PRO, FO 371, 19947, C8249/3928/18. For French air estimates see Colyer to Wigram, 19 November, ibid., C8324/3928/18. For French army estimates, cf. Gauché (EMA) to

air staff, 16 October 1936, SHAA, B 73. Evidently the army had added the 500 Luftwaffe reserve planes to the 1,700 figure used by air intelligence.

15. Tournoux, *Haut commandement*, 237, 260-271, 290-292; Gamelin, *Servir*, I, 243-244, II, 249-250, III, 11-30; M. Ribet, *Le procès de Riom* (Paris: Flammarion, 1945) 373; *Daily Telegraph*, 4 February 1937.

16. And this despite Daladier's subsequent, and one would think dubious, claim that he had warned the high command repeatedly that the Ardennes region was "extremely dangerous." Riom testimony, 28 February 1942, Blum, 3BL/Dr15/sdr a.

17. Poydenot, pt. 2, 28-29.

18. CSDN meeting, 22 November 1935, SHA, Carton 8.

19. "Note sur la mobilisation industrielle," 5 April 1939, Daladier, 4DA4/Dr1.

20. CPDN meeting, report of Ramadier, 9 October 1937, SHA; *Handbook of the French Air Forces*, app. 18 (January 1939) PRO, Air 10/1648.

21. For information on French stockpiles in 1936 see the note on "Mobilisation industrielle," 27 June 1936, Daladier, 4DA1/Dr4/sdr a.

22. The British are even reported to have threatened France on the subject of coal purchases, arguing that inadequate peacetime purchases could jeopardize wartime supply arrangements. Cf. J. Néré, "La France devant la guerre économique et la coopération franco-anglaise," Anglo-French Colloquium, 1972.

23. Note on "Mobilisation industrielle," 27 June 1936, and a collection of six studies appearing under the cover note of 29 June 1936, Daladier, 4DA1/Dr4/sdr a.

24. CPDN meeting, 29 July 1936, SHA.

25. For earlier remarks on the CPDN and the HCM, see Chapter 1.

26. Cf. M. Gowing, "Anglo-French Economic Collaboration up to the Outbreak of the Second World War" and "Anglo-French Economic Collaboration before the Second World War," Anglo-French Colloquium, 1971 and 1972.

27. Cf. Gowing, ibid., 1971; CPDN meetings, 5 December 1936, 9 July 1937, 3 November 1937, *SHA*. Paul Ramadier was under-secretary of state for mines, electricity, and liquid fuel in the Blum government, and under-secretary of state for public works in the Chautemps government of June 1937.

28. Ribet, *Procès de Riom*, 363; R. Jacomet, *L'armement de la France, 1936-1939* (Paris: Editions Lajeunesse, 1945) 114, 288.

29. "Evolution des forces aériennes," no date, Daladier, 4DA2/Dr1/report 1A. The French navy experienced a similar increase during this period: 2 capital ships, 4 cruisers, 2 destroyers, 12 torpedo boats, 2 submarines, plus a modest increase of some 100 planes for the fleet air arm. Cf. note of 7 October 1939 ibid.

30. For Denain's views on the air industry—fairly similar to those of Cot—and his assessment of his own ministry, see Riom deposition, 21 April 1941, Daladier, 4DA14/Dr1.

31. Cf. my "The Strategic Dream: French Air Doctrine in the Inter-War Period, 1919-39," JCH, 9.4 (October 1974) 57-76.

32. See Chapter 2.

33. For the general outrage expressed by the bourgeoisie against so many of

the government's measures, and for the durability of the hostile *mur d'argent*, see T. Kemp, *The French Economy, 1919-1939* (London: Longman, 1972) 115-128.

34. *Evénements*, Testimony, I, Jacomet, 209-210. Jacomet says the air force averaged 27% between 1918 and 1936, compared to 42% for the navy and 31% for the army. Between 1937 and 1939, the air force share rose from 32% to 42% to 51%. Cot's figures for 1937-39 are much lower, 22% (1937), 27% (1938), 27% (1939). See R. W. Krauskopf, "French Air Power Policy, 1919-1939" (Ph.D. dissertation, Georgetown University, 1965) 407.

35. See the key deposition by Jauneaud, 21 March 1941, Daladier, 4DA14/Dr3, and Cot's *Triumph of Treason*, *L'Armée de l'Air*, and "The Defeat of the French Air Force," *FA*, 19.4 (July 1941) 790-805; "War in the Air—A Forecast," *News Chronicle*, 14 July 1938.

36. Jauneaud deposition, ibid., and entry of 8 February 1937 (Mémentos) Schweisguth, 351/AP3/Dr11.

37. *Evénements*, Testimony, I, Cot, 276.

38. CPDN meeting, 15 February 1937, SHA.

39. Cot, *Le procès de la république* (New York: Editions de la Maison Française, 1944) II, 170.

40. Flandin, *Politique française*, 69; Tabouis, *Cassandra*, 153.

41. See his undated "L'armement de la France," Daladier, 1DA7/Dr4/sdr a.

42. Ibid.; Ribet, *Procès de Riom*, 363; Jacomet, *L'armement de la France*, 114, 288.

43. Gamelin to Daladier, 10 July 1936, Note C, Daladier, 4DA1/Dr4/sdr b.

44. Gamelin to Daladier, 25 June 1936, *DDF*, ser. 2, vol. II, no. 357, pp. 536-537; Gamelin, *Servir*, II, 241-243.

45. Gamelin to Daladier, 10 July 1936, Daladier, 4DA1/Dr4/sdr b.

46. For the role of these mobile forces see the remarks entitled "Nature des grandes unités nouvelles" in a note of 1 June 1936, called "Le problème militaire français," Daladier, 4DA1/Dr4/sdr a.

47. Gamelin to Daladier, 10 July 1936, note B (relating to Paul Reynaud's proposals) Daladier, 4DA1/Dr4/sdr b. For Bourret's refutation of these ideas see his note, 21 July 1936, *DDF*, ser. 2, vol. III, no. 9, pp. 17-23. See also chap. 4, pp. 165-211, of J. Connors, "Paul Reynaud and French National Defense, 1933-1939" (Ph.D. dissertation, Loyola University of Chicago, 1977).

48. Note D ("Comment notre organisation actuelle pourrait être améliorée") Daladier, 4DA1/Dr4/sdr b. Cf. also annex 3 ("La division cuirassée") of the note entitled "Le problème militaire français," 1 June 1936, Daladier, 4DA1/Dr4/sdr a and Gamelin's remarks in the CSG, 29 April 1936, SHA.

49. See "La Division Cuirassée," ibid.

50. Ministère de la Guerre, Etat-Major de l'Armée, *Instruction sur l'emploi tactique des grandes unités* (Paris: Lavauzelle, 1940) 17-18, 27-28, 46. The contrast between this infantry-oriented document and that released by the cavalry in 1935 is worthy of note. See J. J. Clarke, "Military Technology in Republican France: The Evolution of the French Armored Force, 1917-1940" (Ph.D. dissertation, Duke University, 1969) 117-118.

51. CSG meeting, 29 April 1936, SHA. These minutes are reproduced in *Evénements*, Report, II, 182-83.

52. Gamelin to Daladier, 27 January 1937, Daladier, 4DA7/Dr1.

53. CSG meeting, 15 December 1937, SHA. For Gamelin's highly conservative views on the use of armor, see J. Clarke, *Military Technology*, 183-198, and Le Goyet, *Le mystère Gamelin*, 82-101.

54. For further information on official readings of the Spanish operations, see M. Astorkia, "Les leçons aériennes de la guerre d'Espagne," *Revue Historique des Armées*, 2.4 (1977) 145-174.

55. For the initial credit distribution of the 1936 program see his note "L'armement de la France," Daladier, 1DA7/Dr4/sdr a. For his advocacy of armored-air cooperation, see his remarks to the CSG, 15 December 1937, SHA.

56. For example, see his remark, "the artillery will remain the decisive arm," to the Finance (Army?) Commission of the Senate, 24 February 1937, Daladier, 4DA2/Dr4/sdr a. His sanguine conclusion on Spain was expressed during the CPDN meeting, 19 May 1937, "Archives du Général Gamelin," SHA.

57. *Evénements*, Testimony, II, Gamelin, 452. For the generally sympathetic reactions of the parliamentary finance commissions to defense expenditures, see F. Boudot, "Sur des problèmes du financement de la défense nationale, 1936-40," *RHDGM*, 81 (January 1971) 49-72.

58. Jean Fabry, *De la Place Concorde*, 87; Jacomet, *L'armement de la France*, 109-114; minutes of the army commission, 1 July 1936, *DDF*, ser. 2, vol. II, no. 375, p. 578; R. Frankenstein, "A propos des aspects financiers du réarmement français, 1935-39," *RHDGM*, 26.102 (April 1976) 1-20.

59. *Evénements*, Testimony, II, Gamelin, 453-454; Gamelin, *Servir*, I, 193-222.

60. *Evénements*, Testimony, I, Gamelin, 454; I, Daladier, 16-19; I, Jacomet, 199; Gamelin, *Servir*, I, 220-222.

61. *Evénements*, Testimony, I, Jacomet, 200; Jacomet, *L'armement de la France*, 277.

62. Cf. W. A. Lewis, *Economic Survey*, 101-102; M. Wolfe, *The French Franc*, 104-171; C. J. Gignoux, *L'économie française*, 275-296; T. Kemp, *French Economy*, 99-128. A. Sauvy, *Historie économique de la France entre les deux geurres* (Paris: Société d'Editions Economiques et Sociales, n.d.) II, 151-223; Sauvy, *De Paul Reynaud à Charles de Gaulle* (Paris: Casterman, 1972) 35-44.

63. Lewis, *Economic Survey*, 102.

64. Cf. Gamelin, *Servir*, I, 210-215; *Evénements*, Testimony, VI, General Happich, 1731; *JO Sénat*, Debates, rapporteur's speech on the air budget, CXXVII, 29 December 1937, 1403; and detailed survey of French air industry, 21 July 1937, PRO, FO 371, 20694, C3411/122/17.

65. Apart from the minister, the members of the CSG were all senior army officers—*général de division* and above—advised on occasion by representatives of the naval and air staffs.

66. Cf. *Evénements*, Testimony, I, Jacomet, 203; I, Daladier, 19; II, Gamelin, 369-70; V, Generals Dassault and Rinderknech, 1459-1462, 1468-1469; VI, Gen-

erals Sablet and Happich, 1579, 1717-1758; VII, General Martignon, 2139-2147; and Gamelin, *Servir*, I, 207-209; II, 188-190; Jacomet, *L'armement de la France*, 27-42.

67. Gamelin, *Servir*, I, 207-208; II, 188-190.

68. *Evénements*, Testimony, VI, General Dassault, 1468-1469; VI, General Sablet, 1579. See also Colyer's report on a conference sponsored by L'Energie Française on the air industry, 14 February 1939, PRO, FO 371, 22915, C1922/130/17.

69. Ribet, *Procès de Riom*, 252; *Evénements*, Report, II, 228. This variant of the S35, known as the Char Automoteur Somua S au 40, was an attempt at a self-propelled artillery weapon. Slower and heavier than the S35, it was to carry a 75 mm cannon mounted on the hull, the turret left unarmed. Cf. *AFV Weapons Profile*, no. 36, ed. Duncan Crow. For Jacomet's testimony regarding one model of an automatic rifle and the 75 mm anti-aircraft gun—each of which took ten years to be developed and produced, see *Evénements*, I, 192. Daladier reported that some four and a half years had elapsed between the initial studies and the production of the 47 mm anti-tank gun. Cf. Riom testimony, 27 February 1942, Blum, 3BL/Dr14, sdr a.

8. Anglo-French Relations, 1938

1. For Hitler's view on German expansion, see the famous Hossbach report, 10 November 1937, *DGFP*, ser. D, vol. I, no. 19, pp. 24-39.

2. Daladier to CSDN, 12 November 1937, SHA; cf. also Petibon's remarks to Beaumont-Nesbitt, 10 January 1938, PRO, FO 371, 21626, C195/95/62.

3. See Chapter 7.

4. These projects, 24-29 November 1937 are included in the documents for the CPDN meeting, 8 December 1937, SHA.

5. Ibid.

6. Ibid. See also CSDN secretariat note of 2 February 1938 and General Billotte (inspector-general of colonial troops) to Daladier, 17 February 1938, SHAA, B1; Colonel Beaumont-Nesbitt's long report, 21 February 1938, PRO, FO 371, 21593, C1230/36/17.

7. CPDN meeting, 8 December 1937, SHA.

8. Bullitt to secretary of state, 23 February to 4 December 1937, *FRUS*, 1937, vol. I, nos. 261-262, 584-588, 1699, pp. 54, 90, 188.

9. Bullitt to secretary of state, 21 February 1938, *FRUS*, 1938, I, no. 278, pp. 25-26.

10. Puaux clearly knew that he was going against "certain attitudes of the Firm." Cf. his note to Massigli, 22 February 1938, *DDF*, ser. 2, vol. VIII, no. 239, p. 465. For Delbos' reticence about Austria, see his dispatch to Puaux, 16 February 1938, ibid., no. 179, pp. 344-345.

11. This incident is recalled by Pierre Renouvin in his two papers on Anglo-French relations for the Anglo-French Colloquium, 1971 and 1972.

12. Gamelin, *Servir*, II, 315. Commandant Petibon, Gamelin's closest aide, had long since admitted that "the fate of Austria was decided" as long as there was no Anglo-French planning. Phipps to FO, 1 February 1938, PRO, FO 371, 21593, C692/37/17.

13. Gamelin, *Servir*, III, 11. This document, with a few marginal comments, has been reproduced under the date of 15 March 1938 in *DDF*, ser. 2, vol. VIII, no. 445, pp. 818-824.

14. *Evénements*, Testimony, I, Daladier, 26-27; Gamelin, *Servir*, II, 316. Cf. also Gamelin's note, 11 March 1938, *DDF*, ser. 2, vol. VIII, no. 381, pp. 730-731.

15. The remark is that of Alexander Cadogan, Vansittart's successor as permanent under-secretary in the Foreign Office. Cf. entry of 15 February 1938 in *The Diaries of Sir Alexander Cadogan*, ed. David Dilks (New York: Putnam, 1972) 47.

16. For Chautemps' claim, see M. A. Wathen, *The Policy of England and France towards the Anschluss of 1938* (Washington: Catholic University, 1954) 174. For Daladier's claim see *Evénements*, Testimony, I, 27, and two undated notes in Daladier, DA7/Dr6/sdr a; and Phipps to Halifax, 28 March 1938, Phipps Papers, I, 1/20.

17. French belief in the probability of an early stalemate in the west is affirmed in Beaumont-Nesbitt's report, 21 February 1938, PRO, FO 371, 21593, C1230/36/17.

18. Handwritten note by Vuillemin, dated 15 January 1938, with a cover note addressed to La Chambre and dated 9 February 1938, La Chambre.

19. Cf. J. Gehl, *Austria, Germany and the Anschluss, 1931-38* (London: Oxford University Press, 1963); and A. J. P. Taylor, *Origins of the Second World War* (Penguin, 1965) 188.

20. For Delbos' most recent assurance that France "will faithfully and unhesitatingly carry out her engagements" to Czechoslovakia, see Phipps to Halifax, 4 March 1938, PRO, FO 371, 22313, R2097/137/3.

21. See Phipps' dispatches and FO minutes, 24 March 1938, ibid., 21713, C2166/1941/18, C2250/1941/18. Bullitt too was afraid that the French "will carry out their pledge to Czechoslovakia as a matter of honor—whatever the cost." Entry of 20 May 1938, O. Bullitt, *For the President*, 262.

22. For the predictions of Delbos and Petibon, see Phipps to Halifax, 4 and 24 March 1938, PRO, FO 371, 22313, R2097/137/3 and 21713, C2166/1941/18. For Phipps' own view, see dispatch of 21 March 1938, ibid., 21674, C1936/132/18.

23. Cf. Maurice Hankey's letters to Chamberlain, 28 and 29 April 1938, and General Ismay's note to Hankey, 26 April, PRO, CAB 21, 14/4/13, 554.

24. Phipps to Halifax, 21 February 1938, PRO, FO 371, 21593, C1230/36/17.

25. See Cabinet Conclusions, 6, 12, 27 April and 25 May 1938, PRO, FO 371, 21653, C2670, C3233, C3561, C4956/37/18, and the "Summarised History of Staff Conversations," PRO, CAB 29/159.

26. For the principal accounts of this meeting see Gamelin, *Servir*, II, 325-331; Paul-Boncour, *Entre Deux Guerres*, III, 88-89. The minutes are most recently reproduced in *DDF*, ser. 2, vol. VIII, no. 446, pp. 824-831.

27. "Information du Président: La question tchécoslovaque," 15 March 1938, Daladier, 4DA8/Dr5/sdr a. This note gives Germany 106 divisions within a week of mobilization—including 33 regular infantry, 4 motorized and 4 armored divisions—of which 36 were likely to be thrown against the Czechs. German first line air strength was reckoned at 2,500 planes, including between 1,300 and 1,400 bombers.

28. Gamelin to Daladier, 16 March 1938, in CPDN documents for 15 March, "Archives du Général Gamelin," SHA. Cf. also Gamelin's note of 14 March, *DDF*, ser. 2, vol. VIII, no. 432, pp. 786-789, and of 21 September 1938, ibid., vol. XI, no. 273, pp. 425-426.

29. Phipps to Halifax, 30 March, 11 April 1938, and Halifax to Phipps, 13 April, PRO, FO 800 (Halifax) 311.

30. Halifax considered Bonnet "not an ideal choice," but he preferred to "imagine that his weaknesses are more the result of personal ambition than misguided principles." Cf. ibid. For other explanations of this appointment, see Paul-Boncour, *Entre deux guerres*, III, 97-101; S. B. Butterworth, "Daladier and the Munich Crisis: A Reappraisal," *JCH*, 9.3 (July 1974) 191-216; A. C. Gay, "The Daladier Administration, 1938-40" (Ph.D. dissertation, Duke University, 1969) 43-73.

31. Gamelin to Daladier, 11 February 1938 covering a CSDN note of 8 February entitled "Les données actuelles du problème militaire français," Daladier, 4DA3/Dr1/sdr a.

32. Daladier to Chamberlain, 5 July 1938, PRO, FO, 371, 21591, C6972.

33. Providing the French honored their pledge to Czechoslovakia—a condition written into the Soviet-Czech treaty of 1935. For French assessments of Czechoslovakia's strategic importance, see "Note du chef d'etat-major général," 9 September 1938, *DDF*, ser. 2, vol. XI, no. 65, pp. 106-110.

34. For French assessments of German economic objectives in the east, see the notes prepared by air intelligence, 28 September and 12 November 1938, entitled "La situation économique de l'Allemagne" and "L'expansion germanique," SHAA, B73, B72.

35. The remark, attributed to an unidentified friend, is recalled in Bonnet's obituary in *The Times*, 19 June 1973.

36. "Pliable yet tenacious, he had but one goal: power." *Le Monde*, 20 June 1973, p. 8.

37. Phipps to Halifax, 13 April 1938, PRO, FO 371, 21590, C2992/13/17; Wilson to secretary of state, 15 March 1938, *FRUS*, 1938, I, no. 431, p. 39.

38. Pertinax [A. Géraud] *The Gravediggers of France* (New York: Doubleday, 1944) 88.

39. Ibid., 102.

40. "Munich" by Daladier, Daladier, 2DA1/Dr5.

42. Gamelin, *Servir*, II, 318-319; *Evénements*, Testimony, I, Daladier, 28.

43. Dominions Office circular, 30 April 1938, PRO, FO 371, 21653, C3693/37/18; Anglo-French Conversations, 28-29 April, *DBFP*, ser. 3, vol. I, no. 164.

44. These talks "could hardly be considered a serious contribution to Anglo-French co-operation." See the paper by Buckley, Neave-Hill, and Haslam,

"Anglo-French Staff Conversations, 1938-1939," Anglo-French Colloquium, 1971. For the restricted scope of these talks see my note 25 above and related text.

45. H. Noguères, *Munich* (London: Weidenfeld and Nicolson, 1965) 55. This interpretation of Bonnet's policy as one which shrewdly used Britain as a stalking horse is best developed in A. P. Adamthwaite's dissertation, "French Foreign Policy."

46. Note Daladier's remarkable emphasis on naval talks. Aware that the navies could do nothing for the Czechs, the British were "taken aback" by this appeal, arguing that Daladier was "attaching an importance to Naval Conversations out of all proportion to their real value" and thus threatening the "success of the Conference." Cabinet Conclusions, 4 May 1938, PRO, FO 371, 21653, C3863/37/18.

47. In this connection, the franc was further devalued in May 1938, this time, however, "linking the franc not to gold but to the pound sterling"—a major departure from previous practice but indicative of French international policy as a whole. See T. Kemp, *The French Economy*, 154.

48. Bullitt to Roosevelt, 20 September 1938, in O. Bullitt, *For the President*, 287-288.

49. Cf. R. Girault, "La décision gouvernementale en politique extérieure," Colloque Daladier, 1975.

50. Cf. annex 2, of "Planning for War with Germany," 2 September 1938, PRO, CAB 53/4, COS 754.

51. One would add to this group the names of Pomaret, Marchandeau, de Monzie, and Chautemps.

52. "The fact is," Phipps complained, "Daladier is inclined to listen to the syren voices of Mandel, Reynaud and Herriot" . . . "the mad and criminal war party . . . , the evil forces working for war." Phipps to Halifax, 23 June 1938, PRO, FO 800 (Halifax) 311, and Phipps to Chamberlain, 30 September 1938, Phipps Papers, I, 3/1. Included in this middle group, ultimately, were Sarraut, Patenôtre, Zay, Queuille, Campinchi, Gentin, La Chambre, Chappedalaine, Julien, and Rucart—the majority of whom began the crisis closer to Reynaud and Mandel than to Bonnet and Chautemps.

53. For studies which discuss these divisions, see Nogueres, *Munich*, 256; Butterworth, "Daladier and the Munich Crisis" *JCH* (1974) 209; R. Young, "French Policy and the Munich Crisis of 1938: A Reappraisal," *Historical Papers 1970* (Canadian Historical Association) 202.

54. Cf. my article, note 53 above and "Le haut commandement français au moment de Munich," *Revue d'Histoire Moderne et Contemporaine*, 24 (January-March 1977) 110-129.

55. Bullitt to Roosevelt, 13 June 1938, in O. Bullitt, *For the President*, 267-272.

56. Compare the army's views in the summer of 1936 (Chapter 7, note 43) with those of March 1938 (this chapter, note 27) and with those expressed by Gamelin in London on 26 September 1938, PRO, FO 371, 21782, C10722/10722/18; CAB 21/595.

57. Georges later wrote, "I felt at the time that our aid to Czechoslovakia

could only be symbolic." Cf. deposition to Riom, 10 September 1941, Daladier, 4DA14/Dr5.

58. Cf. note 54 above. Although Gamelin did not encourage Daladier to resist, he did support the premier's attempts to stiffen British resolve. Thus he appeared far more firm to the British than to Daladier. Cf. Phipps to Halifax, 4 and 17 September 1938, PRO, FO 371, 21595, C9239/36/17; 21596, C10082/36/17; Director of Plans to CAS, 8 September 1938, PRO, Air 8/248; and the record of Gamelin's London visit, see note 56 above.

59. French estimates gave a German total of 6,000 machines versus 1,500 aircraft in France, or first-line strengths at 2,000 versus 500-700. Cf. French air staff note, 13 August 1938, PRO, Air 9/95; *Evénements*, Testimony, II, La Chambre, 312-313; Vuillemin's 1940 depositions to Riom, Daladier, 4DA19/Dr3; Bullitt to Roosevelt, 28 September 1938 in O. Bullitt, *For the President*, 297-300.

60. "Munich" by Daladier, Daladier, 2DA1/Dr5. Bonnet reported that Vuillemin had threatened to resign in the event of war. Phipps to Halifax, 3 November 1938, PRO, FO 371, 21613, C13372/1050/17.

61. "That is why" it was necessary to avoid war. "General Vuillemin's opinion had a major influence on the policy that I chose." Bonnet's Riom depositions, 27 August 1940 and 29 April 1941, Blum, 3BL/Dr10/sdr a; and his letters to the author, 2 November 1967, 11 March 1967, 4 March 1970.

62. For example, see the works by Noguères, Adamthwaite, and Girault.

63. For Daladier's suspicions of communism and Stalin, see Phipps to Halifax, 2 September 1938, *DBFP*, ser. 3, vol. II, nos. 750-751, pp. 219-220, and Brauer to Berlin, 7 September 1938, *DGFP*, ser. D, vol. II, no. 439, p. 713. For recent works on domestic considerations, see Girault "La décision gouvernementale," Colloque Daladier, 1975, and J. B. Duroselle, "L'influence de la politique intérieure sur la politique extérieure de la France, Anglo-French Colloquium, 1972; and for the French press and Munich, see J. Bouillon and G. Vallette, *Munich 1938* (Paris: Colin, 1964).

64. On the eve of Munich the French had some 900,000 men under arms, half of whom were mobilized reserves. See the detailed study of continental military measures in September 1938, prepared by the British War Office, 3 November 1938, PRO, FO 371, 21670, C13563/65/18.

65. At the time, Daladier refused to use the discomforting assessments which he had received from Gamelin and Vuillemin, just as earlier he had "affected hardly to have heard" the pessimistic air reports circulated by the itinerant Charles Lindbergh. Cf. the Anglo-French conversations, 25 September 1938, *DBFP*, ser. 3, vol. II, no. 1093, pp. 522-527; and Phipps to Halifax, 17 September 1938, PRO, FO 800 (Halifax) 311.

66. Cf. letter from Colonel Goutard to Daladier, 11 July 1961, and Daladier's "Munich" in Daladier, 4DA8/Dr1/sdr a and 2DA1/Dr5. Phipps later wrote: "François-Poncet told me under the seal of secrecy that during August and part of September he received constant messages from emissaries of the Army [German] . . . urging France to be firm and unyielding and declaring that in case of war the Nazi regime would collapse. *François-Poncet never informed his government of*

these messages. He felt that their origin made them suspect and that they might unduly strengthen the hands of the warmongers in France," Phipps to Halifax, 31 October 1938, PRO, FO 800 (Halifax) 311.

67. "Munich" Daladier, 2DA1/Dr5; Gamelin's Riom Mémoire #10, December 1940, Blum, 3BL/Dr12.

68. Cf. Air Ministry note to the French, 4 July 1938 (PRO, FO 371, 21654, C6694/37/18), pt. 1 of which concludes: "This frank exposition of the capacity of the Royal Air Force . . . is offered to the French air staff in the strictest confidence, in order that they should be under no illusion as to our readiness for war."

69. Campbell to Sargent, 11 August 1938, PRO, FO 371, 21592, C8578/13/17.

70. Report by Group Captain Bottomley, 29 September 1938, PRO, Air 2/2952.

71. CID to Strang, 18 November 1938, PRO, FO 371, 21592, C14287/13/17; FO minute (Mallet) 16 December 1938, ibid., 21597, C15514/36/17; "Summarised History of Staff Conversations," ibid., CAB 29/159; Compte Rendu of air staff talks, 21 November 1938, MAE.

72. Minute, 17 October 1938, PRO, FO 371, 21612, C12162/1050/17.

73. Bullitt to Roosevelt, 6 February 1939, in O. Bullitt, *For the President*, 308-311. "It was tough, very tough" he confessed to Gamelin. "For a moment I thought that I was going to wreck everything." Poydenot, p. 65.

74. Gamelin to Vuillemin, 14 October 1938, SHAA, B94.

75. Corbin to Bonnet, 8 November 1938, Daladier, 2DA4/Dr3/sdr a.

76. Phipps to Halifax, 12 October 1938, PRO, FO 371, 21785, C12144/11169/18; Minute (Harvey) on Phipps to Halifax, 26 October 1938, ibid., 21613, C13356/1050/17; FO memo, 18 November 1938, ibid., C15093/1050/17; Phipps to Halifax, 7 December 1938, ibid., 21597, C15175/37/17; Halifax to Phipps, 1 November 1938, Phipps Papers, I, 1/21.

77. Cf. German record of this meeting in Paris, *DGFP*, ser. D, vol. IV, nos. 370, and 372, pp. 471-477, 481-482; A. P. Adamthwaite, *France and the Coming of the Second World War* (London: Cass, 1977) 280-300.

78. Included in this clean-out were Massigli and Comert, both of whom had criticized Munich. These changes evoked various reactions, all of which speak to the existence of serious divisions. Bonnet was "pleased" to get rid of Massigli and Comert; François-Poncet regretted that Léger had not been dropped for his anti-Italian bias; Léger was happy to stay and "keep watch over M. Bonnet" and Massigli was delighted to have a post (Ankara) "as far away as possible from Paris." Cf. Phipps to Halifax, 26 October 1938, PRO, FO 21613, C13356/1050/17; and 1 November 1938, FO 800 (Halifax) 311, FO minute (Strang) 17 November 1938, PRO, FO 371, 21592, C14252/13/17.

79. Gamelin, *Servir*, II, 359. See also Chapter 2.

80. Cf. my "The aftermath of Munich," *FHS*, 8.2 (Fall 1973) 305-322. For French concern about German colonial ambitions, see EMAA note, 1 October 1938, SHAA, B72; and Gamelin to Vuillemin, 14 October 1938, SHAA, B94.

81. Domestically, there may well have been a connection between Daladier's new irritability, arising from Munich, and his breaking of the general strike in

November 1938 in an attempt to restore the authority of the state and so to clear the way for increased working hours and accelerated military production. Cf. T. Kemp, *The French Economy*, 157-158.

82. Vuillemin, for one, was prepared to advocate a "complete break with the Soviets" in order to secure a rapprochement with Italy. Vuillemin to Gamelin, 25 October 1938, SHAA, B94. For information on offensive planning against Italy between September and December 1938, see CSDN records, SHAA, B1.

83. For their part, the French also suspected the British, Daladier referring to betrayal as "the customary fate of allies of the British." Cf. Bullitt to Roosevelt, 6 February 1939, in O. Bullitt, *For the President*, 308-311. In this context, one may note Chamberlain's statement of December 1938 that the British guarantee did not apply to the French empire. See Renouvin, "Les relations de la Grande-Bretagne et de la France avec l'Italie en 1938-39," Anglo-French Colloquium, 1972.

84. FO minute (Vansittart) 19 December 1938, PRO, FO 371, 22922, C358/281/17. For the more critical way in which Britain, as opposed to France, was treated in the German press, see de Montbas (Berlin) to Bressy, 21 March 1939, MAE.

85. Record of Anglo-French Conversations, 24 November 1938, MAE and *DBFP*, ser. 3, vol. III, no. 325, pp. 285-311; Note de la section d'outre-mer, EMA, 13 October 1938, MAE.

86. Cf. General Lelong's note, under cover of Corbin to Bonnet, 10 November 1938, MAE.

87. EMA (3e bureau) to Daladier, 23 November 1938, Daladier, 2DA4/Dr3 and Cabinet de Ministère de la Défense Nationale to Daladier, 22 November 1938, ibid.

88. Ibid. In urging completion of the defenses opposite Belgium and Switzerland, Gamelin remarked: "France must be able to wage her war from behind this fortified system as England does from behind the Channel." Gamelin to Vuillemin, 14 October 1938, SHAA, B94.

89. Corbin to Bonnet, 8 October 1938, MAE; "Aide à demander à la Grande-Bretagne," no date, Daladier, 2 DA4/Dr3. See also "Etude sur les opérations aériennes initiales," 19 December 1938, SHAA, B92. For the 1935 proposals see Chapter 5.

90. CSDN secretariat to Daladier, 22 November 1938, Daladier, 2DA4/Dr3.

91. See the exchange of letters between Gamelin and Vuillemin, 14 and 25 October 1938, SHAA, B94.

9. 1939: Preparing for War

1. Phipps to Halifax, 14 February 1939, PRO, FO 371, 22922, C1930/281/17; CID to Strang, ibid., 22923, C2751/281/17.

2. This accord was concluded in April 1938, with ratification contingent upon an Italian withdrawal from Spain. This condition was effectively dropped after Munich and the accord ratified on 16 November 1938. Cf. Middlemas,

Diplomacy of Illusion, 211-213.

3. For example, see WO to Strang, and accompanying FO minutes, 8 February 1939, PRO, FO 371, 22958, C1822/13/18.

4. Cf. Phipps to Halifax, 12 October 1938, ibid., 21785, C12144/1169/18; French notes (translated) to air ministry, 8 December 1938, Air 9/93. In point of fact, however, French army intelligence had concluded that Germany's offensive strength was being concentrated in the east, and not the west. Note of EMA (2e) 30 November 1938, MAE.

5. Cf. French minutes of Anglo-French talks, 22-24 November 1938, Daladier, 2DA4/Dr3/sdr b; Halifax to Phipps, 16 December 1938, PRO, FO 371, 21627, C15647/95/62; "Summarised History of Staff Conversations," 24 March 1939, ibid., CAB 29/159.

6. Phipps to Halifax, 7 January 1939, PRO, FO 371, 22922, C345/281/17; WO to Halifax, 9 January 1939, ibid., 22915, C359/120/17; FO memo, 16 January 1939, ibid., C800.

7. COS Sub-Committee, 25 January 1939, PRO, CAB 53/44, p. 6.

8. CID to FO, 27 January 1939, ibid., FO 371, 22922, C400/130/17.

9. Ibid.

10. FO minute (Strang) 12 January 1939, ibid., 22915, C400/130/17.

11. COS Sub-Committee, 25 January 1939, PRO, CAB 53/44, pp. 3, 6.

12. FO memo (Strang) 16 January 1939, PRO, FO 371, 22915, C800.

13. Newton to Halifax, 14 January 1939, ibid., 22903, C1720/1720/12; Kennard to Halifax, 24 January 1939, ibid., 23143, C842/842/55; Phipps to Halifax, 31 December 1938 and 21 January 1939, ibid., 22912, C150/90/17 and 23143, C842/842/55.

14. For evidence of this debate see Phipps to Halifax, 16 and 31 January 1939, PRO, FO 371, 23792, R388/22, and 22912, C1254/90/17; FO minute (Jebb) 21 March 1939, ibid., 23794, R1939/7/22.

15. Phipps to Halifax, 22 February 1939, ibid., 22922, C2239/281/17.

16. Lord de la Warr to FO, 6 February 1939, ibid., C2060/281/17; FO memo (Roberts) 14 February 1939, 22958, C2058/13/18; Mack (Paris) to Strang, 14 February 1939, ibid., 23055, C1953/1237/18.

17. Note (Halifax) 17 February 1939, ibid., 22922, C2192/281/17.

18. Regarding the precedent, cf. Hollis to Nicholls, 15 February 1939, ibid., C2188/281/17, and to Strang, 8 March 1939, 22923, C2751/281/17. Regarding German plans see WO to Strang, 8 and 28 February 1939, ibid., 22958, C1822/C2450/13/18.

19. See Phipps to FO, 3 and 8 March 1939, ibid., 23793, R1491/R1584/7/22, and Charvériat's remarks during the weekly meeting of soldiers and diplomats at the Quai d'Orsay, 1 March 1939, MAE. For French planning against Italy, cf. CPDN meeting, 24 February 1939, "Archives du Général Gamelin," SHA.

20. Phipps to Sargent, 8 March 1939, PRO, FO 371, 23143, C2787/842/55.

21. Some six weeks later the British government reintroduced conscription, the most serious gesture—in French eyes—of a genuine commitment to the continent. For evidence of how British opinion had been hardening against Germany

since Munich, enough to both encourage and accept the government's action after 15 March, see D. C., Watt, "British domestic politics and the onset of War," Anglo-French Colloquium, 1972.

22. Gamelin to Vuillemin, 14 October 1938, SHAA, B94; CPDN meeting, 5 December 1938, "Archives du Général Gamelin," SHA.

23. Gamelin to Vuillemin, 14 October 1938, SHAA; CSG meeting, 2 December 1938, SHA. In effect, Gamelin seems to have opted for the conservative Duffieux line. See Chapter 7 notes 52 and 53 and related text. For evidence of more progressive views in other military quarters, see the dissertations of Clarke and Gunsburg.

24. CSG meeting, 13 March 1939, SHA.

25. Ibid. For warnings of an imminent coup against Prague see dispatches from the French embassy in Berlin, 11 March (de Montbas) and 13 March (Coulondre), MAE.

26. Gauché of army intelligence claimed the Germans had collected 600 excellent tanks, 750 aircraft, 1,800 anti-tank guns, 1,500,000 rifles, and 2,200 guns of all calibers. Indeed, the general believed that this materiel had been a key motive for Hitler's latest action against the Czechs. Phipps to Halifax, 28 March 1939, PRO, FO 371, 22958, C4325/13/18. Cf. also Lieutenant Colonel Dideret (Berlin) to Daladier, 21 March 1939, MAE and Lieutenant Colonel Albord (Prague) to Daladier, 27 March 1939, MAE.

27. EMA (2e bureau) 17 March 1939, "Note pour le Commandement," Daladier, 2DA4/Dr4/sdr b.

28. Corbin to Bonnet, 4 April 1939, MAE.

29. Corbin's telegram to Bonnet, 28 March 1939, MAE, establishes French awareness of the British proposal, which is presented here as being conditional on French consent. See also Bonnet to embassies (Warsaw, Bucharest) 29 March 1939 and Corbin to Bonnet, 31 March 1939, MAE.

30. Phipps to Halifax, 18 March 1939, DBFP, ser. 3, vol. IV, nos. 404-405, p. 373. One may note that since 15 March the French had been trying to negotiate a Polish guarantee for Roumania in exchange for any new pledge to Poland. W. Jedrzejewicz, ed., Diplomat in Paris, 1936-39 (New York: Columbia University Press, 1970) 174-189.

31. Cf. Chapter 6. The liabilities of France's longstanding reserve toward the USSR were clearly recognized and proclaimed by the military attaché in Moscow, General Palasse, in his note of 13 July 1939, MAE.

32. For Daladier's involvement in the February 1939 mission of Paul Baudouin to Rome, see Evénements, Testimony, VII, Baudouin, 2056-2060; IX, Bonnet, 2728-2731; François-Poncet to Bonnet, 16 February 1939, Daladier, 2DA5/Dr2/sdr a; de Villelume, Journal, 83; resumé of Baudouin's talks with Ciano, 2-3 February 1939, MAE.

33. K. de Courcy to Chamberlain, PRO, FO 371, 23794, R2193/7/22; Perth (Rome) to Halifax, 6 April 1939, ibid., R2393/7/22; Phipps to Halifax, 7 April 1939, ibid., R3106/7/22 and 20 April, R3078/7/22.

34. For Phipps' predilection for the imagery of confrontation see dispatches of

7 April, ibid., R2508/7/22 and of 17 April in *DBFP*, ser. 3, vol. VI, no. 194, pp. 222-223. Further to the Bonnet-Phipps collusion see ibid., nos. 48, 132, 162, 273, 326, 428, and appendix 5.

35. Meeting at war ministry, 9 April 1939, Daladier, 2DA4/Dr5/sdr a. See also Vuillemin's "Instruction particulière sur l'exécution des opérations aériennes contre l'Italie," 14 April 1939, SHAA, B80 and La Chambre to the Marine, prepared by Vuillemin, 11 May 1939, ibid.

36. Halifax to Phipps, 2 May 1939, *DBFP*, ser. 3, vol. V, Appendix 5, p. 801. For Daladier's resistance to any new overtures to Italy, see Bonnet's note, 2 May 1939, MAE.

37. For the British record of these conversations on 20 May, see ibid., no. 569, pp. 608-614 and the French record in Daladier, 2DA6/Dr3. Six months earlier, in December 1938, the Italians had unilaterally dissolved the Franco-Italian accord. See Poncet to Bonnet, 17 December 1938, Daladier, 2DA5/Dr2/sdr b.

38. For the Spanish-French negotiations see Bérard to Bonnet, 20 February 1939, *MAE* and Text of the Bérard-Jordana Declaration, 25 February 1939, ibid. See also Bonnet's *Quai d'Orsay*, 222-225, and *Fin d'une Europe* (Geneva: Bourgin, 1946) 217-234.

39. Phipps to Halifax, 16 and 18 March 1939, PRO, FO 371, 22912, C3233/C3378/90/17. For reports of the Polish government's stunned reaction to the coup in Prague, its "astonishment, worry and discomfort," see Noel to Bonnet, 21 March 1939, MAE.

40. The British avoided the term "vital interests" in favor of the expression "threat to Polish independence." The Anglo-Polish and Franco-Polish conventions were not signed until 25 August and 4 September respectively. Cf. FO minute (Malkin) 23-25 May 1939, PRO, FO 371, 23143, C7788/842/55; Bonnet, *Fin d'une Europe*, 217-234; Gamelin, *Servir*, II, 423-435; Henri Michel, "France, Grande-Bretagne et Pologne, Mars-Août 1939," Anglo-French Colloquium, 1972.

41. Thirteenth meeting of Anglo-French Staff Conversations, 3 May 1939, PRO, COS 900 (JP), CAB 53/48. Unlike Lelong, Gamelin said that the Franco-German frontier was the only front for an early offensive. See his directive of 31 May 1939, *Servir*, II, 426.

42. In this connection, not only was Lelong contradicted on the direction of the offensive but also by the official French assurance to London, of 20 May, that a German attack on Poland would indeed trigger a French offensive. See P. Le Goyet, "Le théâtre d'opérations du nord-est," Anglo-French Colloquium, 1973.

43. Gamelin admitted to giving the military accord "the most flexible form possible, without committing ourselves beyond that which we could reasonably promise, but without running the risk of discouraging our allies." Cf. his Mémoire #6, paper 2, of 25 February 1943, Daladier, 4DA25/Dr1. For information on the more ambitious air staff talks with the Poles, see "La collaboration Franco-Polonaise, 1933-39," SHAA, Cote C/2, pp. 10-12.

44. In his "Rapport général," Anglo-French Colloquium, 1972, Pierre Renouvin noted that the Poles do not appear to have pressed the French on the details of

the promised offensive. For the convention and accompanying minutes of the conversations, see "Protocols of the Polish-French General Staff Conferences in Paris, May 1939," *Bellona*, 2 (1958) 164-179.

45. See Chapter 6.

46. Phipps to Halifax, 28 March 1939, *DBFP*, ser. 3, vol. IV, no. 555, 535, and 7 April 1939, ibid., vol. V, appendix 1, p. 797; *Evénements*, Testimony, II, La Chambre, 315-321.

47. See H. Michel, "France, Grande-Bretagne et Pologne," Anglo-French Colloquium, 1972. On the subject of Russo-Polish relations, see two recent articles, S. Stanislawska, "Soviet Policy toward Poland, 1926-39," and A. Cienciala, "Polish Foreign Policy, 1926-1936," *Polish Review*, 20.1 (1975) 30-38, 42-57.

48. Hitler had renounced the German-Polish nonaggression pact of 1934 on 28 April 1939. For Poland's critical deficiencies in aircraft, heavy artillery, tanks, gasoline reserves, and investment capital, see Noel to Bonnet, 6 April 1939, MAE.

49. An Anglo-Turkish declaration of solidarity in the event of war in the Mediterranean was issued on 12 May 1939.

50. By an "arrangement" of 23 June 1939, the French accepted the annexation of the Syrian sanjak by Turkey. For an outline of the sanjak question, see Massigli to Bonnet, 6 February and 13 March 1939, MAE. Cf. also Massigli's memoirs, *La Turquie devant la guerre* (Paris: Plon, 1964), and the reports of General Weygand (May 1939) and General Huntziger (11 August 1939) in MAE.

51. Corbin to Bonnet, 8 March 1939, MAE.

52. Gamelin to Daladier, 16 May 1939, MAE.

53. Cf. J. M. d'Hoop, "La politique militaire de la France dans les Balkans de l'accord de Munich au début de la deuxième guerre mondiale," *Studia Balcanica*, 71 (1973) 79-89; P. Le Goyet, "Méditerranée orientale et Mer Rouge," Anglo-French Colloquium, 1973.

54. Bonnet to Payart (Moscow) 5 April 1939, MAE; Bonnet *Quai d'Orsay*, 238-239, and *Evénements*, Testimony, IX, 2667-2670. Bonnet has recalled his initiative in a letter to the author of 2 February 1967.

55. Léger reported these rumors during the Paris talks of 20 May. See French record of this meeting with Halifax, Daladier, 2DA6/Dr3.

56. For these negotiations see Jean Laloy, "Remarques sur les négociations Anglo-Franco-Soviétiques de 1939," Anglo-French Colloquium, 1972; R. Wheatley, "Britain and the Anglo-Franco-Russian Negotiations in 1939," ibid; the reports of Jacques Bardoux to the Senate's foreign affairs committee, December 1939 and February 1940, Daladier, 2DA6/Dr1/sdr b; and the Quai's diplomatic correspondence, May-July 1939, ibid., 2DA6/Dr1/sdr c.

57. *Evénements*, Testimony, IX, Bonnet, 2617, 2669; Bonnet, *Quai d'Orsay*, 145-146, 148. Bonnet reaffirmed his belief in the Schweisguth report in a letter to me of 2 November 1967.

58. Bonnet to Corbin, 6 July 1939, Daladier, 2DA6/Dr5. Cf. also his appeals to Halifax and Corbin, both of 19 July, and Corbin's report of Halifax's regret that Britain could not go "as far as the French government with respect to Molo-

tov's demands," ibid.

59. For Daladier's instructions see A. Beaufre, *Le drame de 1940* (Paris: Plon, 1965) 124. The British instructions are in PRO, CAB 54/10 and 11. These instructions were communicated to the French who quickly noted the British intention to carry out the negotiations "with great slowness." Note (Hoppenot), 3 August 1939, MAE.

60. Gauché of army intelligence warned on the eve of war, "At no time in her history has France ever become involved in a war at the outset of which conditions were so unpromising." Gauché, *Le deuxième bureau au travail, 1935-40* (Paris: Amiot-Dumont, 1953) 104.

61. Beaufre, *Le drame*, 124; also see long report by the French naval delegate to Moscow, Captain Willaume, undated but clearly post-3 September 1939, MAE.

62. Gamelin to Doumenc, 27 July 1939, MAE; Beaufre, *Le drame*, 113-186.

63. Beaufre, *Le drame*, 135-139; appendix 2, *DBFP*, ser. 3, vol. VII, 588-614.

64. Beaufre, *Le drame*, 140-145.

65. Doumenc to Daladier, 14 August 1939; Naggiar to Bonnet, 14 August 1939, Daladier, 2DA6/Dr6/sdr a.

66. Naggiar to Bonnet, 17 August 1939, ibid.

67. Ibid., sdr b.

68. Bonnet to Noel, 16, 19, 20 August 1939, ibid.

69. Beaufre, *Le drame*, 155-160; Léon Noel, *L'agression allemande*, chap. 9; Musse to war ministry, 18, 19, 20 August and Noel to Bonnet, 19 August 1939, Daladier, 2DA6/Dr6/sdr b. For the talks of 19-20 August between Musse, the Polish General Stachiewicz, and Britain's Lieutenant Colonel Sword, see Kennard (Warsaw) to Halifax, 24 August 1939, *DBFP*, ser. 3, vol. VII, no. 256, pp. 208-212.

70. For Daladier's attempt of 21 August, see *Evénements*, Testimony, I, Daladier, 47. For Bonnet's assurance to Naggiar of 23 August: "The Polish Government has just given full powers to General Doumenc to deal with (*traiter*) the Soviet authorities," see Daladier, 2DA6/Dr6/sdr c.

71. Naggiar to Bonnet, 21 August 1939, Daladier, 2DA6/Dr6/sdr b. The text of the treaty can be found in *Nazi-Soviet Relations, 1933-41* (Washington: Department of State, 1948) 76-78.

72. In this connection one might mention the interest also shown by the French in Russia's potential military contribution in the Far East against Japan. See Le Goyet, "Les relations militaires Franco-Britanniques et le Japon, mars-septembre 1939," Anglo-French Colloquium, 1973.

73. Cf. note 70 above.

74. Bonnet, *Quai d'Orsay*, 253.

75. Bonnet later admitted that had the committee members agreed, it would have been necessary, in concert with Britain, "to try to get a breathing space and, at the price of sacrifices imposed on Poland, a settlement." See his Riom deposition, 7 July 1941, Blum, 3BL/Dr10/sdr a.

76. For the key and conflicting accounts of this meeting see the original, hand-

written minutes of General Decamp, Daladier, 4DA3/Dr5; a second set of minutes, which does not show Decamp in attendance, ibid., 2DA7/Dr1; Colson's deposition, ibid., 4DA13/Dr3; Gamelin's depositions, ibid., 4DA24/Dr5/sdr a; 4DA25/Dr1/piece 17; 4DA25/Dr5/piece 76; Bonnet's depositions, *Blum*, 3BL/Dr10/sdr a; "Note sur la réunion de 23 août," La Chambre; Gamelin, *Servir*, I, 24-43; *Evénements*, Report, II, 276-278.

77. Campbell to Halifax, 23 August 1939, PRO, FO 371, 22923, C11832/90/17. This was completely in accord with the views of General Dideret in Berlin who argued that, since German and Italian war potential would increase more rapidly than that of the western powers until 1940-42, it would be better for the latter to accept war in 1939. Dideret to Daladier, 11 April 1939, MAE.

78. Mémoire #6, paper 2, 8 May 1941, *Blum*, 3BL/Dr12. For a similar statement see his remarks to the Riom trial session of 28 September 1940, Daladier, 4DA24/Dr5/sdr a, and his Mémoire #2, August-September 1940, ibid., 4DA24/Dr6/sdr b.

79. Gamelin clearly recognized the implications of giving advice against fighting for Poland: "Given the circumstances in which France found herself committed, we did not wish to be responsible for asking the government *not to stand with England*" (my italics) Mémoire #2, August-September 1940, Daladier, 4DA24/Dr6/sdr b.

80. For instance, see the long but guarded report by Commandant Bailly on the first stage of the air staff talks between 29 March and 4 April, undated, MAE.

81. Select references to this topic must include, PRO, CAB 29/159 and 160; Air 9/104, 105, 116; ADM 116/3767; ADM I/9905, 9962, 9898; "Conversations d'état-major, 1938-39," 0190 (ii) 0192, SHA; Buckley, Neave-Hill, Haslam, "Anglo-French Staff Conversations, 1938-39," Dennis Richards, "RAF Narrative" (Air Historical Branch, unpublished narrative); P. Fridenson and J. Lecuir, *La France et la Grande-Bretagne face aux problèmes aériens, 1935-mai 1940* (Vincennes: SHAA, 1976); J. Brown, "Anglo-French Naval Conferences 1939," Anglo-French Colloquium, 1973; N. H. Gibbs, *Grand Strategy*, I, *Rearmament Policy: History of the Second World War*, United Kingdom Military Series (London: HMSO, 1976), chap. 17, 653-684.

82. Le Goyet, "La coopération franco-britannique en temps de guerre," Anglo-French Colloquium, 1971; Neave-Hill, "Franco-British Strategic Policy, 1939: Command," ibid., 1972.

83. See Nicholls' report of visit to Paris, 20 April 1939, PRO, FO 371, 22916, C6004/130/17; French minutes of meetings, 9 February 1939, MAE and 27-28 June 1939 PRO, FO 837/390; also FO 837 (Ministry of Economic Warfare) 389; Paul Morand to Bonnet, 8 June 1939, MAE; Le Goyet, "Les relations économiques," Anglo-French-Colloquium, 1971. For information on the Industrial Intelligence Centre, the agency which supplied Nicholls with the bulk of his information, see my "Spokesmen for Economic Warfare," *European Studies Review*, 6.4 (October 1976) 473-489.

84. Cf. Ismay to Nicholls, 3 July 1939, regarding discussion with General Jamet (Secretary General of the CSDN) PRO, FO 371, 22917, C9299/130/17;

M. Gowing, "Anglo-French Economic Collaboration," Anglo-French Colloquium, 1971.

85. Daladier to Chamberlain, 24 July 1939, Daladier, 2DA5/Dr4.

86. For British insistence on restricting bombing operations over Germany, see General Lelong to Colonel Aymé (CSDN) 16 August 1939 Vuillemin to Gamelin, 24 August and Gamelin to Daladier, 26 August 1939, SHAA, B1. For Gamelin's emphasis on Mediterranean security, see his notes to Lelong, 21 and 22 April, as reported by Le Goyet, "Les relations militaires franco-britanniques et le Japon," Anglo-French Colloquium, 1973. For discussion of a Balkan campaign via Salonika, see CPDN meeting, 16 June 1939, SHA and the report on stage III, 3 September 1939, PRO, CAB 29/159, pp. 12-13.

10. Dénouement, 1940

1. Campbell to Halifax, 2 November 1939, PRO, FO 371, 22918, C17813/25/17.

2. According to Poydenot, following the Anglo-French staff meeting of 4 September General Gamelin reported that "the main English fear was of seeing us getting bogged down like fools' between the Rhine and the Moselle," Poydenot, pt. 2, 51.

3. Gamelin's Riom testimony, 30 August 1941, 28 September 1940, Daladier, 4DA24/Dr5/sdr a.

4. General Erich von Manstein was then chief of staff to von Rundstedt's Army Group A. For accounts of the now famous Mechelin Incident, see B. Bond, *France and Belgium 1939-40* (London: Davis-Poynter, 1975) 63-92.

5. H. Michel, *The Second World War* (London: Deutsch, 1975) 20.

6. Clearly, too, there was a fear that an early offensive might backfire as it had on Joffre in 1914—committing the army to action in one direction before ascertaining the enemy's intentions. Cf. Le Goyet, *Le mystère Gamelin*, 232-234.

7. Cf. Bond, *France and Belgium*, 43-62; D. W. Alexander, "Repercussions of the Breda Variant," *French Historical Studies*, 8.3 (Spring 1974) 459-488.

8. General Heinz Guderian, commander of the nineteenth panzer corps in Army Group A. General Reinhardt, commander of the forty-first panzer corps in Army Group A.

9. Cf. Le Goyet, *Le mystère Gamelin*, 299 et seq.

10. One recalls, for instance, the way in which the counterattack at Arras on 21 May shook German confidence and contributed in large part to the costly German delays which permitted the evacuation at Dunquerque. Cf. B. H. Liddell Hart, *History of the Second World War* (London: Cassell, 1970) 80-81.

11. For recent works on the French collapse, see Shirer, *Collapse of the Third Republic*; G. Chapman, *Why France Collapsed* (London: Cassell, 1968); A. Horne, *To Lose a Battle* (London: Macmillan, 1969); J. Williams, *The Ides of May* (New York, 1968); L. Mysyrowicz, *Autopsie d'une défaite* (Lausanne: Editions l'Age d'Homme, 1973); J. Cairns, "Some Recent Historians and the 'Strange

Defeat' of 1940," *JMH*, 46.1 (March 1974) 60-85; P. M. H. Bell, *A Certain Even-tuality: Britain and the Fall of France* (London: Saxon House, 1974).

12. This regime, with Vichy as its capital of unoccupied France and Marshal Pétain as its chief of state, succeeded the Third Republic in 1940. It collapsed under the weight of the Resistance and the allied invasion of the continent in 1944. See the most recent work by Robert Paxton, *Vichy France* (New York: Norton, 1975).

13. Sartre, *Iron in the Soul* (Penguin, 1967) 280.

14. Gamelin's Mémoire #2, August-September 1940, Daladier, 4DA24/Dr6/ sdr b.

15. The thrust of this argument would have come as no surprise to readers of the already famous *Annales d'histoire sociale et économique*, of which Bloch had been a founding father. For further information on Bloch and the *Annales*, see the illuminating issue of the *Journal of Modern History*, 44.4 (December 1972). Bloch's *Strange Defeat: A Statement of Evidence Written in 1940* is now most readily available in the Norton Library Series.

16. Sartre, *Iron in the Soul*, 79.

17. O. Bullitt, *For the President*, 369; *Sunday Times*, 27 August 1939; Janet Flanner, *Paris Was Yesterday, 1925-1939* (New York: Viking Press, 1972) 222.

18. Michel, *The Second World War*, 14-15. Yet one wonders if such a simple fact can ever hope to prevail over the effective but misleading imagery of those like Monsieur Sauvy: "Having entered the first war with a determined dive, fol-lowed by a vigorous and stimulating swim, the French entered the war of 1939 like a timid bather, inching forward, toes first, teeth chattering." *De Paul Rey-naud*, 97.

19. Cf. R. H. S. Stolfi, "Equipment for Victory in France in 1940," *History*, 55.183 (February 1970) 1-20.

20. Gunsburg, *Vaincre ou Mourir*, 623-624.

21. See, for example, J. McVickar Haight, Jr., *American Aid to France, 1938-1940* (New York: Atheneum, 1970).

Bibliography

Unpublished Primary Material

French Archives

Ministère des Affaires Etrangères (MAE). Research on documents being assembled for publication in volume 12 et seq. (1938-39) in the second series of *Documents Diplomatiques Français*, and for publication in the first series of DDF certain documents relating to 1935.

Private Papers of Edouard Daladier and Léon Blum (Fondation Nationale des Sciences Politiques), General Victor Schweisguth (Archives Nationales), Monsieur Guy La Chambre

Unpublished memoires of General Olivier Poydenot

Service Historique de l'Armée (SHA)

    CSDN, vol. III (1931-35)

    HCM, p-v (1932-35)

    CSG, p-v, vols. XVI-XVII (1926-38), Annexes (1939)

    CPDN, Archives du Général Gamelin (1932-39) p-v (1936-37)

    Etat-Major de l'Armée. 3e Bureau. "Conversations Franco-Britanniques, 1936-39," SHA, 0179, I and II; 0190, II; 0192.

Service Historique de l'Armée de l'Air (SHAA)

    Series B (1919-39)

    Series D1 (1939-40)

    Anonymous. "La collaboration franco-polonaise, 1933-39." Unpublished study, SHAA, n.d.

    Wassmer, "Evolution de la Luftwaffe de 1935-39." Unpublished study, SHAA, 1971.

Bibliography

Service Historique de la Marine (SHM)
    HCM, p-v (1935-36)
    CPDN, Documentation (1936-37)
    Reussner, A. *Les conversations franco-britanniques d'état-major, 1935-39.*
        Printed, undistributed official study, SHM, 1969.

British Archives
Private papers of Sir Basil Liddell Hart, Sir Eric Phipps, and Sir Maurice Hankey

The following derive from the Public Record Office (London):

War Office (WO)
    WO 32, Registered Papers: General Series
    WO 190, Appreciation Files: Director of Military Intelligence

Air Ministry (AIR)
    Air 8, Chief of Air Staff
    Air 2, Correspondence
    Air 9, Director of Plans
    Air 5, Air Historical Branch Records, Series II
    Air 10, Publications
    Air 19, Private Office Papers

Admiralty (ADM)
    ADM 116, Cases
    ADM 1, Papers

Foreign Office (FO)
    FO 371, General Correspondence
    FO 408, Confidential Print Series: Germany
    FO 425, Confidential Print Series: France (1930-33)
    FO 432, Confidential Print Series: France (1934-39)
    FO 418, Confidential Print Series: Russia
    FO 837, Ministry of Economic Warfare
    FO 800, Private Collections: Ministers and Officials (including papers of
        Cadogan, Halifax, Hoare, Simon, Sargent and Cranborne)

Cabinet (CAB)
    CAB 2, Committee of Imperial Defence
    CAB 23, Minutes
    CAB 24, Memoranda
    CAB 21, Registered Files
    CAB 29, Anglo-French Staff Conversations (1939)

CAB 47, Advisory Committee on Trade Questions in Time of War
CAB 53, Chiefs of Staff Committee
CAB 54, Deputy Chiefs of Staff Committee
CAB 55, Joint Planning Committee

Prime Minister's Office
Premier I, Correspondence and Papers

Miscellany
Handbook of the French Army (WO, 1932)
Notes on the French Army (WO 1936 and amendment #1, November 1937)
Richards, Dennis. R.A.F. narrative: "The Campaign in France and Low Countries: September 1939-June 1940" (London, Air Historical Branch, unpublished narrative)

German Archives (Foreign Office Library, London):
Po 1, Frankreich, "Akten betreffend politsche Angelegenheiten Frankreich" Geheim. 5.36-11.38, Serial 1586/383213-253.
Po 2, Frankreich, "Militärattaché, Paris" 1.33-5.36, Serial 5606/E401633-890.
Po 1, Frankreich, "Allgemeine auswärtige Politik (auch Friedensplan des Führers und Wiessbuch)," 5.36-12.38, Serial 605/247695-793.
Po 2, Frankreich, "Eintreten des A. Rechberg für eine deutsch-französiche Verständigung," 6.36-10.39, Serial 2498/D518159-431.
Po 2, Frankreich, "Politische Beziehungen Frankreich zu Deutschland," 5.36-10.39, Serials 621/250263-810; 3406/E013680-912; 6658/E505242-250; 7698/E548594-603; 2459/D515640-656.

Interviews and Correspondence
Interviews with Guy La Chambre, General Olivier Poydenot, Major C. A. de Linde, Air Marshal Douglas Colyer, Colonel H. F. Heywood.
Correspondence with Guy La Chambre, Georges Bonnet, Pierre Cot, René Massigli, Generals André Beaufre, Jean Petibon, Olivier Poydenot, René Bouscat, and René de Vitrolles.

Press Library (Royal Institute of International Affairs, Chatham House, London)

Dissertations
Adamthwaite, Anthony P. "French Foreign Policy, April 1938-September 1939, with Special Reference to the Policy of M. Georges Bonnet." University of Leeds, 1966. While most of my references are to this unpublished work,

Bibliography

Adamthwaite's *France and the Coming of the Second World War* has now appeared in print. See entry under Historical Studies.

Belugou, Sylvie. "Les français et l'aviation militaire française de 1936 à 1939." Mémoire de Maîtrise. University of Paris I, 1973.

Clarke, Jeffery. "Military Technology in Republican France: The Evolution of the French Armoured Force, 1917-1940." Duke University, 1969.

Connors, Joseph. "Paul Reynaud and French National Defense, 1933-1939." Loyola University, 1977.

Coox, Alvin D. "French Military Doctrine, 1919-1939: Concepts of Ground and Aerial Warfare." Harvard University, 1951.

Gay, Albert C. "The Daladier Administration, 1938-40." Duke University, 1969.

Greene, Fred. M. "French Military Leadership and Security against Germany, 1919-1940." Yale University, 1950.

Gunsburg, Jeffery A. "*Vaincre ou Mourir*: The French High Command and the Defeat of France, 1919-May 1940." Duke University, 1974.

Harvey, Donald J. "French Concepts of Military Strategy 1919-1939." Columbia University, 1953.

Krauskopf, Robert W. "French Air Power Policy, 1919-1939." Georgetown University, 1965.

Schweitzer, T. A. "The French Colonialist Lobby in the 1930's: The Economic Foundations of Imperialism." University of Wisconsin, 1971.

Stark, B. C. "A Political History of the Maginot Line." Columbia University, 1971.

Szaluta, Jacques. "Marshal Pétain between Two Wars, 1919-1940: The Interplay of Personality and Circumstance." Columbia University, 1969.

Young, Robert J. "Strategy and Diplomacy in France: Some Aspects of the Military Factor in the Formulation of French Foreign Policy, 1934-1939." University of London, 1969.

Colloquia Papers

"Relations between France and Great Britain between 1935 and 1940," known more simply as the "Anglo-French Colloquium" (1971, 1972, 1973, 1975).

"La France sous le gouvernement Daladier, Colloque." Fondation Nationale des Sciences Politiques, December 1975.

"Colloque franco-allemand." Comité d'Histoire de la Deuxième Guerre Mondiale. March 1977.

"Colloque sur la politique économique extérieure de la France, 1924-1937." University of Paris X-Nanterre. March 1977.

Note: Whereas all my references are to these papers in their unpublished form, the reader may wish to note that most of the papers from the 1971 and 1972 Anglo-French colloquia have now been published under the title *Les relations franco-britanniques de 1935 à 1939* (Paris: CNRS, 1975). Similarly, the first volume of papers from the Daladier Colloquium has now appeared under the title *La France sous le gouvernment Daladier* (Paris: Fondation Nationale des Sciences Politiques, 1977). See my entries, by author, under Historical Articles.

Bibliography

Published Primary Material

Official Documents

Belgium
Documents diplomatiques belges, 1920-1940. 5 vols. Brussels: Palais des Académies, 1964-1966.
The Official Account of What Happened. Published for the ministry of foreign affairs by Evans Bros., London, n.d.
Rapport de la commission d'information, instituée par S.M. le Roi Léopold III, le 14 juillet 1946. Luxembourg: L'Imprimerie St. Paul, 1947.

France
Assemblée Nationale Constituante. *Journal officiel de la république française.* Séance du 18 Juillet 1946. Speech delivered by Edouard Daladier.
Assemblée Nationale. Session de 1947. No. 2344. *Rapport fait au nom de la commission chargée d'enquêter sur les événements survenus en France de 1933 à 1945,* by Charles Serre. 2 vols. Paris: Presses Universitaires de France, 1947.
Rapport fait au nom de la commission chargée d'enquêter sur les événements survenus en France de 1933 à 1945. Annexes (Dépositions). Témoignages et documents recueillis par la commission d'enquête parlementaire. 9 vols. Paris: Presses Universitaires de France, 1947.
Journal Officiel de la République Française. Chambre des Députés. Débats parlementaires et documents parlementaires. Paris: Imprimerie des Journaux Officiels.
Journal Officiel de la République française. Sénat. Débats parlementaires et documents parlementaires. Paris: Imprimerie des Journaux Officiels.
Ministère des Affaires Etrangères. *Documents diplomatiques français.* First and second series (1932-1938). Paris: Imprimerie Nationale, 1963- .
Ministère des Affaires Etrangères. *Négociations relatives à la réduction et à la limitation des armements, 14 octobre 1933-17 avril 1934.* Paris: Imprimerie Nationale, 1934.
Ministère des Affaires Etrangères. *Le livre jaune français: Documents diplomatiques, 1938-1939.* Paris: Imprimerie Nationale, 1939.
Ministère de la Guerre. Etat-major de l'armée. *Instruction provisoire du 6 octobre 1921 sur l'emploi tactique des grandes unités.* Paris: Charles Lavauzelle, 1925.
Ministère de la Guerre. Etat-major de l'armée. *Instruction sur l'emploi tactique des grandes unités.* Paris: Charles Lavauzelle, 1940. Issued August 1936.

Germany
Documents on German Foreign Policy 1918-1945. Series C and D. London: HMSO, 1957 et seq.
White Book No. 2. *Documents on the Events preceding the Outbreak of the War.*

315

Bibliography

New York: German Library of Information, 1940.

White Book No. 3. *The German White Paper: Polish Documents Issued by the German Foreign Office.* New York: Howell Soskin, 1940.

Auswärtiges Amt. 1939/41. Nr. 6 *Die Geheimakten des französischen Generalstabes.* Berlin: Deutsche Verlag, 1941.

Britain
Documents on British Foreign Policy 1919-1939. Second and Third series. London: HMSO, 1946 et seq.

Russia
New Documents on the History of Munich. Published by the ministry for foreign affairs of the Czechoslovak Republic and the ministry for foreign affairs of the Union of Soviet Socialist Republics. Prague: Orbis, 1958.

United States
Foreign Relations of the United States. Diplomatic Papers. Washington: Government Printing Office, 1946-1953.

League of Nations
League of Nations: Armaments Year-Book (annual)
League of Nations: Official Journal
League of Nations: Treaty Series

Political Trials
Haute Cour de Justice. *Procès du Maréchal Pétain.* Paris: Imprimerie des Journaux Officiels, 1945.

Le procès Flandin devant la haute cour de justice, 23-26 juillet, 1946. Paris: Librairie de Medicis, 1947.

Le procès Laval. Compte rendu sténographique. Paris: Albin Michel, 1946.

Les procès de Collaboration. Fernand de Brinon, Joseph Darnand, Jean Luchaire. Compte rendu sténographique. Paris: Michel, 1948.

Aujol, J. *Le procès Benoist-Méchin.* Paris: Albin Michel, 1948.

Coquet, James de. *Le procès de Riom.* Paris: Fayard, 1945.

Mazé, Pierre, and Roger Genebrier. *Les grandes journées du procès de Riom.* Preface by Edouard Daladier. Paris: La Jeune Parque, 1945.

Ribet, Maurice. *Le procès de Riom.* Paris: Flammarion, 1945.

Tissier, P. *The Riom Trial.* London: Harrap, 1942.

Documentary Collections
Degras, Jane, ed. *Soviet Documents on Foreign Policy.* Vol. III, 1933-1941. London: Oxford University Press, 1953.

Documents and Materials Relating to the Eve of the Second World War. Vol. II

Bibliography

(Dirksen Papers), 1938-39. Moscow: Foreign Languages Publishing House, 1948.

Documents on Polish-Soviet Relations, 1939-1945. Vol. I, 1939-43. London: Heinemann for the General Sikorski Historical Institute, 1961.

Survey of International Affairs. Published for the Royal Institute of International Affairs, annually, by Oxford University Press.

Documents on International Affairs, see *Survey* above.

Sonntag, R. J. and J. S. Beddie. *Nazi-Soviet Relations, 1939-1941.* Documents from the Archives of the German Foreign Office. Washington: Department of State, 1948.

International Military Tribunal. *Trial of the Major War Criminals before the International Military Tribunal.* 42 vols. Nuremberg, 1947.

International Military Tribunal. *Nazi Conspiracy and Aggression.* Washington: United States Government Printing Office, 1946.

Diaries, Memoirs, Contemporary Documents

French

Armengaud, General Jean. *Batailles politiques et militaires sur L'Europe: Témoignages 1932-40.* Paris: Editions du Myrte, 1948.

Auriol, Vincent. *Hier . . . demain.* 2 vols. Tunis: Charlot, 1944.

Bardoux, Jacques. *Journal d'un témoin de la troisième.* Paris: Fayard, 1957.

Beaufre, André. *Le drame de 1940.* Paris: Plon, 1965.

Bérard, Armand. *Un ambassadeur se souvient.* Paris: Plon, 1976.

Beuve-Méry, Hubert. *Réflexions politiques, 1932-1952.* Paris: Seuil, 1951.

Billotte, Pierre. *Le temps des armes.* Paris: Plon, 1972.

Blondel, Jules. *Au fil de la carrière: Récit d'un diplomate, 1911-38.* Paris: Hachette, 1961.

Blum, Léon. *L'exercise du pouvoir.* Paris: Gallimard, 1937.

——— *L'histoire jugera.* Montreal: Editions de l'Arbre, 1945.

Bonnet, Georges. *Défense de la paix.* 2 vols. Geneva: Bourgin, 1946.

——— *Quai d'Orsay: 45 Years of French Foreign Policy.* Isle of Man: Times Press, 1965.

——— *Le Quai d'Orsay sous trois républiques, 1870-1961.* Paris: Fayard, 1961.

——— *Vingt ans de vie politique, 1918-1938.* Paris: Fayard, 1969.

Bret, Paul. *Au feu des événements.* Paris: Plon, 1959.

Brinon, Fernand de. *Mémoires.* Paris: L.L.C., 1949.

Chambrun, Charles de. *Traditions et souvenirs.* Paris: Flammarion, 1952.

Charles-Roux, François. *Huit ans au Vatican, 1932-1940.* Paris: Flammarion, 1947.

Chauvel, Jean. *Commentaire.* 3 vols. Paris: Fayard, 1971-73.

Conquet, Alfred. *Trente ans avec Pétain.* Paris, Plon, 1959.

———— *Auprès du Maréchal Pétain*. Paris: Editions France-Empire, 1970.

Cot, Pierre. *Le Procès de la république*. 2 vols. New York: Editions de la Maison Française, 1944.

Coulondre, Robert. *De Staline à Hitler*. Paris: Hachette, 1950.

Daladier, Edouard. *The Defence of France*. London: Hutchinson, 1939.

Darlan, Alain. *L'Amiral Darlan parle*. Paris: Amiot-Dumont, 1953.

De Gaulle, Charles. *Mémoires de guerre*. Vol. I, *L'appel, 1940-42*. Paris: Plon, 1954.

Fabre-Luce, Alfred. *Journal de la France, mars 1939-juillet 1940*. Paris: Imprimerie J.E.P., 1940.

———— *Vingt-cinq années de la liberté*. 3 vols. Paris: Julliard, 1962-64.

Fabry, Jean. *De la Place Concorde au cours de l'Intendance*. Paris: Editions de la France, 1942.

Faure, Paul. *De Munich à la cinquième république*. Paris: Editions de l'Elan, 1949.

Flandin, Pierre Etienne. *Discours*. Paris: Gallimard, 1937.

———— *Politique française*. Paris: Editions Nouvelles, 1947.

François-Poncet, André. *Au palais Farnèse: Souvenirs d'une ambassade à Rome, 1938-1940*. Paris, Fayard, 1961.

———— *Souvenirs d'une ambassade à Berlin*. Paris, Flammarion, 1946.

Galtier-Boissière, J. *Mémoires d'un parisien*. 3 vols. Paris: Table Ronde 1960-63.

Gamelin, Maurice G. *Servir*. 3 vols. Paris: Plon, 1946.

Gauché, General Maurice. *Le deuxième bureau au travail, 1935-1940*. Paris: Amiot-Dumont, 1953.

Herriot, Edouard. *Jadis*. Vol. II. Paris: Flammarion, 1952.

Jacomet, Robert. *L'armement de la France, 1936-1939*. Paris: Editions Lajeunesse, 1945.

Jeanneney, Jules. *Journal Politique: Septembre 1939-Juillet 1942*. Paris: Armand Colin, 1972.

Jouhaud, E. *La vie est un combat*. Paris: Fayard, 1974.

Lagardelle, Hubert. *Mission à Rome*. Paris: Plon, 1955.

Laroche, Jules. *Au Quai d'Orsay avec Briand et Poincaré*. Paris: Hachette, 1957.

———— *La Pologne de Pilsudski: Souvenirs d'une ambassade, 1926-1935*. Paris: Flammarion, 1953.

Laval, Pierre. *Laval parle . . . Notes et mémoires rédigés à Fresnes d'août à octobre 1945*. Paris: Librairie Ch. Béranger, 1948.

———— *The Unpublished Diary of Pierre Laval*. London: Falcon Press, 1948.

Lazareff, Pierre. *Dernière édition*. Montreal: Valiquette, 1942.

Lebrun, Albert. *Témoignage*. Paris: Plon, 1945.

Massigli, René. *La Turquie devant la guerre: Mission à Ankara, 1939-40*. Paris: Plon, 1964.

Minart, Jacques. *Le drame de désarmement français, 1918-1939*. Paris: La Nef de Paris, 1959.

Monzie, Anatole de. *Ci-devant*. Paris: Flammarion, 1941.

Noel, Léon. *L'Agression allemande contre la Pologne*. Paris: Flammarion, 1946.

Bibliography

Paul-Boncour, Joseph. *Entre deux guerres*. 3 vols. Paris: Plon, 1945-46.

Réquin, General Edouard. *D'une guerre à l'autre, 1919-1939: Souvenirs*. Paris: Lavauzelle, 1949.

Reynaud, Paul. *Au coeur de la mêlée*. Paris: Flammarion, 1951.

—— *Mémoires*. Vol. I, *Venu de ma montagne*. Paris: Flammarion, 1960.

Sauvy, Alfred. *De Paul Reynard à Charles De Gaulle*. Paris: Casterman, 1972.

Serrigny, General Bernard. *Trente ans avec Pétain*. Paris: Plon, 1959.

Seydoux, François. *Mémoires d'Outre Rhin*. Paris: Grasset, 1975.

Stehlin, Paul. *Témoignage pour l'histoire*. Paris: Laffont, 1964.

Tabouis, Geneviève. *They Called Me Cassandra*. New York: Scribner, 1942.

Tardieu, André. *L'année de Munich*. Paris: Flammarion, 1939.

Vallat, Xavier. *Le nez de Cléopâtre: Souvenirs d'un homme de droit, 1919-1944*. Paris: Les Quatre-Fils-Aymon, 1957.

Varé, Daniel. *The Two Imposters*. London: Murray, 1949.

Villelume, Paul de. *Journal d'une défaite, août 1939-juin 1940*. Paris: Fayard, 1976.

Weygand, Jacques. *The Role of General Weygand: Conversations with His Son*. London: Eyre & Spottiswoode, 1948.

Weygand, Maxime. *Mémoires*. 3 vols. Paris: Flammarion, 1957.

—— *En lisant les mémoires de guerre du Général de Gaulle*. Paris: Flammarion, 1955.

Zay, Jean. *Souvenirs et Solitude*. Paris: Juilliard, 1945.

Others

Abetz, Otto. *Das offene Problem*. Cologne: Greven, 1951.

—— *Histoire d'une politique franco-allemande, 1930-1950*. Paris: Librarie Stock, 1953.

Aloisi, Baron Pompeo. *Journal*. Paris: Plon, 1957.

Avon, Earl of. *The Eden Memoirs: Facing the Dictators*. London: Cassell, 1962.

Baynes, Norman H. *Hitler's Speeches*. Toronto: Oxford University Press, 1942.

Beck, Joseph. *Final Report*. New York: Speller and Sons, 1957.

Benes, Edward. *From Munich to New War and New Victory*. London: Allen and Unwin, 1954.

Bond, Brian, ed. *Chief of Staff: The Diaries of Lieutenant-General Sir Henry Pownall*. Vol. I, 1933-40. London: Leo Cooper, 1972.

Bullitt, Orville, ed. *For the President: Personal and Secret*. London: Deutsch, 1973.

Chatfield, Lord. *It Might Happen Again*. London: Heinemann, 1947.

Ciano, Count Galeazzo. *Diary 1937-38*. London: Methuen, 1952.

—— *Diary 1939-1943*. London: Heinemann, 1947.

—— *Diplomatic Papers, 12 June 1936-30 April 1942*. London: Odhams, 1948.

Davies, Joseph E. *Mission to Moscow*. New York: Pocket Books, Inc., 1941.

Davignon, Vicomte J. *Berlin 1936-40: Souvenirs d'une mission*. Paris: Editions Universitaires, 1951.

Bibliography

Dilks, David, ed. *The Diaries of Sir Alexander Cadogan, 1938-45*. New York: Putnam, 1972.

Dodd, William E. *Ambassador Dodd's Diary*. New York: Harcourt Brace, 1941.

Dorlodot, R. de. *Souvenirs*. Vol. II. Bruxelles: Ad Geomaere, 1964.

Duff Cooper, A. *Old Men Forget*. London: Hart-Davis, 1954.

Eden, Anthony. *Foreign Affairs*. London: Faber and Faber, 1939.

—— *Days for Decision*. Boston: Houghton Mifflin, 1950.

Flanner, Janet. *Paris Was Yesterday, 1925-1939*. New York: Viking Press, 1972.

Gafencu, Grigore. *The Last Days of Europe*. London: F. Muller, 1947.

Gladwyn, Lord. *The Memoirs of Lord Gladwyn*. London: Weidenfeld Nicolson, 1972.

Guariglia, Raffele. *La diplomatie difficile: Mémoires 1922-46*. Paris: Plon, 1955.

Halifax, Earl of. *Speeches on Foreign Policy*. London: HMSO, 1941.

—— *The Fullness of Days*. London: Collins, 1957.

Harvey, John, ed. *The Diplomatic Diaries of Oliver Harvey, 1937-40*. London: Collins, 1970.

Hassell, Ulrich von. *The Von Hassell Diaries, 1938-44*. London: Hamish Hamilton, 1948.

Henderson, Nevile. *Failure of a Mission*. New York: Putnam, 1940.

—— *Water under the Bridges*. London: Hodder and Stoughton, 1945.

Hoare, Samuel (Lord Templewood). *Nine Troubled Years*. London: Collins, 1954.

Hymans, Paul. *Mémoires*. 2 vols. Bruxelles: Editions de l'Institut de Sociologie Solvay, 1958.

Ironside, Sir Edmund. *The Ironside Diaries, 1937-1940*. Ed. R. Macleod and D. Kelly. London: Constable, 1962.

Ismay, Lord. *The Memoirs of General the Lord Ismay*. London: Heinemann, 1960.

Jedrzejewicz, Waclaw, ed. *Diplomat in Berlin, 1933-39*. New York: Columbia University Press, 1968.

—— , ed. *Diplomat in Paris, 1936-1939: Papers and Memoirs of Juliusz Lukasiewicz*. New York: Columbia University Press, 1970.

Jones, Thomas. *A Diary with Letters, 1931-1950*. London: Oxford University Press, 1954.

Kirkpatrick, Ivone. *The Inner Circle*. London: Macmillan, 1959.

Kordt, Erich. *Nicht aus den Akten*. Stuttgart: Union Deutsche Verlag, 1950.

Liddell-Hart, Basil H. *The Memoirs of Captain Liddell-Hart*. 2 vols. London: Cassell, 1965-1966.

Londonderry, Marquis of. *Wings of Destiny*. New York: Macmillan, 1943.

Minney, R. J. *The Private Papers of Hore-Belisha*. London: Collins, 1960.

Overstraeten, General R. van. *Albert I-Leopold III: Vingt ans de politique militaire belge, 1920-1940*. Bruges: Desclée de Brouwer, n.d.

Papen, Franz von. *Memoirs*. London: Deutsch, 1952.

Peterson, Sir Maurice. *Both Sides of the Curtain*. New York: Macmillan, 1951.

Rauschning, Hermann. *Hitler Speaks*. London: T. Butterworth, 1939.

Bibliography

Ribbentrop, Joachim. *The Ribbentrop Memoirs.* London: Weidenfeld and Nicolson, 1954.

Schacht, Hjalmar. *My First Seventy-Six Years.* London: Wingate, 1955.

Schmidt, Paul. *Hitler's Interpreter.* London: Heinemann, 1951.

Schuschnigg, Kurt von. *Austrian Requiem.* London: Gollancz, 1947.

Simon, Viscount. *Retrospect: The Memoirs of the Rt. Hon. Viscount Simon.* London: Hutchinson, 1952.

Slessor, Sir John. *The Central Blue.* London: Cassell, 1956.

Spears, Sir Edward. *Assignment to Catastrophe.* Vol. I. London: Heinemann, 1954.

Starhemberg, E. R. von. *Between Hitler and Mussolini.* London: Hodder and Stoughton, 1942.

Strang, Lord William. *Home and Abroad.* London: Deutsch, 1956.

Strong, Sir Kenneth. *Intelligence at the Top: The Recollections of an Intelligence Officer.* London: Cassell, 1968.

Szembeck, Comte Jean. *Journal 1933-1939.* Paris: Plon, 1952.

Vansittart, Sir Robert. *The Mist Procession.* London: Hutchinson, 1958.

Van Zuylen, Paul. *Les mains libres: Politique extérieure de la Belgique, 1914-1940.* Brussels: Editions Universèlles, 1950.

Weizsacker, Ernst von. *The Memoirs of Ernst von Weizsacker.* London: Collins, 1951.

Wheeler-Bennett, Sir John. *Knaves, Fools and Heroes.* London: St. Martin's Press, 1974.

Biographies

Angot, E., and R. de Lavergne. *Le Général Vuillemin: Une figure légendaire de l'aviation française de 1914 à 1940.* Paris: La Palatine, 1965.

Antériou, Jacques, and Jean Baròn. *Edouard Herriot au service de la république.* Paris: Editions du Dauphin, 1957.

Aubert, Octave. *Louis Barthou.* Paris: Librairie Quillet, 1935.

Besseige, Henri. *Herriot parmi nous.* Paris: Magnard, 1960.

Birkenhead, Earl of. *The Life of Lord Halifax.* London: Hamish Hamilton, 1965.

Bullock, Allan. *Hitler: A Study in Tyranny.* New York: Harper Torchbooks, 1962.

Butler, Ewan. *Mason-Mac: The Life of Lieutenant-General Sir Noel Mason-Macfarlane.* London: Macmillan, 1972.

Chaigne, Louis. *Jean de Lattre, maréchal de France.* Paris: Lanore, 1952.

Coblentz, Paul. *Georges Mandel.* Paris: Editions du Bélier, 1946.

Cole, Hubert. *Laval: A Biography.* London: Heinemann, 1963.

Colton, Joel C. *Leon Blum: Humanist in Politics.* New York, Knopf, 1966.

Colvin, Ian. *Vansittart in Office.* London: Gollancz, 1965.

Docteur, Admiral Jules. *La grande énigme de la guerre: Darlan.* Paris: Editions de

Bibliography

la Couronne, 1949.

Droit, Michel. *De Lattre: Maréchal de France*. Paris: Editions de Flore, 1952.

Feiling, Keith. *The Life of Neville Chamberlain*. London: Macmillan, 1946.

Griffiths, Richard M. *Marshal Pétain*. London: Constable, 1970.

Herzog, Wilhelm. *Barthou*. Zurich: Verlag die Liga, 1938.

Héring, General Pierre. *La vie exemplaire de Philippe Pétain*. Paris: Editions Paris-Livres, 1956.

Lapaquellerie, Yvon. *Edouard Daladier*. Paris: Flammarion, 1939.

Laure, General Auguste. *Pétain*. Paris: Berger-Levrault, 1942.

Le Goyet, Pierre. *Le mystère Gamelin*. Paris: Presses de la Cité, 1975.

Macleod, Iain. *Neville Chamberlain*. London: F. Muller, 1961.

Mallet, Alfred. *Pierre Laval*. 2 vols. Paris: Amiot-Dumont, 1955.

Martel, Francis. *Pétain: Verdun to Vichy*. New York: Dutton and Co., 1943.

Middlemas, Keith, and John Barnes. *Baldwin*. London: Weidenfeld and Nicolson, 1969.

Mikes, George. *Darlan: A Study*. London: Constable, 1943.

Planté, Louis. *Un grand seigneur de la politique: Anatole de Monzie*. Paris: Raymond Clavreuil, 1955.

Privat, Maurice. *Pierre Laval: Cet inconnu*. Paris: Fournier-Valdès, 1941.

Raissac, Guy. *Un soldat dans la tourmente*. Paris: Albin Michel, 1963.

Ray, Oscar. *General Gamelin*. London: Pilot Press, 1940.

——— *The Life of Edouard Daladier*. London: Pilot Press, 1940.

Roskill, Stephen. *Hankey: Man of Secrets*. Vol. III. London: Collins, 1974.

Sherwood, John. *Georges Mandel and the Third Republic*. Stanford: Stanford University Press, 1970.

Stokes, R. L. *Léon Blum: Poet to Premier*. New York: Coward McCann, 1937.

Torrès, Henri. *Pierre Laval: La France trahie*. New York: Brentano's, 1941.

Varenne, Francisque. *Mon patron, Georges Mandel*. Paris: Editions Défense, 1945.

Varennes, Claude. *Le destin de Marcel Déat*. Paris: Editions Janmaray, 1948.

Vichniac, Marc. *Léon Blum*. Paris: Flammarion, 1937.

Waterfield, G. *Professional Diplomat: Sir Percy Loraine of Kirkharle*. London: John Murray, 1973.

Warner, Geoffrey. *Pierre Laval and the Eclipse of France*. London: Eyre and Spottiswoode, 1968.

Weygand, Jacques. *Weygand, Mon Père*. Paris: Flammarion, 1970.

Wingate, Sir Ronald. *Lord Ismay: A Biography*. London: Hutchinson, 1970.

Contemporary Studies

Allard, Paul. *Le Quai d'Orsay*. Paris: Editions de France, 1938.

Alléhaut, General Emile. *Etre prêts*. Paris: Berger-Levrault, 1935.

Allerme, Colonel Marie. *Les causes militaires de notre défaite*. Paris: Publications du Centre d'Etudes de l'Agence Inter-France, n.d.

Armstrong, Hamilton F. *When There Is No Peace*. London: Macmillan, 1939.

Bacon, Reginald, and F. E. McMurtrie. *Modern Naval Strategy*. London: Muller, 1941.

Barjot, Pierre. *L'aviation militaire française*. Paris: J. de Gigord, 1936.

Bénazet, Paul. *Défense nationale, notre sécurité*. Paris: Grasset, 1938.

Butler, Harold. *The Lost Peace*. London: Faber: 1941.

Cameron, Elizabeth. *Prologue to Appeasement: A Study in French Foreign Policy*. Washington, D.C.: American Council on Public Affairs, 1942.

Castex, Admiral Raoul. *De Gengis-Khan à Staline*. Paris: Editions Géographiques, Maritimes et Coloniales, 1935.

Chauvineau, General Narcisse. *Une invasion: Est-elle encore possible?* Paris: Berger-Levrault, 1939.

Cot, Pierre. *L'armée de l'air*. Paris: Grasset, 1939.

Dans les coulisses des ministères et de l'état-major, 1932-40. Paris: Les Documents Contemporains, n.d.

Davis, Shelby. *The French War Machine*. London: Allen and Unwin, 1937.

Déat, Marcel. *Le front populaire au tournant*. Paris: Editions du Journal *La Concorde*, 1937.

Debeney, General Eugène. *La guerre et les hommes*. Paris: Plon, 1937.

—— *Sur la sécurité militaire de la France*. Paris: Payot, 1930.

De Gaulle, Charles. *The Army of the Future*. London: Hutchinson, n.d.

D'Ormesson, Wladimir. *France*. London: Longmans, 1939.

Driault, Edouard. *La paix de la France, 1918-1935*. Paris: Librairie Recueil Sirey, 1937.

Duval, General Maurice. *Les leçons de la guerre d'Espagne*. Paris: Plon, 1938.

Earle, Edward Mead, ed. *Makers of Modern Strategy*. Princeton: Princeton University Press, 1943.

Frédérix, Pierre. *Etat des forces en France*. Paris: Gallimard, 1935.

Halévy, Daniel. *1938: Une année d'histoire*. Paris: Grasset, 1938.

Kérillis, Henri de, and Raymond Cartier. *Laisserons-nous démembrer la France?* Paris: Nouvelle Revue Critique, 1939.

Leeds, Stanford B. *These Rule France*. New York: Bobbs-Merrill, 1940.

Liddell Hart, Basil H. *The Remaking of Modern Armies*. London: Murray, 1927.

Lombard, Paul. *Le chemin de Munich*. Paris: Editions de France, 1938.

Machray, R. *The Little Entente*. London: Allen and Unwin, 1929.

Maroselli, André. *Le sabotage de notre aviation*. Paris: Gedalge, 1941.

Maurin, General Louis. *L'armée moderne*. Paris: Flammarion, 1938.

Micaud. Charles A. *The French Right and Nazi Germany, 1933-39*. Durham, N.C.: Duke University Press, 1943.

Monteilhet, Joseph. *Les institutions militaires de la France, 1814-1932*. Paris: Librairie Alcan, 1932.

Mordacq, General Jean Jules. *Les leçons de 1914 et la prochaine guerre*. Paris: Flammarion, 1934.

—— *La défense nationale en danger*. Paris: Editions de France, 1938.

———— *Faut-il changer le régime?* Paris: Albin Michel, 1935.

Pertinax [A. Gèraud]. *The Gravediggers of France.* New York: Doubleday, 1944.

Pickles, Dorothy M. *The French Political Scene.* London: Thomas Nelson, 1938.

Pol, H. *Suicide of a Democracy.* New York: Reynal and Hitchcock, 1940.

Reynaud, Paul. *Le problème militaire français.* Paris: Flammarion, 1937.

Royal Institute of International Affairs. *Political and Strategic Interests of the United Kingdom.* London: Oxford University Press, 1939.

Ripka, Hubert. *Munich, Before and After.* London: Gollancz, 1939.

Seversky, Alexander P. de. *Victory through Air Power.* New York: Simon and Schuster, 1942.

Sharp, Walter Rice. *The Government of the French Republic.* New York: Van Nostrand, 1938.

Schuman, Frederick L. *War and Diplomacy in the French Republic.* New York: Whitesley House, 1931.

———— *Europe on the Eve: The Crises of Diplomacy, 1933-39.* New York: Knopf, 1939.

Tabouis, Geneviève. *Blackmail or War.* London: Penguin, 1938.

Tardieu, André. *France in Danger.* London: Dennis Archer, 1935.

Temperley, A. G. *The Whispering Gallery of Europe.* London: Collins, 1939.

Vauthier, Colonel P. *La doctrine de guerre du Général Douhet.* Paris: Berger-Levrault, 1935.

———— *Le danger aérien et l'avenir du pays.* Paris: Berger-Levrault, 1930.

Vidéo [pseud.]. *L'armée et la politique.* Paris: Librairie d'Action Française, 1937.

Werner, Max. *The Military Strengths of the Powers.* London: Gollancz, 1939.

Werth, Alexander. *France and Munich.* London: Hamilton, 1939.

———— *The Destiny of France.* London: Hamilton, 1937.

Weygand, General Maxime. *La France est-elle défendue?* Paris: Flammarion, 1937.

Wheeler-Bennett, Sir John W. *Disarmament Deadlock.* London: Oxford University Press, 1934.

Wiskemann, Elizabeth. *Undeclared War.* London: Constable, 1939.

Periodicals Screened

Année Politique Française et Etrangère, American Historical Review, American Political Science Review, Bellona, Canadian Historical Association Proceedings, Cahiers d'Histoire, European Studies Review, English Historical Review, Esprit International, Foreign Affairs, French Historical Studies, Forces Aériennes Françaises, History, History Today, Historical Journal, International Affairs, International Relations, Journal of Central European Affairs, Journal of Modern History, Journal of Contemporary History, Journal of European Studies, Military Affairs, Middle East Journal, Nouveau Candide, Polish Review, Political Science Quarterly, Quarterly Review, Recherches Internationales à la Lumière du Marxisme, Royal United Services Institute Journal, Revue Hebdomadaire, Revue des

Bibliography

Deux Mondes, Revue Militaire Générale, Revue de France, Revue de Paris, Revue de l'Armée de l'Air, Revue Universelle, Revue Historique, Revue d'Histoire de la Deuxième Guerre Mondiale, Revue de Défense Nationale, Revue d'Histoire Moderne et Contemporaine, Studia Balcanica, Social Research, Slavonic Review, Transactions of the Royal Historical Society, United States Naval Institute Proceedings, Western Society for French History Proceedings, World Politics, World Affairs Quarterly.

Contemporary Articles

Armengaud, General J. "L'armée de l'air et les autres armées." RMG, 1 (1937) 59-68.

———— "La défense aérienne." Pts. 1 and 2. RDDM (1, 15, April 1934) 525-546, 820-838.

———— "La Tchécoslovaquie devant l'Allemagne." RDDM (15 April 1938) 766-779.

———— "Les leçons de la guerre d'Espagne." RDDM (15 August 1937) 754-769.

———— "Vers l'équilibre aérien." RDDM (1 April 1939) 536-555.

Auboin, Roger. "The Blum Experiment." International Affairs, 16.4 (July-August 1937) 499-518.

Azan, General Paul. "L'organisation de la défense nationale." RMG, 4 (1938) 253-258.

Baratier, General Victor. "Force et faiblesse de notre armée." La Revue de France, 5 (1 September 1935) 116-136.

Bidou, Henry. "Que sera le haut commandement." La Revue de Paris, 1 (January-February 1937) 70-80.

Brinquier, P. "De Paris à Munich." RDDM (15 November 1939) 451-459.

Buchet, Colonel Charles. "Après le coup de force allemand." La Revue de France. 3 (1 May 1936) 114-132.

Carr, Philip. "The Outlook in France." International Affairs, 16.1 (January-February 1937) 70-96.

Chambe, René. "L'armée de l'air, garde du pays." RDDM (15 August 1934) 752-770.

Clinton, A. C. "The Trend of Development in Aircraft: Some Impressions of the Paris Exhibition, 1936." RUSI, 82 (1937) 113-124.

"Contre l'attaque brusquée." RDDM (15 December 1934) 742-764.

Cot, Pierre. "The Defeat of the French Air Force." FA, 19.4 (July 1941) 790-805.

Darlan, Vice Admiral François. "Composition et puissance de la flotte: Son rôle dans la défense nationale." RMG, (January 1938) 31-42.

Debeney, General Eugène. "Encore l'armée de métier." RDDM (15 July 1935) 279-295.

———— "La motorisation des armées modernes." RDDM (15 March 1936) 273-291.

———— "Le problème de la couverture." RDDM (15 November 1936) 268-293.

Bibliography

———— "Nos fortifications du nord-est." *RDDM* (15 September 1934) 241-261.

De Watteville, H. "The French Army." *RUSI*, 85 (1940) 213-220.

D'Ormesson, Wladimir. "L'Espagne et les puissances." *La Revue de Paris*, 4 (July-August 1937) 481-494.

Doukas, K. A. "Armaments and the French Experience." *American Political Science Review*, 33 (April 1939) 279-291.

Duchêne, General Emmanuel. "L'attaque brusquée et le danger aérien." *RDDM* (1 March 1937) 116-127.

Duval, General Maurice. "L'armée française de 1938." *La Revue de Paris*, 16 (August 1938) 721-747.

———— "La convention aérienne." *L'Esprit International*, 9.35 (July 1935) 306-319.

Etienne, P. "La doctrine officielle de l'aviation militaire française." *Revue de l'Armée de l'Air*, 79 (February 1936) 123-129.

Faucher, General. "Some Recollections of Czechoslovakia." *IA*, 18.3 (May-June 1939) 343-360.

Fabry, Jean. "La défense nationale." *RMG*, 4 (January 1938) 19-30.

Gamelin, General Maurice. "Hier et Demain." *RMG* (January 1937) 25-28.

"General Vuillemin." *RUSI*, 85 (1940) 237-238.

Géraud, André [Pertinax]. "France and the Anglo-German Naval Treaty." *FA*, 14 (1935-36) 51-61.

———— "France, Russia and the Pact of Mutual Assistance." *FA*, 13.2 (January 1935) 226-235.

———— "Gamelin." *FA*, 19 (1940) 310-331.

———— "The Anglo-French Alliance." *FA*, 18 (1939-40) 601-613.

———— "What England Means to France." *FA*, 17.2 (January 1939) 362-373.

Giraudon, A. "L'organisation de l'armée rouge." *RDDM* (15 August 1935) 751-779.

Grandclément, Captain R. "La politique mondiale du pétrole." *RMG*, (May 1938) 591-623.

Grasset, Colonel A. "La défense nationale et l'effort nécessaire." *RDDM* (15 June 1938) 820-846.

Heywood, Brigadier T. G. G. "General Gamelin." *RUSI*, 85 (1940) 221-225.

Ismay, Major General H. L. "The Machinery of the Committee of Imperial Defence." *RUSI*, 84 (1939) 241-257.

Kovacs, Arpad F. "Military Origins of the Fall of France." *Military Affairs*, 7.1 (Spring 1943) 25-40.

Krebs, Armand. "Considérations sur l'offensive." *RMG*, (September 1937) 324-365.

Lavergne, Bernard. "La crise européene de 1938 ou la grande défaite des démocraties." *L'Année Politique Française et Etrangère*, 13 (April 1938) 185-243.

Milyukov, P. "Edward Benes." *Slavonic Review*, 17.50 (1937-38) 297-328.

Niessel, General Henri. "Les forces militaires de l'U.R.R.S." *La Revue Universelle*, 74.9 (August 1938) 281-294.

———— "Valeur militaire de la Pologne." *RDDM* (15 September 1935) 286-296.

Bibliography

—— "Les effectifs de l'armée allemande." *RDDM* (1 January 1934) 35-50.

—— "La Pologne et la paix." *RDDM* (1 May 1934) 80-95.

—— "Chars, anti-chars et motorisation dans la guerre d'Espagne." *RMG*, 3 (1938) 745-760.

—— "La semaine de quarante heures et la défense nationale." *RDDM* (15 December 1937) 892-898.

—— "Aux grandes manoeuvres italiennes." *RDDM* (1 October 1935) 652-661.

—— "Préparation militaire de la nation." *RDDM* (15 January 1935) 380-395.

—— "La protection contre le danger aérien." *RDDM* (1 June 1934) 531-546.

"Notre armée de l'air." *RDDM* (August 1936) 521-537.

Pétain, Marshal Philippe. "La sécurité de la France au cours des années creuses." *RDDM* (1 March 1935), i-xx.

Pickersgill, Jack W. "The *Front Populaire* and the French Elections of 1936." *Political Science Quarterly*, 54 (1939) 69-83.

Possony, Stefan. "Organized Intelligence: The Problem of the French General Staff." *Social Research*, 8 (May 1941) 213-237.

"Que pourrait encore la force française devant le péril allemand." *La Revue Hebdomadaire*, 45 (March 1936) 391-396.

Regnault, Jean. "L'évolution du rôle militaire et maritime de l'empire colonial français." *RMG* (February 1938) 191-219.

Rosay, Simone. "Admiral Darlan." *RUSI*, 85 (1940) 234-236.

Serrigny, General Bernard. "Le réarmement allemand: essence et carburants." *RDDM* (1 April 1936) 662-675.

Stewart, Oliver. "The Doctrine of Strategical Bombing." *RUSI* (February 1936) 95-101.

—— "The Air Forces of France." *RUSI*, 85 (1940) 239-244.

"Tanks in the Attack: French and German Tactical Theories." *Royal United Services Institute Journal*, 83 (1938) 743-747.

Tollemache, E. D. H. "French Military Training for Defeat." *Quarterly Review*, 277 (October 1941) 180-191.

Utley, T. E. "French Views on the German Problem." *IA*, 20.2 (April 1944) 243-249.

Werth, Alexander. "After the Popular Front." *FA*, 17.1 (October 1938) 13-26.

Weygand, General Maxime. "L'état militaire de la France." *RDDM* (15 October 1936) 721-736.

—— "L'armée d'aujourd'hui." *RDDM* (15 May 1938) 325-336.

—— "How France Is Defended." *FA*, 18.4 (July-August 1939) 459-477.

Historical Articles

"Protocols of the Polish-French General Staff Conferences in Paris, May 1939." *Bellona*, 2 (1958) 165-179.

"Les négociations militaires entre l'U.R.S.S., la Grande-Bretagne et la France en août 1939." *Recherches Internationales à la Lumière du Marxisme*, 12 (March-April 1959) 130-220.

Adamthwaite, Anthony P. "Bonnet, Daladier and French Appeasement, April-September 1938." *IR*, 3.3 (April 1967) 226-241.

—— "Reactions to the Munich Crisis." In *Troubled Neighbours*. Ed. Neville Waites. London: Weidenfeld and Nicolson, 1971, 170-199.

—— "The Franco-German Declaration of 6 December 1938." *Les relations franco-allemandes, 1933-1939*. Colloques Internationaux du CNRS no. 563, 1977, 395-409.

Albrecht-Carrié, René. "Four Power Pacts: 1933-1945." *Journal of Central European Affairs*, 5 (April 1945) 17-35.

Alexander, Donald W. "Repercussions of the Breda Variant." *FHS*, 8.3 (Spring 1974) 459-488.

Askew, W. C. "The Secret Agreement between France and Italy on Ethiopia, January 1935." *JMH* (March 1953) 47-48.

Astorkia, Madeline. "Les leçons aeriénnes de la guerre d'Espagne." *Revue Historique des Armées*, 4.2 (1977) 145-174.

Auphan, Rear Admiral Paul. "The French Navy Enters World War II." *United States Naval Institute Proceedings*, 82 (June 1956) 592-601.

Bankwitz, Philip C. F. "Maxime Weygand and the Fall of France: A Study in Civil-Military Relations." *JMH* (September 1959) 225-242.

Baumont, Maurice. "French Critics and Apologists Debate Munich." *FA*, 25.4 (July 1947) 685-690.

Bédarida, François. "La 'gouvernante anglaise.' " Colloque Daladier, 1975.

—— "Convergences et divergences stratégiques franco-britanniques." Anglo-French Colloquium, 1975.

Boudot, François. "Sur des problèmes du financement de la défense nationale (1936-40)." *Revue d'Histoire de la Deuxième Guerre Mondiale*, 81 (January 1971) 49-72.

Boeninger, Hildegard. "Hitler and the German Generals 1934-38." *JCEA*, 14 (April 1954) 19-37.

Braddick, H. B. "The Hoare-Laval Plan: A Study in International Politics." In *European Diplomacy between Two Wars, 1919-39*. Ed. H. Gatzke. Chicago: Quandrangle Books, 1972, 152-171.

Brooks, Russell. "The Unknown Darlan." *United States Naval Institute Proceedings*, 81 (August 1955) 879-892.

Brown, J. "Anglo-French Naval Conferences 1939." Anglo-French Colloquium, 1973.

Buckley, P., C. Neave-Hill, and E. B. Haslam. "Anglo-French Staff Conversations, 1938-39." Anglo-French Colloquium, 1971.

Buffotot, P. "Le moral dans l'armée de l'air française." *Recueil d'Articles et Etudes, 1974-1975*. Vincennes: SHAA, 1977, 167-196.

—— and J. Ogier. "L'armée de l'air pendant la bataille de France—du 10 mai à l'armistice." *Recueil d'Articles et Etudes, 1974-1975*. Vincennes: SHAA, 1977, 197-226.

Bibliography

Burdick, C. B. "German Military Planning and France, 1930-1938." *World Affairs Quarterly*, 30.4 (1960) 299-313.

Butterworth, Susan B. "Daladier and the Munich Crisis: A Reappraisal." *JCH*, 9.3 (July 1974) 191-216.

Cairns, John C. "Along the Road Back to France 1940." *AHR*, 3 (April 1959) 583-603.

—— "Some Recent Historians and the 'Strange Defeat' of 1940." *JMH*, 46.1 (March 1974) 60-85.

—— "March 7, 1936 Again: The View from Paris." In *European Diplomacy between Two Wars, 1919-39*. Ed. H. Gatzke. Chicago: Quadrangle Books, 1972, 172-192.

—— "A Nation of Shopkeepers in Search of a Suitable France: 1919-1940." *AHR*, 79.3 (June 1974) 710-743.

Carlton, David. "Eden, Blum and the Origins of Non-Intervention." *JCH*, 6.3 (1971) 40-55.

Castellan, Georges. "Les Balkans dans la politique française face à la réoccupation de la Rhénanie (7 mars 1936)." *Studia Balcanica* (1973) 33-44.

Castex, Admiral Raoul. "L'Afrique et la stratégie française." *Revue de Defénse Nationale*, 14 (May 1952) 523-534.

Chapman, Guy. "The French Army and Politics." In *Soldiers and Governments*. Ed. M. E. Howard. London: Eyre and Spottiswoode, 1957, 53-71.

Child, C. J. "Great Britain, France and Non-Intervention in Spain, July-August 1936." Anglo-French Colloquium, 1973.

Chiper, I. "L'expansion économique de l'Allemagne nazie dans les Balkans, 1933-39." *Studia Balcanica* (1973) 121-127.

Christienne, General C., and P. Buffotot. "L'armée de l'air française et la crise du 7 Mars 1936." Colloque Franco-Allemand, Comité d'Histoire de la Deuxième Guerre Mondiale, March 1977.

—— "L'industrie aéronautique française de septembre 1939 à juin 1940." *Recueil d'Articles et Etudes, 1974-1975*. Vincennes: SHAA, 1977, 141-166.

—— P. Buffotot. "L'aéronautique militaire française entre 1919 et 1939." *Revue Historique des Armées*, 4.2 (1977) 9-40.

Cienciala, Anna. "Polish Foreign Policy, 1926-1939." *Polish Review*, 20.1 (1975) 42-57.

Coghlan, F. "Armaments, Economic Policy and Appeasement: Background to British Foreign Policy, 1931-37." *History*, 57 (1972) 205-216.

Cohen, William B. "The Colonial Policy of the Popular Front." *FHS, Studies*, 7.3 (Spring 1972) 368-393.

Daladier, Edouard. "Munich: Vingt-trois ans après." *Le Nouveau Candide* (September-October 1961).

Deakin, F. W. "Anglo-French Relations and the Italo-Ethiopian Crisis (December 1934-December 1935)." Anglo-French Colloquium, 1972.

—— "Anglo-French Relations and Italian Neutrality, September 1939-June 1940." Anglo-French Colloquium, 1975.

Debicki, Roman. "The Remilitarization of the Rhineland and Its Impact on the

French-Polish Alliance." *Polish Review*, 14.4 (Autumn 1969) 45-55.

Deborine, G. "Les négociations anglo-franco-soviétiques de 1939 et le traité de non-agression germano-soviétique." *Recherches Internationales à la Lumière du Marxisme*, 23-24 (January-April 1961) 139-166.

Dhers, Pierre. "Du 7 mars 1936 à l'Ile d'Yeu." *RHDGM*, 5 (January 1952) 17-26.

D'Hoop, Jean Marie. "La politique française du réarmament, 1933-1939." *RHDGM* (April 1954) 1-26.

—— "La politique militaire de la France dans les Balkans de l'accord de Munich au début de la deuxième guerre mondiale." *Studia Balcanica*, 7 (1973) 79-89.

—— "La coopération franco-britannique devant le problème italien." Anglo-French Colloquium, 1975.

Dinerstein, H. S. "The Impact of Air Power on the International Scene, 1933-1940." *Military Affairs*, 19.2 (Summer 1955) 65-71.

Dreifort, John. "France, Britain and Munich: An Interim Assessment." *Proceedings of the First Annual Meeting of the Western Society for French History*. New Mexico State University Press, 1974.

—— "The French Popular Front and the Franco-Soviet Pact, 1936-37: A Dilemma in Foreign Policy." *JCH*, 9 (1976) 217-236.

Dugowson, Jacques. "La déclaration franco-allemande du 6 décembre 1938." *Recherches Internationales à la Lumière du Marxisme*, 23-24 (January-April 1961) 113-138.

Duroselle, J. B. "L'influence de la politique intérieure sur la politique extérieure de la France." Anglo-French Colloquium, 1972.

Fergusson, Gilbert. "Munich: The French and British Roles." *IA*, 44.4 (October 1968) 649-665.

Frankenstein, Robert. "A propos des aspects financiers du réarmement français, 1935-1939." RHDGM, 26.102 (April 1976) 1-20.

French, G. S. "Louis Barthou and the German Question: 1934." *Canadian Historical Association Report*, 1964, 120-135.

Fridenson, Patrick. "Forces et faiblesses des conversations aériennes franco-britanniques." Anglo-French Colloquium, 1972.

Gallagher, M. D. "Léon Blum and the Spanish Civil War." JCH, 6.3 (1971) 56-64.

Gasiorowski, Zygmunt. "The German-Polish Nonaggression Pact of 1934." *JCEA*, 15 (April 1955) 4-29.

Gibson, Irving M. "The Maginot Line." *JMH*, 2 (June 1945) 130-146.

Girault, René. "La décision gouvernementale en politique extérieure." Colloque Daladier, 1975.

—— "Léon Blum: La dévaluation de 1936 et la conduite de la politique extérieure de la France." Colloque, Politique Economique Extérieure de la France 1924-1937. University of Paris X-Nanterre, March 1977.

Goldman, Aron L. "Sir Robert Vansittart's Search for Italian Cooperation against Hitler, 1933-36." JCH, 9.3 (July 1974) 93-130.

Gowing, Margaret. "Anglo-French Economic Collaboration up to the Outbreak of the Second World War." Anglo-French Colloquium, 1971.

—— "Anglo-French Economic Collaboration before the Second World War."

Anglo-French Colloquium, 1972.

Gretton, Sir Peter. "British Naval Policy during the Spanish Civil War." Anglo-French Colloquium, 1973.

Haslam, E. B. "Anglo-French Conversations: Air Staff Views on Preparations for the North East Theatre of Operations." Anglo-French Colloquium, 1972.

——— "The French Aircraft Industry before 1939." Anglo-French Colloquium, 1973.

Helmreich, Jonathan. "The Negotiation of the Franco-Belgian Military Accord of 1920." FHS, 3.3 (Spring 1964) 360-378.

Hill C. J. "Great Britain and the Saar Plebiscite of 13 January 1935." JCH, 9.2 (April 1974) 121-142.

Johnson, Douglas. "Léon Blum and the Popular Front." History, 55 (1970) 199-206.

——— "Britain and France in 1940." Transactions of the Royal Historical Society, 22 (1972) 141-157.

Joll, James. "Anglo-French Relations, 1935-1939." Anglo-French Colloquium, 1971.

Kaspi, André. "Les relations franco-américaines, octobre 1937-septembre 1939." Anglo-French Colloquium, 1973.

Kraehe, Enno A. "Motives behind the Maginot Line." Military Affairs, 8.1 (Spring 1944) 138-152.

Laloy, Jean. "Remarques sur les négociations Anglo-Franco-Soviétiques de 1939." Anglo-French Colloquium, 1972.

Lammers, Donald. "From Whitehall after Munich: The Foreign Office and the Future Course of British Policy." Historical Journal, 16.4 (1973) 831-856.

Lecuir, Jean, and Patrick Fridenson. "L'organisation de la coopération aérienne franco-britannique, 1935-mai 1940." RHDGM, 73 (January 1969) 43-71.

Le Goyet, Pierre. "Evolution de la doctrine de l'emploi de l'aviation française entre 1919 et 1939." RHDGM, 19.73 (January 1969) 3-41.

——— "La coopération franco-britannique en temps de guerre." Anglo-French Colloquium, 1971.

——— "Les relations économiques franco-britanniques à la veille de la 2è guerre mondiale." Anglo-French Colloquium, 1971.

——— Les relations militaires franco-britanniques et le Japon (mars-septembre 1939)." Anglo-French Colloquium, 1973.

——— "Le théâtre d'opérations du Nord-Est." Anglo-French Colloquium, 1972.

——— Méditérranée orientale et Mer Rouge." Anglo-French Colloquium, 1973.

Loizeau, General Lucien. "Une mission militaire en U.R.S.S." RDDM (15 September 1955) 252-276.

Haight, John McVickar. "Les négociations françaises pour la fourniture d'avions américains." Pt. I. Forces Aériennes Françaises, 198 (December 1963), 807-839.

——— "France, the United States and the Munich Crisis." JMH, 4 (December 1960) 340-358.

Marder, Arthur. "The Royal Navy and the Ethiopian Crisis of 1935-36." AHR, 5

(June 1970) 1327-1356.

Martel, André. "Le poids de la stratégie controverses et données contestées." Colloque Daladier, 1975.

Masson, P. "Les premières conversations militaires franco-britanniques, 1935-36." Anglo-French Colloquium, 1972.

———— "La marine française et la guerre d'Espagne." Anglo-French Colloquium, 1973.

———— "Moral et Propagande." Anglo-French Colloquium, 1975.

Medlicott, W. N. "De Munich à Prague." RHDGM (January 1954) 3-16.

———— "La politique britannique et la crise de la Tchécoslovaquie." RHDGM (July 1962) 29-40.

Michel, Henri. "Le Front Populaire et l'U.R.S.S." Anglo-French Colloquium, 1971.

———— "France, Grande-Bretagne et Pologne (mars-août 1939)." Anglo-French Colloquium, 1972.

Neave-Hill, W. B. "Franco-British Strategic Policy 1939: The Decision to Send the BEF to France." Anglo-French Colloquium, 1972.

———— "The Development of Anglo-French Strategy, 1939-40." Anglo-French Colloquium, 1975.

Néré, J. "La France devant la guerre économique et la coopération franco-anglaise." Anglo-French Colloquium, 1972.

———— "L'aspect économique de la guerre et la coopération franco-anglaise." Anglo-French Colloquium, 1973.

Nish, Ian. "Japan and Britain—The Thirties in Review." Anglo-French Colloquium, 1973.

Osgood, Samuel H. "Le mythe de 'la perfide Albion' en France, 1919-1940." *Cahiers d'Histoire*, 1 (1975) 5-20.

Parker, R. A. C. "The First Capitulation: France and the Rhineland Crisis of 1936." *World Politics*, 8.3 (April 1956) 355-373.

———— "Great Britain and the Ethiopian Crisis, 1935-36." *English Historical Review*, 89.351 (April 1974) 293-332.

———— "Economics, Rearmament and Foreign Policy: The United Kingdom before 1939—A Preliminary Study." JCH, 10.4 (October 1975) 637-648.

Renouvin, Pierre. "La politique anglaise pendant la crise de Munich." *Revue Historique*, 205 (1951) 260-271.

———— "Les relations franco-anglaises, 1935-39." Anglo-French Colloquium, 1971.

———— "Rapport général présenté à la séance du 28 septembre 1972." Anglo-French Colloquium, 1972.

———— "Les relations de la Grande-Bretagne et de la France avec l'Italie en 1938-39." Anglo-French Colloquium, 1972.

———— "La genèse de l'accord de non-intervention dans la guerre civile espagnole (août 1936)." Anglo-French Colloquium, 1973.

Richardson, Charles O. "French Plans for Allied Attacks on the Caucasus Oil Fields, January-April 1940." *FHS*, 7.1 (Spring 1973) 130-156.

Bibliography

Robertson, J. C. "The Hoare-Laval Plan." JCH, 10.3 (July 1975) 433-464.

Sakwa, George. "The Franco-Polish Alliance and the Remilitarization of the Rhineland." *Historical Journal*, 16.1 (1973) 125-146.

Savu, A. "Munich et la situation de la Roumanie." *Studia Balcanica* (1973) 211-215.

Seabury, Paul. "Ribbentrop and the German Foreign Office." *Political Science Quarterly*, 66 (1951) 532-555.

Sorlin, Pierre. "Les perspectives aéronautiques dans la crise Tchécoslovaque de 1938." *Forces Aériennes Françaises*, 12 (November 1958) 601-635.

Stanislawska, S. "Soviet Policy toward Poland, 1926-1939." *Polish Review*, 20.1 (1975) 30-38.

Stolfi, R. H. S. "Equipment for Victory in France in 1940." *History*, 55.183 (February 1970) 1-20.

Taboulet, Georges. "La France et l'Angleterre face au conflit sino-japonais (1937-39). D'après les archives diplomatiques de la France." Anglo-French Colloquium, 1973.

Tournoux, General Paul Emile. "Les origines de la Ligne Maginot." RHDGM, 33 (January 1959) 3-14.

Vanku, M. "La politique de gouvernement jugoslave à l'égard de l'Anschluss et de l'accord de Munich en 1938." *Studia Balcanica* (1973) 217-231.

Vial, J. "La défense nationale: Son organisation entre les deux guerres." RHDGM, 18 (April 1955) 11-32.

Vnuk, F. "Munich and the Soviet Union." *JCEA*, (October 1961) 285-304.

Wall, Irwin M. "The Resignation of the First Popular Front Government of Léon Blum, June 1937." *FHS*, 6.4 (Fall 1970) 538-554.

Wallace, W. V. "The Foreign Policy of President Benes in the Approach to Munich." *Slavonic Review*, 39.93 (1960-61) 108-136.

———— "The Making of the May Crisis of 1938." *Slavonic Review*, 41.98 (1962-63) 368-390.

Warner, Geoffrey. "France and Non-Intervention in Spain, July-August 1936." *IA*, 38.2 (April 1962) 203-220.

———— "The Decline and Fall of Pierre Laval." *History Today*, 9.12 (December 1961) 817-827.

Watt, Donald C. "An Earlier Model for the Pact of Steel." *IA*, 33.2 (1957) 185-197.

———— "The Anglo-German Naval Agreement of 1935: An Interim Judgment." *JMH*, 2 (June 1956) 155-175.

———— "The Secret Laval-Mussolini Agreement of 1935 on Ethiopia." *The Middle East Journal*, 15 (1961) 69-78.

———— "The Reoccupation of the Rhineland." *History Today*, 6.4 (April 1956) 244-251.

———— "British Domestic Politics and the Onset of War: Notes for a Discussion." Anglo-French Colloquium, 1972.

———— "Britain, France and the Italian Problem, 1937-39." Anglo-French Colloquium, 1972.

Bibliography

———— "Anglo-American Relations, 1933-39." Anglo-French Colloquium, 1973.

———— "The British Image of French Military Morale, 1939-40: An Intelligence Failure?" Anglo-French Colloquium, 1975.

Wauquier, Commandant A. "Les forces cuirassées dans la bataille: L'emploi des chars français." RHDGM, 10-11 (June 1953) 150-164.

Weinberg, Gerhard L. "Secret Hitler-Benes Negotiations in 1936-1937." *JCEA*, 19 (January 1960) 366-374.

———— "The May Crisis of 1938." *JMH*, 3 (September 1957) 213-225.

———— "Germany Policy and Poland, 1937-38." *Polish Review*, 20.1 (1975) 5-23.

Wheatley, Ronald. "Britain and the Anglo-Franco-Russian Negotiations in 1939." Anglo-French Colloquium, 1971.

Young, Robert J. "French Policy and the Munich Crisis of 1938: A Reappraisal." *Historical Papers 1970* (Canadian Historical Association) 186-206.

———— "Preparations for Defeat: French War Doctrine in the Inter-War Period." *Journal of European Studies*, 2.2 (June 1972) 155-172.

———— "The Aftermath of Munich: The Course of French Diplomacy, October 1938 to March 1939." *FHS*, 8.2 (Fall 1973) 305-322.

———— "The Strategic Dream: French Air Doctrine in the Inter-War Period, 1919-1939." *JCH*, 9.4 (October 1974) 57-76.

———— "Spokesmen for Economic Warfare: The Industrial Intelligence Centre in the 1930's." *European Studies Review*, 6.4 (October 1976) 473-489.

———— "Le haut commandement français au moment de Munich." *Revue d'Histoire Moderne et Contemporaine*, 24 (January-March 1977), 110-129.

I. Historical Studies

Adamthwaite, Anthony P. *France and the Coming of the Second World War, 1936-39.* London: Frank Cass, 1977.

———— *The Making of the Second World War.* London: Allen and Unwin, 1977.

Albrecht-Carrié, René. *France, Europe and the Two World Wars.* New York: Harper, 1961.

Aster, Sidney. *1939: The Making of the Second World War.* London: Deutsch, 1973.

Baillou, J, and P. Pelletier. *Les affaires étrangères.* Paris: Presses Universitaires, 1962.

Bankwitz, Philip C. F. *Maxime Weygand and Civil-Military Relations in Modern France.* Cambridge, Mass.: Harvard University Press, 1967.

Baumont, Maurice. *La faillite de la paix.* Paris: P.U.F., 1951.

———— *The Third Reich.* New York: Praeger, 1955.

———— *Les origines de la deuxième guerre mondiale.* Paris: Payot, 1969.

Beck, Earl R. *Verdict on Schacht: A Study in the Problem of Political Guilt.* Tallahassee: Florida State University, 1955.

Beloff, Max. *The Foreign Policy of Soviet Russia, 1929-1941.* London: Oxford University Press, 1947.

Bibliography

Bell, P. M. H. *A Certain Eventuality: Britain and the Fall of France*. London: Saxon House, 1974.

Benoist-Méchin, Jacques. *Histoire de l'armée allemande depuis l'armistice*. 3 vols. Paris: Albin Michel, 1964.

Bloch, Charles. *Hitler und die europäischen mächte 1933-1934*. Frankfurt: Europäische Verlagsanstalt, 1966.

Bond, Brian. *France and Belgium, 1939-40*. London: Davis-Poynter, 1975.

Bonnefous, Edouard. *Histoire politique de la troisième république*. Vol. V, *La république en danger, 1930-36*. Paris: P.U.F., 1962.

Bouillon, J, and G. Vallette. *Munich 1938*. Paris: Colin, 1964.

Bourget, Pierre. *Témoignages inédits sur le maréchal Pétain*. Paris: Fayard, 1960.

Bouvier, J., and J. Gacon. *La vérité sur 1939: La politique extérieure de l'U.R.S.S., d'octobre 1938 à juin 1941*. Paris: Editions Sociales, 1953.

Braubach, Max. *Der Einmarsch deutscher Truppen in die entmilitärisierte Zone am Reich im März 1936*. Westdeutsche Verlag, 1956.

Brook-Shepard, Gordon. *Anschluss: The Rape of Austria*. London: Macmillan, 1963.

Bruegel. J. W. *Czechoslovakia before Munich: The German Minority Problem and British Appeasement Policy*. Cambridge: At the University Press, 1973.

Budurowycz, Bohdan. *Polish-Soviet Relations, 1932-39*. New York: Columbia University Press, 1963.

Castellan, Georges. *Le réarmement clandestin du Reich, 1930-1935*. Paris: Plon, 1954.

Cattel, David. *Soviet Diplomacy and the Spanish Civil War*. Berkeley: University of California Press, 1957.

Celovsky, Boris. *Das Münchener Abkommen, 1938*. Stuttgart: Deutsche Verlagsanstalt, 1958.

Challener, Richard D. *The French Theory of the Nation in Arms, 1866-1939*. New York: Columbia University Press, 1955.

Chapman Guy. *Why France Collapsed*. London: Cassell, 1968.

Chastenet, Jacques. *Histoire de la troisième république*. Vol. VI. Paris: Hachette, 1962.

Cienciala, Anna. *Poland and the Western Powers, 1938-1939*. Toronto: University of Toronto Press, 1968.

Colvin, Ian. *The Chamberlain Cabinet*. London: Gollancz, 1971.

Connell, John [pseud.]. *The "Office": A Study of British Foreign Policy and Its Makers, 1919-1951*. London: Allen and Wingate, 1958.

Conquet, General Alfred. *L'énigme des blindés (1932-1940)*. Paris: Nouvelles Editions Latines, 1956.

Coverdale, John. *Italian Intervention in the Spanish Civil War*. Princeton: Princeton University Press, 1975.

Cowling, Maurice. *The Impact of Hitler: British Politics and British Policy, 1933-1940*. Cambridge: At the University Press, 1975.

Craig, Gordon A., and Felix Gilbert. *The Diplomats, 1919-1939*. Princeton: Princeton University Press, 1953.

Debicki, Roman. *Foreign Policy of Poland, 1919-1939*. New York: Praeger, 1962.

De la Gorce, Paul M. *The French Army: A Military-Political History*. New York: George Braziller, 1963.

Dennis, Peter. *Decision by Default: Peacetime Conscription and British Defence, 1919-1939*. London: Routledge and Kegan Paul, 1972.

Dreifort, John. *Yvon Delbos at the Quai d'Orsay: French Foreign Policy during the Popular Front, 1936-38*. Lawrence: University Press of Kansas, 1973.

Duroselle, J. B., ed. *Les relations germano-soviétiques de 1933 à 1939*. Paris, 1954.

Earle, Edward Mead. *Modern France: Problems of the Third and Fourth Republics*. Princeton: Princeton University Press, 1951.

Emmerson, J. T. *The Rhineland Crisis, 7 March 1936*. London: Temple Smith, 1977.

Erickson, John. *The Soviet High Command: A Military-Political History, 1918-1941*. London: Macmillan, 1962.

Farnsworth, Beatrice. *William C. Bullitt and the Soviet Union*. Bloomington: Indiana University Press, 1967.

France. *Les relations militaires franco-belges, 1936-1940*. Paris: CNRS, 1968.

―――― *Les relations franco-britanniques, 1935-1939*. Paris: CNRS, 1975.

Fridenson, Patrick, and Jean Lecuir. *La France et la Grande-Bretagne face aux problèmes aériens, 1935-mai 1940*. Paris: SHAA, 1976.

Furnia, Arthur H. *The Diplomacy of Appeasement: Anglo-French Relations and the Prelude to World War II*. Washington: Washington University Press, 1960.

Gatzke, Hans. *European Diplomacy between Two Wars, 1919-1939*. Chicago: Quandrangle Books, 1972.

Gehl, Jurgen. *Austria, Germany and the Anschluss, 1931-38*. London: Oxford University Press, 1963.

Gibbs, Norman H. *Grand Strategy*. Vol. I, *Rearmament Policy: History of the Second World War*. United Kingdom Military Series. London: H.M.S.O., 1976.

Gignoux, C. J. *L'économie française entre les deux guerres, 1919-1939*. Paris: Societé d'Editions Economiques et Sociales, n.d.

Gilbert, Martin. *The Appeasers*. London: Weidenfeld and Nicolson, 1963.

Girardet, Raoul. *La société militaire dans la France contemporaine, 1815-1939*. Paris: Plon, 1953.

Gladwyn, Lady Cynthia. *The Paris Embassy*. London: Collins, 1976.

Goguel-Nyégaard, François. *La politique des partis sous la troisième république*. Paris: Editions du Seuil, 1946.

Gounelle, Claude. *Le dossier Laval*. Paris: Plon, 1969.

Goutard, Col. Adolphe. *The Battle of France, 1940*. New York: Ives Washburn, 1959.

Guérard, J. *Criminel de paix*. Paris: Nouvelles Editions Latines, 1953.

Hébrard, Jacques. *Vingt-cinq années d'aviation militaire, 1920-1945*. 2 vols. Paris: Albin Michel, 1946-47.

Henig, R. B., ed. *The League of Nations*. Edinburgh: Oliver and Boyd, 1973.

Hildebrand, Klaus. *The Foreign Policy of the Third Reich.* Berkeley: University of California Press, 1973.

Hofer, W. *War Premeditated.* London: Thames, 1955.

Hoptner, J. B. *Yugoslavia in Crisis, 1934-1941.* New York: Columbia, 1962.

Horne, Alistair. *To Lose a Battle: France 1940.* London: Macmillan, 1969.

Howard, Michael. *The Theory and Practice of War.* London: Cassell, 1965.

—— *Studies in War and Peace.* London: Temple Smith, 1970.

—— *The Continental Commitment.* London: Temple Smith, 1972.

Hughes, Judith M. *To the Maginot Line: The Politics of French Military Preparation in the 1920's.* Cambridge, Mass.: Harvard University Press, 1971.

Jenkins, E. H. *A History of the French Navy.* London: Macdonald and Jane's, 1973.

Joll, James, ed. *The Decline of the Third Republic.* London: Chatto and Windus, 1959.

Jordan, W. M. *Great Britain, France and the German Problem, 1919-1939.* London: Oxford University Press, 1954.

Kayser, Jacques. *De Kronstadt à Khrouchtchev: Voyages Franco-Russes, 1891-1960.* Paris: Colin, 1962.

Kemp, Tom. *The French Economy, 1919-1939.* London: Longman, 1972.

Kennan, George. *Soviet Foreign Policy, 1917-1941.* Princeton: Van Nostrand, 1960.

Kieft, David O. *Belgium's Return to Neutrality: An Essay in the Frustrations of Small Power Diplomacy.* Oxford: Clarendon Press, 1972.

Kimche, Jon. *The Unfought Battle.* London: Weidenfeld and Nicolson, 1968.

Klein, Burton H. *Germany's Economic Preparations for War.* Cambridge, Mass.: Harvard University Press, 1959.

Komjathy, Anthony T. *The Crises of France's East Central European Diplomacy, 1933-1938.* Boulder: East European Quarterly. Distributed by Columbia University Press, 1977.

Lammers, Donald N. *Explaining Munich: The Search for Motive in British Policy.* Stanford: Hoover Institution, 1966.

Larmour, Peter J. *The French Radical Party in the 1930's.* Stanford, Stanford University Press, 1964.

Laurens, Franklin D. *France and the Italo-Ethiopian Crisis, 1935-1936.* The Hague: Mouton, 1967.

Lewis, W. A. *Economic Survey, 1919-1939.* London: Allen and Unwin, 1949.

Liddell Hart, Sir Basil H. *History of the Second World War.* London: Cassell, 1970.

Mack Smith, Denis. *Mussolini's Roman Empire.* New York: Viking Press, 1976.

Manévy, Raymond. *La presse de la troisième république.* Paris: J. Foret, 1955.

Marcus, John T. *French Socialism in the Crisis Years, 1933-1936.* New York: Praeger, 1958.

McVickar Haight, Jr., John. *American Aid to France, 1938-1940.* New York: Atheneum, 1970.

Medlicott, W. N. *The Economic Blockade.* Vol. I. London: H.M.S.O., 1952.

Bibliography

────── *The Coming of the War in 1939.* London: Routledge and Kegan Paul, 1963.

Merkes, M. *Die deutsche Politik gegenüber dem spanischen Bürgerkrieg, 1936-1939.* Bonn: Rohrscheid, 1961.

Michel, Henri. *The Second World War.* London: Deutsch, 1975.

────── *La drôle de guerre.* Paris: Hachette, 1971.

Middlemas, Keith. *Diplomacy of Illusion: The British Government and Germany, 1937-1939.* London: Weidenfeld and Nicolson, 1972.

Miller, Jane K. *Belgian Foreign Policy between Two Wars, 1919-1940.* New York: Bookman Association, 1951.

Milward, Alan S. *The New Order and the French Economy.* Oxford: Clarendon Press, 1970.

Minart, Jacques. *Le drame du désarmement français, 1919-1939.* Paris: La Nef de Paris, 1960.

Miquel, Pierre. *La paix de Versailles et l'opinion publique française.* Paris: Flammarion, 1972.

Montgomery Hyde, H. *British Air Policy between the Wars, 1918-1939.* London: Heinemann, 1976.

Mourin, Maxime. *Les relations franco-soviétiques, 1917-1967.* Paris: Payot, 1967.

Mysyrowicz, Ladislas. *Autopsie d'une défaite: Origines de l'effrondrement militaire français de 1940.* Lausanne: Editions l'Age d'Homme, 1973.

Namier, Louis. *Diplomatic Prelude.* London: Macmillan, 1948.

────── *Europe in Decay.* London: Macmillan, 1950.

Noguères, Henri. *Munich: The Phony Peace.* London: Weidenfeld and Nicolson, 1965.

Noguères, Louis. *Le véritable procès du maréchal Pétain.* Paris: Fayard, 1955.

Osgood, Samuel M., ed. *The Fall of France.* Toronto: Heath, 1972.

Paxton, Robert O. *Vichy France: Old Guard and New Order, 1940-1944.* New York: Norton, 1972.

Powers, Barry D. *Strategy without Slide-Rule: British Air Strategy, 1914-1939.* London: Croom Helm, 1976.

Pratt, Laurence R. *East of Malta, West of Suez: Britain's Mediterranean Crisis, 1936-1939.* Cambridge: At the University Press, 1975.

Quester, George H. *Deterrence before Hiroshima.* London: J. Wiley, 1966.

Renouvin, Pierre. *Histoire des relations internationales.* Vol. XVIII, *Les crises du XXe siècle,* pt. 2, *De 1929 à 1945.* Paris: Hachette, 1958.

Reynolds, P. A. *British Foreign Policy in the Inter-War Years.* London: Longmans, Green, 1954.

Robertson, E. M. *Hitler's Prewar Policy and Military Plans, 1933-1939.* London: Longmans, 1963.

Robertson, E. M., ed. *The Origins of the Second World War.* London: Macmillan, 1971.

Rock, William R. *Appeasement on Trial: British Foreign Policy and Its Critics, 1938-39.* Hamden, Conn.: Archon Books, 1966.

Bibliography

Rosé, A. C. *La politique polonaise entre les deux guerres.* Neuchâtel: Editions de la Baconnerie, 1948.

Roskill, Stephen. *Naval Policy between the Wars.* Vol. II, 1930-1939. London: Collins, 1976.

Rowe, Vivian. *The Great Wall of France.* London: Putnam, 1960.

Rowse, A. L. *Appeasement: A Study in Political Decline, 1933-1939.* New York: Norton, 1961.

Salvemini, Gaetano. *Prelude to World War Two.* London: Gollancz, 1953.

Saundby, Sir Robert. *Air Bombardment: The Story of Its Development.* London: Chatto and Windus, 1961.

Sauvy, Alfred. *Histoire économique de la France entre les deux guerres.* 2 vols. Paris: Société d'Editions Economiques et Sociales, n.d.

Schoenbrun, David. *As France Goes.* New York: Harper Brothers, 1957.

Scott, George. *The Rise and Fall of the League of Nations.* New York: Macmillan, 1973.

Scott, William E. *Alliance against Hitler.* Durham, N.C.: Duke University Press, 1962.

Seabury, Paul. *The Wilhelmstrasse.* Berkeley: University of California Press, 1954.

Seton-Watson, Hugh. *Eastern Europe between the Wars, 1918-1941.* Hamden, Conn.: Archon Books, 1962.

Shirer, William L. *The Collapse of the Third Republic.* London: Heinemann, 1970.

Slessor, Sir John. *The Great Deterrent.* London: Cassell, 1957.

Tabouis, Geneviève. *Vingt ans de suspense diplomatique.* Paris: Albin Michel, 1958.

Tarr, Francis de. *The French Radical Party, from Herriot to Mendès-France.* London: Oxford University Press, 1961.

Taylor, A. J. P. *The Origins of the Second World War.* London: Hamilton 1961.

Taylor, Telford. *The Sword and Swastika.* New York: Simon and Schuster, 1952.

Thomson, David. *Two Frenchmen: Laval and de Gaulle.* London: Cresset Press, 1951.

Tournoux, General Paul Emile. *Haut commandement: Gouvernement et défense des frontières du nord et de l'est, 1919-1939.* Paris: Nouvelles Editions Latines, 1960.

Waites, Neville, ed. *Troubled Neighbours: Franco-British Relations in the Twentieth Century.* London: Weidenfeld and Nicolson, 1971.

Wallace, L. P., and W. C. Askew. *Power, Public Opinion and Diplomacy.* Durham, N.C.: Duke University Press, 1959.

Walters, F. P. *A History of the League of Nations.* London: Oxford University Press, 1952.

Wandycz, Piotr S. *France and Her Eastern Allies, 1919-1925.* Minneapolis: University of Minnesota Press, 1962.

Warner, Geoffrey. *Pierre Laval and the Eclipse of France.* London: Eyre and

Spottiswoode, 1968.

Wathen, Sister Mary A. *The Policy of England and France toward the "Anschluss" of 1938.* Washington: Catholic University, 1954.

Watt, Donald C. *Too Serious a Business: European Armed Forces and the Approach to the Second World War.* London: Temple Smith, 1975.

Webster, Charles, and Noble Frankland. *The Strategic Air Offensive against Germany, 1939-45.* Vol. I. London: H.M.S.O., 1961.

Weinberg, Gerhard L. *Germany and the Soviet Union, 1939-41.* Leyden: Brill, 1954.

—— *The Foreign Policy of Hitler's Germany, 1933-36.* Chicago: University of Chicago Press, 1970.

Wheeler-Bennett, J. W. *Munich: Prologue to Tragedy.* London: Macmillan, 1948.

—— *The Nemesis of Power.* London: Macmillan, 1953.

Wiskemann, Elizabeth. *The Rome-Berlin Axis.* London: Oxford University Press, 1949.

Wolfe, Martin. *The French Franc between the Wars, 1919-1939.* New York: Columbia University Press, 1951.

Wolfers, Arnold. *Britain and France between the Wars.* New York: Harcourt, Brace, 1963.

Wood, Derek, and Derek Dempster. *The Narrow Margin: The Battle of Britain and the Rise of Air Power, 1930-1940.* New York: McGraw-Hill, 1961.

Index

341

Index

Index

Naggiar, Paul Emile, 236, 239, 240
Nazi-Soviet Pact (1939), 241
Nicholls, John W., 244
Niessel, General Henri, 48
Noel, Léon, 143, 239

Pact of Steel, 231
Palasse, General, 303n31
Paul-Boncour, Joseph: on disarmament, 43, 48; Czech crisis, 199, 202; reference to, 67, 74, 121, 124, 125, 204
Pétain, Marshal Philippe: on Belgium, 32, 139; German threat, 48, 56, 169; reference to, 50, 59, 63, 89
Peterson, Sir Maurice, 102
Petibon, Colonel Jean, 284n76, 269n12
Peyerimhoff, Henri de, 45
Phipps, Sir Eric: on Bonnet, 202, 227; Daladier, 202, 231; Delbos, 156, 199; France, 4, 109, 225; Germany, 95, 107; Laval, 99, 108
Piétri, François, 56
Pilsudski, Marshal, 66, 87
Poincaré, Raymond, 4, 231
Poydenot, General Olivier, 169
Puaux, Gabriel, 195

Ramadier, Paul, 172
Rambouillet accord, 143, 234
Requin, General, 209
Reichswehr, see Wehrmacht
Reinhardt, General Walter, 250
Reynaud, Paul, 180, 208, 211
Rhineland crisis, 114-129, 131, 133, 178, 179, 195, 196, 208, 256
Ribbentrop, Joachim von, 72, 97, 216, 240
Ribes, Auguste Champetier de, 208
Riom trials, 6, 64, 187
Rivollet, Georges, 56
Rome Agreements (1935), 82-84
Rome-Berlin Axis, 137
Rommel, Field-Marshal Erwin, 180
Roosevelt, Franklin, 254, 257
Royal Air Force, *see* Great Britain; France: Military conversations
Royal Navy, *see* Great Britain; France: Military conversations
Rundstedt, General Karl von, 248

Saar question, 73, 79, 80, 88, 170, 276n5
Sablet, General, 190
Saint-Quentin, Count René, 102
Salonika project, 134, 235, 285n7, 285n10
Sargent, Orme, 85, 87, 108, 213, 214-215, 216
Sarraut, Albert: on Rhineland crisis, 117, 118, 120, 121, 122, 128, 129, 131, 133, 134; reference to, 46, 141
Sartre, Jean-Paul, 1, 252, 253
Schacht, Hjalmar, 154-155, 156
Schlieffen Plan, 15, 248
Schuschnigg, Kurt von, 195
Schweisguth, General Victor: on Rhineland crisis, 119, 120, 122, 127; Russia, 145-149, 176, 234, 236
Semenov, General, 148, 149
Serrigny, General Bernard, 26
Siegfried Line, 233
Simon, Sir John, 45, 68, 70, 87, 95, 96, 97, 101
Smigly-Rydz, Marshal Edward, 143
Spanish Civil War, 132, 136, 157, 182, 256
Stalin, Joseph, 59, 87, 93, 94, 146, 149, 155, 225, 234, 236, 240
Standard Oil Company, 172
Stresa front, 89, 96, 97, 98, 100, 101, 114, 116, 118, 123, 128

Tabouis, Geneviève, 64, 177
Tardieu, André, 50, 55, 56, 64, 69
Third Republic, *see* France
Thomas, Lloyd, 288n50, 289n61
Titulescu, Nicholas, 144
Trenchard, Major-General Sir Hugh, 175
Tyrrell, Sir William, 37, 43

Vansittart, Sir Robert: on French disarmament policy, 47; Laval, 108, 109-110; Léger, 43; reference to, 47, 87, 96, 223
Versailles, treaty of, 7, 9, 15, 16, 33, 37, 46, 55, 86, 114
Vichy regime, 187, 251, 309n12
Villelume, Commandant Paul de, 148, 289n52
Vitrolles, Captain de, 90
Vorochilov, Marshal, 149, 238, 240

Index